BOUND LABOR IN THE TURPENTINE BELT

UNIVERSITY PRESS OF FLORIDA

Florida A&M University, Tallahassee
Florida Atlantic University, Boca Raton
Florida Gulf Coast University, Ft. Myers
Florida International University, Miami
Florida State University, Tallahassee
New College of Florida, Sarasota
University of Central Florida, Orlando
University of Florida, Gainesville
University of North Florida, Jacksonville
University of South Florida, Tampa
University of West Florida, Pensacola

Bound Labor in the Turpentine Belt

Kinderlou Camp and Misdemeanor
Convict Leasing in Georgia

Thomas Aiello

UNIVERSITY PRESS OF FLORIDA

Gainesville/Tallahassee/Tampa/Boca Raton
Pensacola/Orlando/Miami/Jacksonville/Ft. Myers/Sarasota

Cover: Black male convicts at the Kinderlou camp, including child convicts, in the early twentieth century. Courtesy of Lowndes County Historical Society.

Publication of this work made possible by a Sustaining the Humanities through the American Rescue Plan grant from the National Endowment for the Humanities.

Excerpt from *The Gilded Auction Block: Poems* by Shane McCrae. Copyright © 2019 by Shane McCrae. Reprinted by permission of Farrar, Straus and Giroux. All Rights Reserved.

Copyright 2024 by Thomas Aiello
All rights reserved
Published in the United States of America

29 28 27 26 25 24   6 5 4 3 2 1

Library of Congress Cataloging-in-Publication Data
Names: Aiello, Thomas, 1977– author.
Title: Bound labor in the turpentine belt : Kinderlou Camp and misdemeanor convict leasing in Georgia / Thomas Aiello.
Description: Gainesville : University Press of Florida, [2024] | Includes bibliographical references and index.
Identifiers: LCCN 2024014804 (print) | LCCN 2024014805 (ebook) | ISBN 9780813079189 (hardback) | ISBN 9780813080826 (paperback) | ISBN 9780813070896 (pdf) | ISBN 9780813073507 (ebook)
Subjects: LCSH: Convict labor—Georgia—History. | Convict labor—Southern States—History. | Turpentine industry and trade—Georgia—History.
Classification: LCC HV8929.G4 A45 2024 (print) | LCC HV8929.G4 (ebook) | DDC 331.5/109758—dc23/eng/20240628
LC record available at https://lccn.loc.gov/2024014804
LC ebook record available at https://lccn.loc.gov/2024014805

The University Press of Florida is the scholarly publishing agency for the State University System of Florida, comprising Florida A&M University, Florida Atlantic University, Florida Gulf Coast University, Florida International University, Florida State University, New College of Florida, University of Central Florida, University of Florida, University of North Florida, University of South Florida, and University of West Florida.

University Press of Florida
2046 NE Waldo Road
Suite 2100
Gainesville, FL 32609
http://upress.ufl.edu

A colored man
came and said he would
Take care of him
good care and pay me   five
Dollars a month his name is my
Brother he is
about fourteen years old his name is James
Robinson and the man who took him his
Name is Dan Cal
Five dollars for his labor his
Name is Dan Cal
I didn't know
. . .
He sold my brother to
a white man named MacRee
They has been working him in prison for twelve month
And they won't send him back to me.

    Shane McCrae, from "After Carrie Kinsey's Letter to Theodore Roosevelt,"
in *The Gilded Auction Block: Poems* (New York: Farrar, Straus and Giroux, 2019)

CONTENTS

List of Figures ix
List of Maps xi
List of Tables xiii
Acknowledgments xv

Introduction 1
1. The McRees of South Georgia 15
2. The Birth of Misdemeanor Convict Leasing 31
3. Felony Leasing and Debt Peonage under Scrutiny 50
4. Misdemeanor Leasing at the Turn of the Century 67
5. The Scandal of 1900–1901 89
6. The State Scandal of 1903 113
7. The National Scandal of 1903 134
8. The Federal Crusade against Peonage 153
9. The Death of Leasing in Georgia 173
10. The Last Twilight of the Kinderlou Dynasty 198

Notes 213
Bibliography 249
Index 269

FIGURES

1.1. The McRee plantation as remembered by a descendant   19
2.1. Structure of Georgia's carceral system, 1892–1908   37
3.1. The rate of increase for Georgia's prison population from 1868 to 1908   53
3.2. The differences in the Black and white male incarceration rate in Georgia, from 1870 to 1935   54

MAPS

2.1. The location of Georgia's misdemeanor camps in 1897   41
9.1. The location of Georgia's private convict lease camps in 1898   174
9.2. The location of Georgia's private convict lease camps in 1902   175
9.3. The location of Georgia's private convict lease camps in 1908   176

TABLES

2.1. County misdemeanor camps, 1897   40

2.2. Private misdemeanor camps, 1897   43

2.3. Private camp deaths (reported), 1896   44

4.1. Felony convict lease camps, 1898   71

4.2. County misdemeanor camps, 1898, divided into public and private camps   72

4.3. Felony convict lease camps, 1899   74

4.4. County misdemeanor camps, 1899, divided into public and private camps   75

4.5. Felony convict lease camps, 1900   80

4.6. County misdemeanor camps, 1900, divided into public and private camps   82

4.7. Felony convict lease camps, 1901   85

4.8. County misdemeanor camps, 1901, divided into public and private camps   86

5.1. Monthly report of misdemeanor chain gang, camp no. 2   101

5.2. Monthly report of misdemeanor chain gang, camp no. 1   103

5.3. Felony convict lease camps, 1902   107

5.4. County misdemeanor camps, 1902, divided into public and private camps   109

7.1. Felony convict lease camps, 1904   145

7.2. Felony convict county road camps, 1904   147

7.3. County misdemeanor camps, 1904, divided into public and private camps   149

8.1. Felony convict lease camps, 1905 155

8.2. Felony convict county road camps, 1905 156

8.3. County misdemeanor camps, 1905, divided into public and private camps 157

8.4. Felony convict lease camps, 1906 159

8.5. Felony convict county road camps, 1906 161

8.6. County misdemeanor camps, 1906, divided into public and private camps 162

8.7. Felony convict lease camps, 1907 165

8.8. Felony convict county road camps, 1907 166

8.9. County misdemeanor camps, 1907, divided into public and private camps 167

9.1. Felony convict lease camps, 1908 183

9.2. Felony convict county road camps, 1908 185

9.3. County misdemeanor camps, 1908, divided into public and private camps 186

10.1. Lowndes County population 203

10.2. Distribution of Georgia prisoners in 1932 209

ACKNOWLEDGMENTS

This project would not have existed without the early work of my former graduate student, Benjamin L. Vieth. Ben wrote a paper on the McRee convict camp in Lowndes County, Georgia, as part of his master's work at Valdosta State University and originally planned to make that work into a thesis. Life, as it often does, got in the way, and Ben had to abandon the project. Years later, he provided me with his preliminary research, which led me to elaborate on his original effort, use some of the data he collected, and ultimately write this book. While many archivists, particularly the librarians at the Georgia Archives in Morrow, Georgia, helped me a great deal in compiling the research that fills these pages, and while I am grateful for their help, *Bound Labor in the Turpentine Belt* would not exist without the impetus provided by Ben Vieth's early efforts in a class project that ultimately found its way into my hands. It is with his blessing and my thanks that I present *Bound Labor in the Turpentine Belt*. And I dedicate it

to Benjamin L. Vieth.

Introduction

"One of the most remarkable phenomena in our industrial world, and one about which comparatively little is known, is the peonage system practiced in the South," explained the *Baltimore Afro-American*, "whereby free Negroes, citizens of the United States who have incurred debt to white men, are compelled to 'work out' their debts, often being retained in harsh servitude long beyond the time represented by the amount of money they owe." It was a system built on legal abuse but also one that facilitated illegal abuse, and "the abuses of the system have been extensive and frightful."[1]

Peonage was a phenomenon throughout the South and in various parts of the country at different times, but it centered primarily on what Pete Daniel has called the "turpentine belt," running along the northern border of Florida and the southern borders of Georgia and Alabama, as well as the Black Belt cotton region running from South Carolina through central Georgia, Alabama, and Mississippi. Kinderlou, a particularly brutal convict camp owned by the McRee family in Lowndes County, Georgia, just miles from the Florida border, was located in the heart of Daniel's turpentine belt and participated overtly in debt peonage. As Fred Cubberly and other federal officials explained in the early twentieth century, the turpentine industry in south Georgia and north Florida was particularly notorious for its use and abuse of debt peons. Alex Lichtenstein has explained that "the fluidity and the constraints of their production process" encouraged turpentine farm owners to rely on a bound labor force. They knew "just where to find their men when they wanted them," said one observer, "which is something of an item in a country where the help is mostly n—s."[2]

The system of debt peonage functioned in several different ways, but usually a white business or plantation owner in need of labor would pay the fines of those convicted of misdemeanors in exchange for a set term of work to pay off the debt. Because the system varied from county to county, state to state, and because records were rarely kept, there are no reliable statistics about the number of peons who experienced this system for the near century of its operation, but easily tens of thousands found themselves in the predicament.[3] Some of them willingly agreed to do the work, labored for their debt, then left the confinement of factory or farm once their ledger was clear. Many others, however, found themselves in shackles, worked tirelessly, abused and beaten, then ultimately kept past the date they were supposed to be free, threatened by employers or confronted with imaginary offenses or fines that justified keeping them well past their release date. Occasionally, they were forced to stay in virtual perpetuity.

Others found themselves kidnapped, taken under false pretenses and supposed private debt that had nothing to do with local or state charges, and sold to plantations or work camps for long terms. While there were white debt peons, the vast majority of them were African American, and all of the known kidnapping victims were Black, white employers being confident that Black travelers away from home could be disappeared with relative ease without the machinery of the white state taking a serious interest in their whereabouts, despite protests of concern from friends and family.

All such horrors existed in the shadow of a broader convict lease system, facilitated by white southern abuses of the Thirteenth Amendment's crime conviction exception. In most southern states following the Civil War, and in every state in the Deep South, governments provided mechanisms for the easy arrest and government lease of felony prisoners to private businesses and planters, claiming that a lack of carceral infrastructure necessitated the diffusion of convicted prisoners to various enterprises throughout the states. In reality, of course, the effort was a scheme to reimpose a version of free bound labor after the constitutional death of slavery in December 1865.[4]

In Georgia, debt peonage and felony convict leasing worked together, with the state doling out prisoners under contract with a select number of corporations and large planters to house those with felony convictions, and the counties allowing local operators to pay the fines of misdemeanants to use as their own form of bound labor on more limited terms. In the 1890s, however, that dual state-county system incorporated two new elements. The first was the development of a new version of county chain gangs, which had been present in the state since before the Civil War but were reimagined in the last decade of the nineteenth century specifically to build a road infrastructure in a decidedly rural area. Misdemeanants given jail time—and many others who were assessed fines for their misdemeanors that they were unable to pay and who were not placed into private hands through debt peonage—would be farmed out to a county camp to build the public works of the region. Unlike privately held farms that worked debt peons, such chain gangs submitted reports to the state and were subject to inspection by authorities to ensure a modicum of fair treatment. Those making such inspections, of course, were the same officials inspecting the felony convict lease camps, so their ability or willingness to ensure a base standard of living was questionable. But there was, it was assumed, a sense of the public good in chain gang labor not present in the felony convict lease system. The addition of the county camps to the system was both insidious and important, because it set the stage for state-controlled felony chain gangs after the death of Georgia's felony convict leasing in 1909.

The second element incorporated into the carceral infrastructure in the 1890s cast less of a historical shadow past the bounds of 1909 but would be even more sinister in its operation, a phenomenon that would become the bane of officials already unproblematically running a racialized for-profit bound labor system. Beginning in 1892, private misdemeanor convict camps would proliferate at the county level, wherein misdemeanants sentenced to a year or less in jail would be leased to local planters, turpentine operations, or sawmills for another version of convict leasing in microcosm, with the exception that unlike felony convict leasing, such private misdemeanor camps were subject to no oversight, no inspection. They operated as their own private fiefdoms, free to abuse their charges as they saw fit, and free to keep prisoners well beyond their sentences by concocting various fines and charges that transitioned misdemeanants to debt peons who could stay in such bondage in virtual perpetuity. And because such camps were completely unregulated, because they were operated at the county level, because the victims did not have felony convictions, such misdemeanor camps were not included in national screeds bemoaning felony convict leasing and the horrors of debt peonage. They operated in the space between felony leasing and peonage, binding the two by incorporating elements of both. In the process, they authored some of the worst abuses of Georgia's entire racialized carceral state.

Private misdemeanor camps have largely been omitted from the historical narrative of convict leasing, but they are vital to that narrative because they provide a connective tissue between the more analyzed elements of felony convict leasing and misdemeanor debt peonage. They were the ghost in the machine, a violent middle ground that hid in plain sight, even as both judicial rulings and media jeremiads attempted to topple the more well-known abuses of the system.[5] The best way to study such middle ground is to focus on a private misdemeanor camp that wasn't able to hide, whose operation incorporated all of the elements of the carceral system, and whose abuses were so egregious that the law and the media were forced to take notice—a camp like Kinderlou.

Kinderlou was owned by the McRee family of Valdosta, Georgia, and simultaneous to the McRees' use of debt peonage workers was their use of both misdemeanor and felony convict labor under the rules of Georgia's convict lease system, providing the worker base for the family's farm, crate factory, and turpentine stills, among other industrial concerns. Of all the private misdemeanor convict camps in Georgia, Kinderlou was perhaps the most diversified, and though the size of its operation was smaller than others, particularly compared to certain lumber concerns in north Florida, its reliance on bound labor and the variety of revenue streams that labor brought made it emblematic of the majority of such convict camps in the region, most of them specializing in agriculture, turpentine, lumber, or ginning. Kinderlou did it all, and the McRees relied on the use and abuse of convict labor, debt peons, and sometimes kidnapping to keep its operation in business. The story of Kinderlou demonstrates the integral interaction of misdemeanor and felony convict leasing and debt peonage. Felony leasing and peonage are often treated separately in the historiography, as two distinct systems that existed at the same time, but both were built on white supremacy and the desire for a version of re-enslavement, both actually fed off of the other, and in Georgia both found succor at the turn of the century in the creation of public and private misdemeanor camps that bound thousands of prisoners every year, the vast majority of them Black men, supplementing felony leasing and facilitating the control of new debt peons. Debt peonage was an easy method for lessees to keep misdemeanor prisoners past their release date, claiming that money owed required longer terms. Runaway peons were charged and became leased misdemeanor prisoners. The McRees moved from felony convict lessees sanctioned by the state to misdemeanor convict lessees sanctioned by the county and back again, all the while including debt peons as supplemental labor in their camp. When the labor of debtors became scarce, they engaged in an organized program of kidnapping Black travelers in south Georgia and north Florida, assuming that the racial mores of the day would give them the benefit of the doubt in any legal disputes resulting from their actions. Such was the addiction to bound labor that developed in the post-Reconstruction Deep South and the permissive nature of a misdemeanor system that did not include state regulation as part of its operation.

The misdemeanor system in Georgia is not entirely unknown, examined most carefully by scholars at the intersection of race and gender. Talitha LeFlouria and Sarah Haley in particular have parsed the consequences of misdemeanor abuse for Black women caught in the system. Their remarkable accounts have been vital to this book's interpretation of the gendered nature of the carceral system in turn-of-the-century Georgia. Their work, however, makes little to no differentiation between private and public misdemeanor camps, a necessary distinction because one was unquestionably legal and subject to regulation (though as LeFlouria, Haley, and others demonstrate, that regulation was often a red herring).[6] Private misdemeanor camps operated on the far edges of the law, and many within the state penal infrastructure argued that they were entirely illegal. The death rates in such camps were almost twice as high as in felony convict lease camps. As the operation at Kinderlou demonstrates, they were staging grounds for uglier incidents of kidnapping and debt peonage. And they included a higher percentage of Black men than any other form of incarceration between the 1890s and 1900s.

That amalgamation of misdemeanor convict leasing and debt peonage, demonstrated in the McRee convict camp at Kinderlou, is described in the chapters that follow. The first introduces the McRee family, the region of Lowndes County in south Georgia, and the birth of the dual systems there. The second chapter provides a fuller analysis of how the private misdemeanor lease system developed in the 1890s, followed by a third chapter that places misdemeanor leasing in the context of felony convict leasing, debt peonage, and county road and public works labor projects, which also traded in bound labor. The fourth chapter carries the narrative of misdemeanor convict leasing through the remainder of the century, describing its interactions with its counterparts in the system. That system, largely unregulated, allowed for substantial abuse, and the fifth chapter describes the McRees' first brush with national infamy in 1900 and 1901 as a result of their abuses of the integrated systems. The sixth and seventh chapters describe a similar controversy in 1903, one that ultimately brought a federal indictment and national infamy to Kinderlou and to the Georgia carceral apparatus at large. Chapter 8 evaluates the federal crusade against debt peonage and the problems inherent in emphasizing one kind of abuse while ignoring other elements of penal thinking that made kidnappings and other harms possible. Ultimately, though, such pressures led to the end of formal convict leasing, both felony and misdemeanor, and the continuation of prison labor in other ways following its demise, a phenomenon described in chapter 9. The final chapter follows the last twilight of the McRees' regional dynasty. Convict leasing and debt peonage programs developed before Kinderlou's years of profitable operation, which began in the 1880s and ended in the first decade of the twentieth century, and they continued in various ways for decades after. This study, emphasizing the McRees and the Kinderlou camp in Lowndes County, focuses on the turn-of-the-century decades of the 1890s and 1900s but also understands their situation in the context of the long history of the broader set of systems, emphasizing private misdemeanor leasing and demonstrating that even though the McRees' infamy and legal troubles made them in many ways exceptional, their camp at Kinderlou was in no way an exception. Theirs was an operation that combined all of Georgia's carceral systems and all of its accompanying abuses.

Georgia's antagonistic relationship with incarcerated individuals began in earnest in 1811 when the state assembly appropriated money to construct a state penitentiary at Milledgeville. Five years later, Georgia developed its first penal code, replacing common corporal punishments with imprisonment. It was a simple, centralized system that worked well until the conclusion of the Civil War. As one 1937 survey of the state's penal system concluded, "Immediately after peace had been established the number of Negro criminals increased at an alarming rate." Vagrancy and other minor crimes subjected those convicted to fines or terms of labor on public works. In lieu of such sentences, prisoners could be "bound out to some person." Many felonies were reduced to misdemeanors in the postwar penal code, but "misdemeanants could also be sentenced to the county camps which had been established both as a matter of expediency and to facilitate the use of the labor of the prisoners." The system built on "the Negroes' ignorance of the nature of their offenses and the capacity of the rebuilt penitentiary." By incarcerating a growing number of freedmen and maintaining only one substantial state prison facility, private convict leasing and misdemeanor county leasing were sold as methods of expediency rather than white supremacy.[7]

Felony convict leasing was inordinately deadly, with mortality rates "typically close to twenty percent and in some places approaching fifty percent."[8] Wilbur Patterson Thirkield, corresponding secretary of the Methodist Freedman's Aid and Southern Educational Society, argued in 1903 that under the dictates of the felony convict lease system, southern states "maintained schools of crime—an organized institution for the training of criminals." They farmed out prisoners and assigned "to the lessee the body and soul of the convicts." They were "quartered in rude stockades without proper sanitation, food or clothing. The average life of these convicts is less than ten years. Old and young are promiscuously chained and herded together." The system was one designed to generate profit for lessees and had no role in rehabilitation, which was the supposed point of incarceration. "Of the fifty boys under 18, nine-tenths of them leave prison much worse than when they come in." Recidivism failures were in part the result of a white supremacy that preyed on the vulnerable, but also because of the role that convict leasing played in the lives of incarcerated people: "Think of a system that has no reformatory element; no system to cure men of crime, but that educates young criminals in crime, and that, by its barbarity, brutalizes and dehumanizes men and sends out those that do not die under the horrors of the system to debauch and degrade society."[9]

Thirkield was not the only leader calling out the vagaries of convict leasing and peonage. "The real foundation of peonage, after all, as it relates to the Negro is the refusal to regard him as a man having rights as other men have them," explained Lafayette Hershaw in 1915. "So far has wrong, and injustice, and oppression gone that not only is the Negro outside of the consideration of the law of the land, but practically outside of the humane and kindly regard of a majority of the white race in the United States. Not only are laws perverted and given a special twist and interpretation in cases where the Negro is a party to litigation, but even words in ordinary use lose their accepted meaning when applied to him."[10] Hershaw was, by design, unaware of the misdemeanor version of convict leasing practiced in Georgia, but his conclusions would apply just as well to that system, as its version of slavery was enacted with technically shorter terms but inherently more brutality than more regulated forms of labor.

And that labor was unquestionably racialized. In the North American colonies, proper slavery began in 1619 when a Dutch ship brought twenty Angolans to Jamestown, but its presence did not immediately begin to dominate as it had in colonies further south in the Caribbean. The transition to slavery's takeover in North America happened in a spare window, generally occurring between 1670 and 1700. In Virginia in 1671, for example, the slave population was less than 5 percent of the non-native total, and white indentured servants outnumbered them three to one. By 1700, however, slaves were at least 20 percent of the population, and the lopsided ratio with indentured servants had disappeared. The process was the result of an interrelated series of factors, but the most prominent was that there had always been an assumption of inferiority among any non-white people, one that continued to grow over time. Black women, for example, almost always worked in the tobacco fields with the men, while most white female indentured servants did domestic work. Black servants didn't have surnames like white servants. Local Anglican priests claimed people of African descent couldn't become Christian. While many early slaves were treated like indentured servants, able to win freedom after serving a series of years in bondage, the racial nature of slavery became more and more prominent over time. In 1662, for example, Virginia doubled the fine for white fornication with a "negro man or woman." The transition to a system rooted in its totality in race-based slave labor was complete by 1705, when Virginia made whipping a white servant illegal, further drawing the distinction and ensuring that the new baseline for social existence was that anyone white was superior to anyone who wasn't. Between 1660 and 1710, American colonies began developing slave codes to further define the new lifelong African slave labor system. Slaves couldn't testify against white people in court, own property, leave their master's estate without a pass, congregate in large groups, enter into contracts, marry, or bear arms. In 1669, the Virginia House of Burgesses passed a law exempting masters from felony charges if they killed a slave while administering punishment. And so by 1700, Africans and African Americans had been reduced to the status of nonhuman animals, with the exception that unlike animals they were held strictly accountable for their own transgressions. The justification for their existence was tied directly to bound labor in aid of white profit.[11]

Slaves, of course, pushed back against the tyranny imposed upon them, shirking responsibilities or slowing down and sabotaging work equipment to get relief from work. Even those efforts, however, demonstrated that work had become the scarlet letter foisted upon those of African descent. Blackness became the hallmark of inferiority, and Black society was defined by labor, leading white people to assume that any labor system was inherently suited to Black employment. So even without a perceived economic need, stringent work codes for freedpeople in the aftermath of slavery would have been probable.

The project of leasing Black workers had been firmly established in the antebellum era, as slave owners sought to monetize their human capital during downtime by renting slaves to a variety of business concerns to recoup some of their investment. It was a process fed by racism, but more than that, it was a process fed by the cyclical nature of farm production.

The growing season between sowing and reaping included, of necessity, waiting for botanical mechanisms to take their course. Idle slaves were financial assets, and the waiting that was part of farm production ultimately affected planters' economic bottom line. With the nascent coal and iron industries in Alabama, with railroad construction leading to more than thirty thousand miles of track in what would become the Confederacy by the onset of the Civil War, and with large-scale plantations always in need of extra work, farmers with monetary need and available hands willingly leased their slaves to supplement income. Though it was part of a brutal slave system, however, the leasing project in slavery was less violent and deadly than the late-nineteenth and early-twentieth-century systems for which it provided precedent, as private deals for the loan of assets inherently assumed the return of those assets in good condition. Plantation agriculture lent itself to slave leasing, but though it was grotesque in its operation, it also lent itself to at least a baseline standard of living for slaves, if for no other reason than financial exigency. Any kind of incentive to protect investments, however, disappeared when slave leasing became convict leasing, when end-of-term health and wellness was removed as an expectation.[12]

After the Civil War ended slavery, white southern leaders recovered in the immediate wake of defeat to create Black Codes, removing bondage designations from previous Slave Codes and imposing similar restrictions on the now freed population.[13] South Carolina planter Henry William Ravenel expressed the sentiment of many white southerners after the war when he argued that the region needed "stringent laws to control the negroes, & require them to fulfill their contracts of labour on the farm."[14] His was an account, like so many others from white southerners of the era, that interpreted a racialized penal policy as a necessary reflection of racial character. Georgia's Black Codes included laws against trespassing, squatting, and hunting on Sundays, efforts that disproportionately targeted former slaves. They were, however, more subtle than those Black Codes in other southern states like South Carolina, the legislature hoping to skirt northern criticism by couching acts in the language of good government reform rather than overt racial retrenchment. At the same time, the legislature increased fines associated with crimes and turned former misdemeanors into felonies, giving state authorities access to a larger potential labor pool.[15] The laws of stringent control, however, fell relatively quickly to the federal government's Reconstruction policy, leaving former Confederates like Ravenel to bitterly sulk until Redemption became possible in the late 1870s. When it did, they began to reimpose many of the restrictions and labor mandates borne of the Black Codes, this time shorn of some of their racial language to maintain constitutionality after the Reconstruction Amendments.

The cornerstone of that effort was a series of vagrancy laws first passed in the years of the Black Codes in every former Confederate state save Arkansas and Tennessee, laws that gave local law enforcement carte blanche to arrest people without labor contracts; and with the exception of North Carolina, those arrested could be subject to convict leasing, playing on the assumed lack of prison infrastructure in states that had made their public arguments for secession based on a desire for local control. And it was, like the Black Codes themselves, a racially coded endeavor. In 1866, Georgia counted 325 felony prisoners, and three hundred of them were Black. Georgia's law survived Reconstruction, and Florida created a new one in its wake, as did its fellow southern states, including Tennessee.[16]

Among them were a series of enticement acts passed in every former Confederate state save Tennessee, laws that imposed felony charges on those seeking to hire workers away from their current employers. Louisiana's law imposed penalties on "any one who shall persuade or entice away, feed, harbor or secrete any person who leaves his or her employer." In Georgia, "offering higher wages or in any other way whatever" enticing a worker became a felony.[17] These were laws that prevented Black workers in particular from engaging in the market economy, tying them as in slavery to labor rather than capital. At the same time, the laws paradoxically accepted Black work as a function of the capitalism they denied, adherents arguing that after centuries of slavery, long-term work contracts were the only possible method of easing freedpeople into the new labor system. Such counterintuitive assumptions found general acceptance even in northern states and even after the nineteenth century had run its course, built on the same assumptions of innate Black degeneracy that had colored white southern thinking for centuries and drove commentary like that of South Carolina's Ravenel.

The largest threat to that system in those early days was a group of labor brokers that southern leaders, accustomed to fretting over "outside agitators," referred to as "emigrant agents." Pragmatic opportunists who saw the contingency of the region's improvised racialized labor market as a chance for profit, emigrant agents would lay bare the problems of the southern system by recruiting labor from one area and moving it to regions of greater need, even if that labor was already under restrictive long-term contracts. After Reconstruction, former Confederate states began passing emigrant agent laws to stop the out-migration of Black labor from the region, but those same states actually relied on labor brokers within the area to house and disseminate those in bondage to plantations and public works projects in need of laborers.[18]

Georgia, for example, required license fees for emigrant agents to try to curb the practice, and when one of them, R. A. Williams, refused to pay, the resulting litigation ended in the Supreme Court in 1900. In *Williams v. Fears* (1900), the court validated emigrant agent laws as constitutional against the protestations of Williams, who argued that they were an unfair tax that interfered with interstate commerce. "These labor contracts were not in themselves subjects of traffic between the States," argued Chief Justice Melville Fuller, "nor was the business of hiring laborers so immediately connected with interstate transportation or interstate traffic that it could be correctly said that those who followed it were engaged in interstate commerce, or that the tax on that occupation constituted a burden on such commerce."[19] At the same time, however, the court also quoted 1897's *Allgeyer v. Louisiana,* which argued that liberty of employment "means not only the right of the citizen to be free from the mere physical restraint of his person, as by incarceration, but the term is deemed to embrace the right of the citizen to be free in the enjoyment of all his faculties; to be free to use them in all lawful ways; to live and work where he will; to earn his livelihood by any lawful calling; to pursue any livelihood or avocation, and for that purpose to enter into all contracts which may be proper, necessary and essential to his carrying out to a successful conclusion" the work he or she chose to do. That liberty, though, was directly connected to contract law, "and this right to contract in relation to persons or property or to do business within the jurisdiction of the State may be regulated and sometimes prohibited."[20] Emigrant agent laws in Georgia were valid, and so too, the court seemed to intimate, were vagrancy laws that punished workers for not having contracts. *Williams* was a victory for Georgia's racialized labor scheme and, in the process, served as a validation of similar systems and the project of white supremacy throughout the South.

Williams was a white man, and most of the emigrant agent laws and enticement acts were aimed at white people attempting to take advantage of freedmen finding themselves in a seemingly new system that supposedly monetized their labor. The vagrancy and work contract laws themselves, however, were designed as a check against such behavior by specifically targeting freedmen, criminalizing their desire to participate as equals in the open market. In Florida, just miles south of Kinderlou, where the McRee family took much of its labor, the state's first work contract law, passed in the era of Black Codes prior to the full force of Reconstruction, punished "willful disobedience of orders," "wanton impudence," or the simple failure to complete assigned tasks as potential felonies, and while most of the Black Codes fell to federal imposition led by a radical Republican congress, Florida's work contract law lasted into the 1890s.[21]

By that time, southern states had also begun passing false-pretenses acts that punished taking an advance contract with the intention of violating it. Florida took its turn in 1891, Georgia in 1903, both seeking less to deal with actual fraud and more to create a separate rubric by which to punish Black workers attempting to void punitive labor contracts.[22] The Supreme Court finally overturned such false-pretenses laws in 1911 in *Bailey v. Alabama*, but Georgia's Supreme Court ruled that the decision did not apply to its own version, and Florida simply modified its efforts to keep the law in line with the Supreme Court ruling, both states maintaining versions of the false-pretenses law until the 1940s.[23]

In Georgia, there was also a criminal surety system sanctioned by state law, one that the McRees used and abused to their benefit, which allowed individual employers and business concerns to pay the fines associated with minor charges like petit larceny or vagrancy, then take possession of the defendants so that they could work off the total of the debt paid.[24] Georgia's 1874 law put petit criminals into the service of "any citizen of this state who pays the amount of said sentence, for said prescribed term." In 1894, the Georgia Supreme Court's *Walton County v. Franklin* decision ruled that the surety law had been invalidated by an intervening convict lease law, but after twenty years of regular practice, the hidebound tradition of surety that allowed a sanctioned version of debt peonage to exist was so ingrained in the minds and practice of white Georgia employers that it continued well past 1894.[25]

By that time, counties had another way to deal with their misdemeanants. An 1892 law allowed county authorities not needing misdemeanor prisoners for public works to send them to other counties "for the purpose of providing material for public roads and other public purposes." Counties realized that selling their misdemeanants to other counties could net them revenue not available to them through the paying of misdemeanor fines. At the same time, there were farmers and other entrepreneurs who did not have the revenue to outbid corporate entities for long-term felony prisoners but did have the ability to pay for short-term misdemeanants at the county level. A broad interpretation of "other public purposes" led some counties to lease their short-term prisoners to private entities instead of other counties, providing an additional revenue stream that played on the assumptions generated at the state level by felony leasing, on the long-held traditions of county chain gangs and private debt peonage, and on the time-worn association of Black male bodies and bound labor dating to the seventeenth century. Misdemeanor convict leasing—unregulated because it was never specifically authorized by the legislature, but still allowed to continue because of the vagaries of legal interpretation—was born.

It was a series of developments that created the crucible for operators like the McRees, whose operation was decidedly profitable but not on the scale of some of the large companies bidding for the state's felony prisoners. The unregulated misdemeanor system would grow the profits of Kinderlou and, at the same time, allow for a variety of stunning abuses. While the nightmares of Kinderlou would burst into public light in a way that many of those at private misdemeanor camps never did, they were not the only nightmares in the system. They were representative of the horrors of convict labor more broadly and of unregulated private misdemeanor convict labor in particular. "Like an infamy resurrected from the Dark Ages," warned Richard Barry in 1907, "a condition of slavery exists to-day, the horrors of which would strain credulity were they not substantiated by most copious and exact facts."[26] What follows is an attempt to substantiate by most copious and exact facts the horrors that took place at the Kinderlou convict camp in Lowndes County, Georgia, at the turn of the twentieth century, demonstrating their dependence on an intersection of debt peonage, misdemeanor convict leasing, and felony convict leasing.

The traditional convict leasing narrative has Georgia's lease system ending in 1909, with prisoners diffused outwardly to county chain gangs after that date. It was a change that changed little, as "punishment was still decentralized" and state officials still served as a "distributing agent, a disciplinarian, and a caretaker of convicts."[27] The problem with that analysis is that felony prisoners had been dispersed to county chain gangs for years by the end of the convict lease system. At the same time, state authorities were not the only ones diffusing prisoners to public and private camps, as those convicted of misdemeanors and sentenced to more than a fine did not become debt peons. Instead, they became part of a large-scale misdemeanor system that combined county chain gangs with unregulated private misdemeanor camps complete with all the brutality of their felony cousins. To be sure, the series of systems in place prior to 1909 did cast a long shadow over the chain gang system that remained after 1909, but taking convict leasing as a singular entity distorts what happened in places like Georgia. Misdemeanor convict leasing served as a conduit between felony leasing and debt peonage, making the transition in 1909 almost a fait accompli, even though its presence was largely shielded from public view. Its insidiousness, then, was both cause and consequence of its invisibility. But misdemeanor convict leasing would finally receive its national public hearing at a farm just west of Valdosta, Georgia, and just north of the Florida border: Kinderlou.

1

The McRees of South Georgia

The convict camp at Kinderlou was borne of a confluence of people and place, of a family and a particular region in south Georgia that fostered the conditions for the kind of abuse to come. It was Francis Jones, along with his brother Berry—both descended from an eighteenth-century Francis Jones, who immigrated from Wales to Virginia, who made his fortune, and whose family became powerful throughout Georgia—who first acquired land in the area in the early nineteenth century, land that only became more valuable when the first railroad was built in the years before the Civil War, passing directly through Jones's property. (He was not alone in benefiting, his brother Berry Jones acquiring much of the land that would become part of nearby Valdosta and the family more broadly controlling much of the land that constituted Lowndes County, of which Valdosta was the seat.) Jones had arrived in the region in 1832 along with Berry and another brother, Tom, who moved to nearby Thomasville and developed the land that would become the Payne Whitney Plantation.[1]

Francis, however, chose for his home base a tract of land six miles outside of the area that would become Valdosta, Georgia, and originally cleared and planted it using Native American labor. He also married a Burke County widow, Rachel Inman Spain, who ran the plantation herself after Francis's death. Spain had one child, John William Spain, from her previous marriage, and he, in turn, had two daughters, Rachel and Sallie, who lived in nearby Brooks County. All, however, were part of the Jones estate in western Lowndes County, orbiting the land like satellites and constantly pulled back to it as the center of gravity for the family.[2]

The railroad made the land even more valuable, gave it even more gravity. Among the railroad crew moving through the Jones property was civil engineer George Randolph McRee. McRee was young, born in January 1838 in Dooly County, a hundred miles north of the place that became known as Jones Crossing. The only child of Edward Lawrence McRee and Elizabeth Young, he grew up in relative privilege and attended Union College in Schenectady, New York, before returning to south Georgia and taking his civil engineering job, where he became part of a railroad survey planning a new route from Savannah to Albany, connecting the two urban centers at the far edges of the southern part of the state.[3]

George's father came from Roberson County, North Carolina, born in 1813, and moved to Georgia at eighteen years old. He married his wife, Elizabeth, in 1830 but didn't have a child for eighteen years. Elizabeth would die just two weeks after giving birth to her only son. Edward Lawrence, however, would remarry two more times after the death of his first wife and ultimately have twelve more children with his subsequent spouses.[4]

The McRees built their antebellum wealth with slave labor, the family holding twenty-one total slaves in 1850. Thirteen of them were men, and eight of them were children. The Jones family was even more dependent upon slaves, counting sixty-six slaves on the large sweep of land that would become Kinderlou.[5]

The white supremacy of the slave system and the lack of value it placed on Black lives created a historical record that didn't include them as individuals, that didn't allow for the kinds of genealogical work this chapter uses to trace the McRee family history. There was no member of that family more meaningful, more historically significant than any of those eighty-seven antebellum lives that live on only in aggregate census data. Our access to their lived experience is not a barometer of their worth, just as a similar lack of access is not a measure of the value of the Black lives caught up in the later misdemeanor lease program. That lack of access is instead a scarlet letter that stands as a testament to the lack of human decency of a place and in a people that appear all too human on the pages that follow, if only because white supremacy allowed them to leave a trace of their existence behind. So let those slaves loom like ghosts over the shoulders of all the white actors in the pages that follow, because the wealth of the McRees and Joneses was dependent upon the exploitation of Black labor. Black hands constructed Kinderlou's buildings, developed the plantation's farming success. Black minds negotiated the challenges associated with antebellum farm life in the Deep South. The Joneses and McRees reaped all the rewards and, in the process, became dependent upon a racialized form of bound labor for all of their perceived prosperity.

With the outbreak of the Civil War, the young McRee abandoned the railroad project to fight for the Confederacy, serving as a first lieutenant in the Twenty-Ninth Georgia Regiment and earning his reputation for valor at the Battle of Chickamauga in 1863. After the fight, he returned to Jones

Crossing to marry Jones's step-granddaughter, Rachel Lavinia Spain, who was, in the cloistered world of south Georgia, his third cousin. After the wedding, the young engineer-turned-army-captain turned again, this time to farming. After the death of the family matriarch, the land transferred to her two granddaughters and their husbands, divided equally between the McRees and the Joneses (Rachel's sister Sallie married another Jones, Mitchell). The McRees took the land with the old Jones residence and the Joneses moved three miles down the principal stagecoach road, creating their own home, known as Wildwood Plantation. It was then, after McRee became a landowner in his own right, that he began leasing prisoners from the state. A small number of the family's former slave population had remained on the farm after emancipation, largely from a lack of better options, but it was a number that needed supplement. As early as 1870, McRee had twenty-five people working on his property, many of them felony prison labor and debt peons. The 1880 census listed McRee as using a total of 312 weeks of "colored" labor in 1879. Those prisoners and peons grew his wealth and his operation just as a different version of racialized bound labor had done prior to the Civil War. And just like them, that labor exists historically as a data set rather than a group of individuals, demonstrating the power of discrete actors and the Redeemer project writ large to disappear generations of distinct lives. McRee used those lives to farm cabbage, tomatoes, and tobacco, then developed a herd of dairy cows. There was a crate factory, a sawmill, and ultimately a large turpentine operation.[6] By 1890, he had 8,015 acres of land valued at $20,000. The total property was worth $25,835, a wealth built in some measure by McRee's ingenuity but dependent entirely on Black labor that received no monetary recompense.[7]

The life created for McRee by that labor allowed George and Rachel to have four sons, William Spain, Edward Jones, Francis Inman, and George Young,[8] all of whom grew up on the family farm and helped work the land along with the prisoners, helping to grow the property to just under twenty thousand acres by the time of George McRee's death in May 1900. And they did so without their mother, who died prematurely in 1875. After her death, McRee invited his sister, Lou G. McRee, to the farm to help him raise his four children. Her faithful service came to define for the McRees the tenor of the white ideal that shaped their thoughts about the family's circumstances. Thus the operation came to be known as Kinderlou, translating from German as "children of Lou."[9]

Lou raised the children and ensured that they were educated, sending William to Virginia's Belview College, Edward to the University of Georgia, Francis, known as Frank, to Georgia Tech, and George to Auburn.[10] All returned after their education to Kinderlou, where the land was divided among them after their father's death in 1900. Built through debt peonage in the 1880s and a combination of peonage and misdemeanor convict labor in the 1890s, the makeshift community began to thrive. Kinderlou got a general store, commissary, and post office. It had a stop on the railroad that George McRee helped establish. Before the patriarch's death, he supplemented his income by selling lumber to the railroad. He sold milk to the government during the Spanish-American War. George also installed the farm's first turpentine still. Then there were the cotton gin and large syrup vats, all operated with the latest technology, as befitted an engineer who educated his sons to be engineers. The family marshaled waterpower to run machines that gave them an advantage over the operations of their neighboring farms. Knowing he needed more skilled laborers for the operation, he built housing and early brought in a variety of non-convict carpenters, masons, blacksmiths, and other skilled workers to help operate the technical parts of the business.[11]

His sons elaborated on their father's ingenuity, inaugurating the crate factory, which supplied fruit and vegetable baskets for their own operation and sold baskets to others for theirs. A sawmill, planing mill, and dry kiln built the family's lumber operation. They designed a cigar factory and expanded the family dairy using their Black bound labor. To get the best cigars they could, the family also brought in laborers from Cuba who knew how to roll cigars properly. Again, as with the original masons and blacksmiths, the first Cubans to take up cigar duties came of their own volition, operating on the same property as those not allowed to leave.[12]

It was a dynamic that would soon change, as the chief source of labor for the operation came from incarcerated people. Under George's nineteenth-century leadership, both Kinderlou and Wildwood became state convict lease camps, maintaining between fifty and one hundred felony prisoners at any given moment in the 1880s. Housed in two barracks, one at Kinderlou and one at Wildwood, the leased prisoners pulled stumps, installed drainage systems, built roads, and dug ditches. Others served as gang agricultural labor and even as servants, cooks, and nurses, all supervised by an overseer who reported directly to the McRee brothers.[13] They were, in other words, two plantations that operated in an almost identical fashion to antebellum slave operations, with bound labor doing all of the traditional tasks foisted upon slaves. Even without the abuses that would plague Kinderlou, the profit of the plantation's diversified operation was built on

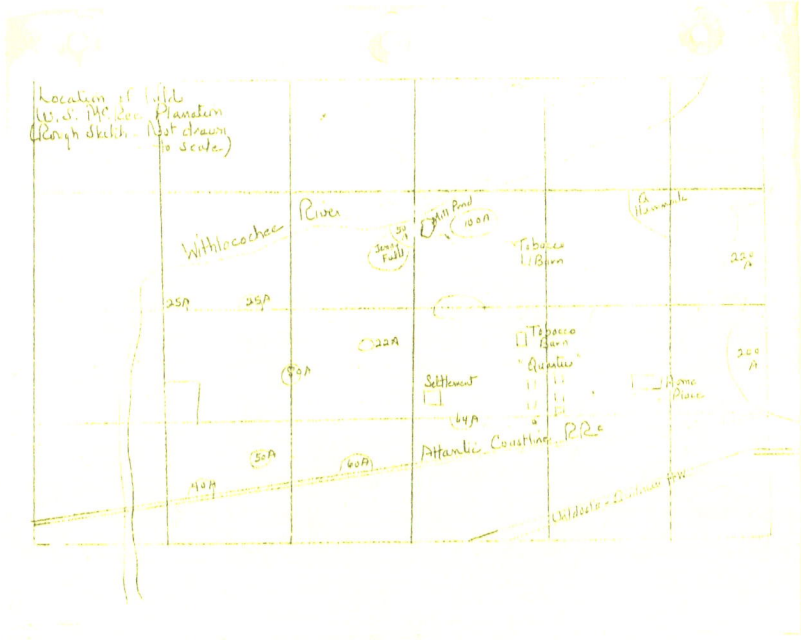

Figure 1.1. Layout of the McRee plantation as remembered by a descendant. Catherine McRee Carter, "History of Kinderlou, Georgia, 1860–1940," December 7, 1940, Lowndes County Historical Society, Valdosta, Georgia, 32.

antebellum bondage assumptions and the white supremacy that sustained them.

Then there were the truck crops.[14] "Eight years ago I was a cotton planter," George McRee explained to a reporter in 1888 in an extended interview that provides the only sustained account of McRee's own voice, his own conception of the business that he spent his life building. "I was perhaps a better farmer than the average, and yet I was able to barely come out even at the end of the year. My land was getting poorer every year, and I was getting older, and both therefore less able to maintain a struggle in which we were then but barely holding our own, as far as the cash went. I was discouraged and thought of giving it up." But soon he "began studying the truck problem. I saw that with the same hands and plows I was obliged to keep for my cotton I could put in a few acres of vegetables and fruit, and did so. But I was so afraid of losing my hold on cotton that I began by preparing my truck patches for cotton, so that I could follow vegetables with cotton. I thus hedged against the diminution of what I considered my money crop." But he turned a profit on the truck crops, and growing them actually helped produce better cotton on the land. Truck farming, McRee explained, actually "increases" the cotton crop. "My experience is this: Where I used to get a bale to three acres, I now get a bale to the acre, and the enriching of the land I always charge to the truck, which always pays for it and more besides. I get six bales of cotton to the land, and the same hand manages the truck crops," he explained. "In short, with truck, you raise more cotton on less ground, and at less cost, for all your fertilizers, and say a half year labor is charged to another crop."[15]

So he began devoting more land to the endeavor. "It has saved me from a life of drudgery and anxiety, and made me independent and happy. What it has done for me it has done for scores of my neighbors. What it has done for us it will do for any others who go at it intelligently." The reason more south Georgia farmers didn't make a similar effort was a bias against truck crops that saw them as less dignified than cotton. Profit, however, was more important than reputation, and McRee gave his interviewer a concise explanation of his operation and the money it generated for his family.

> I could say safely that I have cleared more than $50 an acre on every acre of melons I have planted in eight years, and this year I have 210 acres. I have averaged $250 an acre on 20 acres of truck clear profit. From present prices I think I will clear nearly $200 an acre on vegetables this year. I cleared $610 on one acre of cucumbers year before last, and made a bale of cotton on the same acre the same year. Last year I cleared over $100 an acre on cabbage. These things vary. One year you hit it on one thing and one year on another. But I have cleared, as I tell you, over $50 on melons for eight years, good and bad, and I am disappointed if I don't average from $100 to $200 on vegetables. My net profits for last year were $15,200 and have increased steadily each year since I began.
>
> But it is not the money that I value most. I have enriched my farm. Besides the money I have taken out of every acre, I have a surplus in the ground in increased fertility. My farm was 10 per cent richer last year—had 10 per cent more reserve in the land—than it had before I took the $15,000 in cash out of it. Or, to make the contrast. Under the old cotton system my farm paid me nothing and got poorer every year. Under truck and cotton it paid me well and got richer every year. Say that it was worth $5,000 eight years ago. I wouldn't take $40,000 for it to-day, even if it were for sale.[16]

That diversification allowed McRee to develop several streams of wealth, growing Kinderlou larger than other Lowndes County farm operations. Like others, he used Black bound labor to make his profit, but unlike them, he created more work for them to do, relying on white specialists for facility design but using Black prisoners for what would traditionally be called unskilled labor. While turpentine operations were common in the region, and cotton farming was ubiquitous, combining those operations with crates and truck crops, sawmills and cigars, made the McRee family one of the most influential in Lowndes County. McRee's ultimate goal was "to bring my place to such a condition that when divided among my four boys it will make each of them independent—as well off as if I left them a fortune of $100,000 each." It was a premonition that bore fruit both literally and figuratively. "I have 8,000 acres of land. Of this 6,500 acres is in woodland, 1,500 acres cleared. Of this latter I have 400 acres in truck and about 1,100 acres rented out. This is the material with which I have to work." Options for tenancy to build profit from his land did not appeal to McRee.

> I think our farmers make a great mistake in renting their lands. While the rent [from sharecroppers] may pay a pretty good interest on the investment, the lands are getting poorer every year. The tenant is usually irresponsible as to payment and to methods. If he makes the money he'll pay you. If he don't make it you can't make him pay. He usually treats the land as if he never expects to see it after the present year, and it consequently gets poorer every crop that is taken out of it. There may be exceptions, but that is the general rule. I shall therefore take my land out of the hands of renters just as fast as I get ready to bring it up.[17]

It was much more efficient to use bound convict workers, almost all of whom were Black, whose lives could be regulated in a way unavailable to those housing sharecroppers.

At the same time, he claimed that he mistrusted Black labor and felt that the best hedge against it was technological development.

> I have studied the labor question pretty closely and have long felt assured that the price of negro labor would be raised and the difficulty of commanding it constantly increased. I therefore thought it wise to fortify myself against it. The first protection suggested was improved machinery. The objection to this was the stumps, which clustered so thick as to prevent its general use. I moved at once against the stumps.

I now have 500 acres of land in which there is not a stump to be seen, and I'm moving on my other land now. Nothing I have done has given me so much confidence as this. I can use on it two-horse cultivators, screw pulverizers and any sort of improved machinery, and am comparatively independent. I intend to make my place as near perfect as I can get it, and equip it with the best stock, implements and buildings that money can buy, if it takes all the profit of my truck farming to do it. An intelligent farmer can put his surplus money nowhere in the world where it will pay him such a large certain and satisfactory dividend as to put it back on his farm.[18]

Unmentioned was that much of that surplus developed from his use of bound convict workers, the very "negro labor" that he claimed to worry would cost him more and that he would need either way. He would certainly find new ways to avoid employment costs, and the acreage would be more than one man could manage. "But I shall bring it up gradually. My truck interest is first, my sheep next, my pasturings and corn crop next, and cotton next, and my overshadowing object is to enrich and improve my farm. By the time I get it into condition, some of my boys will be ready to take part of it and so it will divide up," he told his interviewer.

I shall let them decide [if they want to be farmers], but I suppose they will stay here. I hope so. There is no life that is happier, more independent, freer from temptation or fuller of hearty enjoyment, and none that is safer or more lucrative. I abandoned civil engineering, and a flattering position too, to come to my farm. I shall never cease to thank God that I did so. My land will give me every year, good or bad, all the money I want, and will carry in its soil every season, a big balance to the credit of my sons. When I die, it will be an inheritance to them that will make them independent and comfortable all their lives, if they will only let it do so.[19]

They would stay, and they would become independent and comfortable, but they would do so by abusing those without such privilege.

McRee tended away from sharecropping partly because of his desire to control the lives and bodies of those working his farm, but also because sharecropping really only turned a profit for those whose land was devoted to traditional farming practices. McRee was a farmer, but he was, more than that, an engineer and a business owner. His diversified operation made sharecropping a virtual impossibility. His bent for mechanization meant that he didn't need the farming experience of sharecroppers. Tightly controlled unskilled labor could reap him the most benefit, and his successful experience with antebellum slavery ensured that he would default when he could to a version of that original model. While farm tenancy was the most common form of farm labor in the region, technology, diversification, and a history of slavery ensured that the former engineer would choose a different route when establishing his operation. And because that diversification provided quick profits on manufactured goods and truck crops, he could afford to pay for prisoners up front rather than relying on tenants to supply crop share after a traditional growing season. All crop production in the region facilitated labor abuse that was often racialized in its exploitative practices, but it was the unique setup of McRee's operation that kept Kinderlou away from more traditional and common forms of labor abuse and moved them to acquire the work of those even more vulnerable than sharecroppers.

And so McRee may not have been satisfied with "negro labor," but he and the sons for whom he was preparing his estate remained greedy to acquire it. In 1890, for example, his son Edward traveled to Albany "after prisoners for his father's convict camp."[20] There was no provision in the state felony lease contracts for collecting prisoners from seventy miles northwest of the Lowndes County courthouse. Edward was traveling to the region's largest city to pay the fines of debt peons, who would supplement the labor already at Kinderlou. The family knew that bringing peons from Dougherty County meant that any risk of potential oversight would disappear with distance, meaning that peonage contracts set for six months could easily be extended without the protest or action of authorities. And the work those peons did could be dangerous. In October 1894, one convict at Kinderlou lost a hand in a feed cutter on the property.[21] To hedge against the potential public relations problems such accidents could create, the family actively engaged in promoting itself as a paragon of civic virtue. Though Edward would become the only McRee to try his hand at formal politics, all of the brothers were political, cultivating a variety of relationships between Valdosta and Thomasville that would ultimately redound to their benefit in growing their business and sloughing off scandal when it eventually came.[22]

The family was very much part of the cultural life of the region and early kept its reputation through activity in social circles, Frank Inman McRee and his brothers spending time at high-dollar events at area clubs, particularly in nearby Thomasville.[23] Likewise, many of the leading figures in Thomasville traveled regularly to spend several days at Kinderlou. In January 1898, Frank married Carrie Chisolm, a Thomasville debutante, to an overflow crowd that left hundreds of onlookers gathered outside of the church because there was no longer any room.[24]

Such is not to say that there weren't problems that were immune to respectability politics. The McRees had trouble with fire on the property, for example, a problem that would continue into the twilight of the family dynasty. In January 1899, Will's new house burned. It was the second home at Kinderlou to have burned in the last two years. The fire began in the kitchen and engulfed the house in minutes. Heavy winds threatened other buildings on the property, but collective work kept it localized to the house.[25]

The apotheosis of their problems, however, would occur just after the turn of the century. It was on May 21, 1900, when George McRee, the patriarch of the family, died after a weeks-long illness. "No man was more universally liked than he," reported the *Thomasville Times-Enterprise*, "and the news of his death will be received with great sadness by all." Or, perhaps, it would be received with great sadness by his white peer group in the southwest Georgia corridor between Thomasville and Valdosta, as there would be little reason for those living under armed guard on the property, Black or white, to view the death as a tragedy.[26]

Post-Reconstruction south Georgia, like the post-Reconstruction South more broadly, was built on an interplay of a racialized caste system and a largely white class system, in which everyone white was considered superior to everyone Black, while gradations of whiteness built on economic and educational largesse ensured that conflict between the classes would leave those on the bottom railing against those on the top, often finding themselves on the wrong end of the criminal justice system as a result. As Charles Flynn has explained, "The white social ideology provided the avenue by which white labor was ambiguously incorporated within the plantation system—simultaneously extending to landless white workers both exploitative practices and dividends from racial discrimination." Meanwhile, all white people saw free Black labor as "at odds with the planters' idea of appropriate relations between labor and capital." Thus Black workers were considered unreliable and undisciplined, lazy and unskilled. In that situation, binding African American labor again in a manner that matched wealthy white conceptions of efficiency became a fait accompli. It played on assumptions that had been in place since the late seventeenth century. That said, felony and misdemeanor convict leasing and debt peonage systems that overwhelmingly targeted Black defendants over the poor white ones who also found themselves defined out of conceptions of proper white prosperity still only included a minority of the Black population, and many white people in control of labor systems on plantations, camps, or factories often complained that laws permitting the leasing of prisoners or the hiring of debt peons were inadequate to their needs, demonstrating that the constant wrangling over the state of convict and peon labor, described in the following chapters, was the result not only of self-flagellating screeds concerning man's inhumanity to man but of the labor demands bred by white class divisions and their intersection with white supremacy.[27]

Lowndes County found itself well within the nexus of class and caste in the late nineteenth century. The cotton crop that had defined the region in the antebellum period was slow to recover in the postwar era, and while it did eventually bounce back, there was a push for diversification to hedge against potential future losses. Commercial fertilizer, sawmills, and naval stores that built from the vast pine forests in Lowndes and surrounding counties provided real profit for large landowners in the region, further centralizing wealth and exacerbating class divisions between groups of white people. Perhaps the most valuable industry that developed from that bounty of timber was the development of turpentine, the extraction of the material used as paint thinner and its accompanying rosin used for glues, paints, and varnishes, all in high demand in the burgeoning Gilded Age national construction boom. "A turpentine laborer was usually in debt to his boss for $200 or $300" in the Lowndes County system, explains local historian Jane Twitty Shelton, and "the next employer paid off the sum to gain a worker."[28] They were labor-intensive industries that fed on each other, demanding more and more bodies to handle the load, and when one operation paid the debt of a peon already on a different operation, it created a chain of peonage, removing the worker even farther from the government and ensuring that his term of indenture could last in virtual perpetuity without any consequence to the white "employers" who were creating that chain. While there was little risk that county officials would have advocated for the peons themselves, the private debt chain created by such transfers provided further insulation to a system designed to reimpose a version of slavery and create profit for wealthy white people.

Valdosta was the seat of Lowndes County, just miles to the east of Kinderlou. The city was founded one month after the election of Abraham Lincoln and four prior to Georgia's secession. After the war, the town became a cotton farming hub for south Georgia, the bulk of former slaves in the region turning to sharecropping to survive. But while sharecropping was a value added for landowners without the resources for acquiring state contracts for felony convict labor, county officials understood that creating a free labor pool more mobile than the proto-feudal tenant system that kept farmers tied to land plots and didn't leave room for the kinds of diversification that entrepreneurs like McRee wanted to enact was a value added to the local economy. Thus, to help farming and industry develop and thrive, Valdosta and Lowndes County would, in the 1880s, begin the process of arresting small-time offenders and sentencing them to fines that could be paid by influential planters, giving those planters a labor force that they could move around as needed for various enterprises rather than waiting and hoping that a farm tenant or sharecropper would have a healthy crop that would yield some measure of profit.[29]

It was a galling, overtly racist use of the criminal justice system, and it was a standard of the Deep South white supremacy that enveloped both the state and the region. "Among all southern states during this era," explain Martha Myers and James Massey, "none exceeded Georgia in the prevalence of repressive mechanisms of social control directed toward blacks." Hundreds of lynchings and legal executions accompanied a Black male incarceration rate that "ranged between two-and-a-half to nine times higher than the rate for white males."[30] But in cases where race was ancillary to the outcome of a criminal decision, Valdosta demonstrated that it could be at least occasionally responsive to Black voices. Historian Bill Boyd describes a 1905 murder case in the town wherein a long-standing family feud boiled over into a murder-for-hire that put a white father and son on trial for a capital killing. The prosecution hinged on the testimony of Alf Moore, a Black farmworker from Tennessee who was first asked to commit the crime, then after refusing witnessed the machinations that ultimately led to the murder. Moore wasn't the only witness, but he was the one with the eyewitness account, and despite being grilled on cross-examination by defense attorneys who tried to play on Moore's race to invalidate his testimony, he was convincing. The white father and son who were being tried for the crime were convicted of capital murder and hanged in the prison across the street from the Lowndes County courthouse, just miles from the McRee family business at Kinderlou. "It may have been the first time in Georgia history," Boyd explains, "that the testimony of a black man put a white man on the gallows."[31]

By that time, the sins of the McRees had pushed them out of the misdemeanor convict business and driven them back to a state contract for felony leasing, so whatever credence an all-white jury gave the testimony of a Black man in one isolated case, white supremacy and virtual slavery were still the order of the day. The racial intransigence of the area would have its most public airing in 1918, when the region permanently earned its national reputation for white supremacist violence. After Brooks County plantation owner Hampton Smith was killed by one of his debt peonage workers for poor treatment, a manhunt instigated by both civilians and law enforcement generated a ruthless race riot in both Lowndes and Brooks Counties, with white mobs killing at least thirteen people and no one held accountable for the rampage. One of those killed was the husband of Mary Turner, who threatened to swear out warrants against her husband's killers. She was brutally killed as a result, and three days after her murder, the police found and killed the murderer of Hampton Smith in Valdosta, leaving the body for another mob to remove its genitals and drag it to a neighboring town, where they held a public burning.[32] Though the race riot occurred a decade after the death of convict leasing in Georgia, it stood as a testament to the racial intransigence of the region, which had engaged in less publicized versions of racial violence every time it placed another convict or debt peon in private hands.

"When I was eight years old," recalled author Louis Lomax, a native of Valdosta, "a white man ordered his bulldog to attack me simply because I was a Negro." A wealthy white family came out of a nearby house and chased away the white man, demonstrating the class divisions in the town, the politics of respectability that governed Deep South relationships. "Valdostans, like most people, are children of fixity; as individuals and as a tribe they find a crag, a limb, a spot of earth—physical or emotional or both—and they cling on for dear life," Lomax explained. "They change without growing, and the more they change the more they remain the same. What frightens them, as with most people, is the sudden discovery that what they are—how they have lived all their lives—stands somehow in the path of history and of progress."[33]

The Black population of Valdosta was not passive in the face of systemic abuse. In April 1893, for example, as the misdemeanor convict lease system would develop to supplement debt peonage at the county level, African American waiters at the city's hotels went on strike for higher wages. While the effort didn't yield results, as the group had no real ability to collectively bargain, it demonstrated a willingness of Black workers to defend themselves, to act.[34] When those seeking recompense were branded as criminals, however, they disappeared from public view, and the assumption of criminality ensured that in a region ruled by racism, the plaintiff cries of those laboring in virtual slavery would go largely unheard.

And even when they were heard, the willingness to engage in self-defense often turned violent. The year following the waiter strike, in nearby Brooks County a white mob embarked on a rampage, killing seven Black men in response to what white citizens claimed were two murders of local white men by Black assailants. Tip Mauldin, "a respectable white man," was killed by two Black men, the white press claimed, and "numbers of negroes exulted over this murder and even went so far as to hold a war dance a few nights afterwards around the spot in the road where the murdered man's life blood oozed out." That was obviously untrue, but it served to rile up the locals. After a Black man was arrested for Mauldin's murder, "it was discovered that a number of negroes had conspired to kill every man that was in the posse" that arrested him, and one of those who died in the plot was white planter Joseph Isham. While it was true that Isham was also killed, there was no evidence that the death was part of a plot by Black locals; but the moral panic that erupted as a result led white mobs in Brooks County to begin terrorizing the region's impoverished Black population, torturing and murdering those who they assumed to be part of the fictitious plot and leading many to seek shelter from the rampage in local swamps. In Quitman, the Brooks County seat just down the road from Kinderlou, Black leaders wired the governor, "[We] are imposed upon by mobbers and we are trying to obtain by the laws of Georgia. What should we do?" The governor, William Yates Atkinson, called out a local branch of the state militia, the Valdosta Rifles, to maintain order, but they turned out not to be necessary. When the white mob made it to the plantation of Mitchell Brice, perhaps the most influential and wealthy of the county's citizens, he shut down the rampage, angry that the mob would go after the Black workers, many of them misdemeanor convict laborers and debt peons, on his farm.[35] It was a particularly telling intersection of wealth, white supremacy, and violence in the area, playing itself out in a brief burst of pseudo-retributive anger. It would also alert the nation to the violent brand of racism that dominated the region.[36] The McRees would also live at the intersection of wealth, white supremacy, and violence, an intersection that would occasionally play out on a national stage, but theirs would play out over years, focusing violence and white supremacy on the very convict laborers who Brice was seeking to protect, all in the aid of furthering the family's wealth.

There were, however, also instances of more immediate violence. In June

1895, for example, a Black misdemeanor convict at Kinderlou, Sam Johnson, who had arrived three weeks earlier from Nashville, Georgia, killed a guard by chopping his head with an ax as he was attempting to chain prisoners together. The other prisoners stopped a second guard from shooting Johnson and then tried to escape as a group. They didn't get far, and Johnson was charged with murder and brought to the Lowndes County jail in Valdosta, where he was quickly tried and executed.[37]

The retributive violence of mistreated prisoners, combined with the misplaced retributive violence of white Brooks County farmers, frustrated a governor often embarrassed by the violent behavior in south Georgia. Atkinson's willingness to push back against such violence with the state militia was matched by his frustration with abuses in the misdemeanor convict situation. He argued that private lessees like the McRees who took advantage of the system to keep prisoners beyond their release dates, or threatened them into remaining quiet about brutality, or used peonage and the payment of court costs to extend sentences beyond those originally intended threatened the viability of the system itself and needed to be stopped. In September 1897, he sent a circular to superior and county court judges instructing them to vigorously enforce the laws pertaining to misdemeanor sentences and the leasing of those incarcerated to private camps like that of the McRees. While there was a measure of blame-shifting among some of those presiding over the state's courts, the judges, for the most part, responded by instructing their clerks to be vigilant about the issue and by writing public letters of assurance that they, too, wanted better enforcement of the misdemeanor convict statutes.[38] While Atkinson's circular and the judges' responses seemed to be positive, they were a shibboleth in three principal regards. First, judges had little ability to keep track of the misdemeanor defendants who came through their courts twelve months after their sentences, allowing abuses to continue relatively unabated. Second, arguing against abuses of the system was itself a validation of that system, which encouraged the leasing of people with misdemeanor convictions to private camps with no substantive oversight. The effort in 1897 was a wolf in sheep's clothing and would allow the predator to attack with relative impunity in the years to come. The McRees' camp at Kinderlou, for example, never appears in the state whipping reports for felony convict leasing in the 1880s, meaning that they were simply not saved properly or that the McRees were derelict in completing the process. In the 1890s, county chain gangs were at least moderately reliable in sending the state whipping reports for their charges, but private misdemeanor camps like Kinderlou operated outside of that requirement. They were able to do so because, third, there was no clear law governing such camps (see chapter 2). Even for county chain gangs, state officials had no authority to make formal changes in problematic behavior, and they had less authority over private misdemeanor convict camps, creating a dangerous lack of oversight that allowed such abuses to occur.[39]

Whatever the epistemological problems of Atkinson's critique, he was right to assert that the state's misdemeanor convict lease system was broken, a critique that would be echoed by the Georgia Prison Commission in the years to come. His screed also demonstrated that the governor saw south Georgia as a unique problem, a source of specific embarrassment in operating a system that was intended largely to be invisible. Misdemeanor convict leasing was supposed to be a kind of shadow lease hidden from public view, but the abuses of the McRees and other camps in south Georgia were bringing such shadows to life.

2

The Birth of Misdemeanor Convict Leasing

After the Civil War, the mass arrest of Black citizens began, as did the system of felony convict leasing. At the same time, however, "several hundred crimes were reduced from felonies to misdemeanors." Those convicted could be fined, whipped, imprisoned in a county jail, and sent to a county camp to engage in labor profitable to the area, helping to rebuild an infrastructure weakened or destroyed by the war. In those early postbellum years, there was no law or precedent allowing misdemeanants to be farmed out to private camps wherein lessees could earn a profit from misdemeanor convict labor outside the bounds of state-run felony convict leasing, but it was a change that would come soon enough. A 1937 report on Georgia prisons attributed the move to create misdemeanors of former felonies to "consideration for the Negroes' ignorance of the nature of their offenses and the capacity of the rebuilt penitentiary." In reality, the misdemeanor system created a cheaper alternative to felony convict leasing, and one without the kind of oversight that employers experienced in the state-run system. It gave counties more bodies to use as they saw fit at the local level.[1] What ultimately developed was a bifurcated penal apparatus, wherein prisoners with felony convictions were pushed into difficult but regulated convict lease labor, and misdemeanants, increasing in number after legislative penalty reductions, were either farmed out to county chain gangs or eventually leased to unregulated private camps.

The formal leasing of felony prisoners to a private contractor began in Georgia in 1868, based on a December 1866 law allowing the practice. It was an effort, at least in part, to curb the state's massive debt load following the Civil War, a debt that had topped 6.5 million dollars by the end of the decade. It was in May 1868 that Georgia's provisional governor, Thomas H. Ruger, leased one hundred Black prisoners to William A. Fort of Rome for work on the Georgia and Alabama Railroad. Fort paid $2,500 to use the prisoners for a year. In July, he leased one hundred more. The next year, Georgia leased the entire state prison to a private railroad construction firm, Grant, Alexander, and Co. It was a situation that was ripe for abuse, as an 1870 legislative investigation demonstrated that incarcerated individuals were given little room and little time to sleep. Water facilities were inadequate, creating a problem with hygiene. Religious services were almost universally neglected. There were cruel and brutal punishments, and whippings needed full state regulation. Still, that did not stop the state from continuing its relationship with Grant, Alexander. The company kept a stranglehold on the state's prisoners until 1874, when the lease was opened to multiple concerns. The following year, Georgia had 926 prisoners and made $10,756.48 through the lease. But the state wasn't satisfied. In 1876, the state again restructured its lease policy, providing long-term leases to three companies at $500,000 over twenty years. At the same time, there were still prisoners being worked on five-year leases from the previous system in fourteen different convict camps across the state. Added to this particular confusion, there was also a continuing litany of abuse claims, reports of poor conditions, and inconvenient and untimely deaths. To temper some of this criticism, in 1881 the state mandated that the net profit from convict leasing would go to the state's common school fund. It was a public relations gesture that did nothing tangible to eliminate the abuse of prisoners (and did little to improve Georgia's public schools), and so that abuse continued. In 1895, the state House of Representatives Committee on the Penitentiary explained, "With a few exceptions we find all the camps in bad condition, and the prisoners not well treated, and we most heartily condemn the present lease system." It was the exclamation point on the end of a particularly brutal sentence, and ultimately it led to the creation of the Georgia Prison Commission (see chapter 3). It was allowed to continue, however, because throughout the 1890s, felony convict leasing in Georgia brought the state an annual revenue of close to one million dollars.[2]

The McRees were able to grow their own convict camp because the original motive for the state's creation of the system was expediency. Without state institutions and infrastructure, and with a perceived need for free labor to salve the economic ills created by the war, Georgia required no more of lessees than housing. Along with other states like North Carolina, Arkansas, and Tennessee, there was no original charge for the prisoners because the state needed a place for them to go. In places like Mississippi and Florida, for example, states actually paid lessees early in the system for the trouble of taking on incarcerated people.[3]

Despite such presumed civic need, the real motive for all such moves was the profit that ultimately came from corporate contracts and the desire for a reimposition of free Black labor, and so Georgia and its southern counterparts passed laws to make felony convictions easier. "The black criminal population represented a threat to the economic supremacy of the white race but also a resource that could be easily exploited," explains historian Christopher Adamson. "Crime control and economic oppression were one and the same thing in the South after the Democrats seized power."[4]

In 1875, Georgia's legislature passed its infamous "pig law," a statute that raised the penalty from a misdemeanor to a felony for hog theft, an important change that served as an exception to the dominant trend of reducing felony crimes to misdemeanors. Two years later, the state's prison population had more than tripled, from 432 to 1,441, and 95 percent of that new population was Black. The following year, in 1878, 1,122 of 1,239 prisoners, more than 90 percent, were Black. In the postbellum period, states across the former Confederacy helped feed their convict populations by instituting a series of "pig laws," where white governments expanded charges of grand larceny to include the theft of farmed animals like pigs and chickens, taking advantage of the hunger and desperation of freedpeople and the tradition of theft among slaves to generate convictions that led to disenfranchisement and the elimination of Black political power. The most infamous "pig law" came from Mississippi in 1876 and stood at the intersection of white supremacy and speciesism, maintaining the property status of nonhuman animals and attempting to return Black humans to the status of property in the immediate post-Reconstruction age.[5] The Mississippi version of the law reduced the grand larceny property value from twenty-five dollars to ten dollars and singled out a variety of stolen farm animals as requiring a charge of grand larceny, even if the human-imposed value of those animals was less than ten dollars.[6] "Any hog, pig, shoat, cow, calf, yearling, steer, bull, sheep, lamb, goat, or kid of the value of one dollar or more" earned the thief a charge of grand larceny, which merited a sentence in the state penitentiary.[7]

In 1947, Vernon Lane Wharton argued that Mississippi's pig law exploded the prison population and fed convict leasing. His characterization held sway until the 1990s, when Matthew J. Mancini's study of convict leasing demonstrated that Wharton's claims did not match actual convict statistics, though there was an increased number of arrests and convictions after the law's passage. It was instead, he argued, convict leasing itself that boosted those numbers. As Mancini explains, the prison population in Mississippi grew from 375 in 1874 to 1,003 in 1877, but by 1883, it was down to 752. When the pig law was repealed in 1888, the prison population was only 499. After the repeal, the prison population in the state exploded again to 990 by 1895.[8] Still, Wharton's analysis cast a long shadow, and there was in Georgia, unlike in Mississippi, a quantifiable explosion in the number of those incarcerated with felony convictions following its earlier version of the pig law. Much of the later scholarship features repetitions of his numbers, despite Mancini's convincing rebuttal.[9]

Whatever the direct cause of increased criminal convictions, passage of pig laws in Georgia, Mississippi, and other southern states was intended not only to punish African Americans—the group of landless poor most likely to steal animals for basic survival—and tie Republican rule in the South to a scourge of lawlessness but also to help earn the loyalty of small white landholders, because their economic position was so tenuous, and their reliance on the few livestock in their possession kept them alive. Those livestock were usually the only meaningful possessions held by poor white southerners. "Landowners were concerned about petty theft not only because of the losses they incurred but also because agricultural theft gave landless laborers independence," writes Pippa Holloway, who has studied these laws in relation to criminalizing the Black population. "Individuals who could survive on their own did not need to depend on their employers for income and food."[10]

States across the South would mimic the laws of Mississippi and Georgia, and the system the victims of those laws faced was usually inordinately brutal. Jesse De Vancey, for example, a Georgia guard who whipped Black prisoner Aaron Byron to death in the early 1870s, was unapologetic. "I whipped him for impudence and for refusing to work," he explained. "I whipped him on the bare skin."[11] Georgia Senator Joseph E. Brown, who had served as the state's last governor under the slave system, had a twenty-year lease in the 1870s and 1880s that promised him three hundred prisoners per year at a rate of seven cents per man. "If there was no collusion of government and businessmen at first," historian Fletcher Green explained in 1949, "it soon developed and high ranking public officials lined their pockets with the sweat, blood, and tears of convict laborers." It was a practice that Brown defended in the U.S. Senate, pointing to the late industrial revolution taking place in northern urban hubs and arguing that under convict lease, "no matter what goes wrong you have no labor strike."[12] The comparison of convict labor to northern metropolitan "wage slavery" would become a common conceit in white southern defenses of the practice.

Those defenses were largely in aid of felony convict leasing, but those incarcerated for misdemeanor offenses were funneled through their own system that served as a kind of connective tissue between felony leasing and debt peonage labor. Misdemeanor chain gangs had been in place in Georgia since the early nineteenth century. The criminal code set the punishment for misdemeanors at fines "not to exceed one thousand dollars, imprisonment not to exceed six months, to work in a chain-gang on the public works not to exceed twelve months," or some combination of the three, at the discretion of the sentencing judge. The fines were there largely to be paid by planters to create a steady supply of debt peons, the prison time to justify the construction of county jails, and the chain gang to facilitate misdemeanor convict labor. The county misdemeanor camps were inspected annually. There were rules in place for their operation. In September 1891, the state legislature passed a law regulating corporal punishment in those public camps. Superintendents were required to hire whipping bosses, and only those two were allowed to administer such punishments. And they could only do so "in cases where the same is reasonably necessary to enforce discipline or compel work or labor by such convict." It was an intentionally broad statute, designed to appear proscriptive for misdemeanor convict abuse but in reality allowing virtually anything under the broad cope of enforced discipline or compelled work.[13] The following month, October 1891, the state made it legal for counties to hire out misdemeanor prisoners to other counties to pay court fees, not allowing private misdemeanor lease but allowing the movement and leasing of misdemeanants across county lines to places in need of chain gang labor for public works.[14]

The move toward a version of private misdemeanor convict leasing began in 1892. In early November, Muscogee County's C. E. Battle introduced a bill in the Georgia House that allowed county authorities with control of misdemeanor chain gangs to send those misdemeanants beyond the bounds of the arresting county, "for the purpose of providing material for public roads and other public purposes." On November 29, the bill passed overwhelmingly, 94–11.[15]

The following day, the House bill arrived at the Senate, and immediately A. T. Hackett of the state's Forty-Fourth Congressional District sponsored an additional bill to provide "for the better care and humane treatment of misdemeanor convicts." Both would eventually pass, the House bill with amendments, which the House would then approve on December 6. That same day, the Senate unanimously passed the better treatment bill.[16]

The official path for prisoners at that point was either time at the state penitentiary in Milledgeville or state contracted convict leasing for those with felony convictions, and county jails, debt peonage, or county-controlled chain gangs for misdemeanants. The new law would expand the chain gang operation of counties by allowing them to lease their misdemeanants to other counties for public road work or, perhaps, to private individuals outside the county for "other public purposes." The broad language of the law did not authorize private misdemeanor camps, but it opened the door to their possibility. Because such camps would function outside of official control, and because of the prevalence of debt peonage as a strategy for obtaining misdemeanants for private labor, it is difficult to know whether or not the law was designed to legalize behavior already in place or to open new avenues of potential county revenue not previously there.

Whether the new law was in aid of the maintenance of something ongoing or the start of a new system, the counties' need for revenue was driving the legislation. Felony convict leasing at the state level in 1892 was divided into seventeen private camps, but they were operated by only a handful of entities. Chattahoochee Brick Company, Dade Coal Company, James M. Smith, T. J. James, and W. B. Lowe had full control of all of the state's felony male prisoners, while W. H. Maddox operated a separate women's camp. There was a functional trust system in place similar to that operated by America's large corporations throughout the Gilded Age, with five operators maintaining their functional independence while ensuring that they held a monopoly on state felony convict labor. There were almost two thousand prisoners under their employ, 90 percent of them being Black. Between 1890 and 1892, 107 official deaths had been reported.[17]

It was a deadly, insidious system, but for white county leaders, it was one that they felt was being denied them because of a combination of state control and corporate hegemony. That left misdemeanants as a potential vehicle for labor and profit. Debt peonage allowed the local elite to maintain a bound Black workforce, but there was little public works labor or profit in it for the counties, with the paid fines of those convicted providing revenue that many saw as inadequate—money, they felt, that could be supplemented with a version of misdemeanor lease.

The following year, the legislature further enhanced county authority over misdemeanants by passing a law allowing counties or municipalities of at least thirty thousand to create a "Reformatory Prison" for those incarcerated for misdemeanor offenses, including minors under sixteen

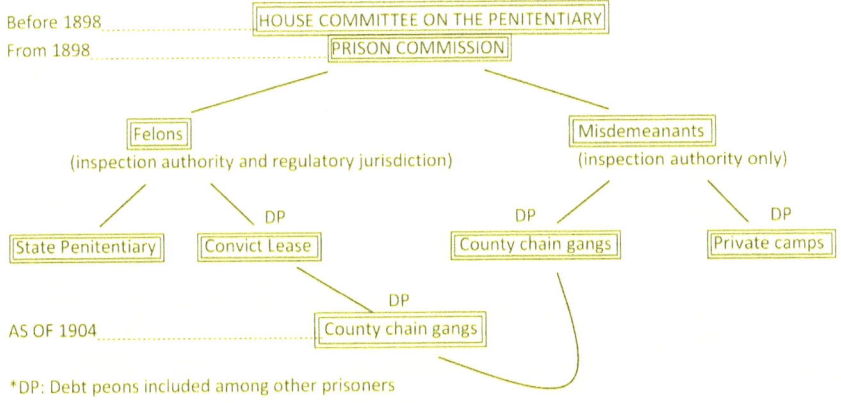

Figure 2.1. Structure of Georgia's carceral system, 1892–1908.

years of age. The "prison" would enact the "punishment, confinement, safe-keeping, humane treatment, protection, profitable employment and reformation of those who may be inmates." Counties were to make the new entities "self-sustaining and self-supporting by the profitable employment of its inmates." To that end, superintendents at such facilities needed to keep the prisoners "constantly at work during week days, allowing the proper time for rest and meals. The kind of work and the number of hours to be worked each day shall be prescribed by the respective authorities" of each county. That said, counties had to engage misdemeanor prisoner labor "as to avoid all competition with free labor."[18] It was a victory for the counties, creating their own misdemeanor fiefdoms within the broader state system. The felony trust might have contracts with the state for long-term prisoners, but the counties were free to create their own camps for misdemeanor labor. And because they didn't have the public odor of convict leasing, and because they were essentially just allowing counties to reap new profit over and above what they were already able to make from debt peonage, the misdemeanor camps would largely develop without state or media oversight.

Another bill that didn't pass in 1892, introduced by John I. Hall, would only exacerbate the county revenue. He proposed that county judges and juries should have the power to reduce felony convictions to misdemeanors, giving county authorities an even greater pool of incarcerated individuals from which to pull. It didn't pass, but it would have made a dramatic impact on the misdemeanor population, driving the supposed necessity of farming out county misdemeanants to private camps. The keeper of the state penitentiary supported the law, arguing in 1894 that it would help reduce the state prison population. That year, there were 2,813 felony prisoners in eighteen camps. While Thomas J. James had become another lessee, the virtual monopoly was still in place. But the large number of prisoners and the different parts of the state where the camps were located made maintenance of the system unwieldy. Creating more discretion for judges and juries at the county level, he argued, could reduce the felony population and still ensure that "criminals would be adequately punished, society fully protected, and the number of felony convicts materially lessened."[19] It also meant, of course, that the counties could use their discretion to stock themselves with misdemeanants for use as they saw fit.

In response to the recommendation, H. A. Jenkins of Putnam County proposed the law again, playing on the momentum in the legislature driven by county authorities. And it passed. As of November 1895, judges and juries convicting defendants of felony charges—with some notable exceptions like treason, insurrection, murder, manslaughter, rape, arson, and others—could in the punishment phase of the trial "reduce the crime of such felony to that of a misdemeanor."[20] The counties now had a mandate to create their own misdemeanor prison camps and a ready assurance that they could attain as many misdemeanants as they needed to make the system profitable at the local level.

But there was always more they could do. The same day that the new misdemeanor law went into effect, George P. Monro of the Twenty-Fourth Congressional District introduced a new bill into the Georgia Senate allowing counties "to hire out misdemeanor convicts to private individuals, upon such terms as may subserve the ends of justice." An amendment was added to ensure that no county could lease its misdemeanants to more than two lessees, but with that change, the bill passed the Senate the following week and was sent to the House.[21] That bill ultimately died in the legislature's other body, prompted by the indefinite postponement proposed by congressman E. J. Reagan of Henry County. Reagan had earlier in the session proposed a law that would have placed county and municipal chain gangs under the control of the state penitentiary department. That law didn't pass either, but it was a clear demonstration of Reagan's concern about a lack of state oversight in the forward progress of misdemeanor legislation that seemed designed solely for the profit and satiation of county authorities. Though he wasn't able to grant the penitentiary officials control over misdemeanor camps, he was at least able to kill broad state sanction for private misdemeanor camps.[22]

Official state sanction, however, was really unnecessary. The momentum of progress in favor of county penal development without any real oversight from the legislature or the penitentiary department ensured that the counties would be able to lease misdemeanants as they wanted without encountering any substantial pushback from state officials. The 1892 law's broad "public purposes" language, the 1893 statute's emphasis on making county misdemeanor facilities self-sustaining, and the 1895 law's emphasis on work all created the possibility of interpreting the law as written as allowing counties to provide misdemeanants to private camps within their borders and across county lines. Wealthy county residents like the McRees, who had local power but didn't have the resources of Dade Coal or Chattahoochee Brick, could enter the convict leasing game at a lower cost and a lower risk, with confidence that their behavior in such private camps would go largely unregulated as long as the county got paid. That lack of oversight, in fact, probably wouldn't have happened if misdemeanor convict leasing had been officially sanctioned by the legislature in 1895, as that mandate would have brought with it the need for some kind of regulatory policy. The counties and the lessees got all the benefits of a small-time version of convict lease, including the ability to turn prisoners with felony convictions into misdemeanants if it suited them, without any of the bureaucracy related to felony convict leasing. It was a victory for everyone in the counties except for those sitting in the defendant's chair at trial.

In 1895, R. F. Wright submitted the first of two comprehensive state government reports on misdemeanor convict camps in Georgia. He found 795 misdemeanor prisoners throughout the state, 749 of whom were Black. There were twenty-seven white men and boys and nineteen Black women and girls. Eleven of the prisoners were under the age of fourteen. The average sentence was nine months with an average of ten hours of work per day.[23]

Perhaps most importantly, of the thirty-three misdemeanor camps in operation, twenty-six of them were in private hands, operating in a way that Wright found to be illegal. Camp owners paid between three and six dollars per month for their prisoners. While the races were not chained together, they did work together and stayed in the same sleeping quarters. "Very little attention is given to the comfort or sanitary condition of the sleeping quarters," Wright reported. The ventilation was poor. Fires were not allowed, even in the coldest months. There were no hospital buildings or medical treatment facilities. Food rations were "scant and meager, and really insufficient to sustain health and strength." There was very little recordkeeping of the prisoners in the camps, which made discovering whether a given prisoner was being kept beyond his term of indenture virtually impossible, though Wright was "satisfied" that "such cases occur not infrequently." Most of the camps had no designated whipping boss as prescribed by law, instead allowing all guards to carry straps, and they "punished the convicts *ad libitum*." The punishments were "cruel, brutal, savage, and barbarous." There were at least twenty-seven documented deaths, more than twice that of the state penitentiary system over the same period, and, Wright assumed, many others that went unrecorded and unremembered. "It is a disgrace to civilization," he reported, "that, when most of the misdemeanor convicts go from the courts to the chaingangs, they are sold bodily for the term of their sentence, often to private parties who are responsible to no one for their treatment."[24]

Two years later, Phill G. Byrd submitted a second report, demonstrating the astronomical growth of the problematic misdemeanor system. By 1897, he counted 1,792 prisoners in the camps, 1,660 of them African American. Seventy-nine of the prisoners were under sixteen years old. While the food situation in the camps seemed to have improved, and while there was variation among the numerous camps across the state, the vast majority of the problems noted in 1895 were still present, and the death rate was still more than double that of the state penitentiary.[25]

The number of county camps had grown precipitously. There were twenty-five camps operated by counties, two by municipalities. But twenty-four camps were still held privately, including Kinderlou.[26]

The misdemeanants employed in those camps were charged with a variety of offenses, ranging from violation of segregation laws to petty theft, from obstructing a bridge to giving liquor to someone within two miles of

Table 2.1. County misdemeanor camps, 1897

Fulton (4)	Bartow	Muscogee	Houston
Chatham (3)	DeKalb	Spalding	Walton
Richmond (3)	Glynn	Laurens	
Bibb (2)	Jefferson	Burke	
Floyd	Dougherty	Greene	

Phill G. Byrd, *Report of Special Inspector of Misdemeanor Convict Camps of Georgia* (Atlanta: Franklin Printing and Publishing, 1897), 4.

Map 2.1. The location of Georgia's misdemeanor camps in 1897.

a polling place on election day. Violating county health regulations was a misdemeanor; so too was cutting turpentine boxes out of season and giving cigarettes to minors. By far the most common racialized misdemeanor charge was vagrancy. "Persons wandering or strolling about in idleness, who are able to work, and have no property to support them" were vagrants. So too were "persons leading an idle, immoral, or profligate life." People who begged on the street, gamblers, people who sold stolen goods, "persons who are able to work and do not work," all were considered vagrants. The vague nature of the statute gave law enforcement the ability to find virtually any poor Black Georgia resident guilty of a misdemeanor charge if the county needed labor.[27]

Most of the prisoners in county camps worked on road development projects, though counties with multiple camps also had county farms. In

Chatham County, the farm was worked predominantly by Black women. Fulton County's "woman camp is located on the Fulton county alms-house farm," as was the case in Richmond and Laurens Counties. Glynn County's farm camp used both women and men, white and Black.[28] While the treatment of prisoners in county misdemeanor camps was far better than that of the private entities, there were still substantial discrepancies between them. Richmond, Glynn, Dougherty, Burke, Houston, Muscogee, Walton, Laurens, and Green Counties only employed incarcerated people from their own counties, but Chatham kept six prisoners from Liberty County and four from Bulloch County and paid nothing to those counties for their charges. Fulton, Floyd, Spalding, and Bartow Counties paid three dollars per month to other counties to employ their prisoners. Bibb County paid $3.33 per month. Jefferson and DeKalb Counties paid $3.50.[29]

The figures demonstrated that misdemeanor camps, even those operated by county officials, could still be substantially diverse. And while counties with small, rural populations like Liberty and Bulloch sent their misdemeanants to larger nearby counties like Chatham, largely because they didn't have the infrastructure to maintain more than a handful of incarcerated people, counties that actively paid for misdemeanants for road work were doing a public version of private camp operations like Kinderlou. And though officials in the leasing counties were ostensibly responsible for misdemeanants from other places, and those misdemeanants were subject to official oversight, they were not subject to the oversight of officials from counties where they were convicted. The county camps were held up as exemplars of what should be done with misdemeanants, engaging them in rehabilitative labor on public works for the broader public good under the watchful eye of county administrators who followed a standardized set of rules. Certainly that structure made them more reliable than their private counterparts in both the felony and misdemeanor systems, but there was still wide variation in the operation of facilities and their method of acquiring bound labor.

Accompanying the county facilities were two small municipal camps, operated by the city governments of Thomasville and Waycross in south Georgia. There were a total of twenty-seven Black prisoners in the camps "employed on the streets of Thomasville and Waycross" along with free labor. They were reported to be "well and cleanly clothed and found to be cheerful and as contented, seemingly, as people of this class could be under similar conditions."[30] It was clear from official support and defense of felony convict leasing that such statements could be misleading, but the

Table 2.2. Private misdemeanor camps, 1897

Jasper (3)	Decatur
Wilkes (2)	Washington
Lowndes (2, both operated by the McRees)	Franklin
Coffee (2)	Lee
Oglethorpe	Pulaski
Clark	Ware
Morgan	Dooly
Oconee	Bulloch
Irwin	Putnam
Emanuel	

Notes: Nine of the camps (101 convicts) operate farms.
Five of the camps (175 convicts) operate turpentine businesses.
One of the camps (nineteen convicts) operates a sawmill.
Two of the camps (forty-three convicts) operate a turpentine business and a farm.
Two of the camps (forty-two convicts) operate a farm and a sawmill.
Two of the camps (51 convicts) operate a farm and make bricks.
One of the camps (123 convicts) operates a farm, sawmill, and turpentine business.
Source: Phill G. Byrd, *Report of Special Inspector of Misdemeanor Convict Camps of Georgia* (Atlanta: Franklin Printing and Publishing, 1897), 4, 6.

municipal camps seemed to be the least problematic operations of a decidedly problematic system.

Most problematic were the private camps, which housed 598 prisoners, 550 of them Black men, twenty Black women, twenty-seven white men, and one white woman, with eighteen of the Black "men" under sixteen years old.[31]

As was the case in 1895, most camps paid between three and six dollars per month to the county for the use of those convicted of a misdemeanor, though there were exceptions, with the average price per prisoner at roughly fifty-five dollars annually. Within that average, however, there was broad differentiation. James Price of Oconee County and G. M. Sherouse and Co. of Bulloch County paid only thirty-six dollars per year for a convict, for example, while S. F. Floyd and Co. of Ware County and A. T. Beach and Co. of Coffee County paid seventy-two dollars per year for a convict, with prices fluctuating based on availability and operator demand.[32]

The previous year, in 1896, the number of prisoners in the county camps ranged from 1,333 at its highest to 688 at its lowest, the average number being 1,010. In the private camps, there were 671 and 389, respectively, with 530 on average. At the same time, however, twenty-three deaths were

Table 2.3. Private camp deaths (reported), 1896

Donaldson & Babb (Decatur)	1 death (31 convicts)
JR Allison & Son's (Lee)	1 death (21 convicts)
George R. McRee & Sons (Lowndes)	**1 death (80 convicts)**
JW Jarell (Oglethorpe)	1 death (22 convicts)
WE Bayne (Jasper)	3 deaths (13 convicts)
RR Jones (Morgan)	2 deaths (12 convicts)
JR Allison & Co. (Irwin)	3 deaths (32 convicts)
JR Allison & Co. (Pulaski)	3 deaths (37 convicts)
Unnamed additional camp	3 deaths
Greer Brothers (Dooly)	2 deaths (115 convicts)

Note: Greer Brothers was the largest private camp, with a low in 1896 of eighty-five prisoners and a high of 135. Byrd's report originally included individual camp reports along with the broader overview, but those reports did not survive.

Source: Phill G. Byrd, *Report of Special Inspector of Misdemeanor Convict Camps of Georgia* (Atlanta: Franklin Printing and Publishing, 1897), 12–13.

reported in the county camps and nineteen in the private camps (2.28 percent and 3.58 percent, respectively.) Not only was the death rate substantially higher in the private camps, but those nineteen deaths in private hands happened in only nine of the camps.[33]

The majority of county camp prisoners worked roughly ten hours a day, with "two or three" working more. Most of the private camps worked the prisoners "from a fourth to a half as many more hours" than ten, meaning they labored between fourteen and fifteen hours a day.[34] The hours worked were a demonstration of the vulnerability of the poor, and particularly the Black poor, in the late nineteenth-century South. The economic need of the region would have driven many to work at the farms and businesses doing the leasing, but fifteen-hour days would have made it hard to recruit employees, and hourly pay would have meant that the private work would have cost the business owners more money. The new private misdemeanor system, then, wasn't a response to a labor shortage in the region. It was a response to dwindling county budgets and the desire of white employers to avoid the costs associated with paying for that labor and creating conditions that would entice it to those farms. In more regulated systems, that lack of enticement would necessitate the financial trade-off of clothing, housing, sheltering, and medicating those who weren't working there by choice, but operating as a kind of shadow system within a broader and already insidious apparatus made those doing the work vulnerable to a lack of basic necessities, as well.

Many of the prisoners in all of these camps "are not properly clothed, and in a few camps, the garments worn by the bare-footed negroes were not only very filthy, but were worn to shreds and were ragged to a shocking degree." The investigator noted that in many of the misdemeanor camps, "the prisoners are not given shoes when they need them." In the south Georgia camps, the barefooted prisoners "assured me that they had shoes at the camps, but preferred to go bare-footed, as it was more comfortable. It is needless to state that the bare-foot convicts were all negroes." Whether such statements were ingenuous or not, the investigator reported that food rations in the northern part of the state tended to be good in all of the camps. "The lessees and superintendents who work convicts, take the practical view that a convict, like a mule, must be fed if you expect paying returns from his labor." In the "pine-belt camps" of the south, however, the prisoners "go from year's end to year's end without a taste of vegetables." Bulk meat and cornbread made up the dominant part of their diets.[35]

The county camps varied as to housing, but all used tents during road construction. Housing at other times seemed to be in good order, with the exception of the Glynn County camp, which required sixty-one men to sleep in a nineteen-square-foot room, with no window or other ventilation. While "a few" of the private camps had facilities comparable to those of the county camps, "quite a number of these private camp prisons are either 'sweat-box' or 'barn,' and are totally unfit for human habitation. Few of them have ever tasted of lime, and white-wash is a stranger." Eight of the camps provided neither bunks nor mattresses. Another eight provided old ratty mattresses with filthy blankets. The final third of the private camp facilities met with the investigator's approval.[36]

There was gender segregation in sleeping quarters when women were present, which was interpreted in reports as a humane response to prevailing gender norms but in reality left women more vulnerable to sexual exploitation in the camps. With the exception of Glynn, Chatham, Bibb, and Jefferson, sleeping quarters in the county camps were racially segregated when white prisoners were present. Fourteen of the twenty-four private camps had only Black prisoners. Of the other ten, four of them kept white and Black prisoners chained together at night. One slept its white prisoners with the free labor, and another slept them with guards.[37]

Two or three camps had running water and bathroom facilities, but most used tubs to gather waste. While some of those facilities made an effort to regularly clean the tubs, many others did not. "The odor emitted from these miniature cesspools, was enough to have killed anyone but a sick misdemeanor convict . . . No [felony] penitentiary camp I have ever visited has anything that could compare with such horrors."[38] Some of the camps had hot water for bathing, others just cold water, and others "appear as if only the showers of heaven were served the poor wretches for ablution."[39]

Of the private camps, only the two McRee camps in Lowndes County and the Jim Price camp in Oconee County had hospital facilities. Obviously the McRees were not paragons of virtue in that regard. Kinderlou had hospital facilities because its time as a felony convict camp left it far more vulnerable to state oversight. The county camps, meanwhile, had better medical care. The investigator deemed Fulton best prepared, with Bibb and Richmond having contracts with local hospitals for emergency medical care for people with misdemeanor convictions. Floyd County had segregated hospital facilities. Chatham had one facility without segregation, as did Houston County. Eleven of the county camps and the two municipal camps had no hospital care. County camps used county physicians, while private camps called in physicians when necessary, and it was regular practice for overseers and superintendents to find them unnecessary. Several of the private camps had not called in a doctor in more than a year, others for multiple months.[40]

The investigator heard several reports of brutal beatings but could find no specific evidence of the claims. Prisoners were unwilling to talk, "lest I might betray that complaint to his master." He separated such brutal beatings from what he considered punishment, for which a leather strap was used. "My observation has been that where the strap has been used least, the best camps exist and the best work has been turned out by the convicts."[41]

In the county camps, "harsh treatment" was "the exception, and not the rule." There was, as an example of such exception, an incident in the Houston County camp in 1896 wherein two guards, acting without the supervision of a superintendent, beat a man named "Buster" Tucker unmercifully. The guards were indicted by the Houston County grand jury, tried, convicted, and sentenced to a fifty-dollar fine. The governor then commuted the remainder of Tucker's sentence as a form of recompense for the victim.[42]

There was far more harsh treatment in the private camps, as "many of the camps are run by men whose object is to make the most money possible out of the convict's labor, regardless of the cost to the poor, and now helpless prisoner." And the condition of such treatment was almost always racial. In the Donaldson & Babb camp in Decatur County, one white convict was boarded at a Donaldsonville hotel, earning money for the camp by painting houses in town. Another white convict was made a guard of the Black prisoners and given keys and a gun. None of the twenty-five Black prisoners had such opportunities. At the R. R. Jones camp in Morgan County, with one of the largest body counts, two of the eight Black prisoners had broken legs. Both claimed that their injuries were accidental, but it was an admission difficult for the investigator to believe.[43]

J. R. Allison had three private camps. He lived in Abbeville but had camps in Pulaski, Irwin, and Lee Counties. There were nine deaths in Allison's camps in 1896. In the Lee County camp, which pulled incarcerated individuals from Lee, Sumter, and Schley Counties, a guard shot and killed Will Morris after claiming the prisoner had drawn an ax and threatened him with it. In another instance, one Black prisoner was sick for several days and died before anyone at the camp called a doctor. In Allison's Irwin County camp, which pulled prisoners from Sumter, Wilcox, Tatnall, and Marion Counties, "the negroes looked worse than at any camp I have inspected." Five prisoners died at the camp in 1896.[44] The Pulaski County camp witnessed three die in 1896. It took its prisoners from Pulaski, Dodge, Wilcox, Sumter, Twiggs, and Montgomery Counties. When guards beat one man to death, one citizen who witnessed the brutality went before the grand jury and explained what he saw, but "Mr. Allison had friends on the jury," and "other citizens on the jury had thought that it would be best to hush the whole deplorable affair up and keep it out of the courts and out of the papers."[45]

But Allison's camps weren't alone. The Wilkes County camp of W. H. and J. H. Griffin was the site where a camp guard named Bob Cannon beat an elderly Black convict, Frank McRay, to death. The "residence" for the prisoners on the property had no windows, no light, no ventilation. "How human beings could confine a fellow being to such an existence, I can't understand." Lizzie Boatwright, an eighteen-year-old sentenced to six months for larceny, told the investigator how she had been whipped by Cannon. In one instance, she and another female prisoner had sore feet, so they stopped on the road to fix the men's shoes they were made to wear. Cannon ordered them to strip and cursed them when they objected because there were so many men present. He made them undress, then he beat them.[46] It was another example of the precariousness of sexual segregation in camps and the vulnerability of women to abuse specifically related to their gender.

Byrd noted that the laws governing misdemeanor convict labor appeared in 1800 and 1801, requiring counties to appoint whipping bosses and set "humane rules and regulations" for the governance of misdemeanor prisoners. But "there are not five camps in the State that have complied" with those rules. Laws in 1884 and 1885 required camps to keep a book wherein the names of all misdemeanor prisoners were listed every day with a record of conduct and that for every instance of good conduct and diligent work, the convict's service time would be shortened four days each month. "There is not a camp in the State that was keeping a book of record."[47]

Of course, the reason for that noncompliance was that those early versions of antebellum penal law did not envision the late-nineteenth-century version of the practice. The 1801 law Byrd referred to was never intended to govern private camps. It was directed specifically at "governing authorities of counties and municipal corporations" that were "employing or having labor performed by convicts." It did, however, require "reasonable and humane, rules and regulations" and mandated that counties appoint a "superintendent, commissioner, guard, whipping-boss, or other person connected with the management of convicts, as to the care, keeping, control, work, and discipline of convicts." That said, the law also stipulated that the whipping boss, superintendent, or other authority figure could not "be personally liable for any injury or damage to any convict."[48] The 1885 law never mentioned anything about public or private camps, assuming "persons having charge of chain-gangs" would be those superintendents, commissioners, guards, or whipping bosses appointed by counties, and it did require the keeping of a book and complete record of the prisoners, just as Byrd described.[49] As the new laws developed in the early 1890s, however, making private misdemeanor lease possible, the records requirement began to be ignored, and only more so after no consequence arrived for not having kept them.

Even without the book, however, many of the county camps were providing time off for good behavior as required, while some provided substantially less than the required amount. In the private camps, the situation was more problematic, with only nine of the twenty-four camps providing at least some time off for good behavior. While in many cases the investigator found written records relating to prisoners in good order, in others "records were very meager and incomplete, while in some instances no records were kept at all."[50]

"These private chain-gangs exist and are being operated against the law, and in spite of the rulings and decisions of the Supreme Court," the investigator explained, and "the average penal camp of the State penitentiary is a heaven, compared to the agony and torture suffered by misdemeanor convicts in many of these joints of suffering." Therefore, "I think it would be to the best interest of the most elements, and the greatest number of people, for the law making private camps illegal, to be repealed, and at the same time legislate all the misdemeanor convict camps in the State under the supervision of the Principal Keeper of the Penitentiary, and provide for their regular inspection."[51]

"God only knows just how badly the misdemeanor convict camps of Georgia need systematizing and regulating. Surely there can be no genuine civilization where man's inhumanity to man is so possible *and so in evidence.*"[52]

In a supplement to his original submission, Byrd reported that he had discovered two additional private camps in Elbert County. One was run by J. C. Hudgins, who had fourteen Black prisoners, all men and boys from Clark County, with only one under sixteen years old. The camp itself was created on March 26, 1897. The other camp, run by Bedford H. Heard and his brother-in-law, J. W. McCalla, who bid for the remaining incarcerated individuals from Elbert County's last court term in August 1897, paid $100 per year for all able-bodied prisoners. The judge who had taken the bid, P. P. Profit, received a letter from the governor explaining that the practice was illegal, and the judge brought the prisoners back to jail.[53]

Byrd found another private camp in Worth County just south of Sylvester. J. W. Tatum was using seventeen Black male prisoners on a turpentine farm as of May 1897, prisoners that he drew from Worth, Terrell, Sumter, and Randolph Counties, paying sixty dollars per year per man. In another county, Tatum operated a camp of felony prisoners, and thus he ran his misdemeanor camp under the regulations he followed for his felony convict lease camp. That he followed the laws for felony convict leasing in his new misdemeanor operation meant that "his individual camp report ranks his camp high, when compared with similar camps in Georgia."[54]

It is significant that the more misdemeanor camps looked like felony convict lease camps, the safer and more comfortable they were. In the years to come, death records would not be reported for misdemeanor camps, but if the trend demonstrated from 1895 to 1987 was any guide, the percentage of dead was roughly double that of felony convict lease, without any oversight or consequence for those abusing prisoners to death.

3

Felony Leasing and Debt Peonage under Scrutiny

Though the McRees would be dependent upon private misdemeanor leasing for the bulk of the 1890s and the early part of the twentieth century, their operation at Kinderlou included at various times felony convict, misdemeanor convict, and debt peonage labor, all acquired through legal means and all of it supplemented with workers taken, often by force, illegally and held completely outside the purview of the machinery of the state. It was, then, a showcase of the interaction of the various systems and their use as vehicles of re-enslavement in the region at the turn of the century. While private misdemeanor leasing existed as kind of a shadow operation within the broader system, it was abetted by the two more public and publicly controversial versions of bound labor in Georgia, each of which built from the other to facilitate the state's carceral apparatus.

Felony convict leasing in its modern form began in February 1876, as Reconstruction fell, replaced by Redeemers who sought to reinstitute a version of slavery for Georgia. Democratic governor James Milton Smith supported and signed the law, which vested the power to regulate the leasing of those with felony convictions in gubernatorial hands.[1] While regulation in those early years of the system was rare, the state did issue circulars providing lessees with rules governing the process. All deaths and escapes had to be reported; stockade prisoners had to be released on Sundays to attend church; men and women had to be segregated. Each convict required sufficient food and clothing. Prison buildings had to allow at least five hundred cubic feet of space per prisoner, and facilities had to be thoroughly cleaned every two weeks; blankets had to be washed every four weeks. There had to be a hospital building, with a steward, a nurse, and a bathtub. Finally, lessees were required to frame the circular and post it in an open area where prisoners could see it and know their rights under the system.[2] The rules were important, but camp inspections to enforce those rules were often inconsistent, giving wide latitude to operators in control of prisoners. Necessarily, abuse would be rampant.

In 1886, the U.S. Labor Commission produced a report on felony convict labor in the South. It was a report less concerned with the racial brutality of the system than with a full comparison of its relationship with free labor. Still, it explained that Georgia's system was among the worst in the physical and mental toll it took on its prisoners. "The convicts are all leased out to three 'penitentiary companies,' at whose hands they are worked to the utmost and barbarously treated from every point of view, moral, physical, and sanitary. The death rate is very high." Among those barbarous private companies was an early incarnation of the McRee prison camp at Kinderlou. It was a system brutal enough in its output that newly elected governor John Brown Gordon, himself a former slaveowner and Confederate general, wrote to the state legislature that year to make the case against felony convict leasing. "It places pecuniary interests in conflict with humanity," he argued. "It makes possible the infliction of greater punishment than the law and the courts have imposed. It renders impracticable the proper care by the state of the health of its prisoners, or their requisite separation according to classes, sexes, and conditions." The system also "reduces to the minimum the chances for reformation," and it "places convict labor in many instances in direct competition with the honest labor of the state." It was a startling admission, and one from the state executive. He was right, of course, that the system had no rehabilitative component, made no effort to reduce recidivism, and gave private companies the ability to avoid private labor in favor of a cheaper option, eliminating the possibility of a free market. But the southern economy had never been a free market, and the system, for all of its faults, was working exactly as it was intended—binding Black labor in virtual slavery and providing pecuniary benefit to the largest landowners and corporations, a modified maintenance of the economic oligarchy of the antebellum slave system. Gordon's missive, then, whether ingenuous or not, would do little to end the practice. Instead, felony leasing would continue with more inspections, and private misdemeanor leasing would develop without any oversight whatsoever, becoming even more deadly than its larger cousin.[3]

In Georgia, convict leasing increased the prison population tenfold over its long life, and while the commission's report ignored the racial nature of the system's brutality, racism underpinned it. Ninety percent of prisoners leased across the South and in Georgia were Black. Matthew J. Mancini concludes that "the response of the criminal justice system to the institution of convict leasing was the sentencing of ever greater numbers of younger men to longer periods of labor. The lease system guaranteed not only a large and reliable labor force, but also a labor force composed of those most fitted for maximum productivity in the work camps."[4] It was a system that fed on its own momentum, that found permission for growth in every new arrest and sentence, but for all the accuracy of Mancini's account, his analysis deals only with the private felony system, the one in which the state had a vested interest.

As of 1890, there were 1,779 prisoners in Georgia felony convict camps. Of that total, only 167 of them were white; 1,612 were Black. The state listed 474 leased prisoners, thirty-seven of whom were white, 437 of whom were Black. Only five of the leased prisoners were listed as residing in Lowndes County, indicating that the felony convict portion of the McRee operation was only a small fraction of the early version of its total bound labor.[5] The McRees were a small-time operation compared to many of the larger corporate entities that contracted with the state for prisoners, so when private misdemeanor leasing became an option in the years to come, Kinderlou would make a transition fitting its size and holding capacity.

The overwhelming majority of both felony and misdemeanor prisoners leased prior to 1909 and those worked in public development projects after it were Black, and this racialized labor division can be mapped. The incarceration rate of Black men began increasing steadily in 1868, after the creation of convict leasing in Georgia, building as it did from the days of slavery that created the association between race and labor. The incarceration rate for white men stayed relatively consistent until its first major jump in 1910, the first full year after the convict lease system had been replaced by chain gang public works labor. Importantly, however, the Black male rate still continued to rise, as well, and witnessed another massive jump in the mid-1920s.[6]

It was a system notorious throughout the country and throughout the world. London's Howard Association, an organization devoted to global criminal justice issues, reported in 1901 that under felony convict leasing "the most abominably cruel sentences continue to be passed upon negroes, in the South, for petty offences, which in other countries would merely involve a reprimand, or a very brief detention." The association noted that "the people of the United States deservedly enjoy a very high position in the world's estimation," but felony convict leasing eroded much of that respect. Many of the nation's most respected leaders were southerners, the group explained, citing George Washington, Henry Clay, and Thomas

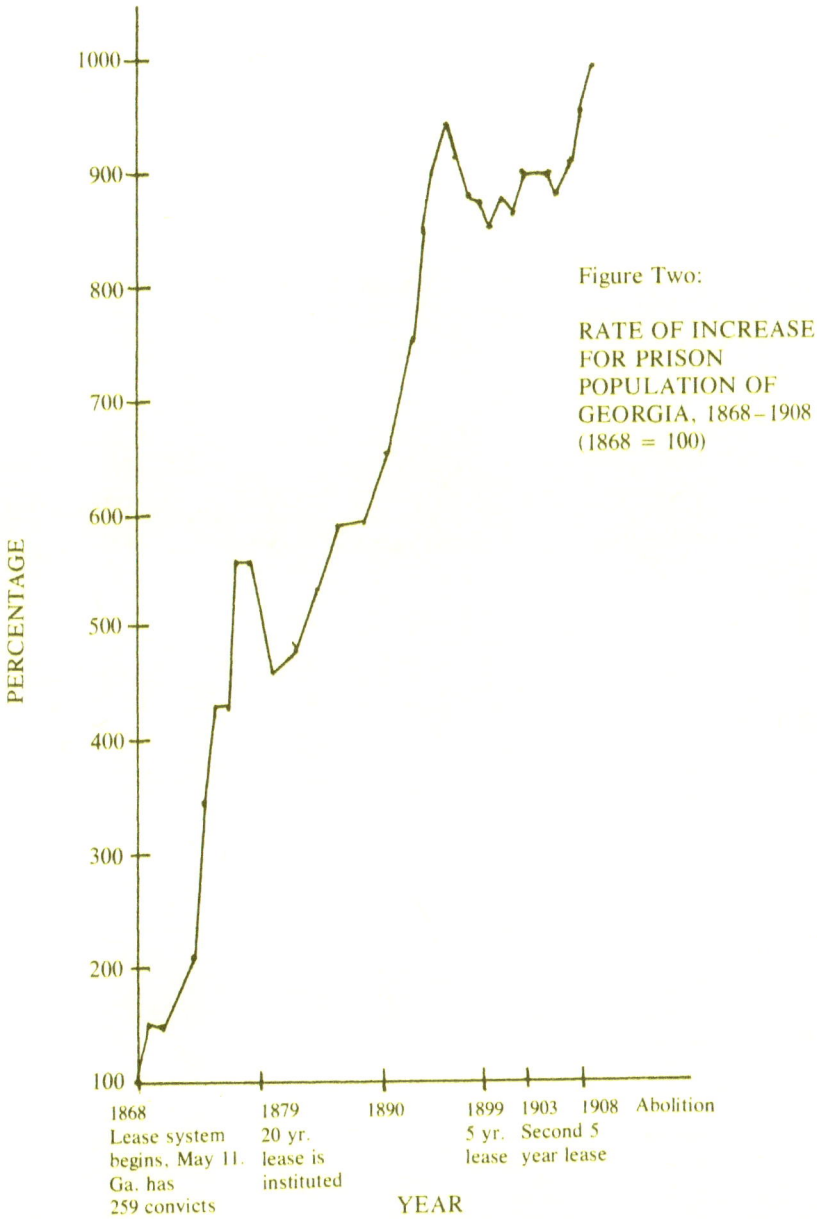

Figure 3.1. The rate of increase for Georgia's prison population from 1868 to 1908. Matthew J. Mancini, "Race, Economics, and the Abandonment of Convict Leasing," *Journal of Negro History* 63 (October 1978): 346.

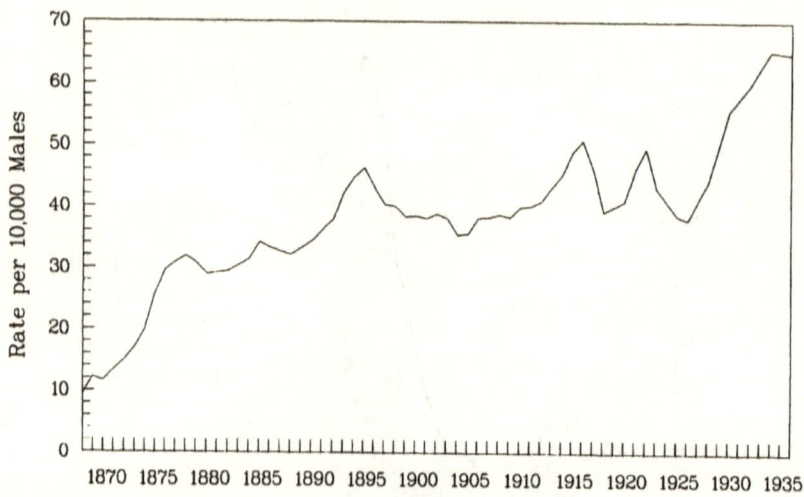

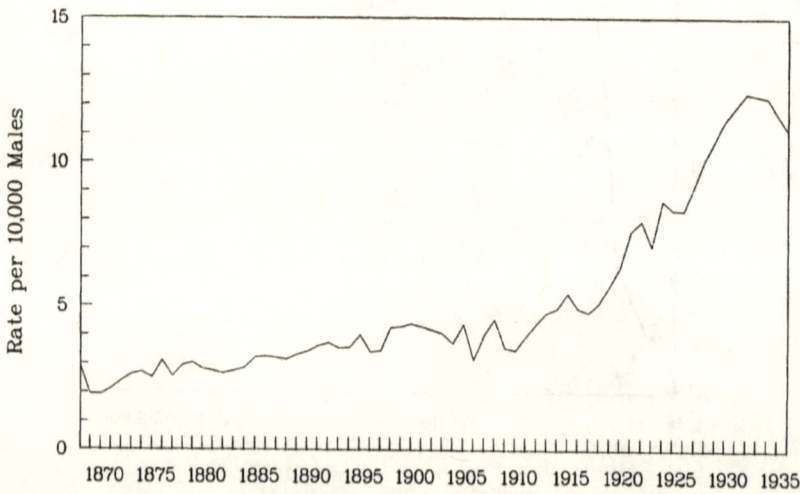

Figure 3.2. The differences in the Black and white male incarceration rate in Georgia, from 1870 to 1935. Martha A. Myers and James L. Massey, "Race, Labor, and Punishment in Postbellum Georgia," *Social Problems* 38 (May 1991): 275.

"Stonewall" Jackson. "The scenes connected with Lynching horrors and Convict Camp vices should be strenuously suppressed by the compatriots and successors of those illustrious men." Convict leasing and lynching were two decidedly different things, of course, but their combination in the Howard Association report wasn't accidental. Each was inordinately deadly, and each was used by white people as a method of racialized social control. The statement evinced no irony in citing slaveowners as exemplary of "illustrious men," but its denunciation of convict leasing was unequivocal.[7]

When the Howard Association and others bemoaned the practice of convict leasing, they did so in relation to the state appropriation of felony prisoners into private hands. They didn't make reference to private misdemeanor leasing because they didn't know it existed. Instead, when jeremiads against racialized bound labor happened in reference to misdemeanants, they targeted a different problem, another that the McRees would abuse in their operation: debt peonage.

As early as 1801, Georgia law mandated that "when any person or persons who now are, or hereafter shall be committed for any debt or damage whatsoever, and shall not be able to satisfy and pay his ordinary prison fees, such fees shall be paid by the person at whose instance such insolvent person may be confined."[8] As it developed over the decades of the nineteenth century, the practice of private individuals paying the debts of misdemeanants punished with fines became commonplace, those payments generally taking place off-the-books and not able to be charted. Misdemeanants punished with incarceration instead of or along with fines for much of the century were shunted to county chain gang camps for labor on public works.

Debt peonage is a phenomenon that the historiography generally considers separately from convict leasing. In these accounts, paying the fines or court costs of misdemeanor defendants is considered an element of local corruption rather than regional or state orthodoxy. There are in the literature nods to the related nature of peonage and leasing, that they were both creating versions of involuntary servitude that targeted poor people of color in the South, but Georgia's system and the operation of Kinderlou demonstrate that in some places peonage and both felony and misdemeanor convict leasing were part of the same system and were inextricably linked, helping to fuel each other and account for labor needs at various levels. While felony leasing provided bound labor for a guaranteed number of years and misdemeanor leasing provided it for up to a year—assuming that the kinds of debt schemes practiced by operators like the McRees didn't keep prisoners there for longer—courthouse peonage, the paying of fines of misdemeanants, provided farms and businesses with a more flexible labor pool that could be obtained at any time to bolster the existing workforce in periods of heavy production. Operators like the McRees didn't require a contract with the state or the county for debt peons, so those peons became the supplemental labor pool for farms and other businesses, some of which had contracts for more stable convict labor and others that didn't. That unique flexibility applied only to the politics of acquisition, however, as upon arrival peons were housed and worked alongside contract-based convict labor. And despite the variances in methods and flexibility of acquisition, when local white elites paid the fines or court costs of misdemeanor defendants, as did the McRees, they did not take advantage of officials on the take; they took advantage of a system designed to benefit them without anyone required to be on the take.

The seminal text on peonage has long been Pete Daniel's *The Shadow of Slavery*, which originally appeared in 1972. While there has been important work on debt peonage in more recent decades, all build from Daniel's work. And Daniel's work makes the argument that debt peonage that built from misdemeanor fines was fundamentally separate from convict leasing. Daniel points out that felony convict leasing in most areas existed at the state level, leaving large economic concerns to divide up prisoners serving criminal convictions at state penitentiaries. Peonage, meanwhile, "originated from local jails and often existed in the absence of supporting laws" and was tied to debt that came from local fines or claims by individual citizens, or debt that was completely fictitious. Sometimes there were laws that sanctioned debt peonage; most of the time the sanction came solely from custom. And in the segment of the peonage system that came with attendant misdemeanor charges, the system "grew out of the corruption of local law enforcement officials."[9]

Daniel was certainly correct for many municipalities in the South. (His principal examples of this particular version of the system come from Alabama and South Carolina.) But the power and skill of his account set the standard for how historians have compartmentalized the region's relationship with postbellum bound labor beyond the borders of Alabama and South Carolina and in the way that private misdemeanant acquisition operated at the county level. That compartmentalization, in turn, has left a gap in the historical understanding of places like Georgia, which engaged in an official peonage system without necessary corruption and worked hand-in-hand with several forms of convict leasing. It is a problem all the more necessary to remedy because Daniel actually describes the McRee operation in his account, accurately describing it as "a gigantic part-convict, part-peonage camp."[10]

One of Daniel's principal critics was William Cohen, who made an early case that the various forms of involuntary servitude that existed in the decades after the Civil War were "a fluid, flexible affair which alternated between free and forced labor in time to the rhythm of the southern labor market," rising and falling in severity and duration based on the economic need of a decidedly white-controlled system. Vagrancy laws that punished former slaves unwilling to sign work contracts made the system of involuntary labor possible, providing a decided advantage to employers who could keep workers on their property for a period of years and a separate advantage to local municipalities who could use law enforcement to round up those who refused to sign restrictive contracts. Those arrested could then "voluntarily" agree to a work contract with an employer eager to take them on, usually for room and board, or they could refuse, giving them criminal liability and forcing them into work through convict leasing. The systems, then, worked in tandem; they were in fact one larger system, that of racialized involuntary labor created by white leadership in southern states, acquired by a variety of means to serve identical ends.[11] It was into that fluid system that private misdemeanor leasing developed, providing an additional form of racialized labor not previously acknowledged by historians, one that reduced such tandem operations to county politics, providing more local control of potential revenue streams and giving more options and flexibility to county businesses and farming operations.

At the same time that Daniel's book appeared describing carceral debt peonage, economic historians Roger Ransom and Richard Sutch described a different kind of debt peonage that created poverty conditions in the region that made such abuses possible. The failure of southern banks after the Civil War, and restrictive banking laws that prevented the creation of new ones, meant that a commercial banking system was largely absent in the region, leaving merchants to control credit for poor farmers, Black and white, transitioning to sharecropping. Because those merchants operated with no real competition, they "introduced inefficiencies and monopoly distortion into the capital markets," not only charging exorbitant interest on commodity loans, keeping most in a state of poverty, but also controlling crop production by preventing "the production of agricultural commodities for home consumption" and forcing "the production of staple crops."[12] This form of "debt peonage," as described by Ransom and Sutch, created a virtual serfdom that drove poor farmers and agricultural laborers into poverty, gave control of the food market to vendors controlled by commodity merchants, and kept the southern economy from entering the capitalist mainstream during the Gilded Age. Ransom and Sutch's original article, published at the same time as Daniel's *The Shadow of Slavery*, was expanded into a book five years later, and *One Kind of Freedom: The Economic Consequences of Slavery* became another seminal text in the understanding of rural poverty in the postwar period.[13] That poverty, in turn, created the conditions for Daniel's version of debt peonage, as economic vulnerability would be the tool by which a more carceral version of re-enslavement could be achieved, as the crop lien system ensured that poor Black tenant farmers would need loans for basic necessities and would be unable to pay any fines imposed on them for the petty crimes manufactured by white southern statehouses.

Robert Toombs, a former senator representing Georgia and the original secretary of state for the Confederacy during the Civil War, was asked later in his life about the future of freedpeople in the post-Reconstruction South. "Peonage," he told his interviewer. "Of course, the negro will remain theoretically a free man, but it is necessary for his preservation that he should be a servant and have a master, call the relation by whatever name you will."[14] Others, however, particularly those in the legal apparatus, were skeptical that racialized bound labor had any tangible relationship to preservation.

"For many years now this infamous 'graft' has been in vogue in different sections of the South," went one commentary in the national *Independent* magazine in 1903, referring to the practice of debt peonage. It was a phenomenon that first entered the national stage in February 1901 with exposure of the practice and its excesses in Anderson, South Carolina. A Black man in Anderson was shot and killed trying to escape a stockade. He had been, the trial discovered, kidnapped, arrested, and taken as a convict without habeas corpus or trial, then forced to work as a virtual slave. Not all such peons were the victims of violent kidnapping, but it became known at trial that on many similar farms, Black workers seeking employment were forced to sign labor contracts that included provisions that the landlord "shall have a right to use such force as he or his agents may deem necessary to require me to remain on his farm and perform good and satisfactory services." The landlord had "the right to lock me up for safe-keeping." The landlord had the right to capture the worker if he ran away; he had the right to "transfer his interest in this contract to any other party." It was a devolution into what the judge in the case called "more than slavery," a system "worthy only of Siberian prisons." He was a white southerner, but he was appalled. Judge William Christie Benet charged a grand jury in Anderson to investigate what he described as a new form of slavery. "I hold in my hand a printed form of contract," he told them. It stated "that the party of the second part binds himself to do all work required at a stipulated salary, and, further, that the laborer agrees that his employers or agents shall have the right to use such force as is deemed necessary to require the laborer to remain on the farm and to perform satisfactory service." If the employee ran away, "the employer shall have the right to offer and pay a reward not exceeding $25 for his capture and return, which amount the laborer, according to the contract, agrees to work out under the rules of the contract." It was a galling scheme, Benet reasoned. "The poor laborer gives the landlord the right to imprison him." It was clear that "by such terms it is manifest that the poor ignorant negroes are subjected to a state that is worse than slavery. I doubt if there ever was such a contract framed or devised before in any civilized or Christian community." And the grand jury needed to investigate it. "Such disgraceful conduct, like those fungus growths which flourish in dark corners, will not stand the light of day."[15]

The grand jury returned three indictments in early March 1901 against three large planters in Anderson County who operated stockades where "negroes guiltless of any felony" were confined. The indictments described "illegal arrests and imprisonment, of cruel whipping, of prolonged imprisonment without even the farce of a trial, of kidnapping negroes from other counties, and even from Georgia, and of poor negroes professing to be satisfied and contented." The case ultimately went nowhere, as the planters pleaded to a lesser charge of assault and battery and paid fifty-dollar fines. But that light punishment also went to highlight the problem to a shocked nation.[16] Unlike in Georgia, the peonage on trial in Anderson came without an actual, physical trial, but with that exception it looked like the McRee operation, including kidnapping innocent Black residents across the state line. Debt peonage had been a subject of legal wrangling before the end of the nineteenth century, but the Anderson case brought it to national attention, alerting much of the country to the racial depravity of the region. And, to be sure, the legal history of debt peonage that led to such rulings did track independently of that of convict leasing.

Congress first dealt with debt peonage in relation to the taking of Mexican peons in the territory of New Mexico. In March 1867, the body passed a law explaining "that the holding of any person to service or labor under the system known as peonage is hereby declared to be unlawful, and the same is hereby abolished and forever prohibited in the Territory of New Mexico, or in any other Territory or State of the United States." Those convicted of holding people in a state of peonage could be fined or imprisoned. It was the first federal interpretation of the new Thirteenth Amendment, but it wouldn't be the subject of an actual criminal prosecution until the early twentieth century.[17]

In the meantime, there would be other federal interpretations. The *Slaughterhouse Cases* (1873), emanating out of New Orleans, gave the Supreme Court its first attempt following the Thirteenth Amendment to reckon with involuntary servitude, though the reckoning dealt with neither convict leasing nor peonage. Still, while adjudicating the existence of a slaughterhouse monopoly and regulatory program granted by the state of Louisiana and the challenge to them brought by the Butchers' Benevolent Association, the court did emphasize that the Thirteenth Amendment not only prohibited African slavery but also "Mexican peonage or the Chinese coolie trade." The Butchers' Benevolent Association had argued that Louisiana violated the privileges and immunities clause of the Fourteenth Amendment but also challenged the state on a Thirteenth Amendment involuntary servitude claim. The Court ruled against the claim but did so on the argument that servitude as described in the Thirteenth Amendment involved only personal ownership rather than a state imposition. And so servitude did include "serfage, vassalage, villenage, peonage, and all other forms of compulsory service for the mere benefit or pleasure of others," wrote Justice Stephen J. Field in his dissent. "Nor is this the full import of the terms. The abolition of slavery and involuntary servitude was intended to make everyone born in this country a freeman, and, as such, to give to him the right to pursue the ordinary avocations of life without other restraint than such as affects all others, and to enjoy equally with them the fruits of his labor. A prohibition to him to pursue certain callings, open to others of the same age, condition, and sex, or to reside in places where others are permitted to live, would so far deprive him of the rights of a freeman, and would place him, as respects others, in a condition of servitude." Though the *Slaughterhouse Cases* were not about peonage, the court used them to clearly argue that peonage was a violation of the Thirteenth Amendment—or, at the very least, a version of peonage that existed without a proscriptive conviction.[18]

A decade later, the Supreme Court declared the Civil Rights Act of 1875 unconstitutional, but in so doing, it sought to differentiate between the power granted to the federal government by the Thirteenth and Fourteenth Amendments to impose its will on the states. While the court saw real limits on the Fourteenth Amendment's ability to make such impositions, thus giving the court license to invalidate the Civil Rights Act, it was more gracious in its interpretation of the Thirteenth. "Under the Thirteenth Amendment," wrote Justice Joseph P. Bradley, writing for an 8–1 majority, "the legislation, so far as necessary or proper to eradicate all forms and incidents of slavery and involuntary servitude, may be direct and primary, operating upon the acts of individuals, whether sanctioned by State legislation or not." Even in the process of gutting protections for freedpeople enacted at the end of Reconstruction, the court remained steadfast in its opposition to all forms of involuntary servitude and in its approval of all federal efforts to bar it.[19]

If debt peonage was a problem under the Thirteenth Amendment, largely because it created a form of involuntary servitude without specific carceral sentence, it would be incumbent on counties like those in Georgia to find another way to get misdemeanants into bondage without drawing the ire of the courts or the media. Applying the long-held concept of chain gang labor to private entities at the county level solved that problem, creating a private misdemeanor convict leasing system that went largely unnoticed in the national and international media even as felony convict leasing and debt peonage continued to be assailed by commentators and judges.

The use of federal charges to combat peonage was prompted by Republican attorney general Philander Chase Knox, who mandated district attorneys who confronted the practice "to hold to strict account every individual upon whom the slightest suspicion of complicity in this system rests—a system which holds in cruel servitude the defenseless of all races."[20] Other federal courts, however, were far more reluctant to make such connections. In an 1899 case in the federal circuit court for the Northern District of Georgia, the judge ruled that the New Mexico law "has no application to the state of Georgia, in which such system never existed." In the reasoning of William T. Newman, the form peonage took in territorial New Mexico was different from the form practiced in Georgia, which was neither slavery as practiced prior to the Civil War nor peonage as practiced in the territories. Georgia did not legally sanction kidnapping, as the McRees would soon discover, but the peonage practices under the dictates of its laws occurred only after misdemeanor conviction, thereby making it something fundamentally different and functionally protected by a Thirteenth Amendment that included a carve out for "punishment of a crime."[21] The decision demonstrated the scope of thinking of much of white Georgia, figuring self-serving technical ways to avoid accountability for the practice. Within federal court jurisdictions, however, Newman's decision proved to be an outlier.

Just after the turn of the century, that original 1867 law finally entered federal court in the Northern District of Florida after Robert W. Lewis was charged with capturing a Black man, George Walker, to a state of peonage near Pensacola. Lewis and two others claimed that Walker owed him "a debt" and thus kidnapped him, beat him, and forcibly placed him in the employ of Lewis. The judge in the case ruled that involuntary servitude as expressed in many cases of peonage was unconstitutional, but not in all cases. Because of those assumed exceptions, the judge passed on ruling on the validity of Walker's peonage claim. Instead, he ruled that the circuit court, which originally ruled against Walker's writ of habeas corpus, had jurisdiction in the case, and therefore argued that the "petitioner is not entitled to the writ of habeas corpus," despite doing so "without expressing any opinion as to the sufficiency, on demurrer, of the indictments in question."[22] It was a nonruling that only gave sanction to further kidnapping practices in the region.

There were also, at the same time, a series of cases moving through the federal circuit court for the Middle District of Alabama in Montgomery, cases that would prompt a judicial action not present in the handwashing of Florida's Northern District. A group of Black defendants in those cases was placed in bondage for breaching a work contract, which was technically a crime under an Alabama statute that punished "any person who has contracted in writing to labor or serve for any given time . . . and who before the expiration of such contract, and without the consent of the other party, abandons such contract."

In response to a series of questions presented by the grand jury on what exactly constituted peonage for the purpose of generating indictments, presiding judge Thomas G. Jones provided an extensive explanation that led him to declare Alabama's 1901 Labor Law, which sanctioned punishment for those who left punitive labor contracts and permitted the proxy payments of various fines for the purpose of generating labor, unconstitutional. "Courts are always reluctant to exercise the delicate power of declaring a statute unconstitutional, and will avoid passing upon such questions when possible," wrote Jones, as if in dialogue with his colleagues in the Northern District of Florida. But "in the phase in which the issue is presented, it is impossible to avoid it." He made clear that Alabama's law violated the Thirteenth Amendment. "It establishes a system of peonage, and uses the arm of the law to keep persons in 'a condition of peonage,' whenever they 'abandon the leased premises,' by coercing performance of the 'obligation' of contracts of 'labor or service' by involuntary service."[23]

"The law delights in the liberty and happiness of the citizen," Jones explained. "No man has any natural right to keep another in involuntary servitude." The 1876 New Mexico statute "struck, at one and the same time, both at the authority to uphold the 'system' by law or usage, and at the holding or returning to a 'condition' of peonage, brought about by the acts of individuals, whether with or without the sanction of state or territorial laws or customs." It was an important distinction, Jones conflating the dicta directed at a territory with binding precedent for states, undercutting many southern arguments that the New Mexico law applied only to federally controlled territories. "Congress never intended, when it denounced the holding to 'a condition of peonage' of 'any person' by 'every person,' that this law for the protection of liberties of citizens of the United States should be partial or local in its operation, or that individuals might violate this general statute of freedom with impunity, unless the state or territory in which the offense occurred attempted to do something it had no power to do."[24]

The Alabama law, he reasoned, ran afoul of congressional holdings: "This statute practically attaints the debtor and makes him a legal pariah if he attempts to exercise his right to labor without another man's consent, and that man his creditor. One of the most valuable liberties of man is to work where he pleases, and to quit one employment and go to another, subject, of course, to civil liability for breach of contract obligations." Jones's ruling was not idealistic; it was pragmatic. There were civil penalties for legitimate contract breach, which still occurred, but debt peonage did not constitute a viable contract. Bondage never could: "It is a fundamental principle of law that the legitimacy of the exercise of the police power, or any other legislative authority concerning the constitutional rights of the citizen, whatever the language employed in the statute, is to be tested and determined by its 'natural and reasonable effect' upon that right."[25] In the vast majority of Alabama counties "all the farm laborers and land renters" had no choice but to "rely upon advances or have work to support themselves and their families at all times. To a man in this condition a dispute or difference with his employer, resulting in the abandonment of the service, no matter what the right of the laborer or renter's contention, is calamitous in the extreme." The Alabama law, then, was not only racist in its motivation but classist in its application. It was "a vicious species of class legislation" that was "designed solely in the interest of the employer or landlord."[26]

Along with violating the 1876 New Mexico statute, peonage provisions like that of Alabama violated both the Fourteenth Amendment's equal protection clause and the Thirteenth Amendment's slavery prohibition: "A person convicted and put to hard labor for violating the provisions of this statute, because he did not give notice of the first employment before entering upon the second, is restrained of his liberty in violation of the Constitution of the United States, and is entitled to discharge on habeas corpus."[27] It was a sweeping ruling but one clearly grounded in existing law, and while Jones's statement did not eliminate peonage from Alabama, it served as an important precedent document for those judges who would wrestle with the phenomenon for years to come.

The *Peonage Cases,* as they came to be known, became a national scandal, opening the country's eyes to a horror many never knew existed. Theodore Roosevelt even commended Jones's statement, though he ultimately pardoned those originally convicted. Back in Alabama, Black leaders were grateful for the decision but knew that it was only a light touch on a sleeping giant. Vagrancy laws and labor roundups of Black citizens continued through the next decades, and debt peonage was in no way going to abate in the face of Jones's ruling, which dealt almost in its entirety with private debt rather than misdemeanor fines paid by those other than the convicted. Booker T. Washington, head of Tuskegee Institute and perhaps the most prominent and influential Black man in the state, contacted Oswald Garrison Villard, editor of the *New York Evening Post* and grandson of William Lloyd Garrison, asking for support to continue pressuring Alabama through a campaign of journalistic shaming, a request Villard was happy to oblige.[28] Paul Lawrence Dunbar was equally incredulous. "The papers are full of the reports of peonage in Alabama," he explained. "A new and more dastardly slavery there has arisen to replace the old. For the sake of re-enslaving the negro, the constitution has been trampled under foot, the rights of man have been laughed out of court and the justice of God has been made a jest."[29]

The Black press was also interested in the decision. "Your Uncle Samuel is sometimes a little slow in getting around, but when he does get a move on him he is apt to make trouble for some one," the *Afro-American* wryly explained. "He is getting in some very good work these days down in Alabama where he has sent a number of farmers to the penitentiary for peonage. Let the good work go on and after a while he will probably get his eyes open to the fact that there are a few other evils down in that part of the country that need his attention."[30] It was a reminder that peonage was systemic and of "what courage is needed to see an honorable end to race barbarism."[31] Of course, one of the principal issues was that there was no penitentiary involved, but the *Afro*'s broader critique remained valid and important, particularly as the focus of national outrage shifted to Mississippi.

The first federal peonage charge appeared in Mississippi in 1904. Shep Griffin had been held in bondage in Kemper County on a claim that he owed white farm owners a dollar. He offered to pay the dollar, but the white people refused, as the charge was just a pretense to bring him under bondage. There he was tortured with whips, and when he tried to escape, one of the white leaders of the camp put a pistol in his mouth. Then "a rope was put around his neck and the other end of it was tied to the pommel of the saddle of one of the pursuers and he was dragged and driven back into Kemper county to the farm from which he had fled." Those running the camp and many of their supporters threatened not only to murder Griffin but to kill any witnesses and any law enforcement that attempted to arrest them. Such was the hegemony of white supremacy in Mississippi, a particularly violent microcosm of the South writ large. "For there can be no peace," the *Baltimore Afro-American* explained, "so long as the skeleton of slavery lurks in the closet, and peonage casts its sombre shadow, and Tillman's pitchfork is in action to keep the Negro down."[32]

The shadow of felony convict leasing, meanwhile, was just as somber, but the status of the those convicted within the system gave them less recourse to the courts. Both systems, however, were assailed regularly in the 1890s and 1900s, and peonage in particular was constantly tested in federal trials in Alabama and north Florida. For many Georgia counties in between those two poles, the lesson learned was that profitable disposal of misdemeanants could happen in a different way, one that hued to the basic theory of felony convict leasing—that work was rehabilitative and could be practiced in any capacity, and that it was particularly suited for Black labor—and the population associated with peonage, that is, misdemeanants convicted at the county level. If counties convicted misdemeanor defendants with jail time, they could lease out the prison to private entities in their own or nearby counties for terms of up to a year, profit off the transaction, and avoid peonage scrutiny in the process. At the same time, since "convict lease" was really only discussed nationally in the context of prisoners with felony convictions, they could also fly under that particular radar, as well. It was clear from the state scrutiny of the 1895 and 1897 misdemeanor reports that private misdemeanor lessees like the McRees couldn't avoid all potential interventions, but they could at least keep a less regulated version of race-based convict slavery that provided profit to the white officials operating smaller-scale systems without the risk and notoriety of federal trials.

Or, at least, they thought they could.

4

Misdemeanor Leasing at the Turn of the Century

Convict leasing of both misdemeanor and felony prisoners was decidedly lucrative for the white people involved in it at both the governmental and private levels, but its death and abuse rates were at least potentially problematic to those involved, if for no other reason than poor public relations. The death rate of private misdemeanor leasing was double that of felony leasing in the years that such records were kept, but all such deaths stood as testaments to the problems of the carceral system of Georgia and of the South writ large. To help regulate the system, the Georgia Prison Commission was organized in December 1897, constituted of three "intelligent and upright citizens," first appointed by the governor, then elected, at a salary of $2,000 per year. "The Commission shall have complete management and control of the State convicts," the law establishing the commission explained, including regulating their working hours, their work itself, their food and clothing, and any other element of their care. The group would "likewise have general supervision of the misdemeanor convicts of the State." The commission would be responsible for regulating felony convict leasing, providing contracts, and conducting the ensuing oversight, but it would only have a supervisory role over misdemeanor camps, both public and private, allowing for what would become rampant abuse in a system that even with regulation was rife with maltreatment.[1] Still, it was sweeping authority, vested in three individuals who maintained control of an entire state system. In 1903, the legislature reauthorized the commission's mandate and added an ability to impose fines on counties for failing to comply with regulations related to misdemeanor chain gangs, but even then it had no authority over the private camps.[2]

The Prison Commission issued its first annual report in October 1898, explaining that oversight for twenty-five penitentiary camps and forty-four misdemeanor camps, private and public, were monitored by one man: state warden Jake C. Moore. Creation of the office of state warden was one of the commission's first activities, part of a larger effort to respond to social reformers from the Populist Party who had advocated for the end of convict leasing and the brutality that accompanied it.[3] Georgia was the home of Tom Watson, a former McDuffie County Democrat who left his party to join the Populist movement in 1891. Understanding the split in votes among poor white farmers, Watson and other Populist leaders attempted to curry favor with Black Republicans, even including Black representatives at the state convention and in the state campaign committee. While Watson and his white counterparts were by no means racial egalitarians, they did overtly campaign against convict leasing as a brutal racial system attempting to reimpose a version of slavery. It was a stand that did bring in some Black votes, but it also allowed white Democrats to charge Watson and the Populists with a version of race traitorism, a charge that helped lose Watson his 1892 gubernatorial bid. The election, however, was close, and the Democrats used open corruption to secure their victory. The pressure on convict leasing exerted by the Populists was palpable and helped spur the creation of the Prison Commission.[4]

Moore was tasked with inspecting every prison camp monthly and every misdemeanor camp quarterly. While the commission's first report praised Moore's efforts, it was clear that such a monumental task would be impossible to complete with any real thoroughness, giving credence to critiques of commentators like Watson.[5]

When the report dealt with those leased after felony convictions, it listed the camps, the lessees, and the operation in which they were working. When it dealt with those convicted of misdemeanors, it described the county where the camp was, the population totals, and the kinds of employment, with "roads and public works" clearly indicating a public county chain gang. Others doing farm or turpentine work were misdemeanor prisoners in private camps who were ostensibly leased for their service without any substantive county supervision and without any categorization that they were leased prisoners. Misdemeanor convict leasing, as practiced at Kinderlou, was hiding in plain sight in the interstitial space between felony convict leasing, on the one side, and public chain gangs and private debt peonage, on the other.[6]

Further masking the place of misdemeanor prisoners, the commission report for 1898, produced the year after Byrd's damning misdemeanor camp report, listed the rules governing misdemeanor chain gangs, but included only statutes related to county camps, further blinding both law enforcement and reformers to the plight of those hidden away. The first of those rules stated that "county authorities, having control of convicts, shall provide suitable places for their safe keeping and their support by the county, and shall employ necessary overseers and guards for their safe keeping, and constant and diligent employment upon the public works."[7] An argument could be made that leasing misdemeanor prisoners to private camps was a method of providing a suitable place for safe keeping, but the counties were not employing the overseers at those private camps, and the work of those incarcerated was not going toward the public works. The private camps themselves, though, were part of the misdemeanor report the previous year and were listed in the Prison Commission's report in 1898. The state knew they were there; they were sanctioned by custom if not by law, largely made possible by the permissibility of debt peonage, which provided a sort of de facto leasing right for misdemeanants and made the private camps a version of the practice for those who received prison time rather than a simple fine.

County authorities, under the listed rules, were to "prepare and have published full and complete, reasonable and humane rules and regulations for the government of convicts under their control." The Prison Commission would have a supervisory role and could advise county or municipal officials about altering their rules. If the counties failed to live up to their rules, the governor and the commission could take individuals convicted of misdemeanors from a county or municipality and send them somewhere else.[8]

Then there were the rules regulating violence. "No punishment shall be administered to a convict" in a misdemeanor camp, "except in cases where it is reasonably necessary to enforce discipline or compel work or labor," the report claimed. It was, like so many of the policies surrounding misdemeanor camps, designed to give administrators wide latitude to excuse most behaviors involved with corporal punishment, because "reasonably necessary" was the kind of null-set signifier that could mean anything depending on the whim of the user or the context in which the term was used.[9]

Included in the rules were requirements for keeping logbooks and registers of those incarcerated, their behavior, and their punishment, as explained in the 1897 report, with time off for good behavior. In line with the revelations from 1897, new rules required each prisoner to have a bunk with "one cotton tick of sufficient width and length for comfort, well filled with clear straw or excelsior, with blankets and other covering sufficient for comfort," with the bedding replaced and washed every two months. Bathing facilities were required, and prisoners had to bathe every week and be given clean clothing every week.[10]

The camps had to be segregated by race and sex. Prisoners could be worked from sunup to sundown on all days but Sunday, with reasonable breaks for lunch. The rules required "ample preparations" for care of sick prisoners: "In cases of sudden deaths, without previous illness, or treatment by physician, a coroner's inquest must be held over the body before interment." Each camp had to produce a monthly report providing a detailed accounting of each prisoner, including health and conduct.[11]

The rules in place were clearly inadequate to the task of protecting those convicted of misdemeanors in many of the county camps, but they were almost mythical in dealing with prisoners in private camps, camps that were listed in the report's accounting but otherwise ignored in every other respect and not even specifically cited as private camps.

The numbers in table 4.2 indicate that privately held misdemeanor prisoners made up a minority of the total of bound labor, with those leased after felony convictions and persons with misdemeanor convictions in county camps greatly outnumbering them, but for those in the system, they existed without any meaningful state oversight, a forgotten group among the several interlocking systems of Georgia incarceration. And those systems were inordinately racial, with the private misdemeanor lease camps having the highest percentage of Black prisoners in their system, more than both the misdemeanor county camps and the felony lease system, a ratio that would continue throughout the life of the practice. When the reported death rate of the previous year is taken into account, it can be assumed that a system fundamentally Blacker than felony convict leasing was killing those Black prisoners at an even higher rate. If the numbers remained consistent in 1898 from the previous recorded years, then the reported felony death rate was 2.3 percent, putting the private misdemeanor death rate above 4.5 percent, meaning that between twenty and twenty-one misdemeanants were killed in private hands.

It is also clear that the misdemeanor system was far more diverse in its operations, be they camps run by counties or private individuals. The state felony convict lease program sent its prisoners to a small and exclusive number of individuals who owned camps spread across the state. While that centralization of convict wealth created its own well-documented series of problems, it did provide a measure of regulatory control that was impossible in the misdemeanor county-based system. The McRees were

Table 4.1. Felony convict lease camps, 1898

Camp	County	Lessee	Employment
Adrian	Emanuel	T. J. James	Sawmilling and farm
Alexanderville	Echols	W. B. Lowe	Sawmilling
Albany	Dougherty	Chattahoochee Brick Co.	Brickmaking
Bostwick	Morgan	J. M. Smith	Farm
Bainbridge	Decatur	Chattahoochee Brick Co.	Sawmilling
Bartow	Bartow	Dade Coal Co.	Mining iron ore
Cole City	Dade	Dade Coal Co.	Mining coal and burning coke
Durham Mines	Walker	Chattahoochee Brick Co.	Mining coal and burning coke
Echo	Bulloch	W. B. Lowe	Sawmilling
Haylow	Clinch	Chattahoochee Brick Co. and W. B. Lowe	Sawmilling and crossties
Hodo	Johnson	T. J. James	Farm
Heardmont	Elbert	W. H. Mattox	Farm
Jachin	Early	J. M. Smith	Turpentine
Kramer	Wilcox	W. B. Lowe	Sawmilling
Oakdale	Fulton	Chattahoochee Brick Co.	Brickmaking
Pitts	Wilcox	Chattahoochee Brick Co.	Sawmilling
Pinetucky	Jefferson	T. J. James	Farm
Richwood	Dooly	W. B. Lowe and Chattahoochee Brick Co.	Sawmilling
Smithonia	Oglethorpe	J. M. Smith	Farm
Saffold	Early	J. M. Smith	Turpentine
Thelma	Clinch	W. B. Lowe and Chattahoochee Brick Co.	Crossties and railroad
Willingham	Worth	Chattahoochee Brick Co.	Turpentine
Worth No. 2	Worth	Chattahoochee Brick Co. and W. B. Lowe	Sawmilling
Worth No. 3	Worth	J. M. Smith	Sawmilling
Woods	Emanuel	T. J. James	Farm

Notes: The felony convict lease camps had a total of 2,228 prisoners, including 239 white men and boys and two white women and girls. There were 1,941 Black men and boys and fifty-five Black women and girls. Fifty-one prisoners died that year in the felony system.

87.1 percent Black men and boys

89.6 percent Black prisoners

Source: First Annual Report of the Prison Commission of Georgia, 1898, Georgia Penitentiary Prison Commission's Reports, 21-1-40, Georgia Archives, Morrow, Georgia, 25–26, 35.

Table 4.2. County misdemeanor camps, 1898, divided into public and private camps

County	WM	WF	BM	BF	Total	Employment
Public						
Baldwin	0	0	17	0	17	Roads and public works
Bartow	8	0	26	0	34	Roads and public works
Bibb	6	0	105	10	121	Roads and public works
Bulloch	0	0	14	1	15	Roads and public works
Chatham	7	0	205	20	232	Roads and public works
Decatur (Bainbridge city)	0	0	5	0	5	Streets
DeKalb	3	0	23	0	26	Roads and public works
Dougherty	0	0	43	2	45	Roads and public works
Elbert	0	0	24	2	26	Roads and public works
Emanuel	0	0	3	0	3	Roads and public works
Floyd	16	0	52	2	70	Roads and public works
Fulton	32	1	260	22	315	Roads and public works
Glynn	0	0	24	2	26	Roads and public works
Greene	0	0	14	0	14	Roads and public works
Houston	1	0	38	0	39	Roads and public works
Jasper	0	0	13	0	13	Roads and public works
Jefferson	0	0	25	0	25	Roads and public works
Laurens	4	0	10	0	14	Roads and public works
Monroe	0	0	41	0	41	Roads and public works
Muscogee	0	0	32	0	32	Roads and public works
Putnam	0	0	17	1	18	Roads and public works
Richmond	3	0	63	8	74	Roads and public works
Spalding	1	0	21	1	23	Roads and public works
Thomas (Thomasville city)	0	0	16	0	16	Streets
Ware (Waycross city)	0	0	17	1	18	Streets
Washington	1	0	13	0	14	Roads and public works
TOTAL	82	1	1121	72	1276	

87.9% Black men and boys
93.5% Black prisoners

County	WM	WF	BM	BF	Total	Employment
Private						
Appling	1	0	14	0	15	Turpentine
Berrien	0	0	16	0	16	Turpentine
Brooks	2	0	58	1	61	Sawmilling and turpentine
Coffee, No. 1	4	0	35	0	39	Turpentine
Coffee, No. 2	1	0	27	1	29	Farm and turpentine
Decatur	0	0	27	2	29	Turpentine
Dooly	0	0	82	1	83	Sawmilling and turpentine
Early	0	0	10	0	10	Turpentine
Elbert	2	0	16	1	19	Farm
Lowndes	**2**	**0**	**56**	**4**	**62**	**Farm**
Oconee	3	0	20	1	24	Farm
Randolph	0	0	3	0	3	Farm
Walton	5	0	28	0	33	Farm
Ware	0	0	21	2	23	Turpentine
TOTAL	20	0	413	13	446	
92.6% Black men and boys						
95.5% Black prisoners						

Source: *First Annual Report of the Prison Commission of Georgia, 1898*, Georgia Penitentiary Prison Commission's Reports, 21-1-40, Georgia Archives, Morrow, Georgia, 36.

part of that private county system, their operation part of the misdemeanor structure, listed as holding sixty Black prisoners and two white prisoners on the Kinderlou farm.[12]

And the system was growing. The Prison Commission's 1899 report the following year showed a sharp rise in the number of misdemeanants, with 550 additional prisoners over the previous twelve months, and put the blame squarely on the legislature: "This increase has been continuous since the passage of the law allowing the juries and judges to reduce certain felonies to misdemeanors." Fitting that analysis, the number of felony prisoners had decreased by twenty-three since 1895. It was clear that the law designed to benefit county coffers had worked exactly as planned. The commission noted that thirty-seven boys under the age of sixteen were in the camps, as were 117 women. "It is unnecessary to say that in many of these institutions these boys and women are not so well cared for or

Table 4.3. Felony convict lease camps, 1899

Camp	County	Lessee	Employment	Num
Cramer	Wilcox	James W. English Jr.	Sawmilling	67
Doe Run	Worth	James W. English Jr.	Turpentine	59
Adrian	Emanuel	James W. English Jr.	Sawmilling	79
Jakin	Decatur	James W. English Jr.	Sawmilling	66
Bartow	Bartow	James W. English Jr.	Mining iron ore	59
Saffold	Early	James W. English Jr.	Turpentine	52
Damascus	Early	James W. English Jr.	Turpentine	22
Cole City	Dade	James W. English Jr.	Mining coal	46
Cole City	Dade	Southern Mining Co.	Mining coal	15
Cole City	Dade	John W. McCalla	Mining coal	50
Cole City	Dade	Canda Lumber Co.	Mining Coal	24
Worth No. 2	Worth	Canda Lumber Co.	Sawmilling	76
Richwood	Dooly	Parrott Lumber Co.	Sawmilling	32
Donalsville	Decatur	Donalson Lumber Co.	Turpentine	51
Fargo	Clinch	GS Baxter & Co.	Sawmilling, RR, and turpentine	345
Alexanderville	Echols	Merritt W. Dixon	Sawmilling	46
Rocky Ford	Bulloch	Merritt W. Dixon	Sawmilling	57
Chattahoochee	Fulton	Chattahoochee Brick Co.	Brickmaking	174
Colquitt	Miller	W. H. Mattox	Turpentine	44
Albany	Dougherty	Cruger & Pace	Brickmaking	50
Worth No. 1	Worth	Enterprise Lumber Co.	Sawmilling	78
Pitts	Wilcox	Enterprise Lumber Co.	Sawmilling	71
Damascus	Early	James M. Smith	Turpentine	48
Durham Mines	Walker	James M. Smith	Coal mining	51
Durham Mines	Walker	Chickamauga Coal & Coke	Coal mining	252
State farm	Baldwin	State farm (men)	Farming	101
State farm	Baldwin	State farm (boys under 15)	Farming	15
State farm	Baldwin	State farm (women)	Farming	71
Total				2,201

Notes: That year, the felony system had 2,201 prisoners and fifty-seven deaths. There were 245 white men and boys and three white women and girls, and 1,885 Black men and boys and sixty-eight Black women and girls.
85.6 percent Black men and boys
88.7 percent Black prisoners
Source: Second Annual Report of the Prison Commission of Georgia, 1899 (Atlanta: Foote & Davies Co., 1899), 20–21, 30.

Table 4.4. County misdemeanor camps, 1899, divided into public and private camps

County	WM	WF	BM	BF	Total	Employment
Public						
Bulloch	1	0	21	0	22	Public roads
Bibb	2	0	55	1	58	Public roads
Baldwin	2	0	31	0	33	Public roads
Burke	0	0	22	1	23	Public roads
Bainbridge	0	0	5	0	5	Public streets
Chatham	10	0	228	35	273	Public roads
Dougherty	0	0	25	3	28	Public roads
Elbert	0	0	18	0	18	Public roads
Emanuel	0	0	6	0	6	Public roads
Floyd	8	1	56	8	73	Public roads
Fulton	26	0	252	17	295	Public roads
Glynn	0	0	30	0	30	Public roads and farming
Greene	0	0	22	1	23	Public roads
Houston	0	0	36	1	37	Public roads
Irwin	3	0	27	3	33	Public roads
Jasper	0	0	13	2	15	Public roads
Jefferson	1	0	38	0	39	Public roads
Laurens	2	0	17	0	19	Public roads
Muscogee	7	0	87	0	94	Public roads
Monroe	1	0	41	0	42	Public roads
McDuffie	0	0	11	0	11	Public roads
Newton	4	0	29	0	33	Public roads
Oconee	1	0	16	3	20	Public roads
Pulaski	0	0	20	0	20	Public roads
Putnam	0	0	24	0	24	Public roads
Richmond	3	0	64	8	75	Public roads
Spalding	3	0	32	1	36	Public roads
Taliaferro	0	0	7	0	7	Public roads
Walton	2	0	27	1	30	Public roads
Washington	0	0	38	0	38	Public roads
Wilkes	0	0	37	0	37	Public roads
Waycross City	0	0	18	0	18	Streets
TOTAL	76	1	1,353	85	1,515	

89.3% Black men and boys
94.9% Black prisoners

(continued)

Table 4.4—Continued

County	WM	WF	BM	BF	Total	Employment
Private						
Banks	7	0	42	4	53	Turpentine
Berrien	0	0	43	0	43	Turpentine
Baker	3	0	65	3	71	Turpentine
Coffee (Sweats)	4	0	40	0	44	Turpentine
Coffee	0	0	30	2	32	Turpentine
Dooly	3	0	95	3	101	Sawmilling, turpentine, farm
Decatur	0	0	35	1	36	Turpentine
Early	2	0	93	0	95	Turpentine
Elbert (M'Calla)	3	0	36	2	41	Farming
Elbert (Hudgins)	2	0	28	2	32	Farming
Elbert (Swift)	8	0	33	2	43	Farming
Lowndes	**2**	**0**	**76**	**5**	**83**	**Turpentine and farming**
Oglethorpe	15	0	51	0	66	Farming
Oglethorpe No. 2	0	0	6	0	6	Farming
Oglethorpe No. 3	7	0	14	2	23	Farming
Oconee	1	0	16	3	20	Farming
Worth	0	0	29	2	31	Turpentine
Wilcox	0	0	13	1	14	Farming
Wilkes No. 2	0	0	28	0	28	Farming
Ware	0	0	25	2	27	Turpentine
TOTAL	57	0	798	34	889	

89.8% Black men and boys
93.6% Black prisoners

Note: This division was not present in the original, as the camps were listed alphabetically by county so as to hide the fact that some of them were in private hands.

Source: Second Annual Report of the Prison Commission of Georgia, 1899 (Atlanta: Foote & Davies Co., 1899), 31.

humanely treated as the same classes are at the farm," meaning the state prison farm that served as part of the felony system. Its report suggested legislation that would put all boys and women under state control, to separate them from a system that was growing out of control.[13]

The commission also worried that the increasing number of misdemeanants translated directly to an increase in the number of private misdemeanor camps, as many of the county chain gangs "have as many as can be profitably used." Private camps, in such instances, were actually a better option than having nowhere for them to go, which ultimately kept misdemeanor prisoners from "their proper punishment, humane treatment, and self-maintenance." It argued, in one of what would become many calls, to place the misdemeanor system under one management, implying that the commission itself would be best equipped to handle such a task: "Except for their shorter terms and consequent larger expenditure for transportation, their labor should be as valuable as felony convicts, whose labor is now in demand at fourteen and one-half dollars per month."[14] The message was clear: these private camps are inhumane and unregulated, but they are also providing profit to the counties that we, the state, could be making, a loss abetted by the felony reduction legislation.

Again, the misdemeanor system was decidedly Blacker than its more notorious felony convict lease counterpart, and the private misdemeanor camps had the largest percentage of Black men and boys (see table 4.4). It is significant, too, that even under the proposed law that would have authorized private camps, Elbert County would have run afoul of it with more than two camps in private hands. And all such private misdemeanor camps were able to operate largely without governmental oversight, meaning that they could treat the prisoners as brutally as they liked without consequence, a phenomenon underscored by the fact that after 1897, death reports for public and private misdemeanor camps never again appeared. If their numbers remained consistent, however, then at least forty-six deaths in private camps can be reasonably estimated for 1899, more than double the number from the previous year.

The Prison Commission report for 1900 proudly portrayed a felony system that had been thoroughly reformed, though it was only barely necessary. "The lease system had become as nearly perfect as it is possible for such a system to be" prior to its adjustment. Of course, "the opportunity, and to some extent the temptation, to make earnings paramount to humane treatment was great," and "occasional acts of inhumanity were discovered." They were infrequent, the report assured readers, but when they happened, "the system and the State were brought into disrepute." The new rules had fixed any inconsistencies, had even ended regular leasing operations: "The convicts are not leased, but contracts for their labor have been entered into, the State through its own officers and employees controlling and working them." Though independent contractors technically controlled the labor of prisoners, "their first duty is to the State, and the proper maintenance and humane treatment of the convicts are made paramount."[15] Standing against such claims were the testimonies of prisoners themselves, but "the Commission must protest against a tendency to exaggerate and sensationalize every reported 'prison horror,' and the proneness to accept such reports as true." The report reminded readers that "a common felon, whose character as a criminal bespeaks him unworthy of confidence and credit, should not be implicitly believed, in preference to his keeper, who has established a character for honesty and truthfulness."[16]

As a demonstration of this humaneness and purported success, the commission reported fifty-four deaths in the felony system during 1900, with eight being "violent and accidental" and forty-six from disease, "a rate of one and four-tenths per cent, which is the smallest death rate ever before recorded in the Georgia penitentiary." There was also a marked decrease in the number of escapes.[17] Despite the obviously disingenuous commentary, the convict counts that can be corroborated make the numbers of the report at least relatively reliable.

Meanwhile, the misdemeanor camps were so bad that the commission couldn't even muster its disingenuous plaudits. The commission's 1900 report acknowledged quarterly inspections of county misdemeanor camps, "but for many reasons this inspection has not been as effective as desired." The commission had no power to compel the camps to make reports. Some camp reports were sporadic, and many others were nonexistent. When old camps closed or new camps opened, the commission received no formal notice; some camps operated for months before state officials knew of their existence. The report admitted to receiving "many complaints" of maltreatment at the camps. The commission attempted to investigate them, but it lacked any enforcement power to actually compel action at the county level.[18]

The frustrated commissioners described three kinds of misdemeanor camps.

"1. Organized under and in conformity with the law, and engaged upon public works.
2. Organized under color of the law, and engaged in work for private individuals.
3. Organized contrary to law, and engaged in work for private individuals."

The camps in the first category, the commission explained, "are the only ones contemplated by the law, and which have any legal status or should be allowed to exist." It noted that the law provided that "county authorities may employ the chain-gang, not to exceed twelve months . . . *provided, that nothing herein contained shall authorize the giving the control of convicts to private persons.*" There was also a provision that even camps under county supervision could not engage in pursuits that would compete with free labor or enterprise. Camps like those of the McRees broke all such rules, keeping incarcerated individuals for well over a twelve-month period, operating privately, and engaging in pursuits that competed in the open market. The commission's conclusion was that all such camps were "unlawful."[19]

Only adding to the abuse, most of the private camps in the second category depended on labor of misdemeanants from counties other than those where the camps themselves were located, paying counties to take prisoners off their hands and out of their borders. The report was careful to absolve county officials, "for they doubtless thought they were acting within the law" but the private lessees were duping them into a form of illegality.[20]

Then there was the third class of camps, "directly in conflict" with the law. The camps were "organized without the order of any county authority, and are under the control of none, and, making no report to any official, have only been discovered by this Commission accidentally." Their existence stood only as testimony to the confusion of the system. The commission reported that there was some recognizable progress in the standard of the camps, but that in no way meant that the standard was "uniformly high." It would never be until "by proper legislation, some one authority has been given complete control thereof and is alone held responsible therefor."[21] The Prison Commission figured itself as the best candidate for the job, but it needed more power from the legislature. As it stood, "rules can be violated without detection, unless the county authorities, who are directly responsible for the control and management of these gangs, ex-

Table 4.5. Felony convict lease camps, 1900

Camp	County	Lessee	Employment	Num
Kramer	Wilcox	James W. English Jr.	Sawmilling	59
Doe Run	Worth	James W. English Jr.	Turpentine	54
Adrian	Emanuel	James W. English Jr.	Sawmilling	75
Jakin	Decatur	James W. English Jr.	Sawmilling	68
Bartow	Bartow	James W. English Jr.	Mining iron ore	121
Saffold	Early	James W. English Jr.	Turpentine	52
Cole City	Dade	James W. English Jr.	Mining coal	46
Cole City	Dade	Southern Mining Co.	Mining coal	7
Cole City	Dade	John W. McCalla	Mining coal	50
Cole City	Dade	Canda Lumber Co.	Mining coal	24
Cole City	Dade	James M. Smith	Mining Coal	50
Durham Mines	Walker	James M. Smith	Mining coal	50
Durham Mines	Walker	Chickamauga Cole & Coke	Mining coal	246
Ensign	Worth	Canda Lumber Co.	Sawmilling	75
Richwood	Dooly	Parrott Lumber Co.	Sawmilling	123
Donalsonville	Decatur	Donalson Lumber Co.	Turpentine	50
Fargo	Clinch	GS Baxter & Co.	Sawmilling, turpentine, etc.	342
Alexanderville	Echols	Merritt W. Dixon	Sawmilling	48
Egypt	Effingham	Merritt W. Dixon	Sawmilling	49
Chattahoochee	Fulton	Chattahoochee Brick Co.	Brickmaking	180
Colquitt	Miller	WH Mattox	Turpentine	49
Albany	Dougherty	Cruger & Pace	Brickmaking	48
Worth	Worth	Enterprise Lumber Co.	Sawmilling	74
Pitts	Wilcox	Enterprise Lumber Co.	Sawmilling	72
State Farm	Baldwin	State Farm (men)	Farming	152
State Farm	Baldwin	State Farm (boys under 15)	Farming	16
State Farm	Baldwin	State Farm (women)	Farming	78
TOTAL				2,258

Notes: That year, the felony system had 2,258 prisoners with fifty-four deaths. There were 255 white men and boys and three white women and girls, 1,925 Black men and boys and seventy-five Black women and girls.

85.3 percent Black men and boys

88.6 percent Black prisoners

Source: *Third Annual Report of the Prison Commission of Georgia, 1900*, Georgia Penitentiary Prison Commission's Reports, 21-1-40, Georgia Archives, Morrow, Georgia, 32–33, 42.

ercise the most constant vigilance." This was especially true for private camps, which were the worst abusers of misdemeanor prisoners and experienced the least supervision, largely because the counties had no vested financial interest in the production coming from the mills and farms that housed the prisoners.[22]

The solution was a change in the law that limited the number of misdemeanor camps and standardized the rules for all of them. There needed to be uniform rules for the treatment of prisoners, for their punishment, for their third-party supervision. Such changes wouldn't eliminate all abuse; abuse occurred even in the best regulated systems. But it would limit the damage caused by multiple systems of imprisonment and supervision, the commission reasoned.[23]

The report also argued that separation of misdemeanants and those with felony convictions was no longer in force. Many misdemeanants were serving sentences for some version of moral turpitude, crimes that would be felonies, "except for the action of the judges and juries fixing the punishment as for misdemeanors." At the same time, many of those convicted of felonies, such as robbery, burglary, and larceny, "are now punished as often in the chain-gangs as in the penitentiary," creating a mixed system that only further blurred jurisdictions and hindered viable oversight.[24] And all of it was abetted by the legislative plot to appease white county stakeholders and provide them additional revenue. The confusion was intentional, counties manipulating sentences to keep prisoner revenue instead of watching it drift to the state system.

It was clear that not only were the misdemeanor camps still significantly Blacker than the felony lease system, and the private camps still had the highest percentage of Black men, but the sheer number of camps was growing as more and more counties and individual investors sought to take advantage of a cheaper, shorter-term version of convict leasing that could be accomplished without state oversight see table 4.6). The diffused system ensured the absence of the monopolistic tendencies of the felony version of convict leasing.

It was the growth in the number of camps that diluted the already sparse inspections and facilitated the abuse that landed the McRee family in its first real state trouble, as reports emerged in 1900 that the Kinderlou camp was abusing its misdemeanor prisoners and doing so without proper governmental supervision. They had even been kidnapping innocent people and keeping them in bondage. By the same statistical sample used in the previous years, at least forty-seven people would have been killed in private

Table 4.6. County misdemeanor camps, 1900, divided into public and private camps

County	Worked By	WM	WF	BM	BF	Total	Employment
Public							
Butts	County	0	0	10	0	10	Roads
Burk	County	0	0	40	0	40	Roads
Baldwin	County	0	0	34	2	36	Roads
Bibb	County	7	0	107	12	126	Roads
Bulloch	County	0	0	13	0	13	Roads
Coffee	County	1	0	9	1	11	Roads
Clark	County	0	0	24	2	26	Roads
Chatham	County	5	2	249	40	296	Roads
Dougherty	County	1	0	20	2	23	Roads
DeKalb	County	2	0	30	2	34	Roads
Elbert	County	0	0	23	0	23	Roads
Emanuel	County	0	0	9	0	9	Roads
Floyd	County	7	0	50	5	62	Roads
Fulton	County	15	0	233	36	284	Roads
Greene	County	0	0	22	1	23	Roads
Glynn	County	0	0	36	2	38	Roads
Houston	County	0	0	27	0	27	Roads
Irwin	County	3	0	12	2	17	Roads
Jefferson	County	2	0	25	0	27	Roads
Jasper	County	1	0	32	2	35	Roads
Laurens	County	1	0	7	0	8	Roads
McDuffie	County	0	0	12	0	12	Roads
Muscogee	County	0	0	28	1	29	Roads
Monroe	County	0	0	15	0	15	Roads
Newton	County	1	0	19	0	20	Roads
Putnam	County	0	0	10	1	11	Roads
Pulaski	County	2	0	22	0	24	Roads
Richmond	County	3	0	73	6	82	Roads
Spalding	County	2	0	34	2	38	Roads
Ware	Waycross city	0	0	27	0	27	Streets
Wilkes	County	0	0	20	0	20	Roads
Walton	County	2	0	15	0	17	Roads
Wilcox	County	0	0	6	0	6	Roads
TOTAL		55	2	1,309	120	1,486	

88.1% Black men and boys
96.2% Black prisoners

Private

Brooks	Brice	4	0	94	6	104	Sawmilling, turpentine
Berrien	J. Brown	0	0	42	1	43	Turpentine
Bartow	IBRR Co.	2	0	21	0	23	Mining iron ore
Baker	T. M. Fleming	1	1	62	1	65	Turpentine
Coffee	A. T. Beed	0	0	25	0	25	Turpentine
Clinch	Simmons & Son	0	0	8	0	8	Turpentine
Clinch	N/A	0	0	7	0	7	Turpentine
Decatur	Chatt. L. Co.	0	0	23	2	25	Turpentine
Decatur	Sharp & D.	6	0	45	2	53	Turpentine
Dooley	Greer & Bro.	3	0	70	2	75	Turpentine, sawmilling
Elbert	F. M. Clark	0	1	11	0	12	Farm
Elbert	Hudgins	0	1	5	0	6	Farm
Elbert	Swift	11	0	73	5	89	Farm
Elbert	McCalla	1	0	26	0	27	Farm
Early	JW Callahan	4	2	107	1	110	Turpentine
Franklin	Little	3	0	9	0	12	Farm
Lowndes	**McRee**	**0**	**0**	**38**	**4**	**42**	**Farm**
Oconee	Price	1	0	16	1	18	Farm
Oglethorpe	J. W. J.	2	0	14	1	17	Farm
Oglethorpe	J. A. B.	2	0	36	0	38	Farm
Oglethorpe	J. M. Smith	8	0	61	0	69	Farm
Sereven	Foy	0	0	8	0	8	Sawmilling
Ware	N/A	0	0	17	0	17	Crossties
Ware	N/A	0	0	22	1	23	Turpentine
Wilkes	Adams & Bro.	0	0	16	0	16	Farm
Worth	Hackly	0	0	15	0	15	Turpentine
Worth	N/A	1	0	10	0	11	Turpentine
Worth	McLend & Co.	1	0	21	2	24	Turpentine
TOTAL		50	5	902	29	986	

91.5% Black boys and men
94.4% Black prisoners

Source: *Third Annual Report of the Prison Commission of Georgia, 1900*, Georgia Penitentiary Prison Commission's Reports, 21-1-40, Georgia Archives, Morrow, Georgia, 43.

misdemeanor camps. But the actual death count in felony convict leasing was surely higher than that reported by the Prison Commission, and any official head count among private misdemeanor camps would not include victims of kidnapping, ensuring that such death estimates were at the low end of what was possible in the system.

Illicit prisoners and kidnapping victims, particularly those at Kinderlou, were a problem considered to exist because of a broader deviation from misdemeanor camp rules. Originally worked within the confines of the law, as of October 1898, the McRee farm had diverged from the intentions of system authorities. It had become a camp in the third category of the Prison Commission's 1900 report, operating "contrary to law." Lowndes County authorities, as of 1901, had not provided guards or official administrators of punishment. The camp had not produced any official reports as required by the commission. The commission's annual report was more equivocal when it came to the kidnapping charges, noting that there was voluminous evidence against the family but that the evidence "tends to connect parties not directly in charge of or interested in the chaingang, and therefore has no bearing on the management thereof by the county authorities." It was a passing of the buck, an argument that such abuses somehow proved that the camp system was itself beyond such behavior.[25]

In its comprehensive annual report for 1901, the Prison Commission made similar oxymoronic statements about the investigation. "It is gratifying to be able to report that this order was promptly obeyed by the Lowndes county authorities, who since then have cheerfully cooperated with this Commission in seeing that this chaingang was conducted according to law," it claimed. At the same time, however, the report claimed that all evidence was turned over to the state's solicitor general "and [has] never been returned, nor has the commission ever received any information as to whether any further investigation was made by the officers charged with the enforcement of the criminal law." It was a handwashing that claimed active engagement, one that "had a salutary effect upon the entire misdemeanor system of the State" (see chapter 5).[26]

Prior to the commission's 1901 report, a new rule adopted early in the year required counties that sent their misdemeanor prisoners to camps in other jurisdictions to provide clothes and transportation to the prisoners after their release so that they could easily return to their home county. It was, perhaps, a valuable rule to those incarcerated people under its auspices, but the new rule did nothing to address the more systemic problems rife throughout the system. And that absence only allowed the camps

Table 4.7. Felony convict lease camps, 1901

Camp	County	Lessee	Employment	Num
Kramer	Wilcox	James W. English Jr.	Sawmilling	60
Doe Run	Worth	James W. English Jr.	Turpentine	48
Adrian	Emanuel	James W. English Jr.	Sawmilling	58
Jakin	Decatur	James W. English Jr.	Sawmilling	63
Bartow	Bartow	James W. English Jr.	Mining iron ore	117
Saffold	Early	James W. English Jr.	Turpentine	50
Cole City	Dade	James W. English Jr.	Turpentine	39
Durham Mine	Walker	James W. English Jr.	Turpentine	24
Durham Mine	Walker	James M. Smith	Turpentine	100
Durham Mine	Walker	Chickamauga C&C Co.	Turpentine	238
Cole City	Dade	John W. McCalla	Turpentine	50
Cole City	Dade	Canada Lumber Co.	Turpentine	24
Ensign	Worth	Canada Lumber Co.	Sawmilling	69
Chattahoochee	Fulton	Chattahoochee Brick Co.	Brickmaking	198
Richwood	Dooly	Parrott Lumber Co.	Sawmilling	124
Donalsonville	Decatur	Donaldson Lumber Co.	Turpentine	46
Fargo	Clinch	GS Baxter & Co.	Sawmilling	336
Egypt	Effingham	Merritt W. Dixon	Sawmilling	51
Lookout	Walker	Merritt W. Dixon	Mining coal	51
Colquitt	Miller	WH Mattox	Turpentine	48
Albany	Dougherty	Cruger & Pace	Brickmaking	51
Worth	Worth	Enterprise Lumber Co.	Sawmilling	67
Pitts	Wilcox	Enterprise Lumber Co.	Sawmilling	72
State farm	Baldwin	State farm (men)	Farming	157
State farm	Baldwin	State farm (boys under 15)	Farming	19
State farm	Baldwin	State farm (women)	Farming	85
TOTAL				2,245

Notes: That year, the felony system had 2,245 prisoners with seventy-five deaths. There were 252 white men and boys and six white women and girls, 1,908 Black men and boys and 79 Black women and girls.
85.0 percent Black men and boys
88.5 percent Black prisoners
Source: Fourth Annual Report of the Prison Commission of Georgia, 1901 (Atlanta: Franklin Printing Co., 1901), 28–29, 37.

Table 4.8. County misdemeanor camps, 1901, divided into public and private camps

County	Worked By	WM	WF	BM	BF	Total	Employment
Public							
Baldwin	County	0	0	20	8	28	Roads
Bibb	County	2	0	56	26	84	Roads
Burke	County	0	0	26	2	28	Roads
Butts	County	0	0	15	0	15	Roads
Chatham	County	3	3	158	76	240	Roads
Clarke	County	0	0	22	2	24	Roads
Coffee	County	1	0	9	0	10	Roads
DeKalb	County	0	0	24	0	24	Roads
Dougherty	County	0	0	20	3	23	Roads
Emanuel	County	0	0	14	0	14	Roads
Floyd	County	14	0	39	3	55	Roads
Fulton	County	12	0	181	29	222	Roads
Glynn	County	0	0	19	2	21	Roads
Greene	County	0	0	20	0	20	Roads
Hancock	County	0	0	12	0	12	Roads
Jasper	County	1	0	5	0	6	Roads
Jones	County	0	0	11	0	11	Roads
Jefferson	County	1	0	17	0	18	Roads
Laurens	County	2	0	20	0	22	Roads
Lowndes	**County**	**0**	**0**	**14**	**0**	**14**	**Roads**
McDuffie	County	0	0	9	0	9	Roads
Monroe	County	0	0	12	0	12	Roads
Muscogee	County	0	0	41	0	41	Roads
Newton	County	2	0	14	0	16	Roads
Putnam	County	0	0	6	0	6	Roads
Richmond	County	2	0	73	0	75	Roads
Spalding	County	0	0	26	0	26	Roads
Terrell	County	1	0	21	0	22	Cutting wood
Walton	County	0	0	9	2	11	Roads
Ware	Waycross city	0	0	17	0	17	Streets
Washington	County	0	0	24	0	24	Roads
Wilcox	County	0	0	13	0	13	Farming
Wilkes	County	0	0	17	0	17	Roads
Wilkes	County	1	0	13	0	14	Farming
TOTAL		42	3	997	153	1,195	

83.4% Black men and boys
96.2% Black prisoners

County	Worked By	WM	WF	BM	BF	Total	Employment
Private							
Baker	John R. Sharpe	4	0	20	1	25	Turpentine
Baker	John R. Sharpe	8	0	47	0	55	Turpentine
Bartow	Ga. I. & C. Co.	6	0	14	8	28	Mining iron
Berrien	E. G. Brown & Co.	2	0	35	0	37	Turpentine
Brooks	M. Brice	8	0	73	2	83	Sawmillinging, etc.
Coffee	A. T. Beach & Co.	0	0	28	1	29	Turpentine
Clinch	G. S. Baxter & Co.	2	0	23	0	25	Sawmilling
Decatur	Sharpe & Drake	3	0	61	1	65	Turpentine
Decatur	Hodges & Powell	2	0	26	1	29	Turpentine
Decatur	Chattah, L. Co.	4	0	27	0	31	Sawmilling
Decatur	L. J. Shingler & Br.	0	0	29	0	29	Turpentine
Dooly	Parrott Lum. Co.	1	0	28	2	31	Sawmilling
Dougherty	Cruger & Pace	2	0	21	0	23	Brick yard
Early	J. W. Callahan	1	0	76	0	77	Turpentine
Effingham	E. E. Toy Mf. Co.	0	0	76	0	76	Sawmilling
Elbert	J. W. McCalla	0	0	8	0	8	Farming
Elbert	Swift Bros.	10	0	35	2	47	Farming
Franklin	C. E. & N. Litts.	0	0	2	0	2	Farming
Irwin	Canada Lum. Co.	1	0	13	3	17	Sawmilling
Lowndes	**McRee Bros.**	**3**	**0**	**36**	**2**	**41**	**Farming**
Miller	John R. Sharpe	0	0	8	0	8	Turpentine
Mitchell	Fleming & Hines	6	0	48	1	55	Turpentine
Oconee	J. D. Price	0	0	6	0	6	Farming
Oglethorpe	J. A. Broach	5	2	25	0	32	Farming
Oglethorpe	James M. Smith	7	1	41	1	50	Farming
Oglethorpe	J. M. Jarrell	1	5	17	0	23	Farming
Ware	Hinson & Co.	0	0	19	0	19	Turpentine
TOTAL		76	8	842	25	951	

88.5% Black men and boys

91.2% Black prisoners

Source: *Fourth Annual Report of the Prison Commission of Georgia, 1901* (Atlanta: Franklin Printing Co., 1901), 38.

to proliferate. As of the 1901 report, there were sixty-one misdemeanor camps, thirty of them in private hands, even though the number of misdemeanants had dropped from 2,451 the previous year to 2,084 (see table 4.8). In the earlier years of the system, the public camps significantly outnumbered the private camps, but now they were virtually equal in number. That growing parity only frustrated the commission more that its recommendation for regulatory legislation had never materialized. It reminded its readers of its "extended reference" in its 1900 report "to the evils existing in the chaingang system, many of which still exist, and recommended legislation on the subject; it therefore feels that it has fully discharged its duty in the premises, and shall only refer the General Assembly to that report." As if to underscore its frustration, the commission used the 1901 controversy at Kinderlou as exemplary of the fractures in the system.[27]

There would be sixty-three estimated deaths in the private misdemeanor camps using the aforementioned formula, a number that continued to rise every year, and Kinderlou surely experienced its share of them. Lowndes County officials were aware of that violence. The county followed the lead of several of its counterparts in 1901 by developing a public roads camp for misdemeanants simultaneous to the private venture of the McRees, pushed at least in part by the controversy surrounding their dealings with Kinderlou. It was a controversy that would reflect poorly on the county and the McRees, but it would also generate publicity that was the first real public exposure of private misdemeanor leasing and the dangers of an absence of regulatory policy.

5

The Scandal of 1900–1901

In September 1900, Brooks County solicitor J. W. Edmonson filed two writs of habeas corpus that led to the release of at least twenty people held without charge on the McRee property. Also in September, Edmonson traveled to Atlanta to file charges against the McRee convict camp with the state Prison Commission. The charges came complete with affidavits from Black victims and prominent white members of the community. Edmonson alleged that the McRees employed "trappers" to capture Black citizens traveling through the area, imprison them, and put them to work on the plantation, knowing that law enforcement would make no real effort to find missing Black people in south Georgia and north Florida. "Under shackles and constant guard," the local Quitman newspaper explained, "men secured in this medieval fashion have been kept in the camp for months and even years."[1]

It was the inherent danger in creating a private misdemeanor system that had no authority to answer to. Along with leasing misdemeanants from county courthouses in the area, the McRees could use several other ways to get prisoners to Kinderlou. First, they could use debt peonage, paying the fines of misdemeanants not sentenced to jail time. Second, they could charge misdemeanants there from lease or there from peonage fabricated prices for meals, services, or fines while in custody, then keep the prisoners well past their scheduled release dates in order to work off such supposed payments, a self-replicating process that could keep the prisoners there in virtual perpetuity. Finally, they could kidnap Black travelers in the area, bring them to the camp, bind them, and force them to work as misdemeanants, knowing that without regulatory oversight, without enforced recordkeeping mandates that the law supposedly required, they could get away with claiming that the prisoners were acquired by legal means if tested on that count. As in Anderson, South Carolina, location was instrumental to the McRee scheme to take advantage of a lack of oversight. Kinderlou was just miles from the Florida border, and the family knew that taking unwitting north Florida citizens and bringing them across the state line would benefit from a lack of law enforcement contact across jurisdictions and state systems, providing additional layers of cover for their criminal plans to take advantage of the loose Georgia state management of private misdemeanor camps. That said, the principal layer of cover came from white supremacy itself, leaving the McRees perfectly comfortable taking Black locals from south Georgia, as well.

The example Edmonson gave in Atlanta was that of Fanny Jackson, who had visited the McRee camp in the early 1890s to see her husband, who was a misdemeanor convict at Kinderlou. When she was leaving, guards arrested her and forced her to work, beating her unmercifully until she agreed to bind her young child to the camp, as well. "I finally had to give up my child to prevent what seemed to me further unendurable beating," she explained in her affidavit. "The skin was beat from my body and the flesh made raw. I was beat first on Sunday and then made to sit in salty water, I suppose to cure the wounds." It was the same thing the next day. "I was then put to work, and Mr. George McRee went into the field and made them let me go to the house. I was sick from the beating nearly four months, too sick to work, and a great deal of the time could not rest at all except on my stomach. Mr. Will has my child yet," said Jackson. "He took it from me by force. I have never been paid any wages."[2]

Mollie Williams had a similar story after bringing a dress to her sister at Kinderlou. James and Will Lewis were kidnapped by two men and taken to Kinderlou by force, then made to sign an eight-month work agreement under threat that otherwise they would be taken to Valdosta on a trumped-up concealed weapons charge. Tom Cole was taken yet another way, convinced by a "recruiter" that there were good wages to be had at the Kinderlou turpentine distillery. When he arrived, though, he was placed in shackles and worked as a convict. Edmonson also charged that the McRees paid the way of several Black prisoners freed by habeas writs to travel to Florida so as to avoid testifying in the investigation.[3]

The charges were a legitimate scandal, leading even the *Atlanta Constitution*, no friend of Black equality, to declare "evidence that innocent men and women, against whom no charge whatever could be raked up, have been apprehended forcibly and compelled under threats to work for years in some cases," a horror "more like a relic of aboriginal barbarity than an actual condition existing in the state of Georgia." The paper argued that the abuses at Kinderlou were not the responsibility of the Prison Commission, "for the law does not give that body direct and entire supervision of that class of camps." The commission made an annual trip to each camp but had no authority to govern the private misdemeanor camps in the way they did felony convict lease camps. For all the problems inherent in the more bemoaned felony leasing, it at least had levels of oversight and requirements for recordkeeping that somewhat tempered its broader abuses. The private misdemeanor camps had no such oversight, no such requirements. Both the commission and the *Constitution* were staunch defenders of felony convict leasing against charges of barbarity, but those defenses centered on the just punishment of crimes committed and the possibility of government intervention if abuses were to occur. That intervention, of course, did not always materialize, but its possibility provided cover to the system. In such a framing, the misdemeanor camps were so problematic specifically because of a lack of state regulatory power: "The evil is not eradicated until the management of the misdemeanor camps is changed and the prison commission is given actual and complete supervision over them."[4] While felony camps and the violence perpetrated in them stood as testament to the reality that commission supervision was not a cure-all for the problems related to convict leasing, the paper was surely right that misdemeanor camps like Kinderlou were dramatically more dangerous than felony camps because of a lack of policy enforcement at the state level. And when abuses did seep into the public discourse, claims of overt criminality justifying harsh treatment were harder to make when the victims were misdemeanants.

Edmonson, for his part, did not want the facts of his charges published, as he believed that more abuses at Kinderlou were ongoing and that publicity would make a coverup easier. Still, some of that testimony was made possible by releases pressured by Edmonson's writs, and along with sure efforts to cover further abuses at Kinderlou, the publicity forced a statement from William McRee. "I agree to notify every hand, man and woman, on the farms of the McRee brothers who is not held under a sentence of court that he is a free man, to go as he pleases and to pay the cost of the two habeas corpus suits now pending in the city court of Valdosta." It was that signed document, Edmonson explained, that released "between twenty and thirty negroes who had been illegally confined in these camps."[5] The charges presented Georgia with a penal problem, but also one of public relations. They threatened to bring private misdemeanor camps under the same scrutiny that felony camps and debt peonage abuses had received, making them a threat to everyone who benefited from a corrupt system, one that was corrupt even before the kidnappings began.

The McRees, for their part, denied the charges and claimed in the press that Edmonson's investigation was motivated by rivalry. Edmonson's brother-in-law, Ed McRee told a reporter, was Mitchell Brice, who operated the private misdemeanor camp in neighboring Brooks County and contracted for access to misdemeanor prisoners in several counties. Brice was the influential planter who had been responsible for stopping the white rampage in 1894 (see chapter 1). But when the McRees sought to obtain misdemeanants from Brooks County and the prisoners "preferred to go to our place," Brice, they claimed, sent Edmonson to investigate and to try and lure the men away from Kinderlou. "He was given access to them," said Ed, "and we found that he had done his utmost to get the men to leave as well as others employed by us, but they refused to do so." It was only after that failure that he moved on to Will McRee's property, "which adjoins ours, but is not a convict camp. Brother Will told him that he was not restraining any one." Edmonson, however, convinced them to file habeas corpus writs "by promises of better pay in Brooks County." The suit failed in the local courts, and afterward, Ed claimed, "the negroes returned voluntarily, and even went to [their] lawyer and begged him to get Will to take them back." Edmondson was "a hostile and malicious representative of a competitive camp with the view of decoying away employees and doing us dirt at all hazards."[6]

Edmonson responded that McRee's statement never denied the charges, instead shifting critique to Edmonson's motives, a non-denial denial that portended a justification of his claims. McRee never mentioned kidnapping, never denied illegally detaining misdemeanor prisoners or innocent citizens being held as prisoners. Edmonson denied having any personal animus toward the Lowndes camp and that he ever sought to influence prisoner testimony. His relationship with Brice did exist, but Brice had no interest in McRee prisoners. Seven different prisoners had left Kinderlou and moved to Brooks County, and none of them were employed or detained by Brice. All quotations that McRee attributed to Edmonson were "absolutely false and not one truthful quotation is contained in the whole interview," as was, surely, the claim that local Black prisoners were eager to work at Kinderlou.[7]

The Kinderlou scheme was the kind of effort that could not exist without the complicity of Lowndes County law enforcement, and Edmonson charged them, too. Governor Allen Candler and Joseph Turner, chairman of the state Prison Commission, responded on October 2 by issuing an order compelling Lowndes County authorities to appear at a Prison Commission hearing in Valdosta two weeks later on October 15.[8] The order repeated Edmonson's claim that "authorities have failed, and are neglecting to comply with the laws of this state, and the rules regulating the control and management of misdemeanor prisoners, and are permitting and allowing many criminal and inhuman acts to be done in connection with and under color of the chain gang of said county, over which they have and should exercise full and complete control." The hearing would decide whether or not the McRee misdemeanor chain gang should be abolished and the victims freed.[9]

Even before the hearing, however, it was clear that Candler was dramatically affected by the charges, and by similar charges around the state. He planned as part of his next annual message to the state legislature a recommendation that the state take those convicted of misdemeanors out of the hands of private labor camps and place them under the jurisdiction of the Prison Commission. It was a plan designed to create better prices for their labor and to ensure better treatment. The state already maintained control over those convicted of felonies, and they tended to prove safer than those convicted of misdemeanors because of the excesses of private lessees.[10] Such had been the clarion call of the Prison Commission since its first report, one that wouldn't be followed despite the public nature of the charges and Candler's seeming intent. That was largely because the counties themselves were making money and didn't want the process to be changed, and because Kinderlou's example of the potential problems with private misdemeanor leasing created a ready foil to use for defending the felony lease system as a regulated and beneficial system compared to its counterpart.

And so the McRees were summoned to answer the charges in front of the state Prison Commission. They were, the *Atlanta Constitution* glossed, "the most serious" charges "in every way of any ever brought in Georgia." But the power of the charges, whatever the conclusion of the commission, would exist almost entirely in public perception. The paper expressed its frustration that "if the rules of the prison commission have been violated, the men who run the camp cannot be touched; the responsibility falls on the commissioners of Lowndes county." It was "remarkable" that "should the charges of kidnapping, inhumanity and criminal brutality be found true, the prison Commission cannot touch the convict camp on that ground. The only recourse for the victim is through the courts, which to people of this particular class are altogether imaginary or else very far off." It was both counterintuitive and counterproductive, promising a scandalous hearing with little teeth at its conclusion. The *Constitution* was adamant that such hearings needed to give the commission the power to say, "Your management of the camp has been brutal and disgusting. From this day on the camp will cease to exist."[11]

In response to the charges against the McRees, the Prison Commission held a three-day hearing in Valdosta in October 1900, interviewing thirty-three witnesses.[12] At the hearing, Turner was joined by C. A. Evans and Thomas Eason, the sitting members of the state Prison Commission. Edmonson was joined in his effort as a de facto prosecutor by Moultrie attorney Colonel W. S. Humphreys. The McRees' representation was led by Captain H. G. Turner, G. A. Whitaker, and Captain S. T. Kingsberry. The attorney for the Lowndes County commissioners was Colonel E. P. S. Denmark. They were some of the most distinguished men of the region, Confederate veterans, lawyers that had carried with them political appointments and local status that benefited from, if not relied on, the status quo of white supremacy. Thus it was that a room full of powerful white people congregated to listen to the testimony of roughly a dozen Black witnesses who had experienced the racialized brutality of Kinderlou. It was a reality that assured the McRees would receive the benefit of the doubt. Black witnesses, for example, were kept cloistered in rooms at the Lowndes County courthouse so that they couldn't hear the testimony of their counterparts, demonstrating a basic a priori distrust of the testimony of those considered broadly less important than white lawmakers and attorneys.[13]

The testimony they gave, however, was powerful and established a basic pattern of life at Kinderlou. Ed and Frank McRee ran the convict camp itself, while their brother Will operated a separate farm and stockade on his own part of the property. There, kidnapped prisoners were detained for years at a time, living in shackles and subjected to a variety of corporal punishments. They were, as the Quitman newspaper explained, "in all respects like ordinary convicts except that they did not wear stripes." The corporal punishment was significant. A case could be made that such private convict camps were legal under Georgia law, but monthly reports were required and each camp was allowed only one whipping boss. The requirements were designed to curb abuses and serve as a de facto watch over a system that was far too large and unwieldy to be policed by a three-person Prison Commission, much less one state warden. But precisely because of the system's largesse and the failure of the commission to provide adequate oversight, the McRees disobeyed both regulations, and "even the negro guards had at various times exercised the right to use the strap."[14]

Little is known about the Black guards at Kinderlou or any other misdemeanor lease camp, but much is known about the self-preservation mechanism prevalent in the existence of antebellum Black overseers and Jewish guards in Nazi concentration camps. Most scholars describe the taking of such roles less as Stockholm syndrome and more as a pragmatic protectionist interest when abused prisoners were faced with difficult choices that could easily lead to death, a phenomenon that Tuvia Friling calls the "politics of survival."[15] The use of long-serving prisoners as guards was itself a form of abuse, a way to break the spirit of those who found themselves in bondage, even if whipping in that context never occurred. The charges, however, claimed that whipping by Black guards did happen.

And the charges only grew from there. Several Black witnesses testified that after they finished serving a regular court sentence at the McRee convict camp, they were, instead of being released, transferred to Will McRee's stockade, where they were continuously beaten, forced to work during the day under armed guard, and housed at night in close quarters without privacy or gender segregation, another violation of the Prison Commission's rules for misdemeanor chain gangs. Attempts to escape prompted manhunts with attack dogs and a swift return to the stockade. Will McRee also employed several Black men to "arrest any roaming or vagabond negroes found in the vicinity, trump up some charge against them," then confine them and put them to work. With two notable exceptions (see chapter 7), nothing is known about these Black bounty hunters, but the same historiography that guides assumptions about Black camp guards would probably apply to them, as well, with the exception that a given survival instinct in this case was not based on maintaining life in incarceration and instead was rooted in an effort to maintain financial solvency and powerful white relationships in an economically depressed and white supremacist climate. Two Brooks County men testified that they had been picked up on this model after being charged with stealing cantaloupes. Despite not being tried for the supposed crime, they were kept and worked for three months each. When they tried to escape, a group of dogs and men forcefully brought them back.[16]

The McRees responded with powerful white witnesses, who would uphold the line of white supremacy and best convince the white authorities. State warden Jake C. Moore argued under oath that he had inspected the McRee camps several times and had found that the prisoners were "well fed and well cared for in every respect." He claimed that he "considered the camps as well managed as any in the state." Thomas Eason, who was part of the commission itself, claimed also to have made a personal inspection of Kinderlou and found good treatment of prisoners. He even "made the convicts strip to discover if [there were] possibl[y] any marks of cruelty or ill-treatment." It was the kind of admission that demonstrated that Black victims of kidnapping and Black prisoners were unlikely to receive justice from white southern judicial bodies, even those bodies that had devoted so much page space to bemoaning the phenomenon of private misdemeanor leasing.[17]

The case occupied the Lowndes County courthouse for days, with every seat taken as crowds sought information on what was a salacious story. But the crowds were white, and they were inevitably on the side of the McRees. "It is the consensus of opinion here," one reporter acknowledged, "that Edmonson's case has gone to pieces and that the camps will be sustained."[18]

J. R. Burton added to the voices of approval in an op-ed. He was the physician hired by the McRees to examine members of the chain gang. He assured everyone that he had "never seen any brutal or inhuman treatment of any convict of either sex or of any color." Black workers who remained at Kinderlou after their sentences were not forced to stay. They "remain there under wages. All are well fed and well clothed," he announced. "I never considered McRee's chain gang a place of punishment, but rather a paradise for vagabond negroes." Any claims to the contrary were "a vile slander upon four excellent young men."[19] Because of its previous incarnation as a felony camp, Kinderlou was cited as a rare exemplar among private misdemeanor lessees for maintaining medical facilities. But if the doctor on call was willing to make statements so demonstrably untrue, even the one credit to the camp's name seemed a shibboleth.

Thus to curry favor with the commission and to plead to a lesser charge, as it were, the McRees admitted to violating the state statute against having only one whipping boss but claimed that they only did so because they did not know about the regulation. Whether true or not, it was a perfectly reasonable claim, since that regulation was technically for public county chain gang camps; the commission had been arguing for years that the kind of camp that the McRees were running was technically against the law and therefore beyond any specific regulation. The family assured the commission that they would pay whatever penalty was required for the whipping boss oversight. Technically, the commission only had supervisory jurisdiction over the convict camp itself. It could not impose penalties, which the family surely understood when making such a concession. The McRees were far more resolute when denying any abuse took place at Kinderlou.

Will McRee brought in an additional series of white witnesses who denied that any mistreatment had occurred. They claimed "that the negroes were not restrained of their liberty but were paid for their labor, and that the wholesale charges of kidnapping, brutal treatment etc., were untrue." With that, the commission returned to Atlanta, promising to work with Governor Candler to make and issue a report in response to the charges and their hearing.[20]

The report finally appeared in late February 1901, "bound in moroccan leather and embrac[ing] over 500 typewritten pages," and it was scathing. The commission's findings explained that Kinderlou was "originally organized and conducted in conformity with the law," with county authorities supervising prisoners on the McRee farm. Since October 1898, however, the date of the first comprehensive Prison Commission report, Kinderlou's operations were "conducted in violation of the law, in that the convicts therein confined were placed entirely in charge of, and worked by, these private individuals." County authorities no longer supervised the work of the prisoners, nor did they hire independent guards. Everything since October 1898 was operated by the McRees without any real supervision, allowing them to "indiscriminately" inflict punishment on their captives. The report claimed that charges that "convicts have been kept longer than the terms imposed by the courts" had "not been satisfactorily proven." The kidnapping charges, however, had far more evidence behind them. The commission's findings did not elaborate substantially on them, publicly arguing that since there was no county oversight, and thus the county authorities played no role, the charges had "no bearing upon the management therefore by the county authorities." Privately, of course, the commission was worried about bad publicity, just as it had been in its earlier comprehensive reports. Still, the group pledged to submit "these matters to the attention of the Grand Jury of Lowndes county, the Solicitor-General of that Judicial Circuit, and other officials who are charged with the enforcement of the laws of the State." This was a tacit admission that despite the claims that such kidnappings crossed state lines and could be considered federal offenses, the commission would not present its findings to federal authorities, fearing actual action and publicity that would redound negatively to its system of race and labor-based apartheid and to the misdemeanor system that had largely escaped national scrutiny up to that point. The report closed with an order for Lowndes County officials to resume oversight of the Kinderlou operation (though the county had never actually begun oversight, and thus there was nothing to resume). It was a report that was both damning and permissive at the same time, noting responsibility and abrogating it in one concise document.[21]

While it did not deal with the charges of kidnapping, or with reports that incarcerated people were held longer than their original sentences, the commission did encourage the local authorities, who had jurisdiction for such matters, to investigate those charges, demonstrating at least a tacit belief in their validity. The evidence on such subjects, the report explained, was "very voluminous and conflicting." Since the would-be kidnappers had no specific relation to the chain gang itself, however, "no attempt has been made to reconcile the conflicting testimony or to pass upon these features of the case." Still, the report sought "to call these matters to the attention" of the Lowndes County grand jury and solicitor general. The report also acknowledged the problems with indiscriminate corporal punishment without a single designated punisher and the lack of written reports required by law. Keeping with the testimony of white witnesses at the hearing, the report concluded that the prisoners had been humanely "fed and clothed and cared for." It was the kind of catering to white witnesses common in the South, but it didn't lead to common conclusions. "It is ordered that the county commissioners of Lowndes county immediately, through proper officers and guards, resume custody and control of the convicts confined in said chaingang." If the county failed in the reclamation effort, "the state warden will remove them from the county of Lowndes."[22]

The report functionally ended the McRees' relationship with the private misdemeanor lease system. With the family's free labor from the state no longer available, they turned to relationships with county sheriffs in the area for debt peons, who were then housed in the stockade constructed for the original convict labor force. Treated as slaves in their work, the debt peons were also treated like slaves when they attempted to flee, tracked down by hunting dogs and whipped as punishment for the effort.[23]

Meanwhile, even as the commission was crafting its report, another charge against the McRees surfaced. A nineteen-year-old Black local who had never been convicted of a crime had been bound at Kinderlou for three years. Unlike many in his situation, he was able to get a lawyer who filed a habeas corpus writ and got him out, but it was yet another documented instance of kidnapping and involuntary servitude initiated by the McRees.[24]

It was all too much for Candler. The governor and the Prison Commission issued an order following its report, mandating that "the county commissioners of Lowndes county must again take charge of the county prisoners now being worked at the McRee camp in that county, and they alone must exercise supervision and control over them."[25] The only misdemeanor camp in Lowndes County, he ruled, had to be a public works chain gang, echoing the proscription in the commission's report.

Candler and the commission issued a series of conclusions to bolster the reasons behind the order that laid bare the problems at Kinderlou: "This chaingang appears to have been originally organized and conducted in formity with the law and was worked by the county authorities for the McRees, on their farm." But "since October 1898, it has been conducted in violation of the law, in that the convicts therein confined were placed entirely in charge of and worked by these private individuals, the county authorities since that date, having neither appointed or paid the guards and other persons in charge thereof, but such guards and other persons being employees of the McRees." Also, "no person has been designated by the county authorities to administer punishment, but it appears that the McRees and their employees, some of the latter being negroes, have indiscriminately inflicted such punishment at will." No reports had been made to either county authorities or the Prison Commission.[26] Candler's statement plagiarized directly from the commission report but was necessary as a public proclamation from a state office to which people actually paid attention.

That said, Candler's order mimicked the Prison Commission report in other ways, as well, hedging on the larger abuses at Kinderlou. "If any convicts have been kept longer than the terms imposed upon them by the courts, it has not been satisfactorily proven." The order acknowledged the charges of "kidnapping and other outrages" but argued that conflicting testimony made accounts irreconcilable. "Nevertheless it is felt to be the duty of the governor and the prison commission to call these matters to the attention of the grand jury of Lowndes county, the solicitor general of that judicial circuit and other officials who are charged with the enforcement of the laws of the state." Though the commission demurred, the charges were "matters of such a serious nature, involving the violation of the criminal laws, the liberty of citizens and the good name of the state and Lowndes county" that they needed to be investigated locally. If nothing else, county officials needed to "resume custody and control of the convicts confined in said chaingang," and if not, the prisoners would be removed.[27]

As repetitive as the statement seemed, it was doing important public work. The order didn't technically abolish the McRee camp. It just required that county commissioners provide oversight and control of those who worked there—the county had to appoint the guard, the whipping boss, and all civilian employees—or it had to house misdemeanants away from a private farm and employ them on public works. Kinderlou would still have access to debt peons, and it would soon return to felony leasing. The problem with the order was that much of the problematic behavior of the family involved holding people illegally, keeping as prisoners citizens who were never convicted of any crime. Threatening to remove legal access to prisoners, in that sense, was cold comfort to those making charges that they had never been duly charged with any misdemeanor or felony. It was particularly troubling because the camp's roughly thirty thousand acres were divided between the four brothers. Edward, Frank, and George engaged in convict labor and abuse. "There is another brother, Will McRee, who has no direct connection with the convict camp, but who works free labor. It was its connection with this work as well as the convict camp, that the charge of kidnapping innocent citizens were made."[28]

State warden Colonel Jake Moore, superintendent of the state penitentiary department, was at the same time as the McRee hearing developing his annual report, which would demonstrate that the state had roughly 2,500 misdemeanor prisoners, housed in sixty-one different camps in fifty Georgia counties, with about half of the total used to build the state's roads:[29] 2,451 misdemeanor prisoners in sixty-one camps; up from 1,834 in 1898 and 2,384 in 1899. Meanwhile, the recognized death rate among those convicted of felonies dropped in 1900 to 1.6 percent. It was a set of statistics that only made the case that misdemeanor prisoners should come under the control of the Prison Commission rather than private camps, with virtually everyone acknowledging that their care would be improved and the exploitation of their labor would be streamlined and cheaper.[30]

The report was even more damning because it came from a largely unreliable narrator. Jacob C. Moore began his career as sheriff of Floyd County, before rising to become assistant keeper of the penitentiary. With the state's reorganization of the prison system, Moore was named state warden in December 1897, "and in his new place he will be in charge of the entire army of guards and inspectors who are to care for the state's convicts."[31] Though it was unknown in 1901, Moore was corrupt (see chapter 9), profiting off the sale of prisoners to supplement his salary and taking bribes to not report abuses against them. Forcing someone with a substantial, if secret, investment in private camps to acknowledge their problems amounted to a canary in an overly dark coal mine.

Table 5.1. Monthly report of misdemeanor chain gang, camp no. 2, Captain J. W. Stephens, February 1901

Name	County	Age/Race/Gender	Crime	Sentence	Behavior	Description	Punish
John Kaigles	???	40 Black Male (B M)	Larceny	12 months	good		
Lorenzo Cheeks	Echols	21 B M	Robbery	12 months	good		
Harry Troy	Echols	20 B M	Robbery	12 months	good		
Will Davis	Lowndes	19 B M	Robbery	12 months	bad	neglect duty	10 licks
John Baker	McIntosh	21 B M	Larceny	12 months	good		
Burton Brisbane	Lowndes	23 B M	Larceny	12 months	good		
John Bird	Lowndes	22 B M	Misdemeanor	12 months	bad		
Charles James	Lowndes	25 B M	Misdemeanor	6 months	good		
Blanche Smith	DeKalb	20 Black Female (B F)	Misdemeanor	12 months	good		
Rich Williams	Lowndes	20 B M	Misdemeanor	6 months	good		
John Stanley	Lowndes	17 B M	Misdemeanor	6 months	fair	neglect duty	10 licks
Will Colbert	Lowndes	27 B M	Misdemeanor	12 months	fair		
Robb Gilbert	Lowndes	25 B M	Misdemeanor	6 months	fair		
John Hicks	Lowndes	26 B M	Misdemeanor	12 months	good		
Ed Fai	Lowndes	23 B M	Misdemeanor	12 months	good		
Mark Beckham	Lowndes	48 B M	Misdemeanor	18 months	good		
Lucius Carter	Lowndes	21 B M	Misdemeanor	6 months	bad	neglect duty	10 licks
Orange Pollard	Lowndes	28 B M	Misdemeanor	12 months	good		
John McCoy	Lowndes	24 B M	Misdemeanor	12 months	good		
Elura Thacel	Lowndes	16 B M	Misdemeanor	12 months	good		
John Hodges	Clinch	26 B M	Misdemeanor	8 months	good		
Jim Johnson	Lowndes	22 B M	Misdemeanor	6 months	good		
Lucius Jackson	Lowndes	23 B M	Misdemeanor	9 months	good		
Tom Gaudidate	Lowndes	Na	Na	Na	good		

Source: "Monthly Report of Misdemeanor Chain-Gang, February 1901, Lowndes County Camp #2," Records of the Georgia Board of Corrections, Record Group 21, 12-18-23-NEWS261, Georgia Archives, Morrow, Georgia.

The later reveal of his criminal behavior, of course, also called into question his testimony that the McRee camp kept its prisoners "well fed and well cared for in every respect." But as Moore's abuses were yet to be known, the McRees managed to avoid a heavy dose of national attention in 1900, though publicity for their own crimes would eventually come. And the strain of the problems in 1900 and 1901 clearly took their toll, as Ed McRee was listed as insolvent on his property taxes for 1901.[32]

The state outrage over Kinderlou and its misuse of misdemeanor convict lease and peonage statutes was matched nationally the following year in the sensational Anderson, South Carolina, murder case (see chapter 3).[33] In Georgia, however, it was a system that surely sounded familiar, and the McRees remained one of the chief offenders. A 1901 profile in the *Savannah Morning News* described the McRee operation, shorn of any controversial elements, in relative detail. The four McRee brothers each owned their own homes on the family property, creating essentially four amalgamated plantations with a diverse farming effort. Timber and turpentine were important, but the Kinderlou farms grew corn, oats, wheat, cotton, rye, peanuts, potatoes, sugar cane, velvet beans, cantaloupes, and watermelons. The family raised cattle for slaughter and operated an advanced dairy with a modern cream separator that helped the family supply butter and milk to Valdosta, Quitman, and smaller surrounding towns. Each brother maintained more than five hundred head of cattle, along with large numbers of sheep and hogs. Then there were the fifteen thousand acres of timber, which the farms fashioned into a variety of crates and boxes, along with providing raw lumber to community builders. There were forty-two springs on the sprawling property accessed by a modern hydraulic ram that provided water throughout. There were also mercantile stores on the property that served both workers on the farm and customers in surrounding towns. The main house on the plantation, the one occupied by Frank McRee, was built by his great-grandfather in 1834, and the elaborate gate that opened onto the property and led to that home was also original to the operation's antebellum beginnings. That particular profile noted the family's reputation for parties and hospitality. When the writer disembarked from his train, the conductor told him that he made it a habit never to announce the name "Kinderlou" at the stop, as "the reputation of the McRees as entertainers" meant that "all his passengers would leave him at once."[34]

Their reputation, however, was by no means pristine. The McRees were controversial, even among their neighbors. Two children of nearby farmer

Table 5.2. Monthly report of misdemeanor chain gang, camp no. 1, Captain J. J. Hines, February 1901

Name	County	Age/Race/Gender	Crime	Sentence	Behavior	Description	Punish
Aaron Smith	Lowndes	26 B M	Misdemeanor	12 months	fair		
Dave Tillman	Lowndes	16 B M	Larceny	12 months	fair		
Jessie Ferguson	Echols	25 B M	Larceny	12 months	fair		
Arthur Jenkins	Lowndes	16 B M	Larceny	12 months	fair		
Henry Shorter	Lowndes	24 M M	Larceny	12 months	bad	neglect	10 licks
Rheuben Fields	McIntosh	26 Br M	...	12 months	bad	impudent	10 licks
Doak Thomas	Lowndes	23 Br M	Gambling	12 months	bad	impudent	10 licks
Ed Henderson	Lowndes	18 M M	Larceny	9 months	good		
Joseph McKinnon	Lowndes	27 B M	Pistol	12 months	fair		
Oscar Spivey	Lowndes	25 B M	Pistol	8 months	fair		
George Morris	Lowndes	15 B M	Larceny	12 months	fair		
Mathis Cain	Lowndes	26 Br M	Gambling	12 months	fair		
Henry King	Lowndes	30 Br M	Larceny	36 months (3xs)	fair		
Sallie Rodgers	Sumpter	25 B F	Larceny	32 months (3 xs)	good		
Anna Willis	Sumpter	25 B F	Larceny	31 months (3 xs)	good		
George Rawlston	Lowndes	28 M M	Misdemeanor	8 months	good		
Tom Woods	Lowndes	16 Br M	Assault/battery	6 months	fair		
Harry Woods	Lowndes	15 Br M	Assault/battery	6 months	fair		
Jeff Dunn	Lowndes	24 M M	Larceny	12 months	fair		
Phillip Ford	Echols	30 B M	Misdemeanor	12 months	fair		
Jack Frazier	Lowndes	33 B M	Larceny	12 months	bad	disobey	10 licks
Alan Bell	Lowndes	24 B M	Larceny	12 months	bad	disobey	10 licks

(continued)

Table 5.2—Continued

Name	County	Age/Race/Gender	Crime	Sentence	Behavior	Description	Punish
Moses Grier	Lowndes	16 B M	Misdemeanor	12 months	fair		
Tom Rease	Lowndes	23 Br M	Misdemeanor	8 months	good		
Joseph Morgan	Liberty	25 W M	Misdemeanor	8 months	good		
Holliston Murphy	Liberty	30 B M	Larceny	12 months	fair		
Joe Martin	Lowndes	40 W M	Misdemeanor	12 months	fair		
Jim Seward	Lowndes	20 B M	Assault/battery	12 months	bad	trying to escape	10 licks
Frank Wade	Lowndes	24 B M	Larceny	24 months (2 xs)	fair		
Ed Russell	Lowndes	35 B M	Gambling	12 months (2 xs)	fair		
Caesar Lessons	Lowndes	30 B M	Misdemeanor	6 months	fair		
Will Robinson	Lowndes	15 B M	Burglary	12 months	fair		
Johnnie Butler	Lowndes	18 B F	Misdemeanor	12 months	fair		
Hexby Johnson	Lowndes	26 M M	Misdemeanor	6 months	fair		
Annie Washington	Lowndes	18 Br F	Larceny	12 months	fair		
John Lew	Lowndes	30 Ch M	Stolen goods	24 months (2 xs)	bad	neglect	10 licks
... Simpkins	Lowndes	30 M M	Misdemeanor	12 months	bad	neglect	10 licks
... Williams	Lowndes	28 Br M	Misdemeanor	9 months	fair		
Ed Mussane	Lowndes	25 B M	Misdemeanor	6 months	fair		
George Branson	Lowndes	25 B M	Larceny	6 months	fair		

Source: "Monthly Report of Misdemeanor Chain-Gang, February 1901, Lowndes County Camp #1," Records of the Georgia Board of Corrections, Record Group 21, 12-18-23-NEWS261, Georgia Archives, Morrow, Georgia.

R. F. Brooks, eleven and thirteen years old, had been working at one of the mills on the McRee property. When Brooks decided to take his children from the mill to have them work on his own farm, mill superintendent Archibald McCranie tried to keep the children in the mill. That led to a confrontation between Brooks and McCranie. The superintendent punched the father, but the father responded by pulling a pistol and shooting his rival in the side. The kids pulled knives and cut McCranie several times. When Ed McRee tried to break up the fight, Brooks's wife hit him in the head with a board. None of the injuries were fatal; both Brooks and one of his children were taken into custody by the local sheriff. But the incident demonstrated the operation's willingness to use captive child labor, even captive white child labor from nearby farms.[35] In the face of controversy over the use of Black bound labor, the family proved willing to try nearby white alternatives, knowing that fights with locals made far fewer headlines than federal indictments.

Captive labor in all of its forms would continue to dog the family, but the vast majority of child labor that found itself at Kinderlou was decidedly non-white. The first juvenile court in the United States did not convene until 1899 in Chicago. Historian Anthony Platt's original study of the phenomenon interpreted it as a way to exert social control on the working class through the legal system, an imposition of distinctly American middle-class values on a largely immigrant population. David S. Tanenhaus revised that analysis in 2004, arguing instead that the movement to create a distinct system of justice for juveniles was prompted by a group of Progressive reformers known as the Child Savers, who claimed with sincerity that children needed a different justice system that defaulted to rehabilitation rather than punishment. In either interpretation, however, Geoff Ward has demonstrated that it was an effort that was decidedly northern in its early development and one that concerned itself almost entirely with white children. Black children in the South, then, found themselves on the outside looking in. They were considered more disposable and less in need of rehabilitation because of white assumptions about their potential to contribute valuable service to society and the racial coding of labor that had been in place since the seventeenth century.[36]

In 1902, fourteen-year-old James Robinson was leased to Kinderlou, his sister Cassie Kinsey writing to Theodore Roosevelt after exhausting all local options to have him released. "Mr. Prassident," she wrote, "They wont let me have him. . . . He hase not don nothing for them to have him in chanes so I rite to you for your help." When the McRees learned of the pending Justice Department investigation of their operation, they allowed Robinson to leave to avoid further scandal.[37]

While it is difficult to have a full understanding of the misdemeanor convict population at Kinderlou, rotating as its population did, records of the prisoners at two of the three separate operations at the McRee plantation in February 1901 remain and provide at least a glimpse of the makeup of the imprisoned workforce (see table 5.1 and table 5.2).

The entries are telling in a variety of ways. First, it is important to note that such listings would only include those who came to the McRees through proper legal channels. Any prisoners who arrived by way of kidnapping or other forms of duplicity would not make the register. Those who did arrive, with the exception of one resident in Camp 2 from DeKalb County, were all from Lowndes County or others in south Georgia. The vast majority were Black men and boys, though the recorder for Camp 1 did include designations for "Brown" and "Mulatto." There was also in Camp 1 one listed "Chinaman," John Lew, whose name was almost certainly spelled incorrectly, serving twenty-four months for two counts of possession of stolen goods. Prisoners were as young as fifteen, and the bulk of them were in their teens or early twenties. Most were incarcerated for misdemeanors, but the vast majority of misdemeanor sentences were no different from those of their felony counterparts, demonstrating that the distinction was cosmetic more than anything else. Most felony convictions were for nonviolent offenses, larceny the most common, followed by burglary and gambling. The count of those who received corporal punishment was almost certainly underreported, if the claims of those who experienced the McRee camp were any indication, but those that were reported cited vague charges of neglect of duty or impudence as reasons for beatings. There were only one white convict and five women across both of the recorded camp logs. The racialized brutality against young men of color for almost universally nonviolent offenses was clear, even in the surely sanitized reports of the camp leaders.

Much of that brutality was made possible by the larceny charge, a law designed specifically to criminalize the Black population and, through such criminalization, disenfranchise those convicted. In an 1880 hearing about Black migration north after Reconstruction, Charles N. Otey, a Black lawyer and newspaper editor headquartered in Washington, D.C., told a Senate committee that disenfranchisement for petit larceny was a principal grievance. "The law was made for the purpose of disfranchising colored men. If a colored man steals a chicken he is pretty liable to be sent to the

Table 5.3. Felony convict lease camps, 1902

Camp	County	Lessee	Employment	Num
Adrian	Emanuel	James W. English Jr.	Sawmilling	55
Heartsease	Berrien	James W. English Jr.	Sawmilling	57
Jakin	Decatur	James W. English Jr.	Sawmilling	57
Bartow	Bartow	James W. English Jr.	Mining iron ore	107
Blakely	Early	James W. English Jr.	Sawmilling	56
Cole City	Dade	James W. English Jr.	Mining coal	27
Durham Mine	Walker	James W. English Jr.	Mining coal	24
Fargo	Clinch	James W. English Jr.	Sawmilling	50
Lookout Mt.	Walker	James W. English Jr.	Mining coal	16
Durham Mine	Walker	James W. Smith	Mining coal	100
Durham Mine	Walker	W. H. Mattox	Mining coal	50
Durham Mine	Walker	Chickamauga C. & C. Co.	Mining coal	256
Cole City	Dade	John W. McCalla	Mining coal	50
Cole City	Dade	Canda Lumber Co.	Mining coal	24
Eensign	Worth	Canda Lumber Co.	Sawmilling	73
Chattahoochee	Fulton	Chattahoochee Brick Co.	Brickmaking	198
Richwood	Dooly	Parrott Lumber Co.	Sawmilling	129
Donalsonville	Decatur	Donalson Lumber Co.	Sawmilling	53
Fargo	Clinch	G. S. Baxter & Co.	Sawmilling	345
Lookout Mt.	Walker	Merritt W. Dixon	Mining coal	50
Egypt	Effingham	Merritt W. Dixon	Sawmilling	50
Albany	Dougherty	Cruger & Pace	Brickmaking	60
Pitts	Wilcox	Enterprise Lumber Co.	Sawmilling	56
Worth	Worth	Enterprise Lumber Co.	Sawmilling	95
State farm	Baldwin	State farm (men)	Farming	177
State farm	Baldwin	State farm (boys under 15)	Farming	15
State farm	Baldwin	State farm (women)	Farming	85
TOTAL				2,315

Notes: That year, the felony system had 2,315 prisoners with sixty-seven deaths. There were 252 white men and boys and five white women and girls, 1,978 Black men and boys and 80 Black women and girls.
85.4 percent Black men and boys
88.9 percent Black prisoners
Source: *Fifth Annual Report of the Prison Commission of Georgia, 1902* (Atlanta: Lester Book and Stationery, 1902), 21–22, 29.

penitentiary," he explained. That trip to the penitentiary then took away his right to vote. "Up North they do not send people to the penitentiary for petit larceny, but they do down there [the South]."[38] Republican politicians in Alabama petitioned Congress in response, claiming that the new expansion of grand larceny had "ulterior purposes" to "persecute and oppress" the Black population by making it easier to imprison and disenfranchise them.[39] "Negroes are frequently arraigned before petty magistrates on the most trivial charges of larceny, and a conviction in these petty courts is sufficient to disfranchise them forever," explained a Republican congressman in South Carolina. "This conviction is readily obtained, and the whole proceedings clearly indicate, in many cases, that the prosecution is merely a pretext to deprive the negro of his vote."[40]

Disenfranchisement was an important element of Redeemer politics, but the principal benefit of larceny charges for families like the McRees was the glut of cheap labor they provided for camps like Kinderlou. In the absence of such charges, of course, there was debt peonage, and when legal recourse to debtors was unavailable, there were extra-legal means at the disposal of camp owners like the McRees. Extra-legal means had landed them in trouble in 1900 and 1901, and they would again two years later, but the immediate consequences of the scandal did seem to have a more salutary effect.

The McRee influence in Lowndes County had been decidedly diminished. In 1902, the parity between public and private misdemeanor camps held, with thirty-three public and thirty-two private camps, the private camps operating, per the Prison Commission, "in most cases contrary to the provisions of the law." Its report for 1902 noted that the body made "more frequent and rigid inspections" of the misdemeanor camps, particularly because of the controversy surrounding Kinderlou. The commission noted that "many abuses continue to exist, especially in those gangs worked for private individuals, and always will exist, more or less, as long as the care and maintenance of the convicts are farmed out illegally to private individuals." The counties, for their part, insisted that the act was legal and refused to stop the practice.[41]

Their argument centered largely on the 1891 debt peonage law (see chapter 2), which allowed "the county authorities" in the area where misdemeanors were committed to transfer those misdemeanor convicts "to any other county or municipal corporation." And when they did engage in such transfers, county officials were "hereby authorized to receive compensation for the labor of said convicts." The law was not intended to create a

Table 5.4. County misdemeanor camps, 1902, divided into public and private camps

County	Worked by	WM	WF	BM	BF	Total	Employment
Public							
Baldwin	County	0	0	23	3	26	Roads
Bibb	County	1	0	59	2	62	Roads
Burke	County	0	0	52	2	54	Roads
Butts	County	0	0	11	0	11	Roads
Chatham	County	8	4	264	47	323	Roads
Clarke	County	1	0	19	1	21	Roads
DeKalb	County	0	0	32	0	32	Roads
Dougherty	County	1	0	19	2	22	Roads
Emanuel	County	0	0	14	0	14	Roads
Floyd	County	13	0	62	4	79	Roads
Fulton	County	10	0	156	21	187	Roads
Glynn	County	0	0	25	0	25	Roads
Green	County	0	0	15	0	15	Roads
Hancock	County	0	0	12	0	12	Roads
Jasper	County	0	0	13	0	13	Roads
Jones	County	0	0	9	0	9	Roads
Jefferson	County	2	0	14	0	16	Roads
Laurens	County	1	0	15	0	16	Roads
Lowndes	**County**	**0**	**0**	**11**	**0**	**11**	**Roads**
McDuffie	County	0	0	15	0	15	Roads
Monroe	County	0	0	16	0	16	Roads
Muscogee	County	0	0	43	0	43	Roads
Newton	County	2	0	14	0	16	Roads
Putnam	County	0	0	6	0	6	Roads
Richmond	County	4	0	62	0	66	Roads
Spalding	County	0	0	9	0	9	Roads
Terrell	County	0	0	35	1	36	Roads
Walton	County	2	0	14	0	16	Roads
Ware	Waycross city	0	0	8	0	8	Streets
Ware	County	0	0	13	0	13	Roads
Washington	County	0	0	30	0	30	Roads
Wilcox	County	0	0	22	0	22	Roads
Wilkes	County	0	0	12	0	12	Roads
TOTAL		45	0	1,124	83	1,252	

89.8% Black men and boys
96.4% Black prisoners

(continued)

Table 5.4—Continued

County	Worked by	WM	WF	BM	BF	Total	Employment
Private							
Baker	John R. Sharpe	1	0	20	0	21	Turpentine
Bartow	Ga. I. & C. Co.	12	0	122	3	137	Mining iron
Berrien	E. G. Brown & Co.	0	0	31	0	31	Turpentine
Brooks	M. Brice	2	0	66	0	68	Sawmillinging, turpentine
Coffee	Beach & Son	0	0	20	1	21	Turpentine
Coffee	A. T. Beach & Co.	0	0	14	0	14	Turpentine
Clinch	G. S. Baxter & Co.	6	0	32	0	38	Turpentine
Decatur	Hodges & Powell	1	0	34	1	36	Turpentine
Decatur	J. W. Callahan	5	0	52	0	57	Turpentine
Decatur	Chat. Lum. Co.	3	0	56	0	59	Turpentine
Decatur	Sharpe & Drake	0	0	18	0	18	Turpentine
Dooly	Parrott Lumber Co.	2	0	55	2	59	Sawmilling
Dougherty	Cruger & Pace	0	0	8	2	10	Brickmaking
Early	J. W. Callahan	1	0	76	0	77	Turpentine
Early	Flowers Lumber Co.	0	0	9	0	9	Sawmilling
Effingham	E. E. Foy Mfg. Co.	1	0	17	1	19	Sawmilling, railroad
Elbert	L. A. Clark	0	0	15	0	15	Farming
Elbert	Swift Bros.	2	0	2	0	4	Farming
Emanuel	E. P. Rentz	0	0	6	0	6	Farming
Franklin	Little Bros.	2	0	10	0	12	Farming
Irwin	Fletcher & Handley	2	0	20	0	22	Naval Stores
Lowndes	**J. B. S. Holmes**	1	0	27	0	**28**	**Farming**
Lowndes	**McRee Bros.**	**0**	**0**	**3**	**0**	**3**	**Farming**
Miller	J.R. Sharpe	0	0	20	1	21	Turpentine

County	Worked by	WM	WF	BM	BF	Total	Employment
Miller	J.R. Sharpe	0	0	19	0	19	Turpentine
Mitchell	Fleming & Hines	1	0	33	0	34	Turpentine
Oconee	J. D. Price	3	0	7	1	11	Farming
Oglethorpe	J. M. Smith	4	0	39	0	43	Farming
Oglethorpe	John Jarrell	2	0	10	3	15	Farming
Oglethorpe	Broach Bros.	5	1	31	1	38	Farming
Worth	McLand & Co.	1	0	9	1	11	Turpentine
Worth	J.S. Bitte & Co.	1	0	5	3	9	Turpentine
TOTAL		56	1	888	20	965	
92.0% Black men and boys							
94.1% Black prisoners							

Source: *Fifth Annual Report of the Prison Commission of Georgia, 1902* (Atlanta: Lester Book and Stationery, 1902), 30–31.

misdemeanor convict lease system. It added that any money received "shall be first applied to the payment of the fees of the officers of the court" and that whatever was left over be "paid into the county treasury for county purposes." The law was facilitating the payment of fines by private individuals to cover the court costs of misdemeanor defendants so as to bring them into a state of peonage, but counties believed that the law gave them cover for an additional profitable venture.[42]

The commission report, meanwhile, focused in particular on prison labor that competed with free labor. It had been part of the law since 1895 that the counties had to take care "to avoid all competition with free labor," and private camps, the commission argued, did just that. It argued that convict labor "is absolutely essential to the reformation of the criminal," as was "conceded by all penologists." But when that labor was marshaled in competition with free labor, the governmental doctrine that strove for "the greatest good to the greatest number" was violated. If counties themselves didn't have the capacity to hold all of their misdemeanants, the commission suggested using them on state roads and highways that moved beyond county borders, which would put them under state control, stop them from competing with free labor, and end the private misdemeanor camps.[43]

In 1898, the state passed a law that allowed counties to requisition prisoners for county road projects at a rate of thirty-six dollars per year, providing that any applicant county not "fail to work its own misdemeanor convicts on the public roads or public works." After the law went into effect, no counties applied, "demonstrating that, at that time, at least, there was no demand by counties or municipalities for such labor." At the same time, though, some counties were hiring misdemeanants from other counties for the same work at thirty-six dollars per year without the intervention of the state government. "Shortly thereafter, however, the demand for such labor, by private individuals, became so great that such convicts are readily disposed of at from ten to fifteen dollars per month." That new profit margin, the commission explained, led to 43 percent of all misdemeanor prisoners working in private camps instead of on public chain gangs.[44]

The chain gangs had records that did not include abuse, the commission claimed, certainly erroneously, but in the private camps "many abuses have occurred and will continue to occur, until a change is made whereby the responsibility for the treatment of such convicts is less divided, and the opportunity to evade the law less easy." It was necessary, because the private camp system itself "is but an evasion of the law."[45] It was another in a long line of screeds from state prison authorities, the same authorities who spent several pages of the same report defending felony convict leasing as the most humane way to deal with state prisoners. The body saw the state convict system as legitimate but private misdemeanor camps as rife with abuse, making private misdemeanor lease a platform for defending state felony leasing and demonstrating how unequivocally inhumane those misdemeanor camps must have been.[46]

As they did every year, the private misdemeanor camps had the largest proportion of Black men, and its estimated number of deaths, as per the rubric established in chapter 4, was fifty-six individuals (see table 5.4). Meanwhile, in the wake of the 1901 Kinderlou scandal, Lowndes County itself was clearly diversifying. There were only three misdemeanants at Kinderlou, while private leasing shifted to Lake Park planter J. B. S. Holmes. At the same time, the county grew its road chain gang to house the remainder of its prisoners, hoping to avoid the kind of public scrutiny that had enveloped them the previous year. It was a hope, however, that would be in vain.

6

The State Scandal of 1903

In early May 1903, the charges originally presented in 1900 by Brooks County's J. W. Edmonson were mirrored in nearby Waycross by the grand jury of Ware County. The presentment there charged that the McRees "are coming into this county, paying the fines of misdemeanor convicts and carrying such convicts to their camps, and there keeping them illegally restrained of their liberty for long terms of servitude, subjecting them to harsh and cruel treatment at the hands of whipping bosses." The grand jury recommended that the Ware County commissioners of roads and revenues investigate whether or not citizens of the county were being held by the McRees, "and if there has been a violation of the penal laws of the state, that prosecution be instituted and carried on." It was a presentment, not an indictment, so the McRees were in no danger of either court date or specific penalty, and there is no evidence that the commissioners of roads and revenues ever took up the grand jury's recommendation. But it was still an official statement by a sworn grand jury, and as the body had not been investigating the McRees, the presentment demonstrated that the behavior was well known enough that it would come up in other more organized investigations and that it could be detailed accurately enough to give the grand jury impetus to mention it in an official, public capacity.[1]

The efforts of officials in Brooks and Ware Counties were all the more significant because they were defending Black citizens and incarcerated people, two groups consistently demeaned by white southerners without criminal records. They were also significant because officials in those counties were unerringly supportive of convict labor as part of a comprehensive public works program. At the same time that the Ware County grand jury was chastising the McRees, the Brooks County grand jury was suggesting the use of county prisoners to help fix the roads (see chapter 7). Ware County already had two different county misdemeanor camps for public works. The expense of labor and the desperate need for better roads made convict labor the only supposed available option, and even in

Brooks County's 1901 complaint, the misuse of convict labor was the stated problem, not the use of convict labor itself. The beating of prisoners by more than one person was at issue, not the beating of prisoners itself. In Ware County, the issue was keeping debt peons beyond the time indicated by county fines and abusing citizens of the county, not the transfer of fined misdemeanants to another county.[2]

The Ware County presentment was news that quickly spread throughout the state, a circular detailing the charges placed on the desk of each member of the Georgia House of Representatives. The *Atlanta Constitution*, misunderstanding the McRees' convoluted relationship with the system, reported that Kinderlou no longer held prisoners on the premises, explaining to its readers that "neither the penitentiary system nor the misdemeanor system figures in this discussion to any degree." The McRees did still control a small number of misdemeanor prisoners, but it was true that Lowndes County officials were required to reimpose supervision over the McRee operation and its use of the prisoners. Ultimately, those officials responded to the need for road construction and the controversy surrounding Kinderlou by removing the misdemeanants from McRee holdings in aid of building a road infrastructure in and around Valdosta and leasing the rest to a private farm in Lake Park. The *Constitution*'s unstated point was that, in the paper's view, debt peonage was something different than felony or misdemeanor leasing and therefore could not be used to stain the state's penal apparatus. The McRees, however, did not turn to debt peonage as a response. The McRees had already been engaged in a form of peonage for years, and while that peonage came constituent with misdemeanor leasing in the first years of the new century, debt peons had previously worked alongside those convicted of felonies and would do so again, as the McRees would soon begin reengaging in traditional convict leasing following the transfer of those convicted of misdemeanors to work on Lowndes County roads.[3] The problem Ware County officials described was not the abomination of debt peonage, a separate insidious system distinct from other forms of convict labor. Instead, they complained that representatives of Kinderlou were abusing the debt peonage system, removing misdemeanor prisoners from their own county, along with Waycross citizens charged with no crime at all, abusing them, and keeping them well past their supposed term for paying off imposed fines or in an unjustified state of kidnapping and bondage. The complaint, as horrifying as it was, was built specifically on the existence of an integrated system that used its formal rules to justify its own horrors. The McRees' crimes were so stunning because they broke a series of statutes designed to allow abuse, and then went beyond those rules and amplified that abuse.

At the time the Ware County charges were made, Edward McRee was serving in the state legislature. He had won election in 1902 to represent Lowndes County and would serve two terms in the body. Forced to respond, he announced that he was willing to submit to a legislative investigation of the practices at Kinderlou. He claimed that his misdemeanor convict program ended in October 1902, after the family's formal contract ended following the devastating report in 1901, and that he had hired no guards and kept no camp since then.[4]

Not only was the statement untrue, but his actions as a legislator at the same time as he claimed to have ended Kinderlou's convict program gave public lie to his denial. Upon arriving in the state legislature in October 1902, McRee was immediately concerned with misdemeanor convict labor. On October 28, he authored "a bill providing for the annual distribution of money arising from the hire of misdemeanor convicts," which was referred to the Committee on Penitentiary. The bill would mandate that the payment of officers of the court, justices of the peace, and constables would come directly from revenue generated from the lease of prisoners. It did not pass, the bill coming out of committee with a negative recommendation on November 8, as it was clear to many that establishing a pay for play system would only encourage abuse and fraud, with local authorities encouraging arrests so as to make more money. The failure of the bill was a small episode in the broader history of Georgia's lease system, but it demonstrated McRee's devotion to that system. If county officials were dependent not only for public revenue but also for individual salaries on leasing misdemeanants, then their willingness to prioritize private entities over and against public road chain gangs would ensure that unregulated private leasing would continue in perpetuity.[5]

And his effort came after Georgia's governor, Joseph Meriwether Terrell, opened the legislative session with a broad denunciation of camps like those of the McRee family. Terrell had replaced Allen Candler and had taken office at the same time as McRee. He was a Progressive Era reformer, concerned with modernizing Georgia's schools and helping all of its children access them. He wanted tax equalization, election reform, and a stronger child labor law. And he wanted an end to misdemeanor convict camps.[6] "The law as originally enacted contemplated only the establishment by counties of county chain-gangs, to be worked by the county for the county," Terrell said. "But by an unwarranted stretch of the law other chain-gangs authorized by county authorities, and nominally under their control, but worked not by the county nor for the benefit of the county, but by private individuals or companies for personal gain, have been established in quite a number of counties, sometimes two or three in the same county." He was adamant that "there is no express provision of law anywhere authorizing the hiring of such convicts to private individuals, nor for working them anywhere except on public works. But because comparatively few counties organized chain-gangs to work on public works, it was often found difficult for the county authorities of counties having no chain-gang to dispose of their misdemeanor convicts." In some of the camps, he argued, with obvious reference to the current McRee debacle, "convicts have been overworked, poorly fed and inadequately clothed, and . . . the punishment inflicted on them has sometimes been cruel, and in one instance that has come to my knowledge even brutal." He received many complaints about prisoners, "and nearly all of them come from this class of chain-gangs," he said. "Nearly all the trouble is in these private unauthorized camps." There was also, again targeting the very concept that McRee would seek to codify into law, "the evil practice, too, which has grown up in many of the counties, of allowing court officers to divide out among themselves in payment of insolvent costs the money derived from the hire of this class of convicts," a practice that was "largely responsible for many abuses." To fix the problem, the governor wanted all convict camps—private, county, and state— brought under the regulatory authority of the Prison Commission, which would hire all physicians, whipping bosses, and overseers. Most importantly to McRee's legislative plans, "The fee system should be abolished and all money derived from the hire of misdemeanor convicts should be paid into the county treasury, and all county judges and all solicitors should be paid salaries out of the county treasury. None of them should be dependent upon fees. Thus the temptation to institute frivolous prosecutions and to impose heavy fines and exact exorbitant costs in trivial cases would be removed, and there would be no ground to charge that any county court is run in the interest of the proprietors of private chain-gangs."[7]

It was a repetition of the annual screed of the Prison Commission, but one forced into broader public light by the Kinderlou kidnapping abuses and not so subtly marshaling them as an exemplar of the system's failings. The problem for Terrell, however, was that arguing for the end of private misdemeanor leasing as a salve against abuse ignored that felony leasing was entirely in private hands. His argument, and that of the commission, was that the formal, overt legality of the felony version of private leasing and the regulation of felony camps by state officials ensured that those entities were operated without the abuse of private misdemeanor camps. It was true that the scant data showing comparative death rates demonstrated that the private county operations were far deadlier than the more publicly notorious felony versions, but there was still a reason why those felony camps were notorious. The idea that state regulation eliminated the problems of private leasing was belied by the sixty-seven cataloged deaths in the felony system in 1902, the seventy-five in 1901, or the fifty-four in 1900.

Terrell was attempting to thread a substantially small needle, claiming that one version of private leasing was abusive and "evil" while the other one, the one that benefited state coffers, was perfectly moral and fitting with modern penal theory. In reality, however, there was no way that everyone in the state legislature could hear such a speech and not associate privatization as a whole—rather than simple misdemeanor privatization—with the foundational problems of Georgia penology. The chief opponent of convict leasing in the state legislature was Thomas S. Felder of Bibb County. In October 1902, he introduced a resolution to create a special committee to investigate the system and propose legislation to deal with it. The Prison Commission had suggested that the current system, which would need to be reauthorized in 1903, should stay as is, but Felder insisted that "the present system was inhuman and brutal, and that acts of cruelty were bound to occur and do occur under a plan by which the labor of the convicts is sold to private parties." He believed that prisoners, both felony and misdemeanor, should stay within the county in which they were charged and be tasked solely with road work or other public works projects. Such was the way it worked in Macon, the seat of Felder's Bibb County, wherein all misdemeanants were used in a county-controlled chain gang building public roads. "Selling convicts for gain" only led to abuse, and despite the governor's assurances, that abuse happened at both the state and county levels when prisoners were in private hands. He was adamant that the very least the legislature could do was authorize an investigation into both the misdemeanor and felony lease systems, and his colleagues agreed, passing his resolution easily to authorize a study of Georgia's convict scheme.[8]

Felder then attempted to build on his success by introducing a bill to kill the state's convict lease system in its entirety, but the effort failed on July 22, 1903. The state felony system would be scheduled to continue for the next five years, with the next revenue from leasing to go to public schools.[9] One alternative, a bill proposed by Interstate Commerce Commissioner Judson C. Clements, renewed the current system without any change but failed.

Then there was a bill proposed by Taylor County's Walter E. Steed and a "Candler compromise" bill brokered by former governor Allen Candler. That was the bill supported by the *Atlanta Constitution*. In its original form, it provided up to ten-year terms for leased felony prisoners, but after failing in the legislature by a narrow two votes, a modification reduced terms to eight years. "No one claims that even then the bill would be acceptable to all the advocates on either side of the recent debates," the paper admitted, "but something must be done to meet the emergency of declaring a policy concerning the convicts and this bill at least presents the desirable opportunity to test opposing theories." Incarcerated individuals sentenced to at least eight years would be leased by the state, and counties could work the rest on public roads, alongside the misdemeanants already occupying county chain gangs. "It does not change by a jot or tittle the authority of the prison commission to follow up, control and regulate the management of the felony convicts retained by such counties as desire to work them." Of most importance to the paper was that the new law "fulfill the exact duties of humanity, the obligations of the state to society, and the least burden upon the people whose rights have been despoiled by these convicts."[10]

When no agreement could be reached, however, yet another bill was proposed by Jonathan Perry Knight of Berrien and W. S. Howell of Merriwether, and though it barely passed a divided house, exhaustion with the process and a desire to lock the felony lease system in place ultimately won out. The Knight-Howell substitute bill would become the new law. It maintained the current felony system with certain modifications. It prohibited, for example, the subletting of prisoners and raised the minimum price for a prisoner to $175 a year, up from ninety-six dollars. Counties were allowed to lease short-term felony prisoners for road work by paying the state a minimum of ten dollars per month or $120 per year and agreeing to cover the expenses of guarding, clothing, and feeding the prisoners. In direct response to violations like those of the McRees, the bill also gave more power to the state Prison Commission to investigate and punish the lessees of misdemeanor prisoners and to abolish abusive convict camps. An officer of the commission would have to inspect camps at least quarterly, and the commission would work with county or municipal authorities to impose rules and punishments, with the governor as the final arbiter of any regulatory disputes. The commission wouldn't have the direct authority over private misdemeanor camps that it wanted, but it would have, at the very least, an influence that it didn't have previously. And at the end of a misdemeanor convict's sentence, "the lessee or county authority leasing said person shall provide him or her a railroad ticket to the home of such person prior to his or her conviction, or to the nearest railway station thereto." Finally, the new law continued the practice of using the state proceeds to build the state school fund, thereby exacerbating the veneer of social good wrapping the more sinister elements of the system, echoing the sentiments of the *Constitution*'s editorial.[11]

The Prison Commission responded by immediately leasing 1,500 felony prisoners, arguing that the deal ensured that the state would net a minimum of $240,000 per year from the new rates. It was a bold claim considering that the previous convict contract leased more than 2,100 felony prisoners, netting roughly $90,000. Under Georgia's new arrangement, the state would average $225.14 per felony convict per year, for $338,119 gross revenue. To make such a deal provide net revenue at the stated share, overhead would have to be considerably lower than had previously been the case, a prognostication that seemed more hopeful than realistic. Still, bids for felony labor stating such high prices were a pleasant surprise—contracts under the previous lease bill averaged only $100—though the aggressive bidding left several lessees who previously worked with the commission out of the running for bound labor. Under the previous iteration, lessees were allowed to sublease prisoners for a profit, but along with having to pay more for each individual, subleasing was no longer allowed, making the new bidding war all the more revealing about the presumed need for bound labor and the fear that the convict lease system, already outlawed in other states, would not last much longer. Among the successful bidders was Edward McRee, who secured one hundred felony prisoners at $220.75 apiece, bringing the family back into the state felony system just as Lowndes County was commandeering misdemeanor prisoners for road work after the family's first major abuse scandal left them out of the running for private misdemeanor leasing. That scandal and the recent Ware County grand jury presentment were not taken into account when awarding the contract, despite the governor's denunciations and despite the family's record of abusing private labor, demonstrating, if nothing else, that such laments about the abuse of private lessees were largely cosmetic rather than substantive. The commission, which had worried over private misdemeanor camps for years and specifically singled out the McRees as violators in the extreme, instead simply took the thirteen highest bids despite knowing precisely the reputation of brutality at Kinderlou.[12]

The measure was immediately popular with counties seeking to use misdemeanor convict labor for their roads, not just because it kept farms like that of the McRees stable with other sources of bound labor but because it also made provisions for counties to supplement their misdemeanor public works workers with short-term felony prisoners. Thirteen immediately applied to the Prison Commission for such incarcerated people for road work after the law went into effect in August. Incarcerated individuals were apportioned based on county population, with one felony convict allowed per 1,100 residents. It was assumed that the heavy demand would ultimately push the leasing price for prisoners up to twenty dollars per month, or $240 per year.[13] The new law also actually encouraged new manifestations of private misdemeanor lease, as counties could accomplish road work with state prisoners and fund the operation by leasing its misdemeanants to private entities to recoup the income, knowing that payments made for state prisoners would return to them in the form of school fund money. And those misdemeanants would often be awarded to operators outside of the counties where they were originally arrested. In September, for example, T. J. Pinson of Sylvester won the bid for Brooks County's misdemeanor prisoners, offering $11.75 per month. Sylvester was in Worth County, and officials in Brooks agreed on the condition that Worth County had an approved convict camp. If there were county chain gangs or private camps that were willing and able to take misdemeanants from other areas, and if counties knew that they could accomplish their road priorities with short-term state prisoners, then there were multiple opportunities for counties to profit off misdemeanants given jail time rather than simple fines, creating an incentive to arrest as many people as possible. And with the overwhelming population of such misdemeanants being Black and male, it made African American men inordinately vulnerable.[14]

The new law, however, was not popular in all corners of the state, not because of potential brutality but instead because of potential loss to county school funds by the prorated pricing of the new system. The *Atlanta Journal* scoffed at the notion, noting that school funds would remain virtually similar. "The fact is, the convicts are worth about $150 each for hire," the *Journal* explained, referring to short-term state prisoners. "This amount reimburses the county for the loss of its pro rate of the school fund." There was also no way, the paper argued, that free labor would be more cost effective: "Let us suppose that a certain county chooses to take convicts in lieu of school money. The county, let us say, would receive under the new system $3,000 per annum—the hire of 20 convicts—as its share of the school fund. When it takes convicts it simply chooses, for a time being, to improve its roads rather than to receive aid from the state for its public schools. The county balance sheet is unchanged."[15] Brooks County leaders had decided not to make an application because of original fears addressed by the *Journal*, but many citizens in Brooks County were supportive of the system, even suggesting that the county pay for felony prisoners from ad-valorem tax money, ensuring that there would be no school money trade-off. "We hope," pressed a group of citizens from the Brooks County town of Dixie, eighteen miles from Kinderlou, "that the commissioners will at their next meeting reconsider their action and make application for the convicts." There could always, they reasoned, be offsets like misdemeanor leasing to places like Sylvester if necessary.[16]

Meanwhile, lost in the debates over the reconstitution of the state's convict leasing was another law passed in August 1903 that would become common in the turpentine belt to justify debt peonage. The statute made it illegal to take money or something else of value "on a contract to perform services, with intent to defraud." While the law seemed like a basic breach of contract statute, it was a Trojan horse designed to give purchasers of debt peons legal recourse to claim that anyone wanting to break a restrictive work or debt peonage labor contract was defrauding their employer and subject to criminal charges that would only force them into longer terms of bound service. Alabama's version of the law would come under scrutiny at the end of the decade (see chapter 7), but Georgia's would prove more durable. It first came before the Georgia Supreme Court in 1905, when Jim Townsend was charged with contravening the law after a work stoppage on a Floyd County peonage farm. Georgia's high court upheld the law as constitutional and unsurprisingly ruled against Townsend, "a common cheat and swindler."[17]

Federal courts were less charitable to the system.[18] Simultaneous to the Georgia Supreme Court decision validating fraud mandates propping up the practice of peonage, the federal circuit court for the Northern District of Florida, a region so pivotal for the McRees' crimes, ruled that "peonage is a form of slavery." It was "compulsory involuntary servitude," and though "many artful methods for evading the effect of this statute have been devised," the court explained that "none of them will avail if the juries of this country will discharge their duties fearlessly and impartially." The practices of peonage "are not only illegal, but have been condemned by all our good people. They are extremely reprehensible because of the lawless condition to which they ultimately lead. In communities where such conditions exist, murders are frequent; in many instances traceable directly to these practices." The court was describing the slippery slope that had carried the McRees into their own criminal acts. Systems of bondage based less on the criminality of the bound and more on the profit and supremacy of the binders inevitably gave way to even greater crimes. The circuit court did not have the power to change north Florida's own system of bondage, but it provided a voice against it, and a counternarrative to that presented by the Georgia Supreme Court.[19]

As south Georgia counties debated how they would use convict labor for civic development, and as new justifications for debt peonage became law, the McRees, the longtime leaders of both private convict leasing and peonage in the region, were indicted by a federal grand jury for illegally holding Black citizens and misdemeanants and selling them into servitude. The case stemmed from a petition sent to federal officials and referred to the Justice Department, detailing the experience of several complainants. Brunswick's Mackey Spencer was convicted of selling liquor without a license and sent to serve his misdemeanor sentence at Kinderlou, where he was held three months after his allotted time had expired. Sam Holmes suffered the same fate. David Smith of Waycross received a thirty-day sentence for stealing a watermelon but was sold to the McRees, who held him for seven months. The same happened to David Brimmage. Waycross's Henry Wilson suffered an even worse fate, acquitted of the charge against him but sold to Kinderlou to pay his lawyer's fee. He was held there for eleven months. The assistant U.S. attorney in charge of the case was worried that "these parties who claim to have been held in involuntary servitude are generally people of no moral character or standing in the community in which they live," making any testimony they provided "easily impeachable by proof of general bad character." Those worries prompted him to request a secret service agent to investigate and provide evidence less "impeachable." The attorney general's office sent Henry C. Dickey, who had helped the investigation in Alabama's *Peonage Cases,* to aid the investigation and verify the complainant's claims before formally making the charges.[20]

Dickey's investigation not only validated the former prisoners' claims but amplified them. "Captain Dickey returned Saturday and reports the condition of affairs which it is almost impossible to credit," Alexander Ackerman reported:

But he seems to be able to substantiate the same with witnesses many of whom are known to me to be honorable and upright men.

McRee Brothers, a firm composed of four brothers, own a farm of 22,000 acres of land in Lowndes County six miles from Valdosta, have a post office of their own known as Kinder Lou and also at this place operate several manufacturing plants. The entire place is posted with trespass notices, which under the Georgia Law prevents outsiders from entering the premises. Prior to the fall of 1900, McRee Brothers depended upon convicts leased from the State in cases of felony, and from various counties in cases of misdemeanor for their labor. At that time charges were filed against them before the prison commission of cruel treatment of these convicts, and the camp abolished by order of the Prison Commission, which deprived them of their right to lease convicts any further.

Being deprived of convict labor it seems that they made arrangements with the County Officers of Lowndes, Brooks, Thomas, Decatur, Clinch, Ware and other Counties, and also with certain city officials in the small cities near their place of business, to arrest strange negroes on petty charges. In some instances the form of a trial would be gone through with and in case of conviction the McRees would pay the fine, and get the negro to sign a contract to work a number of months for them, in case of acquittal they would pay the attorney fee, and make a similar contract with the negro to reimburse them for the attorney fee advanced, in other instances they would pretend to settle the case with the officers and make a similar contract with the negro to work out the money advanced to effect a settlement. These preliminaries settled, they would handcuff the negroes and take them to their place, usually on night trains and put them to work under a guard, keeping them locked in the old convict stockade at night. When one of the negroes got away they would chase him with dogs and when cought [sic] would whip him severely. These poor unfortunates, usually ignorant women and boys[,] were kept long over their contract time in some instances for several years.[21]

While the federal government had created a Southwestern District of its circuit court system that became active on January 1, 1903, most of the McRees' crimes occurred before that date, and thus the trial would come under the jurisdiction of the Southern District in Savannah. "It seems to me," Ackerman reported, "that such an outrageous state of affairs calls for a vigorous prosecution, not only of the McRees, but of all others who have aided them." The plan of Ackerman and Dickey was to "let the matter drop apparently" until a few weeks before the convening of the grand jury. Then Dickey would return "with a lot of blank subpoenas, returnable instanter, and bring in such witnesses as he thinks would be of benefit, and keep them in Savannah, where they could not be tampered with, nor intimidated, until they were put before the grand jury, and then hold them until the trials before the traverse juries." Ackerman had learned well that Black witnesses in such cases often went missing before trial dates and wanted to prevent it.[22]

As reported by the *Augusta Chronicle,* Edward McRee gathered his prisoners together after being notified of the charges "and told them they were free and that all who wished to go could do so. There were about forty. Some of them left. Others thought it was a trick and waited until night, when they 'escaped.'" Edward, William, and Frank McRee were indicted along with two residents of Ware County and another two from Montgomery County. Even though Edward was still a member of the legislature, the brothers pleaded guilty before Judge Emory Speer in Savannah on November 24 and each accepted a $1,000 fine on two of the charges.[23] It was an admission made even more problematic by Edward McRee's legislative denials in July, even encouraging another state investigation.

Speer would play a prominent role in the assault on felony and misdemeanor convict camps in Georgia and on the debt peonage process that was a constituent part of that system. Born in Culloden, Georgia, in 1848, Speer served in the Confederate cavalry as a fifteen-year-old. After the war, it was on to the University of Georgia, then a career in law and politics. In 1873, he became solicitor general of Georgia's western circuit.[24] In 1878, he won a seat in Congress as an "independent" Democrat, the moderate wing of the party opposed to the more vitriolic Bourbon Redeemers in the post-Reconstruction period. He won reelection in 1880 but lost a bid for a third term in 1882 because his associations with national representatives of the Republican Party alienated him from the more overtly racist Democratic contingent. The Republican Party even endorsed his reelection bid in 1882, a well-intended act that ultimately doomed his candidacy. In the wake of his loss, however, his strong relationships with Republicans paid off in an appointment by Republican president Chester A. Arthur to serve as U.S. attorney for the Northern District of Georgia.[25]

He immediately began prosecuting cases of racial violence in his new role. When a series of white men in Banks County terrorized and beat several Black men in 1883, Speer indicted them, convicted them, and watched as the Supreme Court upheld the conviction in a case that became known as *Ex parte Yarbrough*. In his closing argument in the district court trial, he asked the jury, "If crimes such as this diabolical, deliberate, premeditated, beating and murder, are to go unwhipt of justice, what baleful and portentous future is there overhanging our country?" Speer was adamant that "if one class of people are debased or degraded, all suffer." It was the kind of thinking that would guide his convict camp decisions years later.[26]

During the Banks County case, John Erskine retired as a federal judge for the Southern District of Georgia, and Arthur appointed Speer to replace him, seeing a champion of racial justice as a valuable asset in a Deep South Jim Crow state. Controversy over the nomination kept Speer waiting until 1885, but he was eventually confirmed.[27] Despite the threat felt by the Redeemers, Speer was no egalitarian. At the Cotton States Exposition in Atlanta in 1895, Speer told the assembled crowd of "the imperious and commanding nature of the Anglo-Saxon race," but argued from the traditional colonial mindset that thus white people were "the trustees for humanity" and had a responsibility to treat lesser races with dignity and respect. As Timothy Huebner has explained, "Speer's devotion to Black rights was more than just political pragmatism. If a common thread ran throughout Speer's career, it was a commitment to using federal law and the Constitution to combat the violence and oppression that plagued his southern homeland." And it was no less effective for emanating from a colonizer's belief in the white man's burden.[28]

Speer's most influential ruling on the federal bench came in the case of the McRees, whose operation at Kinderlou by 1903 was, in the words of Douglas Blackmon, "operating on a scale no antebellum slave-owner could have comprehended."[29] Assistant district attorney Alexander Ackerman prosecuted the case for the government, traveling to Atlanta in preparation for the trial to examine the Prison Commission records from the family's first federal charges two years prior. Instances of those previous abuses were important precedent, but they were ultimately unnecessary.[30]

The current stories presented in the McRee charges were harrowing enough. Lula Frazier, for example, was among those from Waycross taken into custody and remarked upon by the Ware County grand jury. She was, like so many others, arrested but never tried for a crime. Instead, with the help of sheriff Thomas McClellan and Frazier's lawyer, William F. Crawley, the McRees paid fifty dollars to acquire Frazier, then worked her for nine months. Crawley was not officially hired by Frazier. He just showed up and said that he would represent her. "I did not see why I owed him anything and I had not stood any trial," she explained. McClellan had originally charged her with living in adultery, though officials soon discovered her protestations were correct and that she was, in fact, legally married. She hired Crawley in the interregnum after being pressured by authorities to do so, in the hope that he could prove her marital status, but she had no money to pay him. So McClellan and Crawley decided that payment for his services amounted to fourteen months of servitude, the attorney wiring Edward McRee to "come to Waycross for woman." Meanwhile, they told Frazier she was guilty and pressured her to agree to bondage to pay her fine.[31] Frazier was not, then, a misdemeanant. She was a debt peon, taken to Kinderlou after intentionally being tricked into her own bondage. When she finally made it to the Ware County Board of Commissioners in Waycross nine months later, returned from Kinderlou by Ware County sheriff Stephen F. Miller, she testified to the horror of the ordeal.[32]

"Were you allowed your freedom when you got there?" the Commission asked.
"I was locked up at night till two weeks ago," she told them.
"How long have you been there?"
"Nine months."
"Did they pay you anything?"
"They never paid me any money while I was there. They promised to pay me $5 a month, but never have paid me anything."
"What did you do there?" the commissioners asked.
"I worked in the field and milked and cooked for the hands."
"Did they whip you any?"
"They whipped me twice with a leather strap wide as your four fingers."
"What did they whip you for?"
"They claimed I was trying to run away one day when I went to the cow-pen, and another time they said I was neglecting my work."

That wasn't all. The McRees also asked her to bind her eight-year-old son to the plantation, as well. When she refused, they told her they would get him anyway, that her presence at Kinderlou was tacit consent to take the boy into bondage as long as she was there. And then there was the forced marriage. "Mr. Ed McRee made me marry a man named Henry Hadley."

"Didn't you tell him you were already married and had a husband here in Waycross?" asked the commissioners.
"Yes, sir, I told him I had a husband here, but he laughed and said it didn't make any difference as I would never see him no more."

"Who married you?"
"A man named Albritton."
"Did you have any license?"
"They had a paper there, but I don't know whether it was a license or not."

She was housed with three other women: Sallie Powell and Maggie Hardy from Waycross and Ida Wilson from Valdosta. The men were kept in separate quarters nearby. "You say you were whipped there," she was asked. "Who whipped you?"

Mr. Ed McRee whipped me one time and Mr. Will McRee whipped me another time. They made me lie down across a bunk and when Mr. Will whipped me he made Ida Wilson hold my hand and Jim Henry hold my feet. He turned my clothes up and whipped me with a leather strap. Ida and Henry Brown held me when Mr. Ed McRee whipped me.

McRee told her that when the authorities came to get her, it would be in her best interest to tell them that she had been treated well and had received her five dollars every month, a not-so-veiled threat to lie on their behalf. When the commission asked her if she felt like a convict at Kinderlou, she told them that she "didn't feel that way till I got that whipping," and when asked if she wanted to go back, she told the commissioners, "I'm afraid to go back, he might kill me." Still, she wanted to make sure that her eight-year-old child and her possessions would make their way back to Waycross as soon as possible.[33]

It was the Kafkaesque horror show that made convict leasing so infamous, and yet Frazier was no convict. She was, in fact, explicitly exonerated of the minor crime for which she had ostensibly been arrested. She did not even owe money to the county for misdemeanor fines. And yet she was legally sold to the McRees for fifty dollars to pay attorney's fees for a supposed crime that would have been easy for the sheriff to check. He didn't check, of course, because the arrest was based less on a concern about the morality of men and women living together without a marriage license and more on the payment that officials knew they could get for Frazier from a McRee camp eager to acquire more free labor.

The white *Waycross Journal*, no bastion of racial egalitarianism, was incensed. "If there be the slightest shade of truth in Lula Frazier's story before the commissioners Tuesday, the times are ripe for revolution and a change in the color of the victim's skin would bring it on." The paper focused in particular on Crawley. If the fee he charged Frazier was "excessive, it is a personal matter and not a matter of public concern, but when Mr. Crawley traded her off to the proprietors of a private convict camp where she was locked up, beaten and even forced into the unlawful state of bigamy, then it becomes a matter of public concern, and the public must demand correction or bear the infamy of such a shame." Crawley's behavior, however, was a symptom of a larger disease. "He is no more to blame than the sheriffs and solicitors all over the state of Georgia, who practice the same methods every day in the year. These are not the only cases, this is not the only place, McRee's is not the only camp. It is practiced all over the state and under the laws of the state and the state of Georgia is behind this barter in flesh and blood. It is the fee system which pays the sheriffs and solicitors and bailiffs and constables and crime-hunters," the editorial explained. And because of those potential paydays, they "dig up cases, real and fanciful, against men, and convict them if possible, whether guilty or not. The fee system forces hundreds into jail who, like Lula Frazier, have committed no crime, but who have to employ counsel and pay for same by long terms of servitude in private convict camps." Lawyers opposed changes to the system because it generated business for them and for everyone else involved in aspects of criminal justice, just as counties opposed changes to the misdemeanor system because of their own potential profits.[34]

They did so, however, at their peril. "It will destroy the comity existing between the officers of the law and proprietors of private convict camps, and when that cordial entente is destroyed, the crimes these private lessees commit by whipping and confining negroes, will no longer be overlooked or condoned, and when they can no longer lock these negroes up and beat them at will, they will no longer contract for such labor." In a particularly prescient prediction, the *Journal* claimed that "the result will be that negro convicts will no longer have their fines paid, and, consequently, they will have to serve out their terms with the counties in which they are sentenced, on the public roads where they properly belong." It was exactly the direction that the state was heading, but the move to labor on public roads would not end the over-policing of Black communities or their abuse while in custody (see chapter 7). Still, "It is time the state of Georgia were going out of the slave business, and when the state stops bartering its citizens to private convict camps, lawyers will sell no more men and women for their fees."[35]

The paper was right, but like the governor before it, journalists were conflating a series of different systems in place simultaneously. Felony convict leasing, felony chain gangs, private misdemeanor leasing, misdemeanor chain gangs, and fee- and fine-based debt peonage were all working simultaneously to create different kinds of "slave business" in Georgia, some more regulated than others, some more public than others, but all of it creating systems of unpaid labor that led to a variety of different abuses of prisoners. Those prisoner abuses were simply easier for papers like the *Journal* to see when they were accompanied by abuses of the system itself.

And those abuses were undeniably gendered in their application. W. E. B. Du Bois reported in 1901 on his investigation of convict leasing in his adopted state of Georgia that women like Lula Frazier "were mingled indiscriminately with men, both working and sleeping, and dressed often in men's clothes. A young girl at Camp Hardmont [Heardmont], Georgia, in 1895, was repeatedly outraged [a euphemism for rape] by several of her guards, and finally died in childbirth while in camp." Lula Frazier wasn't housed with men, as was the girl at Camp Heardmont, but being forced to marry one of the men at the Kinderlou camp despite already being legally married was its own form of sexual exploitation. One hundred years later, another influential sociologist, Angela Davis, explained that "black women endured the cruelties of the convict-lease system unmitigated by the feminization of punishment; neither their sentences nor the labor they were compelled to do were lessened by virtue of their gender."[36] Frazier experienced those cruelties, however, with a decided feminization of punishment, her vulnerability all the more pronounced because of the sexual outlet she could provide to rapists unwilling to countenance her humanity and the satisfaction she could give to a new husband foisted upon her as part of her supposed punishment.

And so her plight existed at the troubled intersection of gender and race. As Sarah Haley has demonstrated, Georgia's carceral imagination interpreted "women" as "white women," even making the differentiation explicit in the transition from convict leasing to chain gang public infrastructure labor, carving out "a separate and unique class of persons, defined as female, who would be protected from the brutal throes of the chain gang, while criminalized Black women, positioned outside of the category female, would be routinely forced to labor on public roads and as domestic servants in white homes." Black women like Frazier found themselves in the throes of a system that ensured that their lives were "defined by the unbearable flexibility of nonbeing." Rape was permissible because Black women fell outside the bounds of white male conceptions of femininity and womanhood, and while the Speer court would push back against such assumptions, at least in part, its penalties were such that misogynistic assumptions of those like the McRees would continue into the public roads program that followed.[37]

Talitha LeFlouria had demonstrated that incarcerated women in Georgia were used in diverse ways, sometimes alongside male prisoners and sometimes segregated away from them. Unlike, for example, Alabama, where incarcerated Black women tended to be relegated to quasi-domestic tasks of cooking and cleaning, Georgia's camps employed their female labor in the same kinds of manual labor expected of male prisoners, all while negotiating the sexual dangers and "intrusive medical procedures" posed to them by the system itself. LeFlouria parses the troubling paradox of Georgia's gendered system by explaining that "the mutability of Georgia's carceral structure thereby expanded the possibilities of Black women's labor in the New South while, simultaneously, immobilizing female detainees." It also provided a staging ground for Black women's resistance against such practices, whether setting fires, slowing work, breaking tools while in bondage, or testifying to abuses, as did Lula Frazier.[38]

Frazier's case became public at the same time that Alabama's peonage cases moved through the Montgomery courts. An exposé on her plight in *Outlook* magazine noted that the defendants in Alabama were, at the least, charged with a crime, no matter how unfair the legislation that created that crime might have been. At the same time, the account remained hopeful that because the abuse of Lula Frazier was discovered and adjudicated locally and did not require the federal intervention undertaken in Montgomery, the magazine felt "assurance that in Georgia there has been no such widespread kidnapping of friendless negroes as has been revealed in Alabama."[39] What the account didn't seem to understand was the dependency of such peonage actions on the maintenance of private misdemeanor convict leasing and other carceral efforts at the county level, leaving little room for any assurance that Georgia's "friendless negroes" would avoid bound labor, even if they could avoid actual kidnapping.

But there was also no reason for assurance in relation to Frazier's peonage case. The lack of federal intervention simply demonstrated a more streamlined system, one far from the state capital or other urban centers, allowing it to hide in plain sight and making any federal attention directed at the south Georgia peonage and misdemeanor convict scheme focused on abuses within the system rather than on the existence of the system itself. As the *New York Times* explained, "the traffic in human beings has been going on for years in certain counties, but the public never hears of it unless it happens to be attended by circumstances of unusual cruelty"—or if it fell under the banner of "convict lease" operated at the state level for felony defendants. In another case, for example, Henry Brimmage and Dave Smith, two young boys, were charged with stealing a watermelon in Waycross in August 1903. The judge was concerned about the possibility of peonage, so he replaced the normal fine with a month on the Ware County road crew chain gang. But the next day, Edward McRee paid the sheriff twenty-five dollars and the boys' lawyer forty dollars, then took the boys to Kinderlou for the next seven months. When Brimmage's older brother Jeff came to defend his sibling, McRee, Crawley, and McClellan took him into custody as well, sending him to Kinderlou with the others. And since the county never got its thirty days, after that seven months, the two original prisoners were still slated to serve a month on the chain gang.[40] It was the literal amalgamation of misdemeanor lease and debt peonage, with lack of Prison Commission regulatory power, even after the new law, allowing for seven months of actual slavery without even the feigned pretense of carceral criminal justification.

Edward was the big story in the controversy because of his place in the legislature. He actually faced thirteen charges of peonage, Speer giving him the $1,000 fine, allowing the other counts "to rest during good behavior." His legislative standing was in question because Georgia law prevented anyone convicted of a felony from serving in state office and defined a felony as a crime that merited imprisonment. Even though federal peonage charges were misdemeanors by definition, had Speer been less charitable, the counts amassed against McRee carried a total potential of $65,000 in fines and up to sixty-five years in prison. That made them felonies by the standard imposed by the law, but no one believed that McRee would lose his job in the legislature.[41]

And part of that assumption came from the light sentence. Alexander Ackerman, the prosecuting attorney, was "a little disappointed at the leniency of these sentences," but "upon the whole I am not prepared to say that the leniency upon the part of the Court in these cases, with a warning to the entire public that no leniency in any future case can be expected from the Court, will not have a more wholesome effect than might any undue severity in the sentences." Others in the press were less circumspect about the judge's leniency, and Speer was sensitive to the criticism that the sentences were inordinately light. "While it was competent for me to impose the severe penalties of the statute, I did not deem it justicious to do so," he explained to the attorney general. He argued that there had never been a similar conviction in the state, and there was no broader understanding of the national law or the legal consequences of such behavior. In addition, "the offenders were young and inexperienced farmers." They pleaded guilty and promised not to continue the practice. Therefore, "I deemed it for every reason best to deal very leniently with the prisoners. This will bring to the court the support of the people and will insure subsequent convictions for a repetition of the offense, whereas a severe penalty under the circumstances would have alienated the jury body, rendered jurors intensely hostile to the law and there could have been hereafter no practical or effective enforcement."[42] With the exception of a misunderstanding of the McRees' time in the business and a misjudgment of their character, Speer's reasoning was defensible, but there was no doubt that his leniency would make the McRees' crimes seem less severe in the eyes of the legislature, particularly relating to Edward McRee's tenure in the state body.

"Will Edward McRee's plea of guilty to thirteen charges of peonage have any affect on his ability to hold office?" the *Augusta Chronicle* asked. "The law provides that a man who has been convicted of a felony cannot hold office or vote." Though he received only a fine, and though the peonage charges against him were technically misdemeanors, "McRee could have been sentenced to a federal penitentiary for a grand total of sixty-five years," but even more pressing was the behavior itself. "His 'camp' has grown up under the vicious system which so many times has been condemned of allowing persons convicted of crime to be turned over to private parties who would pay their fines." Kinderlou "was not organized under any law and persons who found their way there were not always committed under any process of the law. They were simply captured and placed in bondage and got out the best way they could."[43]

The other concern was about the remaining misdemeanor and felony prisoners. Despite the peonage charges, contracts for misdemeanor and felony convict labor were given to the highest bidder, and while the McRees' behavior had eliminated their access to misdemeanants, they were still winning state felony contracts. Their ability to continue participating in that system should have been questioned after the federal charges, but the consensus seemed to be, despite the *Chronicle*'s public concern, that the McRee contracts would not be negated after the guilty pleas.[44]

After the case was resolved, Ackerman traveled to Atlanta as a guest of the state supreme court, where he described the results of the investigation against the McRees. He paid particular attention, as did so many, to the case of Frazier. He also told the story of Brimmage and Smith's watermelon theft charge. It was a significant presentation, as many such stories got lost in court testimony, not really presented in a public forum. Ackerman's speech in Atlanta gave the tales of the McRee tactics a public audience and did so in close proximity to Edward's legislative office.[45] It was the kind of state publicity that should have created more consequences for Kinderlou, state publicity that had remained relatively consistent and entirely problematic for the previous three years. That state publicity, however, was about to become national.

7

The National Scandal of 1903

At the end of May 1903, the *New York Times* brought the McRee debacle to a larger audience, reporting on the Ware County Grand Jury's description of more than a dozen of its citizens being taken illegally and worked in the Kinderlou camps, "treated just as slaves were in the ante-bellum days." The paper put the onus for action on Georgia governor Joseph Meriwether Terrell, who the grand jury urged to order the men's release. The *Times* compared the case in south Georgia to that of the *Peonage Cases* in Alabama. With the help of law enforcement officials like McClellan, the McRees "watch the courts, pay the fine of every misdemeanor convict, and transport him to the turpentine and lumber camps, where a long term of servitude is begun." And everyone saw a benefit but the prisoners themselves: "The Prosecuting Attorneys of the State profit by this method of disposing of convicts, as all fines are applied to the payment of costs and find their way into the pockets of the State Prosecuting Attorneys and other officials." It was a "treasure trove for the court officials, when a dealer in human blood presents himself, pays the fines of the convicts, and transports them to his stockade." While the report noted that the practice existed throughout Georgia, "it is practiced to a greater extent and more flagrantly in the southern counties, where the lumber and turpentine camps are located. In that section there is the stockade, the bloodhounds, the whipping boss, and every other adjunct of the slave trade as it was practiced in the days of old."[1]

"The system thrives and arouses no general protest because the State sanctions the leasing of her convicts," the *Times* explained, "and has been at the business so long that it is small wonder that men greedy for dollars buy the services of those convicted of misdemeanors and hold them long after their terms of service have expired." When grand juries made reports like the one in Ware County, and when they included prominent names like those of the McRees, there was a momentary sensation caused by the ordeal, "but after a while the matter lapses and the slave buying and the slave driving go on as before."[2] That was certainly true, but the *Times* report, like so many others, conflated the different sets of systems that existed. Georgia officials, for example, would have countered that they had been fighting against such misdemeanor abuse for years, that every Prison Commission report, proclamations by the governor, and recent legislative action were all in aid of reigning in those misdemeanor practices, whether private lease or debt peonage, from which the state did not profit and which only provided bad publicity for a state felony system that they wanted to keep clean of public scandal. Still, while journalistic conflations problematized the technical accuracy of such accounts, their broader moral accuracy was decidedly prescient, particularly in relation to Kinderlou.

Judge Emory Speer, for his part, understood that the influence of Edward McRee and his status in the state legislature played a decisive role in the case. "That a chairman of a penitentiary committee of the Georgia Senate appeared for the prisoners [the McRee brothers]; that a member of the House judiciary committee in Congress, from the district of the prisoners, contributed a brief in their behalf; that a solicitor general of the state court in their state judicial district, charged with the prosecution of such offenses under the state law, sat with the prisoners and their counsel during the hearing," Speer wrote, "taken altogether is somewhat persuasive of the conclusion that if there is no system of peonage de jure, to which the statute applies, there is yet a de facto system of some equivalent sort."[3] The *Atlanta Constitution* echoed Speer, noting that the McRees were "among the most prominent citizens of Valdosta and both there and in Savannah, as well as throughout the state, have many friends."[4]

The federal indictment came down in November 1903, the McRees charged along with McClellan and William F. Crawley, a prominent young lawyer and University of Georgia graduate. The McRees were charged with holding people in bondage in violation of the Thirteenth Amendment, while McClellan and Crawley were charged with seizing them. The charges coincided with others for Clayton B. and John A. McLeod and Lester Williamson, Montgomery County planters charged not only with keeping Black workers in a state of bondage in violation of the Thirteenth Amendment but also with abusing those workers while under their thumb. The McRee brothers originally claimed that they didn't know they were breaking the law, that this had been a common practice for them and for many in south Georgia—that private misdemeanor camps were a regular and accepted practice, so paying the fines of non-jailtime misdemeanants and estimating a possible work schedule for them in private hands was really a modification of that practice and a legitimate supplement to it. They paid the fines of those convicted of misdemeanors and then worked them at Kinderlou, just as did many others. Because their service time wasn't imposed specifically by a judge, and because those prisoners often earned additional fines and charges while serving, time in bondage could necessarily vary. While it was an argument that attempted to highlight the vagaries of a nuanced system usually misunderstood as relatively monolithic, it was really beside the point of the McRees' abuse of that system. It was a bad argument, and ultimately the family pleaded guilty to thirteen counts.[5]

But the real focus of Speer's ire was McClellan and Crawley. Their indictment focused on the case of John Wesley Boney, taken by the pair in Ware County and sold for an alleged debt to the McRees, where he was held in a state of illegal bondage.[6] Speer dismissed a demurrer rejecting the charges against them based on legal insufficiency. The Thirteenth Amendment and the 1867 anti-peonage statute provided both cause and jurisdiction for the charges.[7] Responding to claims that the 1867 law applied only to territorial exigencies like that of New Mexico, Speer quoted his own decision in *Ex Parte Yarbrough,* his most significant legal success prior to becoming a judge, that "what is implied is as much a part of the instrument as what is expressed." Congressional action "may start out to do one thing and do much more." Among that "much more" was an understood prohibition against kidnapping and terror. "Is it not involuntary servitude to seize by force," Speer asked, "to hurry the victim from wife and children, to incarcerate him in a stockade, and work him in range of the deadly muzzle of the shotgun, or under the terror of the lash and continue this servitude as long as resentment may prompt, or greed demand?" It obviously was, Speer believed, and McClellan and Crawley had engaged in all of it by selling "helpless and pathetic Negroes" to the McRee camp. They were "violent and lawless men" selling innocents to other similarly violent and lawless men. "What hope can the respectable Negro have, what incentive to better effort, or better life if he, his wife, his daughters or his sons may in a moment be snatched from his humble home and sold into peonage?" he asked. "Let us for a moment put ourselves in his place, and imagine our furious indignation and hopeless despair if our loved ones or ourselves could be subjected to such a condition of involuntary servitude." The formal system might have been problematic, but this was behavior beyond the bounds of even the worst parts of that system. McClellan and Crawley understood that they would find no sympathy in Speer's court and pleaded guilty to four of the twelve counts. Speer fined them $1,000 each but later reduced the fines. Though they served no jail time and never experienced their own version of involuntary bondage at the hands of Georgia officials, the conviction was the first such instance in Georgia and would set a precedent for the following year, when attorney Fred Cubberly brought his own case in *Clyatt v. United States* (1905) (see page 140).[8]

Speer explained from the bench that "some talk wildly and extravagantly of the shotgun policy" in southern race relations, referring to the use of violence and intimidation to control the Black population first put into place with the notorious Mississippi Plan at the end of Reconstruction, "but they do not represent the higher classes of the South."[9] Others, however, would disagree.

The *Northwestern Christian Advocate* saw through such claims, arguing that "the enslavement of negroes under the form of peonage is chiefly due to the convict lease system which regards a convict, whether white or black, as the slave of the state during his term of imprisonment." The systems were intertwined, argued the *Advocate,* despite not understanding the role of the state in the corresponding misdemeanor lease. The systems fed off of one another and ultimately led to abuse. "The lease system is for the convict, however, worse than chattel slavery," the *Advocate* explained, "for slaveowners were prompted by self-interest to have some respect for the health of their slaves, whose sickness or death would involve a financial loss to the owners. The lessee of convicts has no such interest in his slaves." The goal of the lessee was to get as much work as possible out of those in bondage, however they arrived in that condition. If they died, "the state is under contract to provide others to take their places. Indeed, it is to the interest of the lessee, when a convict is taken ill, to hasten his death and thus save the expense of caring for him." It was dangerous on its face, but the *Advocate* understood that "thousands of innocent negroes" were involved in that brutal system without ever being convicted of crimes, pushed by debt peonage into situations similar to that of felony prisoners, only with even more vulnerability because there was no vested state interest in oversight of their terms or adequate measurements that ensured that stated durations matched the fines originally paid by lessees.[10]

Of course, the state was not under contract to replace misdemeanants who died in private or public camps, and it was the misdemeanor structure that was the closest neighbor to debt peonage, both practiced at the county level far from felony convict camps more closely regulated by the Georgia Prison Commission. Such national conflations were understandable. Misdemeanor leasing was designed to exist in the shadows of the system, and it was in those shadows where illicit debt peonage deals happened, deals not sanctioned by a law that was already willing to countenance all sorts of violence in the more formal, front-facing system. Like the *Times* before it, the *Advocate*'s analysis was, then, technically wrong but morally right, adding fuel to the justified national outrage about such carceral behavior but leaving the historical record with a misunderstanding of the relationships between peonage and felony leasing.

It was not an analysis shared by many white residents of south Georgia. "They paid them a small pittance in cash each month, but necessarily the negroes had to be guarded and detained by force," the Thomasville *Times-Enterprise* explained sympathetically. Still, that sympathy stemmed from the reality "that they should have been chosen from the long list of offenders" who also participated regularly in the practice. "We nevertheless congratulate Georgia that the practice of peonage will now cease to exist." The paper absolved the McRees of any wrongdoing toward the debtors but admitted that the practice could lead to inhumane conditions. "The state should cease to barter in human labor." It was a case easy for the paper to make because Thomas County, close to Lowndes and home of Thomasville, had no private misdemeanor camp, public misdemeanor chain gang, or state felony camp.[11]

The region's representative in the federal House, William Gordon Brantley, was far more demonstrative in his defense of the practice. He responded to the indictment by taking to the floor of Congress to denounce federal enforcement of peonage statutes. He argued that the federal law based on the territorial New Mexico case did not apply to residents of actual states like the McRees in Georgia. Peonage, he argued, "is something authorized, recognized, or maintained by the State or Territory. An individual can not create it. Once created by the State or Territory, the individual can 'hold' or 'return' a person to it, or 'arrest' a person who has fled from it."[12] That being the case, Brantley argued, since Georgia had not developed a formal "system" of peonage, then individuals like the McRees were not participating in a system, and since the federal statute only criminalized systems, it had no right to prosecute individuals because they were not the target of the original law. What he didn't mention, of course, was that misdemeanor leasing and chain gangs were themselves systems, of which peonage was essentially an extension. In addition, none of the three were being challenged legally, only abuses of those operations, which, despite public approbation, actually provided them with a kind of legal sanction. Accompanying such convoluted claims were reifications of the antebellum interposition doctrine and cries of states' rights in order to defend acts of peonage in Georgia.[13]

At the same time, perhaps counterintuitively, Brantley took pains to demonstrate that the state had its own laws that regulated such behavior. He pointed to the provision in the Georgia constitution that said, "There shall be no imprisonment for debt," then cited a series of legal cases wherein county authorities were ruled to have no power to lease prisoners as proof that the state had the so-called peonage problem well in hand.[14] The problem with such reasoning, common as it was among white Georgians, was that peonage was not the product of county authorities, that the misdemeanor system in the state absolutely did countenance county authorities to lease prisoners, and that the Prison Commission had been making a sustained case for stopping that countenancing for years. Just as disenfranchisement laws were worded to eliminate the Black right to vote without ever mentioning "race, color, or previous condition of servitude," Brantley's recitation of Georgia's dutiful regulation of his conflated understanding of peonage and misdemeanor convict labor was itself a method of covering the white ability to control Black bodies and restore a version of racialized bound labor without the state's constitutional or case law running afoul of Thirteenth Amendment claims against their behavior.[15] Unlike the exposés of the *Times* or the *Advocate,* Brantley's was an intentional conflation designed to disingenuously defend the system rather than a misreading of its intricacies from outside.

Brantley's duplicity in defending Georgia peonage against federal prosecution was taken up by Maine Republican congressman Charles Littlefield two weeks later. He accused Brantley of using his congressional pulpit "largely as a brief" in the Ware County case in front of Emory Speer and reveled in submitting Speer's decision in the case into the Congressional Record, arguing that it was the perfect response to Brantley's claims. He also submitted two letters from assistant U.S. attorneys, one for Georgia's Northern District and one from its Southern, decrying Brantley's speech and giving lie to its claims by providing examples from their own experience of the problems of kidnapping and cruelty present in the peonage system that existed in counties throughout the state. Brantley's address was "a very elaborated and learned speech," Littlefield explained, "although, in my judgment, not entirely convincing and conclusive." Speer's decision, however, was both learned and convincing. Its presence in the Congressional Record as part of the debate surrounding peonage demonstrated the reach that the McRees' behavior had, not just in the national press but in the halls of Congress itself.[16]

And it came accompanied by other legal action that gave further evidence of the problem in the turpentine belt of south Georgia and north Florida. *United States v. Clyatt,* for example, was making its way through the courts in Pensacola and New Orleans while Kinderlou was under scrutiny. The case charged Samuel M. Clyatt of Tifton, Georgia, forty-five miles north of Valdosta, with capturing Will Gordon and Mose Ridley from Florida and returning them to Tifton, to a state of peonage, where they worked for Clyatt, his brother D. T. Clyatt, and H. H. Tift, leaders of the turpentine firm Clyatt & Tift. The case was brought by Fred Cubberly, a U.S. attorney for the Northern District of Florida, a reformer imbued with the spirit of the Progressive Era. It was in early 1901 that J. R. Deen, owner of a naval stores camp in north Florida, told Cubberly about several of his workers being kidnapped at gunpoint. Cubberly's ensuing investigation led him to Tifton and to Clyatt. What he uncovered was not just misbehavior by Clyatt but complicity in the system by the legal apparatus. The workers who Clyatt and his men abducted had formerly worked for him before moving to Deen's camp in Florida. To get them back, Clyatt swore out warrants against them for gambling. Upon arriving in Florida, he gave the warrants to the local sheriff, who without even reading them agreed to arrest both Gordon and Ridley, and then turned them over to Clyatt to take back to Georgia. The case, then, involved south Georgia and north Florida turpentine concerns ostensibly kidnapping people and bringing them into peonage with the aid of law enforcement. The defense, rather than refute the claims of the prosecution, argued that what they were doing was not an organized "system" of peonage and that the 1867 law against the practice only applied to the territory of New Mexico and did not thus transfer to actual states. It was another version of the argument made by Brantley in the House of Representatives. Clyatt, in fact, never attempted to refute the facts of the case. Though he benefited from the mysterious disappearance of Ridley and Gordon, who could not be found to testify and only added to the venality assumed by many in the case, a Tallahassee jury found Clyatt guilty.[17]

The trial was a sensational one, dealing as it did with kidnapping and the mysterious disappearance of the victims of the crime, and coming on the heels of the McRee prosecution in Savannah. It aroused local and national upheaval as the more disturbing elements of the camps in south Georgia and north Florida came to be known. Even without kidnapping claims, the lives of those in private bound labor were brutal. The area's turpentine business was particularly egregious. Those workers were charged for their supplies and food, and when their store debt rose above the meager pay they were allotted, time was added on to the term of their indenture, keeping them in virtual slavery for years at a time. Again, however, there was a broader public misunderstanding of the system that was in place. This particular version of kidnapping and peonage was directly the result of misdemeanor leasing. The prisoners being kidnapped were returned to Tifton because they had originally been farmed out to the camp after misdemeanor convictions. As in the case of Kinderlou fifty miles south, private leasing didn't run parallel to peonage kidnapping; it directly abetted such behavior. "Were they white men the sympathy of the state would be aroused in behalf of the laborers," explained one north Florida editorial, "but being negroes, in the language of Chimmie Fadden, 'what d'ell' will be the general comment, "Tisn't right."'[18]

"It is highly satisfactory to know that the southern states have not stopped active efforts for the suppression of peonage since the quieting down of the general discussion of the subject throughout the country," said an editorial in the *Chicago Record-Herald*. The Clyatt conviction was among several in Georgia, Florida, and Louisiana in the second half of 1903, and the paper wrongly assumed that "an effective public sentiment in the South" would "protect the Negro from the new form of slavery." It was an ill-founded and ahistorical hope. "However insistent the south may be as against social pretensions of the Negroes, and however much injustice it may do while establishing what it deems to be a vital principle, there is much to show that in the end it will give the Negro a chance industrially."[19] While, in fact, there was little chance of that, the editorial demonstrated the positivity bred by a willingness to convict white defendants who abused Black lives and bodies, a willingness not present in cases of lynching or other forms of racial violence.

The *Clyatt* case finally reached the Supreme Court in 1905. The Court was at pains in the case to deal with the factual presentments, as David Josiah Brewer, writing for the majority, concluded simply that "the testimony discloses that the defendant, with another party, went to Florida, and caused the arrest of Gordon and Ridley on warrants issued by a magistrate in Georgia for larceny, but there can be little doubt that these criminal proceedings were only an excuse for securing the custody of Gordon and Ridley and taking them back to Georgia to work out a debt." Still, the justices felt constrained to rule on a technicality that the charges proclaimed that the two were returned to a state of peonage, and "there is not a scintilla of testimony to show that Gordon and Ridley were ever theretofore in a condition of peonage." Though it seemed to be a dodge, the justices declared, "We are constrained, therefore, to order a reversal of the judgment, and remand the case for a new trial."[20] The misdemeanor charge, then, conditioned and justified the kidnapping. Misdemeanor leasing made the state of peonage judicially justifiable.

The case ultimately died on remand, as white locals felt no compunction for further prosecution and the U.S. attorneys in charge of the case were unable to locate their original witnesses, who mysteriously disappeared from the area.[21] But in June 1903, Governor Terrell responded to calls from the Ware County grand jury, the scandal of Kinderlou, and the trouble emanating from Tifton, ordering an investigation of misdemeanor convict camps and the alleged brutality and abuse fostered there. The investigation began with a camp in Oglethorpe County run by J. R. Broach and W. P. Broach, singled out as particularly barbaric in its corporal punishment of those leased and in its denial of "proper food, clothes, tobacco, and sleep quarters as required by law." The Broach Brothers camp, however, was presented by Terrell as the tip of a large and problematic iceberg that included, among others, the camp of legislator Edward McRee, already charged by a grand jury with similar infractions.[22]

Weeks later, the legislature took its turn, singling out McRee and adopting a resolution to investigate the brutality at Kinderlou. Introduced by William C. Glenn of Whitefield, the resolution created a joint committee of four members of the House and three from the Senate to review evidence particularly related to the case of Lula Frazier, which had received national publicity. Frazier's affidavit was distributed to members of the legislature, and it was damning. Frazier claimed to have been used as a prostitute to service other residents of the camp, then forced to marry one of them, despite already having a husband, after being whipped until she agreed. The testimony placed before the legislators reiterated that Frazier had committed no crime and was there only to pay her supposed legal debt to her lawyer after being exonerated of the crime of adultery.[23]

It was an issue that would continue to press on the statehouse. The same month, July 1903, state senator-elect John Foy and his father were indirectly involved in an Effingham County peonage charge. Titus Mitchell and Henry Jones came to work in Effingham County from Savannah on the promise of a dollar a day and three meals. When they arrived, however, they were given only eighty cents a day and were required to furnish their own meals. When they left after discovering that they were required to pay for the meal they received, they were captured and charged with "larceny of one meal, value 30 cents" and sentenced to a thirty-dollar fine or six months in a work camp. The Foys were the original employers and thus part of the suit.[24] Though they faced no substantial punishment, the case was yet another example of influential white citizens taking advantage of the common acceptability of peonage for their own ends, their influence ensuring that not only would they go unpunished but that lawmakers would be in no hurry to remedy the problem legislatively—because Foy, like Ed McRee, was one of the legislators. It was also further evidence that the behavior of the McRees was not an outlier in a system built for racialized slave labor. Kinderlou found itself in the crosshairs of the state government in 1901 and of the federal government in 1903, but its behavior was consistent with many of the private misdemeanor camps and debt peonage practices throughout the state. And now, even as *Clyatt* was moving through the courts, Kinderlou had been allowed to return to the felony convict lease system.

At the same time that the Foy case was being adjudicated, several Black victims of the state's felony system were testifying before the Prison Commission that they were beaten and kept in bondage well after their term was supposed to have been completed.[25] It was a reminder that peonage cases existed under the cope of a larger convict lease regime that sanctioned such behavior and allowed it to continue even in the areas that were more closely monitored by the state. It also demonstrated that commission oversight was not a cure for prisoner abuse, despite its formula being held as an exemplary model as compared to county misdemeanor behavior, which continued to be just as problematic as it had always been.

Though the system's scope was defined by racial considerations, so too was it bound by class lines, and those could even drive Black accomplices to take part. At the end of the year, in December 1903, a Black Valdosta physician named Maurice Hugh Cobb was arrested by federal marshals on a peonage charge after claiming to be a girl's legal guardian and selling her to the McRees at Kinderlou. Cobb, one of the would-be bounty hunters also implicated in the earlier Frazier prosecution, was born in Jefferson County, Florida, in June 1868, a thirty-five-year-old physician, one of two Black doctors in the town. A widower at a young age, in 1901 he married his second wife, Mettie Hill, eleven years his junior, and the two moved to a large house on S. Patterson Street, Valdosta's main thoroughfare. There they rented rooms to Black boarders needing a place to stay in the segregated city.[26]

Lula Durham was only fifteen years old, on her way to White Springs, Florida, from her home in Vienna, Georgia. She stopped at the Valdosta boardinghouse run by Cobb and, at the time, his mother-in-law. Seeing an opportunity, however, Cobb accused Durham of sleeping with a local man and used the charge to blackmail the girl, telling her that he would forgive the affront if she paid him twenty-five dollars. She didn't have the money, so he and a partner, George Hart, called Frank McRee, claiming that Durham had been a patient of his medical practice who owed him the twenty-five dollars for his services. He, Hart, and McRee then pressured the girl to agree to serve time at Kinderlou to pay her supposed debt, keeping her in bondage for three months. Durham's mother hired a lawyer to attempt to free her, but they were forced to fight not on the blackmail charge but instead on the manufactured claim of restitution for medical services. Ultimately, the mother had to pay the McRees three-fourths of her "debt" before her daughter was released.[27] There had been instances of Black emigrant agents prosecuted under laws of southern states, but those labor brokers were working to move Black labor out of the region. They were serving a liberatory function.[28] This was something different. The stories were horrifying, and it was precisely that horror that drew the charges. Peonage itself was sanctioned by the state. Instead, it was Cobb's collusion with the McRees to abuse the system, not the system itself, that brought him under legal scrutiny.[29] Cobb and Hart received federal charges and appeared before Emory Speer in Savannah.[30] "This sort of thing is bad enough when done by white people toward a member of your own race, but it is a great deal worse when done by colored people," Speer told them in a case finally decided in March 1905. "I am afraid if you had remained in Africa that you both would have become leaders of bands of slave catchers, who swoop down on the unprotected kraals of the Hottentots or Congo and seize the defenseless people and bear them off and sell them into slavery."[31] Cobb, who originally pleaded not guilty, eventually changed his plea and was ultimately fined $300 in lieu of prison time in Chatham County.[32]

That year, Emory Speer again crusaded against the Georgia penal system, this time taking on county misdemeanor convict chain gangs. The case involved Henry Jamison, a Black man arrested on a drunk and disorderly charge in Macon who was immediately convicted and fined sixty dollars or seven months on the county chain gang. The court, of course, knew

Table 7.1. Felony convict lease camps, 1904

Contractor	Name	Location	Employment	Number
Hamby & Toomer	Fargo	Fargo	Sawmilling	
Hamby & Toomer	Fargo No. 2	Fargo	Turpentine	219 (aggregate)
Hamby & Toomer	Babcock	Babcock	Sawmilling	69
Hamby & Toomer	Alexanderville	Alexanderville	Turpentine	45
Hamby & Toomer	Dormine	Pickren	Turpentine	29
Hamby & Toomer	Millwood	Millwood	Turpentine	26
Hamby & Toomer	Waycross	Waycross	Turpentine	98
Durham Coal & Coke Co.	Durham Mines	Pittsburg	Mining coal	198
Chattahoochee Brick Co.	Chattahoochee	Chattahoochee	Brickmaking	182
J. W. English, Jr.	Palmer	Atlanta	Brickmaking	51
J. W. English, Jr.	Lookout Mtn.	Pittsburg	Mining coal	92
Edward J. McRee	**Sirmans**	**Sirmans**	**Turpentine**	**35**
Edward J. McRee	**Stanley**	**Valdosta**	**Turpentine**	**26**
Edward J. McRee	**Fenders**	**Valdosta**	**Turpentine**	**26**
Cruger & Pace	Albany	Albany	Brickmaking	74
Flowers Lumber Company	Jakin	Jakin	Sawmilling	46
Flowers Bros. Lumber Co.	Blakely	Blakely	Sawmilling	52
John W. Callahan	Saffold	Saffold	Turpentine	35
J. Lee Ensign	Canda	Willingham	Sawmilling	50
G. V. Gress Co.	**Milltown**	**Milltown**	**Sawmilling**	**51**
E. E. Foy Mfg. Co.	Oakfield	Oakfield	Turpentine	23
E. E. Foy Mfg. Co.	Pinsons	Summer	Turpentine	24
State farm (men)	State farm	State farm	Farming	177
State farm (boys)	State farm	State farm	Farming	21
State farm (women)	State farm	State farm	Farming	92
State farm (girls)	State farm	State farm	Farming	1
			TOTAL	1,742

Source: *Seventh Annual Report of the Prison Commission of Georgia, 1904*, 23, Georgia Penitentiary Prison Commission's Reports, Georgia Archives, Morrow, Georgia, 23.

that Jamison didn't have sixty dollars. That was the point. After several days of hard labor, his lawyer filed a habeas corpus petition. Speer's concern was whether the punishment deprived Jamison of liberty and subjected him "to an infamous punishment without due process of law." The chain gang was decidedly cruel and infamous, Speer argued, explaining the role of whipping bosses and the "heavy leathern strap" they used on the prisoners, a strap that was mandated by law as the authorized mechanism of punishment: "We may judge that the agony inflicted by this implement of torture is not surpassed by the Russian knout, the synonym the world around for merciless corporal punishment." Only exacerbating such horrors was the reality that both those convicted of felonies and those convicted of misdemeanors were so used, as many county chain gangs were now supplementing their misdemeanor convicts with state prisoners. "One guilty of burglary, arson, manslaughter, or any crime on the calendar, however heinous," Speer said, "has been accorded a copy of the accusation against him, trial by jury, the opportunity to appeal—in short, due process of law. Not so with the lad who loiters on the streets or is overcome by sleep in the depot." Speer's colloquy was an important reminder that the alternative to camps like that of the McRees was not a panacea for their problems. Chain gangs, supervised by county officials, had fewer instances of bondage past scheduled incarceration dates, but their brutality during the official time of service could be just as harsh and deadly. "Never in the history of the world has any considerable class of people been debased and degraded by force and lawlessness, but that the entire people suffered because of that degradation," Speer explained. "The white people of this country control the government, state and federal. They enjoy every conceivable advantage. They have superiority in wealth, education, social influence, everything. A magnanimous people, a just people, they owe it to themselves to be magnanimous and just to the colored people."[33] Again Speer ruled from feeling the white man's burden, but it was an important and bold statement for a white judge in the Deep South to make. It was, however, a drop in a large bucket, unable to flood the minds of white residents of Georgia who most needed to hear it.

Still, many Black residents were grateful for Speer's ruling. "This is one of the best and most righteous decisions rendered in the South for many years and is one of the many straws which shows that there are better days in store for the black man in the South after all," the Baltimore *Afro-American* reported. "It also shows that all hope is not lost and with each recurring incident of this kind, the Black man is lifted to a higher and more

Table 7.2. Felony convict county road camps, 1904

County	Number of convicts
Bibb	12
Burke	28
Clarke	15
Coffee	16
Coweta	23
Columbia	9
Dougherty	13
DeKalb	17
Elbert	17
Floyd	27
Fulton	101
Green	13
Jackson	22
Jefferson	14
Johnson	9
Jones	12
Laurens	21
Lee	8
Lincoln	6
McDuffie	9
Morgan	14
Monroe	17
Oglethorpe	17
Pulaski	16
Richmond	43
Spalding	16
Terrell	9
Walton	10
Wilkes	9
TOTAL	573

Notes: There were 2,315 felony prisoners in the state system and ninety-eight deaths in 1904. There were 249 white men and boys, seven white women and girls, 1,973 Black men and boys, and eighty-six Black women and girls.

85.2 percent Black men and boys

88.9 percent Black prisoners

Source: Seventh Annual Report of the Prison Commission of Georgia, 1904 (Atlanta: Lester Book & Stationery, 1904), 15–16, 24.

elevated plane in the future life of the nation."[34] All hope was not lost, but there was still a long way to go. Of all the components of the Georgia penal system, county chain gangs had been the least controversial. They were held up as the model of how private misdemeanor camps should behave. Their rules were the rules that people like the McRees were abusing. They were the stated ideal in an apparatus with multiple parts and decidedly low bars. But Jamison's case and Speer's ruling demonstrated that a simple transition out of private leasing into county chain gangs was not the solution that the Georgia Prison Commission often made it out to be. Abuse was rampant in each area of the carceral structure, and just because it was most heinous in private misdemeanor leasing did not mean that trading one bad system for another was a substantive and moral remedy to its ills.

The Prison Commission did not submit a detailed comprehensive report for 1903, as the McRees were undergoing their second round of intense scrutiny and the Jamison case was making its way to Speer,[35] but its 1904 report seemed to validate Speer's skepticism and demonstrated that Edward's place in the legislature had paid dividends. The McRee operation at Kinderlou had returned to its place as an official contractor for felony prisoners with the state, with three distinct convict turpentine camps, all within the bounds of the Kinderlou property, one with thirty-five officially counted prisoners and the other two with twenty-six (see table 7.1). The ignominy that came from the 1900 investigation never appeared after that of 1903 because of the family's political stature, insulating them, to the dismay of reformers like Speer, from any real consequences for their actions other than moving from private misdemeanor lease to private felony lease, labor that was supplemented with a debt peonage that fell beyond the Prison Commission's remit. Lake Park's J. B. S. Holmes remained the county's repository for privately held misdemeanants, along with a growing county chain gang dedicated to road work (see table 7.3).[36]

By 1904, the system had grown and evolved. There were twenty-five felony convict leasing institutions, twenty-nine felony road camps, and forty misdemeanor camps, twenty-five of which were privately held. The ninety-four different entities held more than four thousand felony and misdemeanor prisoners. At the same time, however, the inspection system had not grown with them, and the commission's report for the year claimed that the budget for inspections would have to increase if the state was to employ at least three inspectors at all times so as to adequately make the rounds to all of the different places where prisoners were held.[37]

The 1904 Prison Commission Report did not provide death figures for

Table 7.3. County misdemeanor camps, 1904, divided into public and private camps

County	Worked by	WM	WF	BM	BF	Total	Employment
Public							
Baldwin	County	0	0	9	1	10	Road work
Bibb	County	1	0	71	8	80	Road work
Burke	County	0	0	46	1	47	Road work
Chatham	County	4	0	108	45	157	Road work
Cobb	County	0	0	22	0	22	Road work
Coffee	County	0	0	14	0	14	Road work
Columbia	County	0	0	5	0	5	Road work
Coweta	County	0	0	3	0	3	Road work
Clarke	County	1	0	19	1	21	Road work
DeKalb	County	3	0	17	0	20	Road work
Dougherty	County	0	0	26	4	30	Road work
Elbert	County	0	0	8	0	8	Road work
Emanuel	County	1	0	10	0	11	Road work
Fulton	County	11	0	225	35	271	Road work
Floyd	County	5	1	41	11	58	Road work
Green	County	0	0	5	1	6	Road work
Glynn	County	3	0	33	1	37	Road work
Hancock	County	0	0	7	0	7	Road work
Irwin	County	1	0	28	0	29	Road work
Jackson	County	0	0	7	0	7	Road work
Jasper	County	0	0	8	0	8	Road work
Jefferson	County	0	0	10	1	11	Road work
Johnson	County	0	0	12	0	12	Road work
Jones	County	0	0	13	0	13	Road work
Laurens	County	0	0	17	0	17	Road work
Lee	County	1	0	20	0	21	Road work
Lowndes	**County**	**1**	**0**	**18**	**0**	**19**	**Road work**
Monroe	County	0	0	12	0	12	Road work
Morgan	County	0	0	25	1	26	Road work
Muscogee	County	0	0	35	0	35	Road work
Oglethorpe	County	4	0	13	0	17	Road work
Newton	County	2	0	13	1	16	Road work
Putnam	County	0	0	3	0	3	Road work
Richmond	County	7	0	72	0	79	Road work
Spalding	County	0	0	21	0	21	Road work
Terrell	County	0	0	11	0	11	Road work
Terrell	County	0	0	31	1	32	Farming
Walton	County	1	0	10	0	11	Road work
Ware	County	0	0	27	0	27	Road work

(continued)

Table 7.3—Continued

Washington	County	0	0	24	0	24	Road work
Wilkes	County	0	0	5	0	5	Road work
Lincoln	County	0	0	2	0	2	Road work
McDuffie	County	1	0	9	1	11	Road work
Pulaski	County	0	0	8	0	8	Road work
TOTAL		47	1	1,123	113	1,284	

87.5% Black boys and men
96.3% Black prisoners

Private

Worth	C. A. Alford	0	0	15	1	16	Turpentining
Coffee	A. T. & W. R. Beach	2	0	23	1	26	Turpentining
Worth	J. S. Betts & Co.	2	0	27	0	29	Farming
Ware	W. R. Beach & Co.	0	0	30	0	30	Turpentining
Berrien	E. G. Brown & Co.	3	0	21	0	24	Turpentining
Lee	W. B. Coxwell	0	0	2	2	4	Farming
Early	J. W. Callahan	1	0	17	0	18	Turpentining
Decatur	J. W. Callahan	1	0	51	2	54	Turpentining
Wilcox	Enterprise Lumber Co.	0	0	13	0	13	Sawmilling
Quitman	Eufala Brick Co.	0	0	14	2	16	Brickmaking
Effingham	E. E. Foy Mfg. Co.	0	0	13	0	13	Sawmilling
Decatur	Greer Hinson & Co.	8	0	33	0	41	Turpentining
Bartow	Ga. Coal & Iron Co.	10	0	37	3	50	Mining iron ore
Mitchell	Higston Lumber Co.	3	0	42	3	48	Sawmilling
Miller	J. W. Hinson & Co.	1	0	36	1	38	Turpentining
Lowndes	**J. B. S. Holmes & Co.**	**4**	**0**	**12**	**0**	**16**	**Farming**
Decatur	Hodges & Powell	2	0	29	0	31	Turpentining and farming
Oglethorpe	J. W. Jarrell	4	0	4	1	9	Farming
Oglethorpe	J. M. Smith	5	0	30	1	36	Farming
Colquitt	Mallet-Gray Lum. Co.	2	0	29	2	33	Sawmilling
Worth	T. J. Pinson & Co.	1	0	36	0	37	Turpentining
Decatur	T. J. Shingler & Co.	8	0	61	1	70	Turpentining
Miller	J. R. Sharpe	0	0	23	0	23	Turpentining
Franklin	Little Bros	1	0	4	0	5	Farming
TOTAL		58	0	602	20	680	

88.5% Black men and boys
91.5% Black prisoners

Note: The camps were not alphabetized by county in the original and therefore are not alphabetized here.
Source: Seventh Annual Report of the Prison Commission of Georgia, 1904 (Atlanta: Lester Book & Stationery, 1904), 25–26.

the misdemeanor camps but argued that the death rate in convict lease was only 1.6 percent, with ninety-eight total deaths in the previous twelve months. It argued that the death rate in Atlanta was 2.66 percent, making prison life healthier than life in the capital city. The low reported death rate was all the more impressive "when it is remembered that eighty-nine per cent of the convicts are negroes, a majority of whom, by reason of their previous surroundings, immoral and unsanitary lives, are received from the jails in a diseased condition."[38] Still, with ninety-eight deaths and 2,315 total prisoners, the 1.6 percentage rate seemed to come from nowhere.

Of those 2,315 felony prisoners, 249 were white men and boys, seven white women and girls, 1,973 Black men and boys, and eighty-six Black women and girls. The commission made no reference to the racial makeup of felony convict deaths, but its racist language in the report made it clear that the vast majority of them were Black.[39]

The number of private misdemeanor camps had grown to 63 percent of the total number of holding sites. Under the estimation rubric used in previous chapters, the death toll in those private camps would be roughly fifty-seven. Still, what is most striking about the composition of the misdemeanor camps in 1904 is the diminished number of misdemeanants in private hands—there were almost double the number of prisoners held on county chain gangs—making it seem as though the criticisms of the Prison Commission were finally getting through to county officials. At the same time, not only was there a new profusion of county misdemeanor camps, but many counties were supplementing their misdemeanor road labor with felony convict labor, as well, again following the example of an earlier Prison Commission jeremiad and fueled by a new law in 1903, making the offer of prisoners to counties for road construction just as it had in 1897. The 1903 law eliminated the 36-dollar-per-year contract price, only requiring that counties not attempt to sublet prisoners to other counties, and limited potential felony convict recruits to those serving less than a five-year sentence. Though the thirty-six dollars in the original law ostensibly fed back to the counties in a school fund, the new law eliminated the cost but also eliminated the money such counties could earn for their schools.[40] Despite the warning from Speer about the state of depravity in which county chain gangs operated, the shift to putting felony prisoners in county hands had begun. The landscape following the McRee scandals was decidedly changing.

That year, in 1904, the portion of Kinderlou run by J. F. Flender actually vacillated between twenty-four and thirty prisoners over the course of the year. Each convict was allotted one coat, one pair of shoes, one hat, two pairs of pants, and two shirts. They received bacon, beef, flour, syrup, salt, and a rotating selection of vegetables. They were provided a modicum of tobacco, as well as soap and lamp oil.[41]

Records also exist for the camp run by S. M. Stanley in 1908 and 1909. The size of the operation vacillated in those years, as well, the camp managing between sixteen and thirty-one prisoners. Food rations remained stable, as did soap and oil, though only one pair of pants and one shirt was issued to each person.[42] Managing the operation in the first decade of the twentieth century had become an institutionalized, regular process built on consistency in record-keeping, even if the family's more brutal excesses never made it into the log books.

The excesses at Kinderlou also stayed out of the national press after their brush with the law in 1903, but the national attention on the system itself didn't abate. Writing in 1905 in *Cosmopolitan* in a grand takedown of debt peonage, Herbert Ward wrongly argued that the system was solely one about labor and capital, not about race and racism. But he was adamant about its evils.

> As long we tolerate in our cities policemen who are abettors of crime and share the burglar's loot—as long as we tolerate in our country legislators who sell their honor for a price—as long as we tolerate railroads that charge a preferred rate to a preferred customer—as long as we tolerate United States senators who trade upon futures because of their connivance at legislation—as long as we tolerate rumsellers to run our municipalities—as long as we tolerate justices of the peace whose living is made out of convictions—as long as we tolerate the slavery of our mines, of our railroads and many of our factories, so long will peonage be a probability in our body politic.

Ward was certain that laws existed to prevent peonage and other forms of organized slavery: "We need only an aroused public opinion and fearless officers to enforce these laws."[43]

Again the national press conflated the varied systems in place in Georgia to govern its form of legalized slavery, but again its advocacy was important, helping to press for "public opinion and fearless officers" to make substantive change in the system, whatever its intricacies. Public opinion and fearless officers, it turned out, were on their way.

8

The Federal Crusade against Peonage

Benjamin Wilenski began working for S. H. Swartz in June 1906 after being recruited by a northern employment agency to travel south for the opportunity, but the pretense under which he was hired soon gave way to the harsh realities of debt peonage in a north Florida turpentine camp. He was taken to an outlying area where he was worked from sunup to well past sundown. "Overseers beat them unmercifully," explained one account. "He was under guard of giant Negroes armed with rifles and shotguns." The Black guards only added to the presumed degradation of the white Wilenski. (For more on Black guards, see chapter 5.) Still, he persevered and eventually made his escape from the camp as bloodhounds trailed behind him. From there, he made his way to New York, where he showed the mass of scars littering his back and testified to the abuses to U.S. commissioner John H. Shields, where the story then reached the national press, again reminding the nation of the grotesquery taking place in the turpentine belt.[1]

Another U.S. commissioner in New York, Nathan A. Brown, presided over a hearing months later of similar debt peons in Georgia, held in forced labor to the Atlanta and Birmingham Construction Company. As with the Wilenski testimony, the case received extra attention because those held were white. "White men were held in slavery and made to work," the *Afro-American* reported with surprise, "when they would not work they were whipped." Everyone, the conceit of the coverage went, was potentially vulnerable, and the Black press was optimistic that stories of white abuse would provide more incentive for federal action to stop the practice. It was, according to the *Afro-American,* "the determination of the Roosevelt administration to stamp out peonage entirely."[2]

The cases were horrifying, but they were abuses beyond the supposed bounds of Georgia authorities, one of them happening in north Florida and the other the result of Georgia's debt peonage process by a company not part of the felony or misdemeanor convict lease systems. If nothing else, debt peonage could at least be monitored if those engaged in it had some formal relation with the state's carceral system, but Atlanta and Birmingham Construction only traded in peons. Meanwhile, the actual penal apparatus carried on, largely untouched by such outside investigations and monitored solely by the state Prison Commission, which could use such cases as exemplars of what could happen without commission oversight. To that end, the body continued its lament against private camps in its 1905 report. It noted that commissioners had the ability under the law of 1897 to advise county authorities on policies governing misdemeanor prisoners and could even fine them up to 250 dollars when those authorities did not comply with imposed rules. But when county authorities had not established their own camp, instead leasing the misdemeanants out to others, often in other counties where there were also no public camps, then the commission had no one under law to take action against, no one to fine. The commission remained of the opinion that "imprisonment in such private chaingangs is illegal," but without legislative or judicial authority, all it could do was scream yet again into the wind in what had become an annual tradition by 1905.[3]

By that year, the McRees were fully divested of the misdemeanor chain gang business, instead relying on felony convict labor. But even that had declined. The three separate camps the family had operated in 1904 had been reduced to one, operated by S. M. Stanley (see table 8.1).

The private misdemeanor camps again had the highest percentage of Black men and boys in 1905 with an estimated death toll of forty-four, but the number of counties using misdemeanor or felony prisoners on roads was dramatically increasing, serving as an inevitable threat to the private camp business as roads became a greater priority in the state (see table 8.3). There were 2,090 total prisoners and misdemeanants devoted to road works in 1905, well more than the 1,707 in private felony camps and the 782 in private misdemeanor camps. Though the end of convict leasing was still several years away, the transition to chain gang labor was well underway. It was not a phenomenon that developed when convict leasing ended; it had developed at the misdemeanor level in the wake of the Civil War and at the felony level in the early twentieth century, and by 1905, even with both forms of private leasing still in effect, those prisoners used in road work already outnumbered those in private hands.

For those who saw public works as the best corrective for convict leasing, the transition was progress. And while its corrective function has rightly been historically questioned, there was, undeniably, progress. In 1906 in Pensacola, six representatives of the Jackson Lumber Company were

Table 8.1. Felony convict lease camps, 1905

Contractor	Location	Employment	Number
Arlington Lumber Co.	Arlington	Sawmilling	27
Babcock Bros. Lumber Co.	Babcock	Sawmilling	110
Bibb Brick Co.	Macon	Brickmaking	47
Cherokee Brick Co.	Macon	Brickmaking	48
Chattahoochee Brick Co.	Atlanta	Brickmaking	167
Cruger & Pace	Albany	Brickmaking	75
T. G. Culbreath	Tarver	Turpentine	25
Dorminy-Palmer Co.	Pickren	Turpentine	23
Durham Coal & Coke Co.	Pittsburg	Coal mining	234
Enterprise Lumber Co.	Pitts	Sawmilling	23
Flowers Lumber Co.	Jackin	Sawmilling	55
Flowers Bros. Lumber Co.	Blakely	Sawmilling	56
Georgia Iron & Coal Co.	Rising Fawn	Iron furnace	31
Georgia Iron & Coal Co.	Ferrobutte	Iron ore mining	41
Gress, G. V. Co.	**Milltown**	**Sawmilling**	**47**
Hamby & Toomer	Fargo	Sawmilling	53
Hamby & Toomer	Fargo	Turpentine	69
Holmes, Dr. J. B. S.	**Lake Park**	**Farming**	**55**
Lookout Mt. Coal & Coke Co.	Pittsburg	Coal mining	93
Palmer Brick Co.	Atlanta	Brickmaking	49
Royster Guano Co.	Macon	Manuf'g guano	47
Stanley, S.M.	**Valdosta**	**Turpentine**	**27**
Toomer, W. M.	Waycross	Turpentine	90
State Farm	Milledgeville	Farming (men)	132
State Farm	Milledgeville	Farming (women)	88
		Total	1,712

Source: *Eighth Annual Report of the Prison Commission of Georgia, 1905* (Atlanta: Lester Book & Stationery, 1905), 20.

convicted on federal charges of peonage. Five of them received thirteen-month sentences and another an eighteen-month sentence.[4] It was a decided change from the cases stemming from Kinderlou, where guilty pleas resulted in fines and no prison time. Using bondage to create a legitimate check against bondage was a new strategy, one that promised the potential end of the system. Richard Barry, presenting an exposé on peonage in Florida for *Cosmopolitan,* lauded the basic effort to fight the abuses but described a system in north Florida almost identical to that in south Georgia: "To complicate the system, each county also has its prisoners, and these are

Table 8.2. Felony convict county road camps, 1905

County	Number of convicts
Bibb	40
Burke	26
Clarke	17
Coffee	14
Coweta	20
Columbia	9
Dougherty	11
DeKalb	19
Elbert	18
Floyd	25
Fulton	102
Green	14
Jackson	21
Jefferson	14
Johnson	10
Jones	12
Laurens	22
Lee	8
Lincoln	6
McDuffie	9
Morgan	13
Monroe	17
Oglethorpe	17
Pulaski	16
Richmond	48
Spalding	15
Terrell	9
Walton	9
Wilkes	12
TOTAL	573

Notes: There were 2,285 felony prisoners in the state system and sixty-four deaths in 1905. There were 284 white boys and men, seven white girls and women, 1,913 Black boys and men, and eighty-one Black girls and women.

83.7 percent Black boys and men

87.2 percent Black prisoners

Source: Eighth Annual Report of the Prison Commission of Georgia, 1905 (Atlanta: Lester Book & Stationery, 1905), 12–13, 21.

Table 8.3. County misdemeanor camps, 1905, divided into public and private camps

County	Worked by	WM	WF	BM	BF	Total	Employment
Public							
Baldwin	County	1	0	12	1	14	Road building
Bibb	County	5	0	68	11	84	Road building
Burke	County	0	0	17	2	19	Road building
Clarke	County	0	0	29	4	33	Road building
Colquitt	County	0	0	14	0	14	Road building
Columbia	County	0	0	9	1	10	Road building
Coffee	County	3	0	22	3	28	Road building
Coweta	County	0	0	15	0	15	Road building
Chatham	County	8	0	216	58	282	Road building
DeKalb	County	1	0	23	0	24	Road building
Dougherty	County	0	0	21	0	21	Road building
Elbert	County	2	0	9	0	11	Road building
Effingham	County	0	0	11	0	11	Road building
Emanuel	County	1	0	16	1	18	Road building
Floyd	County	2	1	15	0	18	Road building
Fulton	County	21	2	301	31	355	Road building
Green	County	0	0	8	2	10	Road building
Glynn	County	3	0	25	3	31	Road building
Hancock	County	0	0	12	0	12	Road building
Irwin	County	0	0	16	5	21	Road building
Jackson	County	0	0	8	1	9	Road building
Jasper	County	0	0	5	0	5	Road building
Johnson	County	2	0	12	2	16	Road building
Jones	County	0	0	6	0	6	Road building
Jefferson	County	0	0	6	0	6	Road building
Laurens	County	0	0	6	0	6	Road building
Lee	County	0	0	16	0	16	Road building
Lowndes	**County**	**5**	**0**	**28**	**3**	**36**	**Road building**
McDuffie	County	0	0	4	0	4	Road building
Monroe	County	0	0	3	0	3	Road building
Morgan	County	1	0	15	0	16	Road building
Muscogee	County	5	0	45	6	56	Road building
Newton	County	1	0	21	0	22	Road building
Oglethorpe	County	1	0	14	0	15	Road building
Putnam	County	0	0	12	0	12	Road building
Pulaski	County	1	0	12	1	14	Road building
Richmond	County	5	0	65	33	103	Road building

(continued)

Table 8.3—Continued

County	Worked by	WM	WF	BM	BF	Total	Employment
Sumter	County	0	0	16	0	16	Road building
Screven	County	0	0	6	0	6	Road building
Spalding	County	0	0	16	6	22	Road building
Terrell	County	0	0	30	0	30	Road building
Washington	County	1	0	19	0	20	Road building
Ware	County	0	0	18	0	18	Road building
Ware	Waycross city	0	0	10	0	10	Street building
Walton	County	1	0	10	0	11	Road building
Wilkes	County	0	0	8	0	8	Road building
TOTAL		70	3	1,270	174	1,517	

83.7% Black boys and men
95.2% Black prisoners

County	Worked by	WM	WF	BM	BF	Total	Employment
Private							
Baker	McDowell & Pool	0	0	18	1	19	Turpentine
Bartow	Georgia I. & C. Co.	22	2	41	0	65	Mining ore
Berrien	E. G. Brown	3	0	13	0	16	Turpentine
Berrien	Gress Lumber Co.	0	0	26	1	27	Sawmilling
Calhoun	Arlington Lumber Co.	0	0	2	0	2	Sawmilling
Clinch	Hamby & Toomer	9	0	4	1	14	Sawmilling
Coffee	W. W. Stewart & Bro.	2	0	18	0	20	Turpentine
Decatur	T. J. Shingler & Bro.	1	0	61	2	64	Turpentine
Decatur	Hodges & Powell	0	0	29	2	31	Turpentine
Decatur	J. W. Callahan	3	0	29	1	33	Turpentine
Decatur	Chattahoochee L. Co.	2	0	36	2	40	Sawmilling
Dougherty	Cruger & Pace	0	0	4	7	11	Farming
Echols	T. G. Culbreath	0	0	1	0	1	Turpentine
Echols	Hamby & Toomer	8	0	27	3	38	Turpentine
Early	J. W. Callahan	1	0	18	1	20	Turpentine
Franklin	Little Brothers	0	0	6	0	6	Farming
Lowndes	**J. B. S. Holmes**	**2**	**0**	**0**	**0**	**2**	**Farming**
Miller	Jasper Hinson	1	0	22	0	23	Turpentine
Miller	T. J. Shingler Bros.	1	0	40	1	42	Turpentine
Mitchell	Higston Lumber Co.	4	0	45	0	49	Turpentine
Oglethorpe	John Jarrell	0	0	4	0	4	Farming
Oglethorpe	J. M. Smith	3	0	24	0	27	Farming
Quitman	Eufaula Brick Co.	0	0	2	0	2	Brick Making
Terrell	C. C. Lunday	0	0	7	0	7	Farming

Thomas	Stetson Lumber Co.	7	0	16	4	27	Sawmilling
Ware	O. H. Lowther	0	0	23	0	23	Turpentine
Ware	W. R. Beach & Co.	3	0	18	0	21	Turpentine
Wilcox	Enterprise Lumber Co.	3	0	6	0	9	Sawmilling
Worth	T. J. Pinson	4	0	25	0	29	Turpentine
Worth	J. S. Betts & Co.	1	0	24	0	25	Farming
Worth	C. A. Alford	2	0	82	1	85	Turpentine
TOTAL		82	2	671	27	782	

85.8% Black boys and men
89.3% Black prisoners

Source: *Eighth Annual Report of the Prison Commission of Georgia, 1905* (Atlanta: Lester Book & Stationery, 1905), 22–23.

Table 8.4. Felony convict lease camps, 1906

Contractor	Location	Employment	Number
Arlington Lumber Co.	Arlington	Sawmilling	29
Babcock Bros. Lumber Co.	Babcock	Sawmilling	129
Bibb Brick Co.	Macon	Brickmaking	50
Cherokee Brick Co.	Macon	Brickmaking	50
Chattahoochee Brick Co.	Atlanta	Brickmaking	177
Cruger & Pace	Albany	Brickmaking	86
T. G. Culbreath	Tarver	Turpentine	25
Dorminy-Palmer Co.	Pickren	Turpentine	19
Dorminy-Price Lumber Co.	Broxton	Sawmilling	21
Durham Coal & Coke Co.	Pittsburg	Coal mining	246
Flowers Lumber Co.	Jakin	Sawmilling	59
Flowers Bros. Lumber Co.	Blakely	Sawmilling	59
Georgia Iron & Coal Co.	Rising Fawn	Iron furnace	29
Georgia Iron & Coal Co.	Ferrobutte	Iron ore mining	41
G. V. Gress & Co.	**Milltown**	**Sawmilling**	**50**
G. S. Baxter & Co.	Fargo	Sawmilling, etc.	124
Dr. J. B. S. Holmes	**Lake Park**	**Farming**	**51**
Lookout Mt. Coal & Coke	Pittsburg	Coal mining	93
Palmer Brick Co.	Atlanta	Brickmaking	55
Royster Guano Co.	Macon	Manf'g guano	51
S. M. Stanley	**Valdosta**	**Turpentine**	**28**
W. M. Toomer	Waycross	Turpentine	93
State Farm	Milledgeville	Farming (men)	123
State Farm	Milledgeville	Farming (women)	85
		TOTAL	1,773

Source: *Ninth Annual Report of the Prison Commission of Georgia, 1906* (Atlanta: Lester Book & Stationery, 1906), 18.

leased by the same villainous patronage, but with the added disadvantage that they have no supervision. The state inspects its camps; the counties do not have even that formality." Thus "the horrors of this convict system," which had "become so heartrending in Florida during the past few years," would continue. "No one can say just where this slavery begins and where it leaves off. It has assailed the fair name of Florida."[5]

It assailed the fair name of Georgia, too. The year 1906 would be the last gasp for private misdemeanor convict labor in Lowndes County, as the Holmes operation in Lake Park had diminished from two prisoners in 1905 to one in 1906, moving instead, like the McRees, to using felony prisoners for a majority of its labor (see table 8.6). By 1907, Lowndes would devote all of its misdemeanants to roads. But that didn't mean that the apparatus itself wasn't working as it was intended, creating systems of virtual slavery and abject misery without the need for kidnappings like those that would draw federal charges in north Florida.

As it had each year before it, the percentage of Black men and boys remained highest in the private misdemeanor camps (with an estimated death total of twenty-five), but the number of prisoners in those camps had dwindled while the number of misdemeanants in public camps had grown, demonstrating the beginnings of a shift away from the practice. There were 1,982 prisoners and misdemeanants tasked with public road work in Georgia, more than the 1,773 in felony convict lease, and the 533 in misdemeanor lease. Part of that shift was the result of the natural progression of a system increasingly devoted to public works, but part of it also was a desire to move away from systems that could draw the kind of federal charges coming from nearby Florida or from other southern locations.

Even as the convictions in north Florida came down, other charges were filed in federal court in Mississippi. A Rankin County farmer kept Dan January, his wife, and his six children in a state of involuntary servitude for two years, then sold January to another farmer, James Patrick, for $1,090.06, claiming that price was the debt that January owed him. Along with allegations of brutal beatings, the charge demonstrated an overt form of slavery, but it also demonstrated the new willingness of the federal government to charge those accused of the crimes.[6] In a message to Congress at the end of 1906, Theodore Roosevelt told the assembled, "I have striven to break up peonage. I have upheld the hands of those who like Judge Jones and Judge Speer, have warred against the peonage because I would hold myself unfit to be President, if I did not feel the same revolt at wrong done a colored man as I feel at wrong done a white man."[7]

Table 8.5. Felony convict county road camps, 1906

County	Number of convicts
Bibb	45
Burke	26
Clarke	16
Coffee	14
Coweta	21
Columbia	10
Dougherty	13
DeKalb	19
Elbert	17
Floyd	30
Fulton	100
Green	13
Jackson	19
Jefferson	15
Johnson	9
Jones	12
Laurens	20
Lee	8
Lincoln	5
McDuffie	9
Morgan	13
Monroe	17
Oglethorpe	17
Pulaski	15
Richmond	41
Spalding	16
Terrell	10
Walton	19
Wilkes	11
TOTAL	580

Notes: There were 2,344 felony prisoners in the state system and fifty-three deaths in 1906. There were 207 white men and boys, six white women and girls, 2,052 Black males, and seventy-nine Black women and girls.

87.5 percent Black men and boys

90.9 percent Black prisoners

Source: Ninth Annual Report of the Prison Commission of Georgia, 1906 (Atlanta: Lester Book & Stationery, 1906), 13–14, 19.

Table 8.6. County misdemeanor camps, 1906, divided into public and private camps

County	Worked by	WM	WF	BM	BF	Total	Employment
Public							
Baldwin	County	0	0	11	0	11	Road building
Berrien	County	1	0	8	0	9	Road building
Bartow	County	0	0	7	0	7	Road building
Bibb	County	3	0	61	5	69	Road building
Bulloch	County	0	0	22	0	22	Road building
Burke	County	0	0	22	0	22	Road building
Clarke	County	0	0	18	6	24	Road building
Columbia	County	0	0	5	0	5	Road building
Coffee	County	4	0	10	0	14	Road building
Coweta	County	0	0	17	0	17	Road building
Chatham	County	8	1	222	63	294	Road building
Colquitt	County	0	0	10	0	10	Road building
DeKalb	County	1	0	10	0	11	Road building
Dougherty	County	0	0	24	1	25	Road building
Elbert	County	1	0	6	0	7	Road building
Effingham	County	0	0	5	0	5	Road building
Emanuel	County	0	0	13	0	13	Road building
Floyd	County	2	0	10	1	13	Road building
Fulton	County	25	0	253	30	308	Road building
Green	County	0	0	7	0	7	Road building
Glynn	County	3	0	21	1	25	Road building
Hancock	County	1	0	19	0	20	Road building
Irwin	County	0	0	10	1	11	Road building
Jackson	County	0	0	2	0	2	Road building
Jasper	County	0	0	3	0	3	Road building
Johnson	County	0	0	6	0	6	Road building
Jones	County	0	0	8	0	8	Road building
Jefferson	County	0	0	8	0	8	Road building
Laurens	County	0	0	6	0	6	Road building
Lee	County	0	0	18	0	18	Road building
Lowndes	**County**	**0**	**0**	**22**	**0**	**22**	**Road building**
Lincoln	County	0	0	3	0	3	Road building
McDuffie	County	0	0	10	0	10	Road building
Monroe	County	0	0	4	0	4	Road building
Morgan	County	0	0	14	1	15	Road building
Muscogee	County	0	0	33	3	36	Road building
Newton	County	0	0	12	0	12	Road building
Oglethorpe	County	0	0	11	0	11	Road building

County		WM	WF	BM	BF	Total	Employment
Putnam	County	0	0	8	0	8	Road building
Pulaski	County	0	0	17	1	18	Road building
Randolph	County	0	0	15	0	15	Road building
Richmond	County	3	0	61	30	94	Road building
Sumter	County	0	0	33	2	35	Road building
Screven	County	0	0	10	0	10	Road building
Spalding	County	0	0	17	0	17	Road building
Taliaferro	County	0	0	7	0	7	Road building
Terrell	County	0	0	32	0	32	Road building
Washington	County	0	0	10	0	10	Road building
Ware	County	0	0	21	0	21	Road building
Walton	County	1	0	10	0	11	Road building
Warren	County	1	0	14	0	15	Road building
Wilkes	County	0	0	4	0	4	Road building
TOTAL		54	1	1,211	145	1,411	

85.8% Black men and boys
96.1% Black prisoners

County	Worked by	WM	WF	BM	BF	Total	Employment
Private							
Appling	Holton & Rogers	2	0	5	0	7	Turpentine
Baker	Bowers & Kendall	0	0	11	0	11	Turpentine
Bartow	Georgia I. & C. Co.	1	0	15	1	17	Mining ore
Berrien	E.G. Brown	1	0	8	1	10	Turpentine
Calhoun	Arlington Lumber Co.	1	0	10	0	11	Sawmilling
Clinch	B.A. & C.O. Burnett	0	0	14	0	14	Turpentine
Cobb	L.D. Yancey & Co.	19	0	34	4	57	Railroad grading
Coffee	Beach, Henderson & Co.	0	0	13	0	13	Turpentine
Coffee	W.W. Stewart & Bro.	1	0	19	0	20	Turpentine
Colquitt	Pinson & Williams	0	0	21	0	21	Turpentine
Decatur	T.J. Shingler & Bro.	0	0	60	0	60	Turpentine
Decatur	Hodges & Powell	1	0	19	0	20	Turpentine
Decatur	Callahan & Davis	0	0	23	0	23	Turpentine
Decatur	J.A. Carlton & Co.	0	0	9	0	9	Turpentine
Dougherty	Tenn. Fertilizer Co.	0	0	2	0	2	Fertilizer
Early	J.W. Callahan	0	0	52	0	52	Turpentine
Franklin	Little Brothers	0	0	4	0	4	Farming
Jeff Davis	A.T. Beach & Co.	0	0	10	0	10	Turpentine
Lowndes	**J.B.S. Holmes**	**0**	**0**	**1**	**0**	**1**	**Farming**

(continued)

Table 8.6—Continued

County	Worked by	WM	WF	BM	BF	Total	Employment
Miller	Bettie Hinson	1	0	13	0	14	Turpentine
Miller	T.J. Shingler Bros.	2	0	6	0	8	Turpentine
Miller	E.D. Hinson	0	0	9	0	9	Turpentine
Oglethorpe	J.M. Smith	4	0	22	0	26	Farming
Quitman	Eufaula Brick Co.	0	0	3	0	3	Brickmaking
Tift	So. Lumber Co.	0	0	10	1	11	Sawmilling
Thomas	Stetson Lumber Co.	0	0	5	0	5	Sawmilling
Thomas	Mills & Williams	0	0	25	5	30	Turpentine
Worth	T.J. Pinson	1	0	16	0	17	Turpentine
Worth	J.S. Betts & Co.	0	0	20	0	20	Farming
Worth	Oakfield N.S. Co.	0	0	16	1	17	Turpentine
Worth	C.A. Alford	0	0	11	0	11	Turpentine
TOTAL		34	0	486	13	533	
91.2% Black men and boys							
93.6% Black prisoners							

Source: *Ninth Annual Report of the Prison Commission of Georgia, 1906* (Atlanta: Lester Book & Stationery, 1906), 20–21.

The effect served as a moral panic that prompted new charges and new stories to appear. In early January 1907, U.S. commissioner E. C. Kinnebrew presided over a charge against George J. Cunningham, former sheriff of Georgia's Oglethorpe County, who, it was claimed, kept a Black woman, Mary Willingham, in custody for twelve years for a debt he claimed her father owed him. Attorney General Charles Joseph Bonaparte claimed to be revolted by the cases appearing in federal court and encouraged their continued prosecution.[8] Cunningham was acting outside of the penal systems of Georgia, but he was acting within a county that was mired in carceral politics. The county had a misdemeanor chain gang, a short-term felony chain gang, and a private misdemeanor lease camp in 1907. The slavery and bondage of Black lives and bodies was a regular part of life in Oglethorpe, surely contributing to Cunningham's behavior.

The Black male trend continued in 1907, as it had every year in the private misdemeanor lease system (see table 8.9). Based on the previous formula, there would have been roughly thirty-two estimated deaths in those camps. Meanwhile, the number of felony convict lessees was far more diverse than it was in the system's earlier years when there was a more

Table 8.7. Felony convict lease camps, 1907

Contractor	Location	Employment	Number
Stetson Lumber Co.	Arlington	Sawmilling	26
Babcock Bros. Lumber Co.	Babcock	Sawmilling	126
Bibb Brick Co.	Macon	Brickmaking	50
Cherokee Brick Co.	Macon	Brickmaking	50
Chattahoochee Brick Co.	Atlanta	Brickmaking	177
Cruger & Pace	Albany	Brickmaking	118
T. G. Culbreath	Tarver	Turpentine	25
Dorminy-Price Lumber Co.	Broxton	Sawmilling	63
Durham Coal & Coke Co.	Pittsburg	Coal mining	250
Flowers Lumber Co.	Jakin	Sawmilling	59
Flowers Bros. Lumber Co.	Blakely	Sawmilling	59
Georgia Iron & Coal Co.	Ferrobutte	Iron ore mining	74
G. S. Baxter & Co.	Fargo	Sawmilling, etc.	150
Dr. J. B. S. Holmes	**Lake Park**	**Farming**	**41**
Lookout Mt. Coal & Coke	Pittsburg	Coal mining	98
Milltown Lumber Co.	**Milltown**	**Sawmilling**	**92**
Palmer Brick Co.	Atlanta	Brickmaking	73
Royster Guano Co.	Macon	Manf'g guano	50
S. M. Stanley	**Valdosta**	**Turpentine**	**29**
H. Stevens & Sons Co.	Macon	Tile making	50
W. M. Toomer	Waycross	Turpentine	51
State Farm	Milledgeville	Farming (men)	121
State Farm	Milledgeville	Farming (women)	78
		TOTAL	1,910

Source: *Tenth Annual Report of the Prison Commission of Georgia, 1907* (Atlanta: Lester Book & Stationery, 1907), 19.

monopolist tendency. There were now 2,224 prisoners working on road-building chain gangs in the state. Lowndes had moved all of its misdemeanants to the county chain gang, but places like Oglethorpe stubbornly clung to several of the state's varied carceral systems and were awash in different forms of bound labor.

At the end of 1907, assistant attorney general Charles W. Russell submitted a "report on peonage" to Bonaparte that castigated the system: "State laws take various forms and are used in various ways to uphold peonage and other kinds of involuntary servitude." Vagrancy laws, contract or fraud laws, employment laws, and debt laws all played a role. All such

Table 8.8. Felony convict county road camps, 1907

County	Number of Convicts
Bibb	38
Burke	25
Clarke	14
Coffee	14
Coweta	20
Columbia	11
Dougherty	11
DeKalb	18
Elbert	17
Floyd	25
Fulton	109
Green	15
Jackson	20
Jefferson	15
Johnson	9
Jones	11
Laurens	24
Lee	8
Lincoln	6
McDuffie	9
Morgan	15
Monroe	18
Oglethorpe	14
Pulaski	17
Richmond	46
Spalding	15
Terrell	10
Walton	9
Wilkes	11
TOTAL	574

Notes: There were 2,484 felony prisoners in the state system and sixty-two deaths in 1907. There were 272 white men and boys, five white women and girls, 2,134 Black men and boys, and seventy-three Black women and girls.

85.8 percent Black men and boys

88.8 percent Black prisoners

Source: Tenth Annual Report of the Prison Commission of Georgia, 1907 (Atlanta: Lester Book & Stationery, 1907), 11–12, 20.

Table 8.9. County misdemeanor camps, 1907, divided into public and private camps

County	Worked by	WM	WF	BM	BF	Total	Employment
Public							
Baldwin	County	2	0	13	1	16	Road building
Berrien	County	1	0	14	1	16	Road building
Bartow	County	4	0	13	0	17	Road building
Bibb	County	1	0	61	6	68	Road building
Bullock	County	0	0	22	0	22	Road building
Burke	County	0	0	19	0	19	Road building
Clarke	County	1	0	34	0	35	Road building
Columbia	County	0	0	5	0	5	Road building
Coffee	County	1	0	9	0	10	Road building
Coweta	County	1	0	22	0	23	Road building
Chatham	County	10	0	163	72	245	Road building
Colquitt	County	0	0	14	0	14	Road building
Decatur	County	0	0	12	0	12	Road building
DeKalb	County	1	0	10	0	11	Road building
Dougherty	County	0	0	29	1	30	Road building
Early	County	0	0	10	2	12	Road building
Elbert	County	0	0	5	0	5	Road building
Effingham	County	0	0	12	0	12	Road building
Emanuel	County	1	0	15	1	17	Road building
Floyd	County	3	0	17	4	24	Road building
Fulton	County	18	0	311	30	359	Road building
Green	County	0	0	9	0	9	Road building
Glynn	County	7	0	36	6	49	Road building
Hancock	County	0	0	19	0	19	Road building
Irwin	County	2	0	27	3	32	Road building
Jackson	County	0	0	5	0	5	Road building
Jasper	County	0	0	12	0	12	Road building
Johnson	County	1	0	10	0	11	Road building
Jones	County	0	0	7	0	7	Road building
Jefferson	County	0	0	7	0	7	Road building
Laurens	County	0	0	20	0	20	Road building
Lee	County	0	0	17	0	17	Road building
Lowndes	**County**	**3**	**1**	**31**	**5**	**40**	**Road building**
Lincoln	County	0	0	3	0	3	Road building
McDuffie	County	0	0	10	0	10	Road building
Monroe	County	0	0	8	0	8	Road building
Morgan	County	0	0	10	0	10	Road building
Muscogee	County	4	0	40	4	48	Road building

(continued)

Table 8.9—Continued

County	Worked by	WM	WF	BM	BF	Total	Employment
Newton	County	1	0	19	0	20	Road building
Oglethorpe	County	0	0	6	0	6	Road building
Putnam	County	0	0	9	0	9	Road building
Pulaski	County	1	0	11	0	12	Road building
Randolph	County	0	0	9	0	9	Road building
Richmond	County	12	0	79	25	116	Road building
Sumter	County	0	0	25	4	29	Road building
Screven	County	0	0	12	0	12	Road building
Spalding	County	0	0	10	0	10	Road building
Taliaferro	County	0	0	9	0	9	Road building
Telfair	County	5	0	1	0	6	Road building
Terrell	County	0	0	29	0	29	Road building
Washington	County	1	0	17	0	18	Road building
Ware	County	0	0	35	0	35	Road building
Walton	County	0	0	11	0	11	Road building
Warren	County	0	0	12	0	12	Road building
Wilkes	County	0	0	7	0	7	Road building
Worth	County	1	0	18	2	21	Road building
TOTAL		82	1	1,400	167	1,650	

84.8% Black men and boys
95.0% Black prisoners

County	Worked by	WM	WF	BM	BF	Total	Employment
Private							
Appling	Walton Holton	0	0	6	0	6	Turpentine
Baker	Bowers & Kendall	0	0	20	0	20	Turpentine
Baker	McConnell Bros.	2	0	11	0	13	Turpentine
Bartow	Ga. Iron & Coal Co.	2	0	9	0	11	Mining ore
Calhoun	Stetson Lumber Co.	7	0	18	0	25	Sawmilling
Coffee	Beach, Henson & Co.	0	0	13	0	13	Turpentine
Coffee	W. W. Stewart & Bro.	2	0	16	0	18	Turpentine
Colquitt	Pinson & Williams	0	0	22	1	23	Turpentine
Colquitt	Corbett & Taylor	1	0	10	0	11	Sawmilling
Decatur	T. J. Shingler & Bro.	5	0	52	4	61	Turpentine
Decatur	Hodges & Powell	0	0	23	2	25	Turpentine
Decatur	Callahan & Davis	0	0	19	0	19	Turpentine
Decatur	Chattahoochee L. Co.	7	1	60	2	70	Sawmilling
Decatur	J. A. Carlton & Co.	5	0	23	0	28	Turpentine
Dougherty	G. B. D. McConnell	0	0	18	0	18	Turpentine
Franklin	Little Bros.	0	0	2	0	2	Farming

Jeff Davis	A. T. Beach & Co.	1	0	7	1	9	Turpentine
Miller	Comoly & Pinson	4	0	11	2	17	Turpentine
Miller	T. J. Shingler & Bro.	6	0	49	1	56	Turpentine
Miller	Whitehead Naval Co.	0	0	5	0	5	Turpentine
Oglethorpe	J. M. Smith	6	0	17	4	27	Farming
Quitman	Eufaula Brick Co.	0	0	3	0	3	Brickmaking
Tift	So. Lumber Co.	1	0	20	2	23	Sawmilling
Thomas	Mills & Williams	1	0	7	1	9	Turpentine
Turner	J. S. Betts & Co.	3	0	42	1	46	Farming
Ware	W. G. Hinson	0	0	5	0	5	Turpentine
Worth	T. J. Pinson	8	0	10	0	18	Turpentine
Worth	Westberry & Perry	1	0	14	0	15	Turpentine
Worth	I. H. Moree	0	0	19	0	19	Turpentine
Worth	Oakfield N. S. Co.	0	0	24	4	28	Turpentine
Worth	C. A. Alford	0	0	5	0	5	Turpentine
TOTAL		62	1	560	25	648	

86.4% Black men and boys
90.3% Black prisoners

Source: *Tenth Annual Report of the Prison Commission of Georgia, 1907* (Atlanta: Lester Book & Stationery, 1907), 21–22.

statutes "were not originally passed to enslave workmen, but in view of the use to which they are put, need amendment in order that they cannot be so abused." The laws "are used to threaten workmen, who have been defrauded into going to an employer by false reports as to the conditions of employment." Russell reported that "these laws have become a trap for the enslavement of white workmen as well as Black, and ought to be repealed, or amended with that fact in view." They had been "passed to force Negro laborers to work, but if so they are now affecting other persons, and the States formerly depending upon Negro laborers exclusively, need twice as many hands, and are resorting to every means to obtain them from Europe, directly or indirectly."[9] It was a play to a white audience to demonstrate the threat to more than just the Black population, despite the fact that the Black population was inordinately affected. The statement also foreshadowed one of the McRees' last-ditch efforts at maximizing free labor that would manifest years later.

Russell understood the incestuous nature of the various systems working in concert. "In Georgia and Florida I have investigated to some extent the connection between peonage and convict leasing, but not as fully as some other aspects of the subject of peonage or involuntary servitude." While he focused the bulk of his interest in Georgia on the area around Atlanta, his work in north Florida led him to "no longer doubt that there is some basis of truth in the statement, the convict lease system has led to this abuse: A prisoner is leased and sublet, and at the expiration of his term of imprisonment is not permitted to depart; in other words, after the law has finished with him he is held in involuntary servitude by the man who has leased him for, say $17.50 per month, or subleased him for two or three dollars more. The State gets no pay for the months he is thus detained, and the lessee gets his labor without having to pay anything." It was a horrifying ordeal, but one that Russell found to be all too common: "It is bad enough to be treated as a 'convict' for being out of work, or the like under the so-called 'vagrancy law,' and perhaps cruelly treated by 'the whipping boss,' but to be afterwards cheated out of one's liberty, when the ministers of justice have finished with their punishment, must be a bitter experience indeed."[10] It was galling morally, but the seeds of the death of the system were already sown in the subleasing practice. The state lost revenue when such subleasing occurred with felony prisoners, but it happened even more frequently to misdemeanor prisoners at the county level. The immorality of the system had not convinced Georgia officials to abandon its carceral project, but the combination of public pressure, federal investigations, and weakening profitability as a result of subleasing certainly could.

The next year, Russell served as the lead prosecutor in a case against four men accused of luring thousands of debt peons into virtual slavery, telling the press that he planned on calling five hundred witnesses to make his case. It was an issue that had finally made its way into the political mainstream. W. E. B. Du Bois, speaking at the annual Niagara Movement convention in 1909, decried the fact that "peonage and prejudice are used to keep our wages low, and education is proposed to fit us only for menial service." The following year he argued for the necessity of "the right of peace. The protection from force and violence in the prosecution of work, and this cannot be done until a stop is put to war and lynching, and peonage and wage slavery." In 1911, Republican New York senator Elihu Root decried peonage and lynching as core constituents of southern attempts to abrogate the Reconstruction Amendments.[11]

When William Howard Taft became president after Roosevelt, his own attorney general, George Woodward Wickersham, committed to the same vigorous prosecution of peonage cases and "the acts of cruelty and oppression which frequently mark" them. He singled out the South as "the chief support of peonage," which "lies in the peculiar system of laws prevailing in some of the southern states intended to compel personal service on the part of laborers." He would challenge "the constitutionality of such laws" whenever possible.[12]

There was also action on the subject in the federal legislature, as in December 1905, Pennsylvania Republican Edward Morrell introduced a bill in the House "to prohibit shanghaiing and peonage in the United States."[13] Hearings on the bill focused principally on a version of peonage performed on seafaring vessels, but the bill was clear in its intention to include the racialized forms of peonage present in the South. It was, in fact, exactly what many Progressive reformers in the South had been hoping for since the beginning of the century. It read, in part:

> Sec. 2. That every officer and employee of any railroad or mining company, and every Individual operating a railroad or private car line or mine within the United States or any of Its dependencies, who shall, by false promises or other fraudulent means, entice any person into any car or mine or mining camp or other place, and shall thereupon forcibly confine or detain such person, with intent to make him a slave or compel him to perform involuntary service of any kind, or deliver him into the custody of any other person or persons with like intent, and every person who shall knowingly aid or abet in such fraud, confinement, or detention, shall be guilty of a felony and be punished by Imprisonment of not less than ten years nor more than twenty years.
>
> Sec. 3. That any person within the jurisdiction of the United States who shall, under the pretext of any contract, covenant, or agreement, hold or attempt to hold or assist in holding, or combine or conspire with others to hold, any person in involuntary servitude to work out a debt or contract, or who shall combine or conspire with others to deprive any person of the liberty of contract, shall be guilty of a misdemeanor, and shall, upon conviction thereof, be punished by a fine not exceeding five thousand dollars or by imprisonment not exceeding five years, or by both, in the discretion of the court: *Provided, however,* That the provisions of this act shall not apply to public officers who, in their official capacities, hold persons to involuntary servitude for crime nor to private citizens whose acts are not in conflict with the thirteenth amendment of the Constitution of the United States.[14]

It was a bill that seemed to be a legitimate payoff on the work of federal district courts and prosecutors, but it would never receive a vote on the floor. In December 1907, Florida representative Frank Clark filed a bill "calling upon the Attorney-General for information regarding investigations of alleged peonage in Florida," but it too fell in committee. The following year, he sponsored a bill "providing for the appointment of a committee to investigate the charges of peonage in Florida and other Southern States." The House Judiciary Committee, however, gave the effort an adverse report.[15] It was clear that the appetite for action demonstrated by federal prosecutors and judges simply didn't exist in the halls of Congress, a body with a large contingent of white southerners, whose wealthiest constituents surely benefited from a penal apparatus designed to create profit rather than rehabilitation. And without Congress, whatever progress was made against the excesses of peonage and convict leasing would be necessarily limited.

Even if such statutes had made more federal headway, however, all of them neglected both felony convict leasing and the private misdemeanor camps that kept so many more in bondage under the guise of a legitimacy that was missed in the moral panic over debt peonage and kidnapping, an omission all the more problematic because of the permissive role that misdemeanor leasing played in allowing camps like Kinderlou to profit from both legal versions of peonage and the outright kidnapping of vulnerable Black residents in Georgia and north Florida. Peonage wouldn't end without toppling the apparatus that allowed it to continue, and Congress's inaction proved that such topplings would have to come from the states themselves.

9

The Death of Leasing in Georgia

Before the end of convict leasing in Georgia, the prison system was divided into state camps for long-term felony prisoners and private and public misdemeanor camps for those assumed to be serving short terms, where debt peons also went. Complaints arose from both institutions, but the misdemeanor camps generated the most documented problems, largely because of the corruption and lack of state supervision that often kept prisoners past their supposed date of release and put many in bondage who had never been convicted of a misdemeanor. Those misdemeanor camps tended to cluster in the south of the state, far from the home of government in Atlanta, and unsurprisingly abuse claims tended to be more frequent in that area. The 1895 and 1897 misdemeanor reports (see chapter 2) plainly described camps in the south as being demonstrably worse in conditions of clothing, food, shelter, and bathing facilities than their northern counterparts.[1] It was a reality made all the more problematic by the slow shift of private camps farther south over time.

Private misdemeanor camps were always more prevalent in the southern part of the state, in the turpentine belt that so relied on peonage and other forms of pseudo-slave practices. But that trend would only grow as the number of private misdemeanor camps increased over the years. At the same time, felony convict lease camps would also begin moving to the south and west, placing the bulk of state prisoners not in Milledgeville in the northeast but instead into a region much closer to Florida and Alabama.

There would always remain a line of felony camps running from Georgia's northwest corner to the coast above Savannah, but the general trend remained a slow trickle southward. The final year of the lease program would show a further clustering in the southwest, the heart of the turpentine belt, where similar combinations of both lease and debt peonage had come under such scrutiny in Alabama, Florida, Tifton, Georgia, and Kinderlou itself.

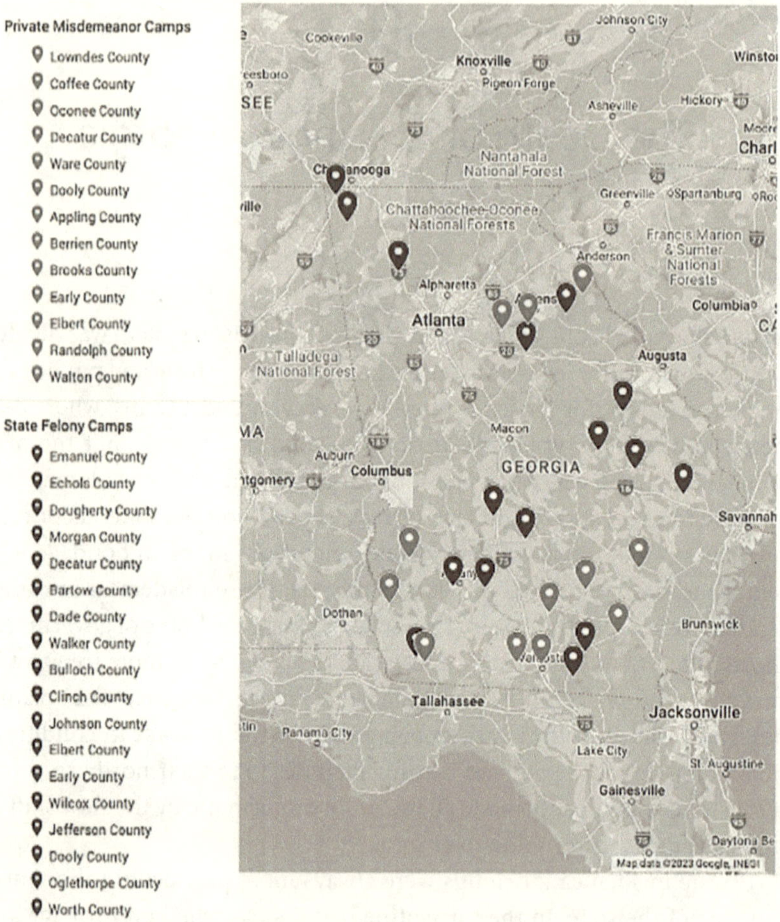
Private Misdemeanor Camps
Lowndes County
Coffee County
Oconee County
Decatur County
Ware County
Dooly County
Appling County
Berrien County
Brooks County
Early County
Elbert County
Randolph County
Walton County
State Felony Camps
Emanuel County
Echols County
Dougherty County
Morgan County
Decatur County
Bartow County
Dade County
Walker County
Bulloch County
Clinch County
Johnson County
Elbert County
Early County
Wilcox County
Jefferson County
Dooly County
Oglethorpe County
Worth County
Knoxville
Pigeon Forge
Asheville
Hickory
Nantahala National Forest
Chattahoochee-Oconee National Forests
Greenville
Spartanburg
Anderson
Francis Marion & Sumter National Forests
Alpharetta
Atlanta
Columbia
Augusta
Talladega National Forest
Macon
GEORGIA
Columbus
Auburn
Savannah
Dothan
Brunswick
Tallahassee
Jacksonville
Panama City
Lake City
St. Augustine
Gainesville
Map data ©2023 Google, INEGI

Map 9.1. The location of Georgia's private convict lease camps in 1898.

That the most violent and abusive area of the state would ultimately become the home of so many of the camps lamented at home by the Prison Commission and outside of Georgia by the Justice Department and national media was indicative of the lack of concern for Black lives demonstrated by an apparatus controlled at both the private and public levels by white men with economic interests built on Gilded Age corporate thinking and racial assumptions left over from the antebellum era and fed by Redeemer politics. It was almost as if the violence endemic in the felony and misdemeanor prison camps of south Georgia acted as a magnet for more and more prisoners, more and more would-be white entrepreneurs seeing

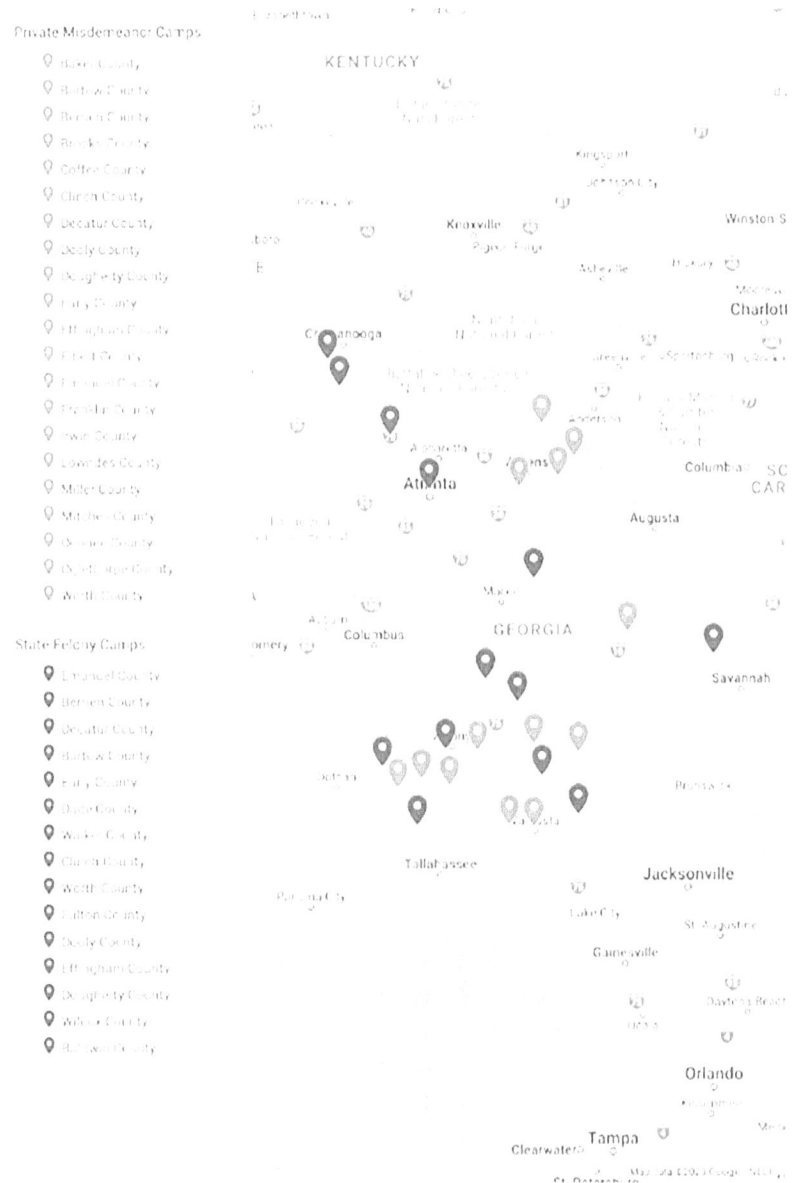

Map 9.2. The location of Georgia's private convict lease camps in 1902.

Map 9.3. The location of Georgia's private convict lease camps in 1908.

opportunity in the financial success of their neighbors and knowing that they could count on their counties to incarcerate enough people to keep the camps stocked with a cheap and continuous source of labor.

There were several reasons for that magnet phenomenon. First, the region was the farthest away from the oversight of the state Prison Commission in Atlanta, allowing for at least the perception of a freer hand with the policing of those incarcerated. Second, the turpentine belt of south Georgia and north Florida consumed bodies on both sides of the state line. The established norms of the industry were built on the work of prison labor, and so the growth of that industry in the early twentieth century led more entrepreneurs into the business using the model that had been established in the late nineteenth century. Finally, because the economy of the region depended on such operations, local law enforcement was more likely to look away from abuses of the incarcerated workers occupying those camps. Or, in the case of the McRees, law enforcement would at times actively collude with them to ensure a ready supply of labor.

The McRees, then, were exceptional, in that their abuses attracted federal attention in a way that most south Georgia camps did not. But the *Clyatt* case demonstrated that Kinderlou was not the only camp in the region engaging in kidnapping and other forms of barbarism. There was never, throughout the trials of 1901 or 1903, any public outcry from white residents of the region, no screeds from other camp owners that the behavior happening at Kinderlou or at Tifton was endangering their ability to continue the leasing practice. The McRees were a powerful family in Lowndes County, but they never had to overtly wield that power to maintain their operation. Law enforcement saw them as a convenient aid to racial control in the area; they didn't need to be convinced of the usefulness of Kinderlou as a mechanism of white supremacy. So the McRees may have been an outlier in the level of their brutality, but brutality itself—in Lowndes County and throughout the convict camps of south Georgia—was the norm.

Once the McRees' abuses of convict labor kept them from qualifying as a state camp and moved them to the misdemeanor category, they became representative of all the problems documented in legal challenges and national exposés. In 1906, however, when the state senate's penitentiary committee traveled Georgia to investigate the abuses reported in both state and misdemeanor camps, Ed McRee was part of the investigative group. That a state senator so compromised could be part of the committee demonstrated the lack of seriousness with which the legislature considered such problems. After one trip to a Decatur misdemeanor camp, the committee announced its indignation that the prisoners would be worked on a Sunday. "Now I think this working of convicts on Sunday is all wrong," said J. A. Bush of Miller County in faux outrage. Miller County was just northwest of Thomasville, another stronghold of timber and turpentine production in southwest Georgia.[2] The cruelty, abuse, and term expansion were not part of his critique, which instead remained solely focused on labor itself happening on Sunday. That kind of duplicity, combined with a willingness to include McRee on the penitentiary committee itself, just one year after the state senator faced federal charges related to kidnapping and real abuse at Kinderlou, was a harbinger that nothing would change as a result of the committee's investigative efforts. It served as a method of validating private misdemeanor leasing by creating a straw man to fight against, thus validating what investigators saw as an otherwise beneficial system, one that had largely avoided the national scrutiny of felony leasing and debt peonage.

But there were many in the state who believed that substantive change needed to happen, a continuation of the earlier Populist effort to end the practice in Georgia. Women were among the leaders of those pushing back against felony convict leasing in the Deep South. Julia Tutwiler of Alabama described the practice as "not only a disgrace" to the state "but a disgrace to civilization." She organized the Anti-Convict League to petition the Alabama state legislature for reform. Other groups in other states would follow her lead. In Georgia, the push was led by Rebecca Latimer Felton.[3] Felton was a former slaveowner, a forceful advocate for women's suffrage, and a white supremacist. She referred to African Americans seeking civil rights as "half-civilized gorillas" with a "brutal lust" for white women. She mused fondly about the antebellum South and its slave system. In a speech to the Georgia State Agricultural Society in 1898, she argued for an increase in lynching to protect white women: "When there is not enough religion in the pulpit to organize a crusade against sin; nor justice in the court house to promptly punish crime; nor manhood enough in the nation to put a sheltering arm about innocence and virtue—if it needs lynching to protect woman's dearest possession from the ravening human beasts—then I say lynch, a thousand times a week if necessary." After the infamous lynching of Sam Hose in 1899—wherein a Coweta County man was murdered by a mob after killing his employer and being accused of raping his employer's wife—she celebrated the act and argued that any "true-hearted husband or father" would have gladly lynched the supposed rapist. Despite her racism, however, she saw convict leasing as a blight on the state, interpreting it as overly cruel and unfair to prisoners. It seemed an incongruous position for a racist of Felton's stripe, but her advocacy against convict leasing came from the same place as did her advocacy for women's suffrage. When she believed something was unfair, she railed against it. And her overt racism, counterintuitive as it may have been, surely helped her credibility in the fight to end prisoner leasing, as it would be impossible for anyone to charge her with race traitorism.[4]

But there were others less vested in the racial status quo who also made a public move against the practice. Loud Black voices railed against forced bondage, for example, led by Ben Davis, publisher of the *Atlanta Independent*. "Reform legislation used to mean remedial and helpful legislation for all the people, and special privileges to none," he wrote in 1907, "but under the present regime at the state capitol it means special favors for white people and the downright outlawry of the Black man's rights." Davis had crusaded against felony convict leasing since at least 1906 and remained a constant thorn in the side of white legislators in Atlanta.[5] Momentum also began building to repeal convict leasing from the state's white media, which had a broader understanding of the reputational damage done by the abuses of the system than individual citizens. The *Atlanta Georgian*, in particular, began a crusade in July 1908 for the termination of the practice: "It is the full purpose of the Georgian to bring from day to day the full light of publicity on the system, not only for the benefit of the readers of this paper, but also for the information of members of the Legislature who are interested in the welfare of their state." The note came accompanied with daily front-page descriptions of reported abuses in convict leasing.[6]

Or, felony convict leasing. Misdemeanor leasing still occupied a place in the shadows of public reporting on leasing, so it never became a constituent part of screeds against the practice. In a pragmatic sense, however, it didn't need to be. The death of private leasing would not only end the felony practice constantly on the tips of state pens, but it would also wipe away its misdemeanor offshoot by default. Kill the head and the body will die.

In response to the publicity, a similar effort to investigate state convict camps in particular was undertaken by a Georgia House of Representatives now decidedly more resolute in its opposition to the practice, which led in July 1908 to a bill that would outlaw felony convict leasing sponsored by investigatory committee chairman John Holder of Jackson. The investigation was concerned in particular with mismanagement and abuse, tasking investigators with seeking out any violation of state contracts or cruelty to resident prisoners. The committee was also concerned, however, with human trafficking, seeking whether any state employee was "receiving or has received any emolument, money, compensation, gift or gratuity from the working, trafficking in or controlling of convicts," whether any warden had received such trafficking kickbacks, or whether lessees themselves were engaging in such behavior regardless of state complicity.[7]

The McRees were not part of the official investigation, even though Kinderlou was again an official felony convict lease camp by 1908. But though Kinderlou avoided investigation, probably through the influence of Ed McRee, the committee did send investigators to several other convict lease camps nearby, and transcripts of interviews with the investigators demonstrated a normalized, routinized lack of concern for prisoners among those tasked with their care in south Georgia. At the Pinson and Williams private misdemeanor lease camp in nearby Colquitt County, just miles from Kinderlou, the commissary had no food and the bedding "was poor and very filthy." They kept no formal records to be examined. Another camp in Colquitt County, just to the north of Brooks and to the northeast of Lowndes, "was the worst camp that we visited." Prisoners were sleeping on the wires of bunks in lieu of mattresses.[8]

An employee at a camp in nearby Cordele (one not listed in the Prison Commission report) testified to the committee that state warden Jake C. Moore demanded a two-hundred-dollar payoff after "inspecting" the camp, refusing a check because "Jake was too smart for that." Instead he "wanted him to go and draw the money out of the bank and give him the cash." The payoff kept Moore from reporting, among other things, on the cruelties that went on at the camp. One of the most vicious overseers there dealt with a Black convict whose ankle was swollen at the shackle that bound it. The overseer "called a trustee that was down there and had him to chain Woodson's other leg up to a bar in the building windows so as to rest all of the weight of the boy's body on this foot; and he kept the man standing on that foot as long as I was in the room. I was in the room 15 or 20 minutes. The negro was standing on that foot. The doctor reported, recommended not whipping the negro, but he was whipped."[9]

At the Milltown lumber camp in Valdosta, a manager admitted to working those convicted of felonies from sunup to sundown without the required two hours rest and often working them at night against restrictions. He admitted to whipping between seven and fifteen prisoners per month.[10] The stories in and around Lowndes County were matched by hundreds more across the state, creating a portrait of a system built on abuse, graft, and violent white supremacy.[11] While the McRees were not named, the stories were representative of the kinds of abuses practiced on the plantation. The one difference in the accounts, perhaps, was that all of the reported prisoners in the legislative investigation were at least there legally, while many at Kinderlou were victims of kidnapping. The testimonies made clear, however, that by whatever means one entered the system, it was one built on a foundation of cruelty and exploitation.

That being the case, the report produced by the committee was damning. State warden Moore, who had been tasked with investigating conditions at the camps since the founding of the state Prison Commission, had "negotiated a number of deals between convict labor lessees for the transfer of lease contracts, receiving compensation" of at least $2,700. "We are utterly unable to conceive how a high-minded State official could close his eyes to the impropriety and reprehensibility of such conduct." But the state itself was also part of the problem. The office of state warden had been invented by the commission, not by state statute, and commission salaries were capped at $100 per month. Moore received his one-hundred-dollar monthly salary as warden, then also received an additional forty dollars per month to inspect the misdemeanor convict camps, a salary that was "improper, illegal, and without authority of law." If that weren't enough, Moore was also a business partner of W. B. Hamby, the state's largest lessee of felony convict labor, co-owned several properties that used convict labor in conjunction with Hamby, and by the time of his resignation was in debt to Hamby. The Prison Commission knew of the relationship but did nothing about it.[12]

Then there were the deputy wardens down the chain of command, "practically all" of whom, "while in the employ of the State and paid as such, received salaries or compensation from the lessees, in one or more instances nearly twice as much as paid by the State." Even the physicians and guards were guilty of taking kickbacks, all with the knowledge of the Prison Commission. In one instance, the commission told one state physician that his salary would be reduced and suggested that he correspond with a lessee whose prison farm he monitored to make up the difference. "There is no excuse which can palliate such conduct in State officials," the report noted in unabashed frustration. "No mere man can serve two masters with conflicting interests. This is the truth of God, as well as human experience. The evidence before us conclusively proves that deputy wardens are not exceptions, and many of the violations of rules and abuses of convicts, clearly established by the evidence, are due to the existence and universal practice of this pernicious custom."[13]

None of those the House investigating committee interviewed admitted to trafficking in prisoners for individual profit, but the investigators were unconvinced, noting that in March 1904, J. M. Strickland, who was a candidate for the Prison Commission that year, charged that "both wardens and guards were receiving money from lessees and that he could substantiate the charge." Strickland was a "reputable citizen," and yet the Prison Commission never investigated, a sin of omission that surely demonstrated knowledge that the charges would have been substantiated. In addition, the conflicts of interest and extra payments to the state warden and his deputies provided them with direct monetary benefit if any of the lessees did in fact traffic illegally in human beings. Lessees were also shown to regularly work employees past the term of indenture, as well as work them on Sundays, and most of them were paying deputy wardens some kind of compensation.[14]

Charges of cruelty were even more plentiful. The investigators "believe from the evidence that charges of cruelty are well founded," but "the truth is, we deem it almost impossible to secure evidence of cruelties." It was largely word against word, as no recorded evidence existed. The committee chronicled cases of brutality nonetheless, emphasizing instances where leased felony prisoners died, because death itself was a form of evidence unavailable in word against word situations. Investigators found less evidence of abuse in misdemeanor county road camps, but abuse still existed despite fewer deaths to provide concreteness to any charges, and the investigators virtually ignored the notorious private misdemeanor camps altogether. The state prison farm at Milledgeville and the Georgia State Reformatory were also being corruptly mismanaged.[15]

The report was a damning indictment of the leasing system as constructed in the early twentieth century, one whose scars drew an obvious scarlet letter on the use and abuse of prisoners for both felony and misdemeanor convictions. But its revelations were not the only reasons that legislators sought to modify the system. Significantly, the 1904 fiscal year, one wherein the McRees had come under scrutiny for all of the problems cited in the 1908 report, was the first that Georgia's convict scheme failed to turn a profit, losing more than $10,000. That would become the norm in the years to come, the system only bringing in more than it doled out in the 1906 fiscal year. For all of the pressure for reform, the models of abandoning convict leasing provided by its fellow former Confederate states, and the description of corruption and abuse cited in the investigative report, another clear motivation for modifying the state's convict plan was its lack of any substantial profitability for the state.[16]

Meanwhile, the 1908 Prison Commission report, the results of which had to be questioned because of the revelatory payoff information provided by the legislative finds, emphasized what it interpreted as the success of felony convict labor on county roads and the public county misdemeanor camps intended for the same purpose, doing its best to act as a counter to the legislature's investigation. Even in that climate, however, the commission used the supposed success of chain gangs to make another in a long line of cases against private misdemeanor camps. They were illegal, and their operation in "open and notorious violation" of the law "brings into disre-

Table 9.1. Felony convict lease camps, 1908

Contractor	Location	Employment	Number
Ashley-Price Lumber Co.	Douglas	Sawmilling	50
Stetson Lumber Co.	Arlington	Sawmilling	43
Babcock Bros. Lumber Co.	Babcock	Sawmilling	134
Bibb Brick Co.	Macon	Brickmaking	50
Cherokee Brick Co.	Macon	Brickmaking	49
Chattahoochee Brick Co.	Atlanta	Brickmaking	172
Cruger & Pace	Albany	Brickmaking	99
T. G. Culbreath	Tarver	Turpentine	26
Dorminy-Price Lumber Co.	Broxton	Sawmilling	40
Durham Coal & Coke Co.	Pittsburg	Coal Mining	234
Flowers Lumber Co.	Jakin	Sawmilling	61
Flowers Bros. Lumber Co.	Blakely	Sawmilling	60
Georgia Iron & Coal Co.	Ferrobutte	Iron ore mining	77
G. S. Baxter & Co.	Fargo	Sawmilling, etc.	151
Dr. J. B. S. Holmes	**Lake Park**	**Farming**	**55**
Lookout Mt. Coal & Coke	Pittsburg	Coal Mining	104
Milltown Lumber Co.	**Milltown**	**Sawmilling**	**101**
Palmer Brick Co.	Atlanta	Brickmaking	44
Royster Guano Co.	Macon	Manf'g guano	52
S. M. Stanley	**Valdosta**	**Turpentine**	**29**
H. Stevens & Sons Co.	Macon	Tile Making	50
Muscogee Brick Co.	Columbus	Brickmaking	40
Southern Lumber Co.	Tifton	Turpentine	25
State Farm	Milledgeville	Farming (men)	129
State Farm	Milledgeville	Farming (women)	74
		TOTAL	1,949

Source: *Eleventh Annual Report of the Prison Commission of Georgia, 1908* (Atlanta: Lester Book & Stationery, 1908), 23.

pute the State's entire penal system." If the private camps were to remain, the commission argued, then "legalize the contracts," provide the necessary restrictions "as will protect the convict, and insure him humane and proper treatment." There was not in 1908 and there had never been proper local supervision over private misdemeanor lessees, a basic aspect even of the felony convict leasing whose corruption had just been laid bare.[17] There was in the commission's rhetoric, presented as it was in the dying days of its long-standing felony system, an attempt to scapegoat private misdemeanor camps as a method of elevating the legitimacy of felony convict leasing, but there were also all the hallmarks of previous reports bemoaning the system that the commission had long interpreted as a violation of law.

Its report acknowledged that "many officers are unfortunately, more or less, dependent upon the fund realized from the hire of misdemeanor convicts for their fees," and so suggested that legalizing "the hiring under proper restrictions would still insure the payment of such fees." The counties could also charge the other counties a fair market price for misdemeanants hired for use on roads and, in the process, make up for the loss of school fund money they willingly forewent by accepting felony road workers without paying into the state coffers.[18] The proposal was the first time that the commission suggested legalizing and regulating the private misdemeanor camps rather than demanding their elimination, a product of the stress on the felony system that would soon end in its own elimination. If felony leasing disappeared, so too would misdemeanor leasing, so why not validate the former by suggesting the latter get in line with its dictates, making felony leasing the model of good government over and against an abused and abusive system.

It was in this final year of felony and misdemeanor convict leasing that the private misdemeanor camps did not hold the highest percentage of Black men in bondage, replaced by the chain gangs that would supplant them the following year (see table 9.3). But even with a reduced number of privately leased misdemeanants, the estimated death toll would still have been roughly forty-one people.

There were 2,486 prisoners, both felony prisoners and misdemeanants, engaged in chain gang labor, by far the largest subsection of prisoners in Georgia's system, continuing a trend that had been developing since 1905. And so representative John Holder's bill in response to the legislative investigation would allocate prisoners proportionally based on county population for road work and other infrastructure projects, further developing the existing trend. "Any county desiring more than its share can take them from the counties not desiring to work their own allotment at a fixed price," Holder wrote. Then "all remaining shall be leased to the highest bidder for a period of five years, with the right reserved to the state of terminating the lease at the end of one year if so desired." A rival bill in the state Senate, sponsored by Thomas Felder, limited convict leasing terms to eighteen months, at which point they would be employed on state road work. A third bill, this one competing with Holder's in the House, mandated the "immediate abolishing of the convict lease system" in favor of using state

Table 9.2. Felony convict county road camps, 1908

County	Number of convicts
Bibb	43
Burke	27
Clarke	18
Coweta	24
Columbia	11
Dougherty	12
DeKalb	21
Elbert	18
Floyd	31
Fulton	110
Green	15
Jackson	23
Jefferson	16
Johnson	10
Jones	12
Laurens	24
Lee	11
Lincoln	6
McDuffie	10
Morgan	14
Monroe	19
Oglethorpe	17
Pulaski	18
Richmond	56
Spalding	16
Terrell	11
Walton	11
Wilkes	11
TOTAL	615

Source: *Eleventh Annual Report of the Prison Commission of Georgia, 1908* (Atlanta: Lester Book & Stationery, 1908), 24.

prisoners on state road construction projects. W. A. Covington of Colquitt, one of the bill's sponsors, argued that the current system was "infamous and a blot on the fair name of the state." He compared convict leasing to Russian serfdom or the horrors of the Spanish Inquisition. While the bills proposed different solutions to the problems of felony convict leasing, all shared a willingness to continue using prisoners as a wellspring of free la-

Table 9.3. County misdemeanor camps, 1908, divided into public and private camps

County	Worked by	WM	WF	BM	BF	Total	Employment
Public							
Appling	County	1	0	1	0	2	Road building
Baldwin	County	0	0	11	1	12	Road building
Berrien	County	0	0	17	0	17	Road building
Bartow	County	0	0	17	0	17	Road building
Bibb	County	3	0	88	5	96	Road building
Bulloch	County	1	0	34	0	35	Road building
Burke	County	0	0	18	0	18	Road building
Ben Hill	County	0	0	8	0	8	Road building
Calhoun	County	0	0	20	0	20	Road building
Clarke	County	3	0	23	8	34	Road building
Columbia	County	0	0	8	0	8	Road building
Clinch	County	1	0	5	0	6	Road building
Coweta	County	0	0	29	0	29	Road building
Chatham	County	7	0	161	60	228	Road building
Colquitt	County	1	0	31	0	32	Road building
Decatur	County	0	0	28	0	28	Road building
DeKalb	County	3	0	21	0	24	Road building
Dougherty	County	4	0	34	0	38	Road building
Early	County	0	0	11	0	11	Road building
Elbert	County	0	0	3	0	3	Road building
Effingham	County	2	0	9	0	11	Road building
Emanuel	County	0	0	15	0	15	Road building
Floyd	County	8	0	17	9	34	Road building
Fulton	County	15	0	336	34	385	Road building
Green	County	1	0	7	0	8	Road building
Glynn	County	1	0	47	5	53	Road building
Hancock	County	0	0	15	0	15	Road building
Irwin	County	1	0	10	0	11	Road building
Jackson	County	0	0	7	0	7	Road building
Jasper	County	1	0	13	0	14	Road building
Jenkins	County	0	0	19	0	19	Road building
Johnson	County	0	0	13	0	13	Road building
Jones	County	0	0	6	0	6	Road building
Jefferson	County	1	0	13	1	15	Road building
Laurens	County	0	0	10	0	10	Road building
Lee	County	0	0	8	0	8	Road building
Lowndes	**County**	**2**	**0**	**23**	**2**	**27**	**Road building**
Lincoln	County	0	0	7	0	7	Road building
McDuffie	County	0	0	7	0	7	Road building

Miller	County	0	0	8	0	8	Road building
Monroe	County	2	0	10	0	12	Road building
Morgan	County	1	0	12	0	13	Road building
Muscogee	County	4	0	41	3	48	Road building
Newton	County	1	0	21	1	23	Road building
Oglethorpe	County	0	0	12	0	12	Road building
Putnam	County	2	0	11	1	14	Road building
Pulaski	County	2	0	9	0	11	Road building
Randolph	County	0	0	8	0	8	Road building
Richmond	County	16	0	72	0	88	Road building
Sumter	County	0	0	48	0	48	Road building
Screven	County	1	0	21	0	22	Road building
Spalding	County	2	0	16	0	18	Road building
Taliaferro	County	0	0	8	0	8	Road building
Telfair	County	0	0	14	0	14	Road building
Terrell	County	0	0	19	0	19	Road building
Thomas	County	0	0	48	0	48	Road building
Turner	County	1	0	7	0	8	Road building
Washington	County	1	0	29	1	31	Road building
Ware	County	0	0	35	0	35	Road building
Walton	County	0	0	13	0	13	Road building
Warren	County	0	0	17	0	17	Road building
Wilkes	County	0	0	4	0	4	Road building
Worth	County	0	0	18	0	18	Road building
TOTAL		89	0	1,651	131	1,871	

88.2% Black men and boys
95.2% Black prisoners

County	Worked by	WM	WF	BM	BF	Total	Employment
Private							
Appling	Beecher & Varnadoe	0	0	8	0	8	Turpentine
Baker	Bowers & Kendall	0	0	18	1	19	Turpentine
Baker	McConnell Bros.	2	0	14	0	16	Turpentine
Calhoun	Stetson Lumber Co.	0	0	18	0	18	Sawmilling
Coffee	W. W. Stewart & Bro.	4	0	19	0	23	Turpentine
Coffee	Riverside Brick Co.	0	0	12	0	12	Brickmaking
Coffee	D. B. Gray	0	0	12	0	12	Turpentine
Coffee	A. B. Fisher & Co.	4	0	30	1	35	Turpentine
Colquitt	Pinson & Williams	3	0	18	0	21	Turpentine

(continued)

Table 9.3—Continued

County	Worked by	WM	WF	BM	BF	Total	Employment
Decatur	T. J. Shingler & Bro.	6	0	55	2	63	Turpentine
Decatur	Hodges & Powell	0	0	10	0	10	Turpentine
Decatur	Chattahoochee L. Co.	9	1	63	1	74	Sawmilling
Decatur	G. L. Davis	0	0	7	0	7	Turpentine
Decatur	Ball Naval Store Co.	4	0	30	1	35	Turpentine
Dougherty	G. B. McConnell	3	0	17	0	20	Turpentine
Franklin	Little Brothers	0	0	6	0	6	Farming
Jeff Davis	A. T. Beach & Co.	1	0	11	0	12	Turpentine
Mitchell	Ball Naval Store Co.	0	0	14	0	14	Turpentine
Oglethorpe	J. M. Smith	9	0	31	3	43	Farming
Oconee	J. D. Price	0	0	5	0	5	Farming
Thomas	Mills & Williams	0	0	5	0	5	Turpentine
Turner	J. S. Betts & Co.	3	0	35	0	38	Sawmilling
Worth	M. G. Dupree	0	0	8	0	8	Turpentine
Worth	J. D. Bridges	0	0	17	0	17	Turpentine
Worth	T. J. Fowler	7	0	12	0	19	Turpentine
Worth	Conly & Pinson	2	0	19	0	21	Turpentine
TOTAL		57	1	494	9	561	

88.1% Black men and boys
89.7% Black prisoners

Source: Eleventh Annual Report of the Prison Commission of Georgia, 1908 (Atlanta: Lester Book & Stationery, 1908), 25–26.

bor for the public good, seemingly ignoring the localized problems and brutality that had nothing specifically to do with the structure of the existing system itself. All plans, in fact, proposed moving felony prisoners into the kinds of county work that had created so much controversy over the previous years.[19]

Ultimately, the legislature crafted a system that looked similar to Holder's original formulation combined with Covington's all-out ban on private leasing of felony prisoners. Counties would be allotted felony prisoners for work on roads, bridges, or other public works projects based on population. If some counties needed or wanted fewer or no prisoners, they would be apportioned to those counties who might need them. If there were prisoners left over, municipalities would be able to hire them from the Prison

Commission for $100 per capita per annum. The new bill provided measures to keep wardens, deputy wardens, inspectors, guards, or physicians from profiting in any way from the work of prisoners and provided increased oversight in an attempt to solve some of the problems in the report. If the county's misdemeanants were not already apportioned to a public works chain gang, they would have to be so encumbered. They were not to be leased to private corporations or entities. Thus it was that the state eliminated private lessees and marshaled the work of both felony and misdemeanor prisoners in service to the state, particularly emphasizing county and state roads and bridges, a program that promised to maintain much of the abuse embedded in the former system, because the only real change was the private holding of state felony convict camps. Misdemeanor road camps would continue to house prisoners for hard work on public works, and public works projects would still require a continuous flow of free labor to complete.[20] Camps like those of the McRees would necessarily lose the ability to house convict labor, because their tasks were not related to public infrastructure, but debt peonage would keep them flush with available workers. This meant that for the majority of misdemeanor prisoners, the new system would provide no relief, no substantive change at all.

The September 1908 legislation that officially ended convict leasing tasked all misdemeanor and felony male prisoners with eligibility to be used by "the several counties and municipalities upon the public roads, bridges and other public works." A county could also, with the blessing of the Prison Commission, "deliver its quota of felony convicts and also its misdemeanor convicts, if it so desires, to another county, to be used in the construction and repair of public roads, bridges or other public works." If there were prisoners left over after such distributions, the Prison Commission could distribute them among the counties as needed. Counties could also maintain a farm to house its working prisoners, "and all products and supplies arising from said farm shall be used in the support of the convicts, improvement of its public roads, bridges and other public works, and in support of the county institutions." The law ensured that the Prison Commission would still have final oversight over all such labor and had the right to inspect camps and farms run by counties as it saw fit, something the commission had been demanding for a decade. In every other way, however, the system looked much the same as its predecessor, with counties running the farms rather than private entities like the McRees. The private leasing of those convicted of felonies and those convicted of misdemeanors would end, but everything else would remain much the same.[21]

There was also a gendered component to the new legislation. "If the convict be a female, the presiding judge may, in his discretion, sentence her to confinement and labor in the woman's prison on the State Farm in lieu of a chain gang sentence, not to exceed twelve months." It was an out for certain women, but the caveat demonstrated that if judges so chose, they were allowed to put women they didn't deem worthy of the segregated State Farm to chain gang labor as well. Which is to say that Black women were eminently vulnerable to the chain gang, the only thing protecting them being a lower rate of incarceration and an assumption of female inability to do the kind of heavy lifting required of chain gang public works labor. As Sarah Haley has demonstrated, the Georgia chain gang system's gender provisions after 1908 were only designed to cordon off white womanhood for something other than hard labor. "Black women's labor was profoundly flexible, the absence of a normative gendered subject position making it possible for authorities to force them to labor on both sides of the gender divide; the Jim Crow carceral regime replicated slavery's gendered economic logic." In 1878, for example, ten years after convict leasing was instituted, Georgia had thirty-four Black women in the system. It was a gender ratio that would be reversed in later litigation, as the most harrowing examples of abuse would come from the voices of Black women.[22]

The federal push for road construction began in 1893 with the Office of Public Road Inquiries, which encouraged a "Good Roads Movement," but Georgia's movement actually began two years prior, with its 1891 Good Roads Law levying a tax for funding the development of a nascent road infrastructure and allowing the use of chain gangs of misdemeanor prisoners to build them. And they did. By the end of the decade, more than eight hundred misdemeanor prisoners were employed on Georgia's roads. The problem with the system as it developed in the early years of the decade was that misdemeanor prisoners, serving between thirty days and twelve months, had little time to actually build roads after the time it took to train them in the needed skills. At the same time, many counties chose to farm out those misdemeanants to private camps to generate revenue instead of building roads. In 1895, for example, the U.S. Department of Agriculture's Office of Road Inquiry held a national conference on the progress of road construction, and they held it in Atlanta. The hosts described for their national audience the great benefits of convict labor to build roads. Judge W. F. Eve, presenting the report for Georgia, extolled the virtues of misdemeanor convict labor, telling his audience that "there is a very general spirit throughout the State among those interested in road improvement to have the legislature place our penitentiary convicts upon the roads," as well. In a 1902 series of forums on roads in the southern states, Georgia representatives worried in particular about rural roads, as an influx of white rural citizens into cities left many counties poor and unprepared for infrastructure. It was the kind of problem that more incarcerated individuals could solve, enough to feed both the private and public systems.[23]

As a remedy, the state passed a new law in 1903, which allowed those convicted of felonies with sentences of five years or less to be included in the pool. S. W. McCallie, state geologist of Georgia, made the case that it was the success of this new venture that ultimately pushed the legislature to end formal convict leasing by law in 1908 and practice in 1909. It was, in this view, the success of felony convict labor on state projects rather than a moral imperative or response to reform advocates that ended the practice. Georgia simply saw a better economic incentive in using forced felony labor for itself. When the new convict law took effect on April 1, 1909, 1,641 felony prisoners and 550 misdemeanor prisoners were transferred from private hands to that of county public works directors.[24]

That 1903 law also reorganized the state penitentiary and put it under the control of the Prison Commission, led by Clement A. Evans, an elderly Civil War veteran who was respected but senile. That senility allowed the second-in-command, Secretary Goodloe Yancy, to run the system as his own private fiefdom. As Dan T. Carter has explained, "the prison administration was a refuge for incompetents, who were protected by their political friends." Nepotism in hiring led to unqualified guards and alcoholic wardens.[25] It also left real historical doubt about the official prisoner counts and low death totals in annual commission reports.

McCallie's interpretation was optimistic in the extreme. While public works and the need for infrastructure labor was a real contributor to carceral reform decision-making, it was not the only contributor. Protests against convict leasing had been happening in Georgia since the program's inception. They became even more fervent in 1906 when Abe Winn, a sixteen-year-old white convict, was whipped to death at the Durham Coal Company camp. The 1908 legislative session was to begin on August 25. In the summer leading to its meeting, labor organizers, the Methodist ministers of Atlanta, and the Georgia Farmers Union all came out in opposition to convict leasing. Even Ben Jones, president of the Bibb County Good Roads Association, argued that convict leasing should end. On August 2, protest meetings against the system took place across the state. The Atlanta meeting adopted a resolution that referred to convict leasing as "a crime against God, a blot on the civilization of the south."[26] It was that climate into which the legislature stepped, ending convict leasing but replacing it with an elaboration of the existing chain gang road system that would bring felony and misdemeanor prisoners under the same umbrella and continue for decades.

Matthew Mancini, however, has argued that such protests were the background accompaniment to more immediate economic issues that ultimately ended the system. As the nineteenth century ran its course, he argues, the sheer number of prisoners grew rapidly; the sentences became longer and the white prisoners virtually disappeared from the system. After 1899, "profits diminished, and private citizens had less of an incentive to manage so unsavory a population," particularly with a prison population expanding exponentially during the existence of convict lease. And in its last years, the prices for the labor of those incarcerated people counterintuitively rose dramatically. Exacerbating such realities, a 1907 economic depression left many potential convict labor projects shuttered, leaving lessees with a crew for whom they had no meaningful work. By that time, Jim Crow segregation had been established, full disfranchisement of the Black population was in the process of becoming complete—the final act of the 1908 general assembly's regular session had been a disfranchisement law—and for a decade better roads programs had demonstrated the effectiveness of the chain gang. When combined with the economic burden on those leasing prisoners and the special session of the legislature, prefaced by public criticism and defined by the damning report of the general assembly's Convict Investigating Committee, the end of the process in Georgia was almost a fait accompli.[27]

Mancini's analysis is, for the most part, right. The state was annually losing money on the felony lease system in its final years. But many counties remained opposed to its end because there was still an overt private demand for misdemeanants that could supplement county revenues. Because the state revenue took precedence in this case, and because of the continuing peonage claims in courts around the state and nation and the complicity of misdemeanor leasing in the abuse of debt peons in misdemeanor camp settings, the voices of county elites and the officials who served them lost out to reformers hoping to use incarcerated people for low-cost infrastructure projects and to remove the negative reputation that Georgia had accrued over the past two decades of violent and embarrassing carceral politics.

Under the newly established system, the Prison Commission engaged with the counties each February, with authorities making requests for a given number of incarcerated individuals, which were then dispersed annually through a prorated system based on total county population. Technically, the prisoners remained under the supervision of the Prison Commission, but the day-to-day expenses of their housing, feeding, and clothing was the responsibility of the counties. McCallie was very pleased with the system and its results, but among his recommendations for future development was the creation of a state Highway Commission that was separate from the Prison Commission, thereby putting infrastructure decisions in the hands of road experts rather than prison officials. It was a plan the state would ultimately adopt in its evolving attempt at balance between the need for infrastructure and the legacy of free Black labor.[28]

In 1916, seven years after the end of Georgia's convict lease program, the Federal Aid Road Act provided federal money for rural road construction. Under the new law, the federal government would pay half the cost of such projects, but since Georgia's constitution prohibited state money being used for internal improvement—part of the small government impetus still left over, like the use of Black convict labor, from the antebellum era—that task fell to counties themselves. But the counties targeted by the program were extremely poor, one of the reasons being that they were rural and without roads, the point of the program in the first place. That being the case, the government allowed counties in Georgia to meet their share of the cost by supplying free convict labor rather than actual dollars. By 1932, Georgia had produced more federally assisted road miles than any other southern state, receiving nearly $34 million in government aid to do so.[29]

And so Georgia abolished convict leasing, both felony and misdemeanor, and directed prison authorities to contract with counties for use of convict labor on road construction, creating a decentralized system with little state oversight for the conduct of overseers of chain gangs and for the work they actually did. "This was practically a return to chaos," Blake McKelvy explained in 1934, "for, what with chains, dogs, and guns, an absence of inspection, and frequently a scarcity of provisions, life in these chain gangs was often more desperate than in the worst camps of the old lease system."[30] Convict leasing, argues Mancini, "is best understood not as part of the history of prisons but as part of the elaborate social system of racial subordination which had previously been assured by the practice of slavery."[31]

The ability of peonage to survive such purges was on display in Alabama when yet another in a long line of cases before the Alabama Supreme Court—at the same time that Georgia was formally ending its convict lease system—prompted Oswald Garrison Villard to again correspond with his friend Booker T. Washington. "This is precisely the kind of a case for which I want my endowed 'Committee for the Advancement of the Negro Race,'" he told Washington. "Sooner or later, we must get that committee going."[32] Villard would do so the following February but would tap Washington's rival W. E. B. Du Bois to help with the creation of what would become the National Association for the Advancement of Colored People (NAACP) rather than his confidant from Alabama.[33]

In October 1909, just months after the creation of the new civil rights group, Will Postell was captured in Florida and carried back to Valdosta. He had escaped from the McRees' convict camp in the 1880s and had spent the last fifteen years on the run. It was a demonstration of the temporal reach of convict leasing, even after it was outlawed by Georgia. Postell's sentence was originally thought to be the common twelve-month misdemeanor term, and as he had escaped after six months at Kinderlou, there was discussion of someone in Florida potentially buying out his remaining six months. His actual sentence, however, was for three years. He had three charges for assault with intent to kill, disturbing public worship, and pointing a gun at another, so despite the one incident, three twelve-month sentences were doled out. He would be forced back into custody for two-and-a-half more years. Convict leasing and its effects still continued.[34]

Earlier that year, in April, the Valdosta city council agreed to lease a contingent of state prisoners to pave and repair town roads. It didn't fall afoul of the new convict law, because the lease would be by the municipality rather than a private company, but it demonstrated that convict leasing was still part of the Georgia system and that Valdosta was still comfortable with its presence in Lowndes County.[35]

Meanwhile, in December 1909, the federal Supreme Court again dealt with debt peonage in the case that had so troubled Villard, and justice Oliver Wendell Holmes Jr. again found a way to excuse the process. In *Bailey v. Alabama* (1909), he argued that Alonzo Bailey, who had signed a work contract with the Riverside Company for twelve dollars a month with a fifteen-dollar advance, had stopped work after one month without refunding the money he had been given. In Alabama, stopping work during a restrictive contract, particularly when the worker was Black, constituted prima facie evidence of intent to defraud the employer. Holmes, writing for the majority, sent the case back to Alabama for a jury trial, arguing that the case was "brought here prematurely by an attempt to take a short cut." A jury trial, he argued, might discover real fraudulent intent. John Marshall Harlan, as he had done in *Clyatt,* responded with a blistering dissent. Punishing a desire to remove oneself from a restrictive work contract could not occur by law without violating the Thirteenth Amendment. Alabama's peonage statute, which allowed the prosecution, was "repugnant to the Constitution and laws of the United States," as "the accused is deprived of his liberty in violation of Federal law."[36]

The *Bailey* case went back to Alabama but wound its way to the Supreme Court again in October 1910. In January 1911, the court ruled again, Charles Evans Hughes writing for the majority that "the state may impose involuntary servitude as a punishment for crime, but it may not compel one man to labor for another in payment of a debt, by punishing him as a criminal if he does not perform the service or pay the debt." Alabama's contract law was an "instrument of compulsion peculiarly effective as against the poor and the ignorant, its most likely victims," and it was unconstitutional under the tenets of the Thirteenth Amendment. Holmes naturally dissented, arguing that laws motivating laborers to behave in a certain way were constitutional and that juries should be the ones to decide whether fraudulent intent existed. He claimed that if a similar law had been passed in New York, it would have been ruled constitutional, making the decision dependent on a specific racialized history of Alabama rather than on the merits of the law itself.[37]

Holmes was in the minority, and Alabama's contract law was struck down, but the decision did not apply to the kind of peonage typically practiced in south Georgia, which ran through fines assessed by local courts rather than restrictive private work contracts. "The effect of the decision of the Supreme Court of the United States in the Bailey case is to render null and of no effect all of these labor laws which either directly or indirectly resulted in compulsory slavery," assumed Lafayette Hershaw, writing as a representative of the American Negro Academy.[38] It was a hopeful assumption, but it was wrong. The system had been bruised, but the system would continue.

Three years later, in 1914, the Supreme Court again dealt with an Alabama peonage law, this one far more similar to that used and abused by the McRees. Ed Rivers had been convicted of petit larceny and fined fifteen dollars, along with $43.75 in court costs. An employer paid his debt and Reynolds signed to work for him for ten months to pay the fine and costs. When he stopped working and refused to fill the contract, he was arrested. He was again convicted, this time for violation of contract, and again fined, which a separate employer paid for fifteen months of work. Again Rivers stopped work, and again he was arrested. The Supreme Court cited its *Bailey* decision and argued that "compulsion of such service by the constant fear of imprisonment under the criminal laws renders the work compulsory." The Court did not deny that a state "has authority to impose involuntary servitude as a punishment for crime," citing both *Bailey* and *Clyatt* in its ruling, "but here the State has taken the obligation of another for the fine and costs, imposed upon one convicted for the violation of the laws of the State. It has accepted the obligation of the surety," explained William R. Day, writing for the majority.

> The surety and convict have made a new contract for service, in regard to the terms of which the State has not been consulted. The convict must work it out to satisfy the surety for whom he has contracted to work. This contract must be kept, under pain of re-arrest, and another similar proceeding for its violation, and perhaps another and another. Thus, under pain of recurring prosecutions, the convict may be kept at labor, to satisfy the demands of his employer. In our opinion, this system is in violation of rights intended to be secured by the Thirteenth Amendment.[39]

States like Georgia, however, simply modified their laws to get around the Supreme Court's Alabama decisions rather than stopping their own systems. It wasn't until 1942 that Georgia had its own reckoning with *Bailey*, when a similar case, wherein a worker who signed a restrictive labor contract stopped working and refused to pay back the money he received, came before the federal judiciary. In *Taylor v. Georgia*, the Supreme Court noted the case's similarity to *Bailey*, arguing that there "is no material distinction between the Georgia statutes" and those from Alabama ruled unconstitutional in 1911. "We are told that the manner in which these sections have been interpreted by the courts of Georgia rescues them from invalidity. It is urged that the phrase 'without good and sufficient cause,'" which the state added to get around the *Bailey* ruling, "in effect requires proof of fraudulent intent at the time of making the contract and obtaining the money. But this argument is wide of the mark." The one principal difference in the cases was that Georgia did allow defendants to make statements of innocence, whereas Alabama denied such statements, "but the opinion in the *Bailey* case leaves no doubt that this factor was far from controlling and that its effect was simply to accentuate the harshness of an otherwise invalid statute. We think that the sections of the Georgia Code upon which this conviction rests are repugnant to the Thirteenth Amendment and to the Act of 1867."[40]

It was decades after Kinderlou had traded in prisoners and debt peons, but Georgia's contract law was finally voided by the Supreme Court. Still, just as in Alabama decades prior, the ruling did not deal with fine payment rules that forced so many into bondage in Lowndes County and its surrounding areas in south Georgia. The consolidation meant that there were no longer five different systems working in tandem—felony convict leasing, felony chain gangs, misdemeanor convict leasing, misdemeanor county chain gangs, and debt peonage—but two: the chain gang system, which worked both felony and misdemeanors on county road projects under the auspices of the Prison Commission, and debt peonage, which kept prisoners in private hands based on fine payments. When felony convict leasing was eliminated, and private misdemeanor camps went away with them, Georgia didn't replace those systems with the chain gang. It simply shifted some of its prisoners into an apparatus that already existed, and the diffusion of that apparatus across 159 counties in Georgia ensured that debt peonage would continue to operate within the reformulated penal system for decades to come.

10

The Last Twilight of the Kinderlou Dynasty

Late in 1904, new complaints against Kinderlou came to the office of Alexander Ackerman. He was constrained in what he could do about them, as Georgia's 1903 fraud law gave the McRees a measure of legal cover for their abuses. They had taken several prisoners and held them on fraud charges based on the new statute, keeping them in a state of bondage against their wills. Ackerman responded by traveling back to Valdosta, where he met with the McRees' attorney. He "reminded him of the fact that there were a large number of pleas of guilty on which sentences were suspended, hanging over his clients," and that "they of all others could not afford to be taking advantage of this statute." He warned them that because of their abuse of the law and the illegally held prisoners, "of which I understand they have instituted quite a number," he would make a motion for the court to enforce their previous suspended sentences.[1]

It was enough to scare the family. William McRee met with Ackerman at his Valdosta hotel, where the prosecutor "frankly told him that the Department of Justice would not brook any oppression of negroes on his part, even under the color of a state statute." McRee promised him "that no more of these prosecutions will be instituted." It was an important coda to the Kinderlou trials, one that reminded the family that even though Edward's place in the legislature shielded them from much of the scrutiny of continuing state investigations, the federal government was still watching. The shadow of their suspended sentences blotted out at least part of the sunlight provided by Georgia's fraud statute. As Ackerman knew all too well, however, promises from the McRees had proven less than trustworthy.[2]

The year 1906 was Edward's last in the legislature, and he died the following year, soon after the 1906 election in 1907.[3] His brother Will served as his executor, the will stipulating that whatever was left of his fortune, valued at more than $100,000, be used to pay any existing debts. He left

$5,000 in escrow to accrue interest for his aunt Lou, who had served as his surrogate mother for so many years. He left any money remaining, along with his property, to Will's children, to be given upon their twenty-first birthday. He left $1,000 to his Black servant, Mamie Taylor, "as evidence of my appreciation of her kindness and care and attention to me during the long illness I have recently suffered." He also provided money for her child, Cy Taylor, to "be given an education in the common school," then to attend Georgia Tech for two years. It was a suspicious bequest, particularly considering that Georgia Tech would not admit a Black student until 1961, but it was also a provocation. In contrast to the money left to the Taylors, and demonstrating the frayed relationships borne of the controversies the family had endured, Edward left his remaining brothers, George and Frank, ten dollars each.[4]

Some of that enmity came from a suit filed in January by Frank against his brothers concerning the main home at Kinderlou. While Ed, Will, and George built their own homes, Frank never did, his father encouraging him to take the plantation's original house. He agreed and had always lived there, but in late 1906, with convict lease ending, peonage controversies hurting the family's reputation, and Ed's tenure in the legislature coming to a conclusion, the brothers claimed that Frank's home was actually their father's, and that they were thus each entitled to a one-quarter division of the building. Frank filed suit to stop them. Even before Edward's death, most assumed that the case would never reach court, but the fight drove a wedge between the brothers, who had already endured the stress of scandal in the preceding years.[5]

And that stress would continue. Frank and George were incensed about receiving only ten dollars in their brother's will. George filed an application for temporary administration of his brother's estate and a formal lawsuit seemed almost destined to end up in court.[6] It did. Frank and George charged a conspiracy between Will and Mamie Taylor to keep them from profiting from their brother's death. They claimed that the housekeeper "sent numerous and anonymous and scurrilous letters to young ladies whom the testator had visited and made every effort to prevent his marriage" and that the cabal between Taylor and Will led to a will signed while Edward was of unsound mind. The contentious nature of the charges and the publicity they received led Will to settle the following day. He agreed to allot $27,000 to his brothers and agreed to stop the lawsuit against Frank over their father's house. Nothing in the settlement mentioned how Taylor would be affected.[7] It was clear that as the racialized convict and peonage system that had sustained the brothers for so many years dissipated, each scrambled in their own way to secure their economic position as the walls came tumbling down.

Meanwhile, in an effort to supplement the loss of convict and debt peonage labor in the face of various lawsuits, the McRees in December 1907 worked with the Georgia Immigration Association to bring fifteen Austrian immigrants to Kinderlou to work the plantation. They were "apparently very intelligent people and splendid physical specimens," noted the *Atlanta Constitution*. They couldn't speak English, "but it is expected that they will not be long in picking up enough of the language to get along on."[8] While the transaction seemed sanguine, it, too, was ancillary to the peonage system. "Immigrants who went to the South on labor contracts during the Progressive era," Pete Daniel explains, "discovered themselves held by force to work out transportation costs while being driven deeper into debt by the usurious commissary system." When Black help began to dry up, the McRees simply turned to another form of bound labor to generate their revenue.[9] The McRees' use of Austrians fit a broader trend mentioned in the 1907 Russell report (see chapter 8), as operations across the state and region looked to new sources of bound labor to maintain the quasi-feudal economy they had always known.

Three years later, the federal Immigration Commission undertook an investigation of the use of immigrants in southern peonage situations. "The peonage cases in the South relating to immigrants have been found to cover almost every industry," the new report concluded. "The chief causes of the abuses have been the systems of making advances to laborers, the operations of contract-labor laws, and the misrepresentations made to laborers by unscrupulous employment agents. The cases of beating and brutal treatment have been exceptional." And yet the vast majority of the cases went unpunished. Congress had never passed a law specifically dealing with the practice, and the federal attorneys and judges in southern states "have been unable to find any provisions in the statutes of the United States imposing penalties for the imposition of slavery unaccompanied by some special feature."[10] It was another effort. Another failure. The system would continue well beyond Kinderlou's ability to sustain it.

Edward's death, however, did not stop the family's use of bound felony convict labor in the last throes of the system. In April 1909, McRee's estate was charged $5,617.11 as the last payment made for felony prisoners before the formal end of the lease system.[11] The death of that system affected the McRees in other ways, as well, as in August, Will McRee, acting as executor for his brother's estate, filed suit against Goodloe Yancey, secretary of the Prison Commission, and W. B. Hamby, one of his fellow lessees, claiming that Yancey and Hamby entered into a conspiracy to deprive lessees of the prisoners they were due and funneling additional prisoners to Hamby. For his part, McRee asked for a judgment of $1,844.26, arguing that his bid was for one hundred felony prisoners based on an estimate of 1,500 total, making his share of the lot one-fifteenth. And yet from 1907 to 1909, at least 1,600 prisoners were leased annually, meaning that Kinderlou should have received a larger share of the workers. Instead, he received only ninety-nine prisoners in 1907 and ninety-eight in 1908, actually less than his contracted numerical share, to say nothing of his percentage of the whole. Meanwhile, Hamby, who contracted for five hundred prisoners, received 626. The suit alleged that Hamby's good fortune was a result of conspiracy between himself and Yancey, facilitated by his corrupt relationship with state warden Jake Moore, depriving the McRees and other defendants of their fair share of the total. The system in its former form was over, but debates surrounding apportionment and the value of bound labor to wealthy white Georgians continued, as was the stain of corruption that had dogged the state's penal apparatus for years.[12]

In 1909, both felony and misdemeanor private convict camps disappeared, replaced by those convicted of felonies farmed to counties for road projects. There were 2,558 felony prisoners that year, 191 of the men and sixty-eight of the women working at the state prison farm in Milledgeville. Everyone else was moved to a county chain gang. Officially reported deaths among felony prisoners in custody shrunk to forty-two, a number decidedly lower than it had been under convict lease, but also a number frighteningly high for the "humane treatment" the Prison Commission claimed the system provided. There were, meanwhile, 2,424 misdemeanants, twenty of them working at the state prison farm and the rest on county chain gangs. Lowndes County, in this new system, employed twenty-two felony prisoners and twenty-two misdemeanants on its roads program.[13] The numbers remained similar the following year, with reported deaths falling further to thirty-two in 1910.[14]

With the timber market faltering, those convicted of misdemeanors working on county roads, and peonage no longer a reliable option, George Young McRee, the youngest of the brothers, decided to change his business model and divide his estate into small tenant farms, which would allow him to harness and profit from the labor of the poor in a new way, a profit he used for "improving his pretty home at Kinder Lou," the *Valdosta Times* remarked. "Those who have seen it since the improvements were made to say that it is the handsomest country home in South Georgia."[15]

Will McRee had done much the same thing, leasing his land to others, including more affluent citizens, ignoring the early advice of his grandfather George, who had claimed that farm tenancy was a sucker's game that provided for less revenue than bound labor. But those early lessons hadn't entirely dissipated. Jasper Mathis, for example, was a white farmer, but he was no tenant farmer. Mathis and his family moved out to Kinderlou to take advantage of the rich farmland. It was an experiment, however, that wouldn't last long. In July 1911, Mathis died at his Kinderlou home on Will's fourth of the property.[16]

Valdosta and its surrounds were in the geographical center of the wiregrass and longleaf pine region of the South, which ran from southern North Carolina down the coast, stretching into the arid heel of Mississippi, a region also known as "the fire forest" because of the controlled burns prompted by the environment itself. In March 1909, the fire forest took its revenge. A fire that started on a nearby farm moved through the Kinderlou plantation, sweeping up timber along a six-mile run of fencing. Will McRee led a large group hoping to stop the blaze. They worked through the night, but the wind and the dry turpentine timber gave them little help. Much of the farm's resources were left in ash.[17]

Frank Inman McRee moved to Valdosta after the original Kinderlou homestead burned, and he died soon after in late 1910. On January 17, his executors held an estate sale. Mules, pigs, and cattle were auctioned, along with wagons, plows, and other farm implements. They sold hay, cantaloupe seed, and three thousand bushels of corn. Frank's legacy was one that included a heavy debt, and in the wake of his death, the farm was dismantled and sold.[18]

In May, the sale continued. J. A. Ewing, a Jacksonville businessman who had made his fortune in naval stores, bought a controlling interest in Kinderlou. Ewing had done business in Valdosta for years and had decided to move to the region. The now-vulnerable McRee estate would be his point of entry.[19]

Ewing's company then divided the property into five acre lots and sold them. About two hundred of the lots would be planted with pecan trees, while others would be residential. The company planned to build a dam across the lake where the McRee brothers' mill once operated, creating a large fishpond that would center the residential area. There would also be a country club for residents. The company had, as of March 1912, already

Table 10.1. Lowndes County population

	White	Black	Total	Percentage Black
1890	7,128	7,974	15,102	52.8
1900	9,347	10,688	20,035	53.3
1910	11,481	12,955	24,436	53.0
1920	12,986	13,535	26,521	51.0
1930	16,211	13,783	29,994	46.0

Source: Statistics in this table aggregated and tabulated from U.S. Department of Commerce, *Twelfth Census of the United States, 1910, Population*, vol. 1, part 1 (Washington: USGPO, 1901), 534; U.S. Department of Commerce, *Thirteenth Census of the United States, 1910, Population*, vol. 2, *Alabama-Montana* (Washington: USGPO, 1913), 389; U.S. Department of Commerce, *Fourteenth Census of the United States, 1920, Population*, vol. 3 (Washington: USGPO, 1922), 215; and U.S. Department of Commerce, *Fifteenth Census of the United States, 1930, Population*, vol. 3, part 1, *Alabama-Missouri* (Washington: USGPO, 1932), 485.

hired a landscape gardener to help beautify the land and ease its transition from productive farm to residential mecca.[20]

In April 1913, George Young McRee, the youngest of George's McRee's four sons, died in Valdosta. He had a heart condition exacerbated by malarial fever. Frank and Ed had already died, leaving only Will remaining. The younger George was raised on the main plantation, then lived on his fourth of the estate after his father's passing for all of his life, excepting the time he spent at college in Auburn.[21] The following year, in November 1914, George's home, now occupied by the manager of what was now the Valdosta Pecan Plantation Company, went up in flames. The servant at the house tried to save what he could, but it was a total loss. It was a symbolic end, the third of the four homes of the four McRee boys. All of them had been engulfed in fire. Kinderlou, in any recognizable form, had been mostly burned to the ground.[22]

The only remaining brother was William, who had avoided convict leasing during its heyday but still trafficked in bound Black labor. In 1914, soon before his brother's former home burned, Will McRee shot and killed Will Porter, one of the Black workers on his portion of Kinderlou land. Porter and a group of other Black workers were having a fight in the housing quarters around ten o'clock on the night of August 16, which brought McRee out. Porter ran out of the room when McRee entered, and McRee claimed that Porter pulled a gun on him as he ran away and was intending to shoot him, despite the implausibility of the claim and the fact that only McRee's gun was fired. Porter ran into the woods with a gunshot wound where he died soon after. McRee didn't go after him. He returned to his house after the shooting. Porter's body was discovered the following morning. Despite no evidence that there was a justifiable reason for McRee's action, the local coroner's jury claimed that the incident was an act of justifiable homicide, ensuring that the killer would face no charges.[23] It was the last documented instance of the McRees skirting justice for their abuse of Black lives and bodies.

It was not, however, Will's last time in court. In 1915, McRee was sued by real estate agent Floyd Frederick, who argued that the two had an oral agreement for commissions on the sale of property that McRee refused to pay. The court ruled in favor of Frederick, but McRee's appeal the following year overturned the ruling on demurrer that a parole contract was too vague and did not fix "a precise length of time for its duration" or exact conditions upon which the agent would sell the property.[24] It was one final example of McRee vindictiveness. It was devoid of the racial animus that defined so much of the problematic behavior on the Kinderlou property. But it was vindictiveness nonetheless, a final signpost of the legacy of a family abetted by a legal apparatus that catered to them through white supremacy to allow them chance after chance to abuse a corrupt system and to abuse all of those who found themselves within it. William McRee, the last surviving brother, died in February 1924.[25]

The wife of William Spain McRee would live far longer than her husband. In 1946, at age seventy-six, she flew for the first time, as her son Jerry McRee, a member of the South Georgia Flying Service, took her up for a half-hour flight.[26] Later that same year, the Taylor-Colquitt Company of South Carolina purchased a large parcel of Kinderlou land that had at one time been part of George Young McRee's holdings. The land deal, 6,670 acres at a total of $280,000 from the current owner, the J. N. Bray Company, was one of the largest regional real estate deals in decades and began the company's and the city's interest in the telephone pole industry, an interest that would remain an integral part of the Valdosta economy into the twenty-first century.[27]

Meanwhile, the region's Black population was left with the remnants of what Kinderlou represented and the county camps that had taken its place. In 1917, the Baltimore *Afro-American* told its readers that as many as 1,500 Black residents of Georgia were absconding for points north every week, pushed in part by "a system of peonage or new slavery." There were other reasons, of course, for the first major wave of the Great Migration, but the paper was undeniably correct that the prospect of becoming bound labor was among the push factors contributing to the exodus. "If there is needed further proof of the Negroes' unrest and dissatisfaction it is furnished in the fact that thousands of them are migrating North on account of their present treatment," argued Benjamin Davis in the Black weekly *Atlanta Independent*.[28]

"Negroes, Leave the South!" commanded a 1920 editorial in the *Messenger*, one of the foundational magazines of the Harlem Renaissance, initiated three years prior by Chandler Owen and A. Philip Randolph. "Go North, East, and West—anywhere—to get out of that hell hole." There were better schools. There was better housing. There was the vote. Convict leasing and debt peonage didn't exist. "All is not rosy here, by any means," the magazine admitted, "but it is Paradise" compared with its southern counterpart. "Besides, you make it better for those you leave behind. Labor becomes scarce, so that the Bourbons of Dixie are compelled to pay your brothers back home more wages." Whatever hardships migrants endured, they would end up benefiting everyone, North and South. "Sell out your stuff quietly, saying nothing to the Negro lackeys, and leave! Come into the land of at least incipient civilization!"[29]

The "land of at least incipient civilization" was, as the name suggests, mostly beneficial to the Black community, but with clear limits on those benefits. The migration of Black southerners to northern urban hubs helped crystallize race as a national issue rather than a regional one at a time when convict leasing and debt peonage, along with Jim Crow segregation, voting restrictions, and lynching horrors, dominated the South. While life in the urban North was certainly difficult, and while many would make the case that northern labor standards would create a version of "wage slavery" not far afield of debt peonage, life in the rural South had proven far more deadly, the racism far more systemic and violent. Such was to be expected from a "hell hole." Thus it was that from 1890 to 1910, roughly two hundred thousand African Americans left the region. In the nineteenth century, most Black southerners were far more likely to emigrate to Africa, to the American West, or to urban hubs within the South than they were to northern cities, but that would change. Between 1910 and 1940, 1.75 million Black migrants left the South, doubling the Black population outside of the region. In this wave, they largely moved north, where they generally worked outside of industry, as janitors, elevator operators, and house servants. There weren't Jim Crow laws in the north, but northern industrialists generally refused to hire Black workers, preferring immigrants from Eastern Europe. It was a vestige of that "incipient civilization," factory owners worrying that hiring Black employees would associate their products with Blackness and thus alienate white customers. Black workers, then, were brought in only as scabs during strikes, making them even less popular in a racist North. That dynamic would change during World War I, as labor shortages created space for Black workers, but even then, charges of wage slavery would draw comparisons with debt peonage in the South.[30]

Lowndes County's Black population, like so many others, would respond to Georgia's carceral abuses by migrating north, though not in the massive numbers of other parts of the state.

From 1900 to 1930, though the county's Black population rose every decade, its growth rate declined at every census measure along the way, demonstrating the effects of the migration (see table 10.1). That the demographic shift wasn't larger was a product, surely, of some of the hard realities of those who had already made the trip. But mostly it was the result of a lack of resources and of binding agents back home. In a carceral operation designed to acquire as many Black bodies as possible in one of several systems working in tandem, the vast majority in Black Lowndes County experienced no more than one or two degrees of separation between themselves and someone important to them in bondage, only adding to the difficulty of attempting to leave. Still, leave they did, as demonstrated by the county's diminishing population rate during the period.

For those in the region slowed by public metaphors tying northern wage slavery to southern debt peonage, those comparisons would gain a new force in 1921, when Georgia's combination of convict leasing and peonage would again find a national spotlight. Jasper County's John S. Williams was charged with the murder of eleven debt peons in his charge. Jasper County sat between Atlanta and Macon, and, fearing that his acquisition of workers from jails in those two cities would come to light, Williams had ten of them killed and murdered another himself. While the shocking crime was unfathomable to many, the process that led to it was all too common. "I am like most farmers that I know," Williams said at his trial, "that at times I have bonded out and paid fines for n—s with actual agreement that they would stay there till their fines were paid, or till he was relieved from his bond." He was guilty of murder, but he was right about the commonality of the process and the inherent racism that accompanied it.[31] While the McRees never effectuated a mass murder on the order of the Williams plantation, theirs was a slow burn mass killing, a comparative serial killing that took place over the long years of the turn of the century on the Georgia-Florida border.

Even as that shocking mass murder was coming to light just north of Kinderlou, just south of it in Dixie County, Florida, the turpentine camp of Alston Brown was perpetrating its own abuses on a mass scale. Brown had a policy that "no negro could leave his camp without his consent," meaning that family members of those held there would also be roped into imprisonment just for attempting to visit. The beatings were brutal and often deadly. When workers died, they were buried without notification to family or even an acknowledgment of the death. Female workers were pimped to men. All food and supplies were charged against the claimed service time of the camp, leaving many in a version of lifetime slavery. Investigators concluded that some workers had been at Brown's camp for more than fifteen years and had never seen anyone outside of it. The Dixie County case in 1921 and 1922 seemed to be the apotheosis of convict labor restrictions in the turpentine belt of south Georgia and north Florida. Like the McRees, Brown worked both misdemeanants and peons at the same time, at the same tasks. They were housed in the same barracks. Peons who attempted escape returned as prisoners. Those who completed their sentences found that commissary charges left them in debt and forced them back into the system as peons.[32] Brown's turpentine camp, a hundred miles south of Lowndes County, was the Kinderlou of the early 1920s.

And brutality begat brutality. Brown's system built from a Kinderlou model just to the north; just to the south of Brown's camp was Rosewood, Florida, where only months following Brown's indictment, in January 1923, white men destroyed the small Black community, killing many and forcing others into hiding.[33] Rosewood had no direct relation to convict camps or debt peonage, but it was another violent outgrowth of a broader system rooted in white supremacy, one that devalued Black lives and gave the benefit of the doubt to white people until the crimes became so systemic and egregious that action became unavoidable. Both were important. Rosewood was egregious, for example, but no one was held to account for the murders because officials could portray the race riot as an outlier. Kinderlou's crimes, and those of Brown in Dixie County, were also egregious, but taken individually they could be excused by a system where those in power benefited. It was only through the maintenance of systems of brutality that any attempt at justice could be created. And even then, the punishments for the taking of innocent lives consisted largely in the removal of imprisonment privileges and negative publicity. In a system weighted racially, governed by the ingrained assumptions of white supremacy, Black suffering was unworthy of much more.

As convict leasing was coming to an end, the Georgia Prison Commission initially preferred the creation of a permanent penitentiary farm for white prisoners to ensure that segregation could be maintained on chain gang labor, as it had been in previous convict labor camps. The new governor, M. Hoke Smith, however, vetoed the idea as too expensive. The whole point of convict labor, after all, was to save the state money. That being the case, as long as chain gang labor remained segregated, white prisoners would be included on road projects. Though the system was still heavily weighted racially, it demonstrated a real change from convict leasing, in which almost all of the lessees were Black. And since much of Georgia's public works efforts were driven by necessity and a shortage of unskilled labor willing to do such thankless, low-paying work, there was no visible accompanying antagonism between free labor and that usurped from prisoners, as there was in other southern states.[34]

In the first annual report of the Georgia Highway Department, published in 1919, the group lamented that "work proceeds very slowly in most of the counties" because the counties' share of the cost "must be supplied by convict labor, as there are no available funds to allow the work to be done under contract."[35] But the report was confident that the system was eminently beneficial for the prisoners. "The counties have provided equipment for housing, feeding, guarding, and working them in a manner that has resulted in great benefit to the convicts themselves, as compared with their former health and treatment under the Lease System," the department report claimed. "They are well clothed and well fed and are given wholesome work in the open. An inspection of the different road camps throughout the State shows them to be in excellent physical condition. When sick they are given the best medical attention and the authorities in charge always treat them in a humane manner." Such was clearly untrue as to the treatment of prisoners. But it was true that taking prisoners out of the hands of private farms like that of the McRees did improve life expectancy and general health. It wasn't beneficial treatment, but it was better than the low standard that was set by convict leasing.[36]

By 1937, Georgia was actively in the process of developing a prison infrastructure at the state and local levels. It had at least a baseline county road system. The process of marshaling prison labor for public works had already begun to decline. In 1933, the state highway board's convict depart-

Table 10.2. Distribution of Georgia prisoners in 1932

	Felons			Misdemeanants		
Race	Total	State farm	Chain gang	Total	State farm	County labor
Black	3,229	331	2,898	3,925	212	3,713
	100%	10%	90%	100%	5%	95%
White	1,196	247	949	273	141	132
	100%	21%	79%	100%	52%	48%
Total	4,425	578	3,847	4,198	353	3,845
% Black	73.0	57.3	75.3	93.5	60.1	96.6

Source: William Cohen, "Negro Involuntary Servitude in the South, 1865–1940," *Journal of Southern History* 42 (February 1976): 58.

ment accounted for only one project; in 1934 it listed thirteen, mostly associated with road grading and bridge building.[37]

While Georgia's Black population was 32 percent of the total in 1930, it composed 83 percent of the prison population two years later (see table 10.2). And those prisoners were more likely to be included in forced labor provisions like the chain gang, the majority of them misdemeanor prisoners tasked with working on county roads, just as they had in previous decades.[38]

"Public authorities never for a moment slaked their thirst for profits from convict labor," Blake McKelvey explained in the waning years of the system. The penal process in the South used its labor in different ways based on the region where it was housed: "The penal systems, whether centering around plantations as in the southwestern part of the section, whether specializing in road labor as in the southeastern states, or developing contract industries within prison walls as in the border states, remained strangely isolated from the vital influences active in northern penology."[39]

The formal end of felony convict leasing would happen in Mississippi in 1890 and Tennessee in 1895. Florida, meanwhile, had a sanctioned version of the system until 1924, North Carolina until 1933.[40] "One reason for the large number of arrests—in Georgia particularly—lies in the fact that the state and the counties make a profit out of their prison system," explained Ray Stannard Baker in 1908. "Demand for convicts by rich sawmill operators, owners of brick-yards, large farmers, and others is far in advance of the supply," meaning the "natural tendency is to convict as many men as possible." Charles Russell concluded that the convict lease system in Georgia and Florida was "largely a system of involuntary servitude—that is to say, persons are held to labor as convicts under those laws who have committed no crime." C. Vann Woodward agreed with his early century predecessors, arguing that "the convict lease did greater violence to the moral authority of the Redeemers than did anything else. For it was upon the tradition of paternalism that the Redeemer regimes claimed authority to settle the race problem."[41]

The carceral system, for both those convicted of felonies and those convicted of misdemeanors, was an exercise in social control, and it worked in concert with similar racialized efforts to ensure white hegemony in the state. Between 1882 and 1936, for example, Georgia officially lynched 389 Black men and surely unofficially lynched many more. The state executed 415 prisoners in that same period, more than any other southern state.[42] When combined with felony and misdemeanor lease and the near-ubiquitous and untallied debt peonage system, white authorities could ensure dominion over those without the political power to stop them. That said, the incarceration, lynching, debt peonage, and death penalty cases were all separate systems. There was no coordinated effort among white people to enact such policies. Coordination was never their strong suit. Instead, each served as its own manifestation of white supremacy that created a dominionist effect.[43]

In 1937, Franklin Roosevelt's Prison Industries Reorganization Administration (PIRA) surveyed the problem with prison labor in Georgia. It recommended abolishing "the present practice of turning state prisoners over to the county convict camps" and instead developing "modern state camps for those inmates selected for road work." There should also be "consolidated camps under state control for misdemeanants." Camps and penitentiaries should be classified for certain types of prisoners and limit their intake. It was a demonstration that even decades after the felony and misdemeanor lease systems had run their course, operation of bound labor at the county level was always more brutal, more prone to abuse, than those camps operated by the state. Investigators encouraged the "establishment of an educational and vocational training program sufficient at least to eliminate illiteracy and to give trade or agricultural training to promising young offenders." All female prisoners should be moved to a "new cottage-type women's institution" separate from that of the men "regardless of length of sentence."[44]

The Prison Commission still controlled convict labor in the state. One group of prisoners was housed at Milledgeville, another in state highway camps. The third and largest group of prisoners was in the county road camps. The commission segregated all prisoners by race and gender, separating "the white and colored completely when not at work and as much as possible while at work."[45] But the addiction to free labor kept the system growing. As of the onset of 1937, the state counted 4,653 felony prisoners and 3,130 convicted of misdemeanors, not including those held in city or county jails, and the population was overwhelmingly Black. PIRA noted that in the immediate wake of Reconstruction, the state's prison population was more than 90 percent Black, a ratio that began to decrease somewhat after the creation of the Prison Commission at the end of the century. For most of the twentieth century, the prison population remained relatively consistent at roughly 75 percent Black.[46]

According to the investigation, the county camps in which the majority of the state's prisoners were housed ranged from clean, decent facilities to inhumane hellholes. "Under Georgia's present system," PIRA noted, "they must all attempt to make a profit from the labor of the prisoners confined in them if they wish to avoid increasing local taxes," which encouraged cutting costs to the detriment of those incarcerated. It was clear to investigators that the Prison Commission was unequipped to "function as an agency to control or properly supervise county camps." Shackles and corporal punishments were still common.[47]

Kinderlou was long gone by the time of PIRA's report in 1937, but its methods and the grounding ideals that governed the camp still dominated in much of the state's penal system. Its amalgamation of felony and misdemeanor convict leasing with debt peonage labor and outright kidnapping would become a precedent document for the state's troubled relationship with Black incarceration not only through the Great Depression but well past it into the late-twentieth and early-twenty-first centuries. In the process, it demonstrated that the systems so often treated separately in the historiography actually developed in a state of mutual dependance, a relationship of tautology, convict leasing in its various forms feeding off of debt peonage and vice versa, the breadth of the system creating a superstructure too large and unwieldy for regular, consistent oversight, which made the kidnapping and graft that supplemented such practices all the more common. Kinderlou as an exemplar of turn-of-the-century Georgia carceral systems also serves as a demonstration of the important role of private misdemeanor convict leasing, a system part of that tautological loop but distinct in its brutality, its percentage of Black male victims, and its ability to hide within the prison infrastructure because of its contested legality, lack of oversight, and operation at the county level. The screeds of the time, both within Georgia and outside of it, emphasized the legitimate horrors of felony convict leasing, debt peonage, and kidnapping, many pundits not understanding the distinct problems of private misdemeanor leasing and its ability to facilitate so many of the other abuses commentators bemoaned. But it was there, creating the model for what would come after 1909 and leaving a gruesome body count in its wake.

It was part of a broader system that included felony leasing, felony chain gangs, misdemeanor county chain gangs, and debt peonage, but because it hid in contemporary jeremiads, it often hides in the historiographical narrative. It was the most brutal part of a brutal system in Georgia, and a version of the same practice occurred in north Florida, as well (see chapter 8). Historians have yet to seek such differentiations in other states, but this book is written in part to prompt that kind of work. Kinderlou was exceptional, but it was not an exception, and its use and abuse of Black labor, along with the incestuous system that facilitated it, can serve as a guide to historians' evolving understanding of the role of bound labor in the turpentine belt and the broader post-Reconstruction South.

NOTES

Introduction

1 *Afro-American,* August 5, 1905, 4.
2 Pete Daniel, "Up from Slavery and Down to Peonage: The Alonzo Bailey Case," *Journal of American History* 57 (December 1970): 656; Fred Cubberly to Attorney General, May 30, 1901, Casefile 909-1898, Reel 1, Peonage Files of the Department of Justice, 1901–1945; Fred Cubberly to Attorney General, July 13, 1901; John Eagan to Attorney General, April 3, 1903, Casefile 5280-1903, Reel 2, Peonage Files of the Department of Justice, 1901–1945; and Alex Lichtenstein, *Twice the Work of Free Labor: The Political Economy of Convict Labor in the New South* (New York: Verso, 1996), 170. *Observer* quoted in Lichtenstein, *Twice the Work of Free Labor,* 170. See also Jeffrey A. Drobney, "Where Palm and Pine are Blowing: Convict Labor in the North Florida Turpentine Industry, 1877–1923," *Florida Historical Quarterly* 72 (April 1994): 411–34.
3 Daniel, "Up from Slavery and Down to Peonage," 655.
4 The literature examining convict leasing dates back to the period of the system itself, but historical examinations really began in earnest in the 1970s. See, for example, William Cohen, "Negro Involuntary Servitude in the South, 1865–1940," *Journal of Southern History* 42 (February 1976): 31–60; Matthew J. Mancini, "Race, Economics, and the Abandonment of Convict Leasing," *Journal of Negro History* 63 (October 1978): 339–352; Christopher R. Adamson, "Punishment after Slavery: Southern State Penal Systems, 1865–1890," *Social Problems* 30 (June 1983): 555–69; Charles L. Flynn Jr., *White Land, Black Labor: Caste and Class in Late Nineteenth-Century Georgia* (Baton Rouge: Louisiana State University Press, 1983); Lichtenstein, *Twice the Work of Free Labor;* Matthew J. Mancini, *One Dies, Get Another: Convict Leasing in the American South, 1866–1928* (Columbia: University of South Carolina Press, 1996); David M. Oshinsky, *Worse than Slavery: Parchman Farm and the Ordeal of Jim Crow Justice* (New York: Free Press, 1996); Mary Ellen Curtin, *Black Prisoners and Their World, Alabama, 1865–1900* (Charlottesville: University Press of Virginia, 2000); and Douglas A. Blackmon, *Slavery by Another Name: The Re-Enslavement of Black Americans from the Civil War to World War II* (New York: Anchor Books, 2008), the bulk of which are cited extensively in the chapters that follow.

5 The concept of the ghost in the machine began as a critique of Cartesian mind-body dualism, first coined by Gilbert Ryle and popularized by Arthur Koestler. Here, however, it serves to describe a seemingly invisible operation that is vital to the system itself. See Arthur Koestler, *The Ghost in the Machine* (originally published 1967; New York: Penguin, 1990).

6 Sarah Haley, "'Like I Was A Man': Chain Gangs, Gender, and the Domestic Carceral Sphere in Jim Crow Georgia," *Signs* 39 (No. 1 2013): 53–77; and Talitha LeFlouria, *Chained in Silence: Black Women and Convict Labor in the New South* (Chapel Hill: University of North Carolina Press, 2015). Misdemeanor labor is mentioned in other studies, as well, either tangentially or as a function of post-1909 chain gang labor after the fall of felony convict lease. See, for example, David Berry, "Free Labor He Found Unsatisfactory: James W. English and Convict Lease Labor at the Chattahoochee Brick Company," *Proceedings and Papers of the Georgia Association of Historians* (1990): 117–25; Christopher Muller, "Freedom and Convict Leasing in the Postbellum South," *American Journal of Sociology* 2 (September 2018): 367–405; A. Elizabeth Taylor, "The Origin and Development of the Convict Lease System in Georgia," *Georgia Historical Quarterly* 26 (June 1942): 113–28; and A. Elizabeth Taylor, "The Abolition of the Convict Lease System in Georgia," *Georgia Historical Quarterly* 26 (September–December 1942): 273–87.

7 Louis N. Robinson, Joseph N. Ulman, Gustav Peck, James P. Davis, and Linton M. Collins, *The Prison Labor Problem In Georgia* (Washington: U.S. Prison Industries Reorganization Administration, 1937), 2–4; and Fletcher Melvin Green, "Some Aspects of the Convict Lease System in the Southern States," in *Essays in Southern History*, ed. Fletcher M. Green (Chapel Hill: University of North Carolina Press, 1949), 115–16.

8 Benno C. Schmidt Jr., "Principle and Prejudice: The Supreme Court and Race in the Progressive Era. Part 2: The Peonage Cases," *Columbia Law Review* 82 (May 1982): 651.

9 *Afro-American*, October 17, 1903, 1.

10 Lafayette M. Hershaw, *Peonage*, Occasional Papers, No. 15 (Washington: American Negro Academy, 1915), 13.

11 Ira Berlin, *Many Thousands Gone: The First Two Centuries of Slavery in North America* (Cambridge, Mass.: Belknap Press of Harvard University Press, 1998).

12 Green, "Some Aspects of the Convict Lease System in the Southern States," 112–15. See also Harlan Greene, Harry S. Hutchins Jr. and Brian E. Hutchins, *Slave Badges and the Slave-Hire System in Charleston, South Carolina, 1783–1865* (Jefferson, N.C.: McFarland, 2004); David Brion Davis, *Inhuman Bondage: The Rise and Fall of Slavery in the New World* (New York: Oxford University Press, 2006); Robert William Fogel, *Without Consent or Contract: The Rise and Fall of American Slavery* (New York: W. W. Norton, 1994); Frederic Bancroft, *Slave Trading in the Old South* (originally published 1931; Columbia: University of South Carolina Press, 1996); Winthrop D. Jordan, *White Over Black: American Attitudes toward the Negro, 1550–1812* (Chapel Hill: University of North Carolina Press, 1968); and Walter Johnson, *Soul*

by Soul: Life Inside the Antebellum Slave Market (Cambridge, Mass.: Harvard University Press, 1999).

13 Theodore Brantner Wilson, *The Black Codes of the South* (Tuscaloosa: University of Alabama Press, 1965), 61–80, 96–115. See also David F. Forte, "Spiritual Equality, the Black Codes, and the Americanization of the Freedmen," *Loyola Law Review* 43 (1998): 569–611; Risa L. Goluboff, "The Thirteenth Amendment and the Lost Origins of Civil Rights," *Duke Law Journal* 50 (2001): 1609–85; Joe M. Richardson, "Florida Black Codes," *Florida Historical Quarterly* 47 (April 1969), 365–79; Alexander Tsesis, *The Thirteenth Amendment and American Freedom: A Legal History* (New York: New York University Press, 2004); and Joel Williamson, *After Slavery: The Negro in South Carolina During Reconstruction, 1861–1877* (Chapel Hill: University of North Carolina Press, 1965).

14 Arney R. Childs, ed., *The Private Journal of Henry William Ravenel, 1859–1887* (Columbia: University of South Carolina Press, 1947), 256.

15 A. E. Raza, "Legacies of the Racialization of Incarceration: From Convict-lease to the Prison Industrial Complex," *Journal of the Institute of Justice and International Studies* 11 (2011): 163; Jonathan M. Bryant, "'We Have No Chance of Justice before the Courts': The Freedmen's Struggle for Power in Greene County, Georgia, 1865–1874," in *Georgia in Black and White: Explorations in the Race Relations of a Southern State, 1865–1950*, ed. John C. Inscoe (Athens: University of Georgia Press, 1994), 18; Wilson, *The Black Codes of the South*; Steven Hahn, "Hunting, Fishing, and Foraging: Common Rights and Class Relations in the Postbellum South," *Radical History Review* 26 (October 1982): 45; and Eric Foner, *Nothing But Freedom: Emancipation and Its Legacy* (Baton Rouge: Louisiana State University Press, 1983), 66.

16 "An Act to punish Vagrants and Vagabonds," Ch. 1467, No. 4, *Acts and Resolutions Adopted by the General Assembly of Florida, 1865* (Tallahassee: Office of the Floridian, 1866), 28–29; "An Act to alter and amend the 4435th Section of the Penal Code of Georgia," March 12, 1866, *Acts of the General Assembly of the State of Georgia, 1865 and 1866* (Milledgeville: Bougton, Nisbet, Barnes & Moore, 1866), 234–35; "Vagrants Defined," §4560, *The Code of the State of Georgia*, 4th edition (Atlanta: Jason P. Harrison & Co., 1882), 1190; "Of Offenses against Chastity, Morality, and Decency," Chapter 8, sec. 24, *Acts and Resolutions Adopted by the Legislature of Florida, 1868* (Tallahassee: Office of the Tallahassee Sentinel, 1868), 99; and Adamson, "Punishment after Slavery," 561.

17 "An Act to provide for the punishment of persons for tampering with, persuading or enticing away, harboring, feeding or secreting laborers, servants or apprentices," No. 16, December 21, 1865, Acts Passed by the General Assembly of the State of Louisiana at the Extra Session, 1865 (New Orleans: J. O. Nixon, 1866), 24–26; "An Act to alter and amend Sections 4596 and 4597 of the Code of Georgia," February 15, 1866, *Acts of the General Assembly of the State of Georgia, 1865 and 1866* (Milledgeville: Bougton, Nisbet, Barnes & Moore, 1866), 235; and Cohen, "Negro Involuntary Servitude in the South," 35.

18 Cohen, "Negro Involuntary Servitude in the South," 39–40; and David E. Bernstein, *Only One Place of Redress: African Americans, Labor Regulations, and the Courts from Reconstruction to the New Deal* (Durham, N.C.: Duke University Press, 2001), 8–27.
19 *Williams v. Fears*, 179 U.S. 270 (1900).
20 *Allgeyer v. Louisiana*, 165 U.S. 578 (1897).
21 "An Act in relation to Contracts of Persons of Color," Chapter 1470, No. 7, January 12, 1866, *Acts and Resolutions Adopted by the General Assembly of Florida, 1865* (Tallahassee: Office of the Floridian, 1866), 32; "An Act to punish Vagrants and Vagabonds," 28–29; and "An Act to extend the provisions of an act entitled an act in relation to Contracts of Persons of Color to all persons without distinction of color," Chapter 1551, No. 18, December 13, 1866, Acts and Resolutions Adopted by the General Assembly of the State of Florida, 1866 (Tallahassee: Office of the Floridian, 1867), 21–22.
22 "An Act in Relation to Obtaining Money or any other Personal Property under False Promises, or for Violation of Contracts, and Providing Penalties therefor," Chapter 4032, No. 23, *Acts and Resolutions Adopted by the Legislature of Florida, 1891* (Jacksonville: Times Union Book and Job Office, 1891), 57–58; "Contracts That Must Be in Writing," Chapter 29, *A Digest of the Laws of the State of Florida from 1822 to 1881*, comp. James F. McClellan (Tallahassee: Floridian Book and Job Office, 1881), 208–210; and "Procuring Money on Contract for Service, No. 345," August 15, 1903, *Acts of the General Assembly of the State of Georgia, 1903* (Atlanta: Franklin Printing and Publishing Co., 1903), 90–91.
23 *Bailey v. Alabama*, 219 U.S. 219 (1911); *Wilson v. State*, 138 Ga. 489 (1912); "An Act to Provide a Penalty to Be Imposed Upon Any Person in This State Who Shall, With the Intent to Injure and Defraud, Obtain or Procure Money or Other Thing of Value on a Contract to Perform Labor or Service, and to Repeal Chapter 5678, Acts 1907," Chapter 6528, No. 108, *General Acts and Resolutions Adopted by the Legislature of Florida, 1913* (Tallahassee: T. J. Appleyard, 1913), 417; *Goode v. Nelson*, 73 Fla. 29 (1917); *Taylor v. Georgia*, 315 U.S. 25 (1942); and *Pollock v. Williams*, 322 U.S. 4 (1944). In the Florida statute, the language stipulated that "the failure or refusal, without just cause, to perform such labor or service or to pay for the money or other thing of value so obtained or procured shall be prima facie evidence of the intent to injure and defraud." "An Act to Provide a Penalty to be Imposed Upon Any Person in This State Who Shall, With Intent to Injure and Defraud, Obtain or Procure Money or Other Thing of Value on a Contract or Promise to Perform Labor or Service and Prescribing a Rule of Evidence Governing Same," Chapter 7917, No. 135, *General Acts and Resolutions Adopted by the Legislature of Florida, 1919* (Tallahassee: T. J. Appleyard, 1919), 286.
24 Daniel, *Shadow of Slavery*, 25–26; Howard Devon Hamilton, "The Legislative and Judicial History of the Thirteenth Amendment" (Ph.D. diss., University of Illinois, 1950), 225–29; and Cohen, "Negro Involuntary Servitude in the South, 1865–1940," 53.

25 "An Act to authorize the hiring of a certain class of Convicts to private citizens, to prescribe the conditions thereof, and to regulate the relations between the parties, No. 25," March 2, 1874, *Acts of the General Assembly of the State of Georgia, 1874* (Savannah: J. H. Estill, 1874), 29; and *Walton County v. Franklin*, 95 Ga. 538 (1894).
26 Richard Barry, "Slavery in the South To-Day," *Cosmopolitan* 42 (March 1907): 481.
27 Martha A. Myers and James L. Massey, "Race, Labor, and Punishment in Postbellum Georgia," *Social Problems* 38 (May 1991): 268; and S. W. McCallie, "Use of Convicts on the Public Roads of Georgia," *Engineering Record* 64 (1911): 157–58. See also Hilda Jane Zimmerman, "Penal Systems and Penal Reform in the South since the Civil War" (Ph.D. diss.: University of North Carolina, 1947), 424–29.

Chapter 1. The McRees of South Georgia

1 *The Heritage of Lowndes County, Georgia* (Valdosta: Lowndes County Historical Society, 2000), 104; and Catherine McRee Carter, "History of Kinderlou, Georgia, 1860–1940," December 7, 1940, Box 122, folder 1, Kinderlou Papers, Archive Row 1, Lowndes County Historical Society, Valdosta, Georgia, 1.
2 Carter, "History of Kinderlou, Georgia, 1860–1940," 1–3.
3 *Fourth Decennial Catalogue of the Chi Psi Fraternity* (New York: Baker & Godwin, 1883), 33; and Carter, "History of Kinderlou, Georgia, 1860–1940," 2–3.
4 One of those children was William Lawrence McRee, and the glut of McRee children not associated directly with Kinderlou and Edward's ultimate bequest of land that virtually ignored them indicates that the family's reach may have been larger than south Georgia. In 1811, for example, a William McRee acquired a one-thousand-acre headright in Clarke County. There is no direct evidence that he is part of the same family, but George's birth in between Lowndes and Clarke Counties, his education, and the naming of one of his sons William gives an indication that the family was monied from its earliest days and might also have maintained land in the Athens area. William McRee, Land Warrant, 1000 acres, Bounty, Georgia Headright and Bounty Documents, 3-4-5, McRee, William, Georgia Archives, Morrow, Georgia. That particular William McRee may have been George's half-brother, one of Edward's twelve additional children. That close relationship to the family might, however, be pyrrhic. In November 1864, for example, William McRee wrote to the governor, J. E. Brown, that "the situation of my family makes it absolutely necessary that I should be at home for the Spring season to wit: I expect my wife to be confined over till the 20th of the present month." His requests through military channels had been refused, and so "I have thought it best to write to you in my behalf." McRee described himself as "a man of ordinary circumstances, I have a large family and want to see after my little effects. I am forty-six years old. I have been a Civil Officer for twelve years." His war service as an enrolling officer proved his devotion to his state and the Confederate cause, but his "ordinary circumstances" were given lie by his thousand acres of land. William McRee to Gov. J. E. Brown, November 2, 1864, Civil War Records, 1847–1865, Governor Joseph E. Brown Papers, 1-1-5, Georgia Archives, Morrow, Georgia; and Sub-Voucher No. 4, Civil War Records, 1861–1865, 022-01-017, Folder 2857, Georgia Archives, Morrow, Georgia. If the William McRee

who settled in Clarke County really was forty-six years old in 1864, he could not be one of Edward's children. The other indicator arguing against the possibility is the fact that George's son William Lawrence McRee is buried in Valdosta. That by no means provides any proof, as much can change from the first half of the nineteenth century to its later years. But if the McRee family's largesse extended north to Clarke County, it was not a branch of the family that was immediately connected to those at Kinderlou. Carter, "History of Kinderlou, Georgia, 1860–1940," 27.

5   U.S. Department of Commerce, *Seventh Census of the United States, 1850,* Schedule 2, Slave Inhabitants in the County of Lowndes (Washington, D.C.: National Archives and Records Administration, 1850), M432.

6   *The Heritage of Lowndes County, Georgia,* 104–106; Carter, "History of Kinderlou, Georgia, 1860–1940," 3, 16; "No. 663 District, Georgia Militia," Real Estate, Lowndes, 1870, 5, Georgia Tax Digests, Georgia Archives, Morrow, Georgia; and U.S. Department of Commerce, *Tenth Census of the United States, 1880,* Schedule 2, *Productions of Agriculture,* Ousley, Lowndes County, Georgia, 20. His land as of 1877 was eight thousand acres valued at roughly $24,000. "No. 1246 District, Georgia Militia," Lowndes, 1877, n.p., Georgia Tax Digests, Georgia Archives, Morrow, Georgia.

7   "No. 1246 District, Georgia Militia, Ousley," Lowndes, 1890, p.3, Georgia Tax Digests, Georgia Archives, Morrow, Georgia; and Fred H. Hodges, *History of Lowndes County, Georgia, 1825-1941* (Valdosta: General James Jackson Chapter NSDAR, 1995), 164–66. That value was up slightly from his eight thousand acres valued at 24,750 in 1887. "No. 1246 District, Georgia Militia, Ousley," Lowndes, 1887, 3, Georgia Tax Digests, Georgia Archives, Morrow, Georgia.

8   William Spain McRee was born on March 17, 1866, Edward Jones on August 22, 1867, Francis Inman on March 29, 1869, and George Young on July 26, 1872. Carter, "History of Kinderlou, Georgia, 1860–1940," 25.

9   Albert S. Pendleton Jr., *Way Back When,* vol. 1 (Valdosta: self-published, undated), 141, available in general collection of the Lowndes County Historical Society, Valdosta, Georgia; and Carter, "History of Kinderlou, Georgia, 1860–1940," 4–5.

10 The claim of attending Belview College in Virginia is reported in the source, but there is scant evidence of a Belview College in Virginia. There are two possibilities about William's potential college. He either attended Belview College in Missouri or he attended the Virginia Agricultural and Mechanical College, which was a few miles from Belview, Virginia and later became known as Virginia Polytechnic Institute, Virginia Tech. Considering the family's emphasis on engineering and its legacy in Virginia, William's attendance at Virginia Tech seems most likely. Carter, "History of Kinderlou, Georgia, 1860–1940," 4.

11 Carter, "History of Kinderlou, Georgia, 1860–1940," 5, 7, 9.

12 Carter, "History of Kinderlou, Georgia, 1860–1940," 6, 8.

13 Carter, "History of Kinderlou, Georgia, 1860–1940," 9–10.

14 Carter, "History of Kinderlou, Georgia, 1860–1940," 10–11.

15 *Bainbridge Democrat,* May 24, 1883, 1.

16 George McRee and Sons produced roughly twenty acres of cantaloupes. *Bainbridge Democrat,* May 24, 1883, 1; and *Thomasville Times-Enterprise,* July 4, 1899, 1.

17 *Bainbridge Democrat*, May 24, 1883, 1.
18 *Bainbridge Democrat*, May 24, 1883, 1.
19 *Bainbridge Democrat*, May 24, 1883, 1. While printed locally in the *Bainbridge Democrat*, the extended interview with McRee first appeared in the *Atlanta Constitution*, May 10, 1883, 5, May 13, 1883, 3.
20 *Thomasville Times-Enterprise*, October 11, 1890, 1.
21 Wayne and Judy Dasher, *Personal Mentions from Our Research Papers*, vol. 2 (s.p.), 154.
22 Carter, "History of Kinderlou, Georgia, 1860–1940," 11–12.
23 *Thomasville Times-Enterprise*, November 25, 1897, 4, February 13, 1898, 4, March 2, 1898, 1, March 6, 1898, 1, May 3, 1898, 4, June 21, 1898, 4, July 7, 1898, 4, May 13, 1904, 1.
24 *Thomasville Times-Enterprise*, November 27, 1897, 1, January 13, 1898, 1, January 15, 1898, 1, June 21, 1898, 4.
25 *Thomasville Times-Enterprise*, January 10, 1899, 1; and *Valdosta Times*, January 10, 1899, 1.
26 Whether the result of his grief or something more prosaic, Frank took ill soon after for much of the summer of 1900. *Thomasville Times-Enterprise*, May 26, 1900, 1, July 7, 1900, 2.
27 Flynn Jr., *White Land, Black Labor*, 5, 24–26, 109–12, quotes from 5, 24; James L. Roark, *Masters Without Slaves: Southern Planters in the Civil War and Reconstruction* (New York: W. W. Norton, 1977), 111–205; and Albert Bushnell Hart, *The Southern South* (New York: D. Appleton & Co., 1910), 280–83.
28 Jane Twitty Shelton, *Pines and Pioneers: A History of Lowndes County, Georgia, 1825–1900* (Atlanta: Cherokee Publishing Co., 1976), 174–203, quote from 201–2; and Fred H. Hodges, *History of Lowndes County, Georgia, 1825–1941* (Valdosta: General James Jackson Chapter NSDAR, 1995), 88–90. For more on the relationship between debt peonage and the turpentine industry, see Michael David Tegeder, "Prisoners of the Pines: Debt Peonage in the Southern Turpentine Industry, 1900–1930" (Ph.D. diss., University of Florida, 1996).
29 For more on the historical development of Valdosta and Lowndes County, see Louis Schmier, *Valdosta and Lowndes County: A Ray in the Sunbelt* (Northridge, Calif.: Windsor Publications, 1988); and Shelton, *Pines and Pioneers*.
30 James L. Massey and Martha A. Myers, "Patterns of Repressive Social Control in Post-Reconstruction Georgia, 1882–1935," *Social Forces* 68 (December 1989): 459.
31 Bill Boyd, *Blind Obedience: A True Story of Family Loyalty and Murder in South Georgia* (Macon, Ga.: Mercer University Press, 2000), 97–108, quote from 105.
32 Christopher Myers, "Killing Them by the Wholesale: A Lynching Rampage in South Georgia," *Georgia Historical Quarterly* 90 (Summer 2006): 214–235. See also Julie Buckner Armstrong, *Mary Turner and the Memory of Lynching* (Athens: University of Georgia Press, 2011).
33 Louis E. Lomax, "Georgia Boy Goes Home," *Harper's* 230 (April 1965): 152–153, quote from 153.
34 *Tifton Gazette*, April 28, 1893, 1.

35 *Savannah Tribune*, December 29, 1894, 1; *Columbus Daily Enquirer*, December 25, 1894, 1; and W. Fitzhugh Brundage, "The Roar on the Other Side of Silence: Black Resistance and White Violence in the American South, 1880–1940," in *Under Sentence of Death: Lynching in the South*, ed. W. Fitzhugh Brundage (Chapel Hill: University of North Carolina Press, 1997), 261–62.

36 *Baltimore Sun*, December 24, 1894, 2; *New York Herald*, December 24, 1894, 1; *New York Times*, December 24, 1894, 1; *Los Angeles Herald*, December 24, 1894, 1; *Illinois State Register*, December 26, 1894, 1; *Illinois State Journal*, December 26, 1894, 1; and *Daily Inter Ocean*, December 25, 1894, 1.

37 *Atlanta Constitution*, June 26, 1895, 3.

38 *Atlanta Constitution*, September 10, 1897, 3, 6.

39 The collection is by no means complete, making the possibility of records being lost eminently plausible. DOC 2759, 021-01-011, Prisons-State Prison Commission-Corporal Punishment Monthly Reports-1884–1886; 1889– (aka Whipping Reports) Consignment # 2000-1022A, Georgia Archives, Morrow, Georgia.

Chapter 2. The Birth of Misdemeanor Convict Leasing

1 Prison Industries Reorganization Administration, *The Prison Labor Problem in Georgia* (Washington: USGPO, 1937), 3–4.

2 Taylor, "The Origin and Development of the Convict Lease System in Georgia," 113–28; Martha A. Myers, *Race, Labor, and Punishment in the New South* (Columbus: Ohio State University Press, 1998), 8; Green, "Some Aspects of the Convict Lease System in the Southern States," 116; Raza, "Legacies of the Racialization of Incarceration," 164; and Mancini, "Race, Economics, and the Abandonment of Convict Leasing," 340–41. Quote from E. J. Reagan, "Report of the Committee on Penitentiary," December 11, 1895, *Journal of the House of Representatives of the State of Georgia, 1895* (Atlanta: Franklin Printing and Publishing Co., 1895), 830.

3 Daniel A. Novak, *The Wheel of Servitude: Black Forced Labor after Slavery* (Lexington: University Press of Kentucky, 1978), 31. For a fuller comparative analysis focusing on one nearby state, see Darnell Hawkins, "State versus County: Prison Policy and Conflicts of Interest in North Carolina," *Criminal Justice History* 5 (1984): 91–128.

4 Adamson, "Punishment after Slavery," 562.

5 Pippa Holloway, "'A Chicken-Stealer Shall Lose His Vote': Disfranchisement for Larceny in the South, 1874–1890," *Journal of Southern History* 75 (November 2009): 937–38; William B. Taylor, *Brokered Justice: Race, Politics, and Mississippi Prisons, 1798–1992* (Columbus: Ohio State University Press, 1993); and Adamson, "Punishment after Slavery," 562.

6 Sharon Dolovich, "State Punishment and Private Prisons," *Duke Law Journal* 55 (December 2005): 451–52; Christopher Waldrep, "Substituting Law for the Lash: Emancipation and Legal Formalism in a Mississippi County Court," *Journal of American History* 82 (March 1996): 1450; and Michael Perman, *The Road to Redemption: Southern Politics, 1869–1879* (Chapel Hill: University of North Carolina Press, 1984), 242–43.

7 "An Act to amend section 2652 and 2653 Revised Code of 1871, in relation to Grand and Petit Larceny," Chapter LVII, *Laws of the State of Mississippi, Passed At a Regular Session of the Mississippi Legislature, Held in the City of Jackson, Commencing January 4th, 1876, and Ending April 15th, 1876* (Jackson: Power & Barksdale, 1876), 51–52; and S. B. No. 214, *Journal of the Senate of the State of Mississippi at a Regular Session Thereof, Convened in the City of Jackson, January 4, 1876* (Jackson: Power & Barksdale, 1876), 495.

8 Vernon L. Wharton, *The Negro in Mississippi, 1865–1890* (originally published 1947; New York: Harper Torchbooks, 1965), 237; and Mancini, *One Dies, Get Another*, 135–36.

9 Adamson, "Punishment after Slavery," 562; Novak, *The Wheel of Servitude*, 32; Perman, *The Road to Redemption*, 243; and C. Vann Woodward, *Origins of the New South, 1877–1913* (Baton Rouge: Louisiana State University Press, 1971), 213.

10 Holloway, "A Chicken-Stealer Shall Lose His Vote," 940, 941.

11 Vancey quoted in Green, "Some Aspects of the Convict Lease System in the Southern States," 120.

12 The moment slavery ended in Georgia, the prison population became Black. Even in 1866, Georgia's prison population was 92 percent Black. That was the year that convict leasing became part of the law, even though it didn't technically start until 1868. Novak, *The Wheel of Servitude*, 32–33; Adamson, "Punishment after Slavery," 562, 563, 565; Green, "Some Aspects of the Convict Lease System in the Southern States," 119; "Statement of Joseph E. Brown," February 12, 1883, *Congressional Record*, 47th Cong., 2nd sess., vol. 14, 1883, 14, p. 2493; and Darnell F. Hawkins, "Trends in Black-White Imprisonment: Changing Conceptions of Race or Changing Patterns of Social Control?" *Crime and Social Justice* 24 (1985): 196. For more on Brown, see Derrell C. Roberts, *Joseph E. Brown and the Politics of Reconstruction* (Tuscaloosa: University of Alabama Press, 1973); and Joseph Howard Parks, *Joseph E. Brown of Georgia* (Baton Rouge: Louisiana State University Press, 1977).

13 1854 §4705, Part IV, Title I, division 13, in *Annotated Penal Laws of Georgia*, ed. John L. Hopkins (Macon: J. W. Burke & Co., 1875), 453; and "Whipping Bosses for County and Municipal Chain Gangs, No. 398," September 11, 1891, *Acts and Resolutions of the General Assembly of the State of Georgia, 1890–'91, Vol. 1* (Atlanta: Franklin Publishing House, 1891), 211–12.

14 "Authorizing Hiring Out of Misdemeanor Convicts, Etc., No. 679," October 16, 1891, *Acts and Resolutions of the General Assembly of the State of Georgia, 1890–'91, Vol. 1* (Atlanta: Franklin Publishing House, 1891), 212–13.

15 *Journal of the House of Representatives of the State of Georgia, 1892* (Atlanta: Franklin Publishing House, 1892), 202–3, 368.

16 *Journal of the Senate of the State of Georgia, 1892* (Atlanta: Franklin Publishing House, 1892), 230–31, 301–2; and *Journal of the House of Representatives of the State of Georgia, 1892*, 447.

17 *Biennial Report of the Principal Keeper of the Georgia Penitentiary, 1890–1892* (Atlanta: Franklin Publishing House, 1892), 3–5.

18 "Providing for Establishment of Reformatory Prisons by Counties or Municipalities," No. 321, Part I, Title 10, December 19, 1893, in *Acts and Resolutions of the General Assembly of the State of Georgia, 1892* (Atlanta: Franklin Publishing House, 1893), 120–23.

19 *Annual Report of the Principal Keeper of the Georgia Penitentiary, 1895–1896* (Atlanta: Franklin Printing and Publishing Co., 1896), 4; and *Annual Report of the Principal Keeper of the Georgia Penitentiary, 1893–1894* (Atlanta: Franklin Publishing House, 1894), 4–5.

20 The full list of exempted felonies was treason, insurrection, murder, manslaughter, assault with intent to rape, rape, sodomy, feticide, mayhem, seduction, arson, burning railroad bridges, train wrecking, destroying, injuring, or obstructing railroads, perjury, false swearing, and subornation of perjury and false swearing. "Prescribing Penalties for Felonies, with Certain Exceptions, and for All Misdemeanors," No. 17, Part I, Title 7, November 27, 1895, in *Acts and Resolutions of the General Assembly of the State of Georgia, 1895* (Atlanta: Franklin Printing and Publishing Co., 1896), 63–64.

21 The final vote was thirty-seven in favor, three opposed, and four not voting. *Journal of the Senate of the State of Georgia, 1895* (Atlanta: Franklin Printing and Publishing Co., 1895), 300, 370–71.

22 *Journal of the House of Representatives of the State of Georgia, 1895* (Atlanta: Franking Printing and Publishing Co., 1896), 284, 608, 869.

23 R. F. Wright, *Special Report of R.F. Wright on Misdemeanor Convicts of the State of Georgia, 1895* (Atlanta: Franklin Printing and Publishing, 1895), 4, Georgia Archives, Morrow, Georgia.

24 Wright, *Special Report of R.F. Wright on Misdemeanor Convicts of the State of Georgia, 1895*, 3–8.

25 Phill G. Byrd, *Report of Special Inspector of Misdemeanor Convict Camps of Georgia* (Atlanta: Franklin Printing and Publishing, 1897), 4–5.

26 Byrd, *Report of Special Inspector of Misdemeanor Convict Camps of Georgia*, 3.

27 $449 "Vagrants," Tenth Division, Article 15, *The Code of the State of Georgia, 1910*, Vol. 2 (Atlanta: Foote & Davies, 1911), 91–92.

28 Byrd, *Report of Special Inspector of Misdemeanor Convict Camps of Georgia*, 5.

29 Byrd, *Report of Special Inspector of Misdemeanor Convict Camps of Georgia*, 5.

30 Byrd, *Report of Special Inspector of Misdemeanor Convict Camps of Georgia*, 4–5.

31 Byrd, *Report of Special Inspector of Misdemeanor Convict Camps of Georgia*, 4–5.

32 Byrd, *Report of Special Inspector of Misdemeanor Convict Camps of Georgia*, 6.

33 Byrd, *Report of Special Inspector of Misdemeanor Convict Camps of Georgia*, 12.

34 The reporter admitted that specificity about regular work hours might be inexact, as he was "forced to base [his] report on information furnished by superintendents and lessees." Byrd, *Report of Special Inspector of Misdemeanor Convict Camps of Georgia*, 6.

35 Byrd, *Report of Special Inspector of Misdemeanor Convict Camps of Georgia*, 7–8.

36 Byrd, *Report of Special Inspector of Misdemeanor Convict Camps of Georgia*, 9–10.

37 Byrd, *Report of Special Inspector of Misdemeanor Convict Camps of Georgia*, 10–11.

38 Byrd, *Report of Special Inspector of Misdemeanor Convict Camps of Georgia,* 11–12.
39 Byrd, *Report of Special Inspector of Misdemeanor Convict Camps of Georgia,* 14.
40 Byrd, *Report of Special Inspector of Misdemeanor Convict Camps of Georgia,* 13–14.
41 Byrd, *Report of Special Inspector of Misdemeanor Convict Camps of Georgia,* 15.
42 Byrd, *Report of Special Inspector of Misdemeanor Convict Camps of Georgia,* 17.
43 Byrd, *Report of Special Inspector of Misdemeanor Convict Camps of Georgia,* 19–20.
44 Byrd, *Report of Special Inspector of Misdemeanor Convict Camps of Georgia,* 21.
45 Byrd, *Report of Special Inspector of Misdemeanor Convict Camps of Georgia,* 22.
46 Cannon was convicted for McRay's murder but was given only a twelve-month sentence. Byrd, *Report of Special Inspector of Misdemeanor Convict Camps of Georgia,* 22, 23–24, 26–27, quote from 23.
47 Byrd, *Report of Special Inspector of Misdemeanor Convict Camps of Georgia,* 15–16.
48 §860 (§715) "Rules for government of convicts, etc.," and §861 (§716) "Superintendent, etc., not personally liable for damage to convict," Seventh Title, Chapter 1, Article 2, *The Code of the State of Georgia, 1910,* vol. 1 (Atlanta: Foote and Davies, 1911), 222. It was also in 1801 when Georgia law first created the possibility of debt peonage. See chapter 3.
49 "Good Behavior of Misdemeanor Convicts," Part I, Title VIII, No. 319, October 9, 1885, in *Acts and Resolutions of the General Assembly of the State of Georgia, 1884–1885* (Atlanta: James P. Harrison & Co., 1885), 89.
50 Byrd, *Report of Special Inspector of Misdemeanor Convict Camps of Georgia,* 16.
51 Byrd, *Report of Special Inspector of Misdemeanor Convict Camps of Georgia,* 27.
52 Byrd, *Report of Special Inspector of Misdemeanor Convict Camps of Georgia,* 28.
53 Byrd, *Report of Special Inspector of Misdemeanor Convict Camps of Georgia,* 30.
54 Byrd, *Report of Special Inspector of Misdemeanor Convict Camps of Georgia,* 30–31.

Chapter 3. Felony Leasing and Debt Peonage under Scrutiny

1 The law was referenced and explained during the amendment process in 1895. "Penitentiary Convicts, Amending Law As to Release of, No. 124," December 14, 1895, *Acts and Resolutions of the General Assembly of the State of Georgia, 1890-'91, Vol. 1* (Atlanta: Franklin Printing and Publishing, 1896), 80.
2 "Orders and Instructions to Lessees of the Georgia Penitentiary," July 1, 1885, Records of the Georgia Board of Corrections, Record Group 21, 3–4, 19–20, Georgia Archives, Morrow, Georgia.
3 U.S. Bureau of Labor, *Second Annual Report of the Commissioner of Labor, 1886: Convict Labor* (Washington, D.C.: USGPO, 1887), 301, 382. For more on Gordon, see Ralph Lowell Eckert, *John Brown Gordon: Soldier, Southerner, American* (Baton Rouge: Louisiana State University Press, 1993). See also Hilda Jane Zimmerman, "Penal Systems and Penal Reforms in the South Since the Civil War" (Ph.D. diss: University of North Carolina, 1947), 119–23.
4 Mancini, "Race, Economics, and the Abandonment of Convict Leasing," 343. See also Myers and Massey, "Race, Labor, and Punishment in Postbellum Georgia," 270–71; Du Bois, "The Spawn Of Slavery," 117–24; and George Washington Cable, *The Silent South* (Montclair, Calif.: Patterson Smith, 1969), 123.

5 Frederick H. Wines, *Report on Crime, Pauperism, and Benevolence in the United States at the Eleventh Census: 1890* (Washington: USGPO, 1895), 15, 118, 121.
6 Myers and Massey, "Race, Labor, and Punishment in Postbellum Georgia," 274–75, 278.
7 Howard Association, "Continuing Cruelties in the Convict Chain Gangs and Camps of the Southern United States," London, 1901; Howard Association, "The Evils of Lynching and Convict Camps," London, undated, Casefile 909-1898, Reel 1, Peonage Files of the Department of Justice, 1901–1945.
8 "AN ACT To Carry into Effect the Seventh Section of the Fourth Article of the Constitution," No. 22, section 6, December 5, 1801, *A Compilation of the Laws of the State of Georgia*, ed. Augustin Smith Clayton (Augusta: Adams & Duyckinck, 1812), 21–23.
9 Pete Daniel, *The Shadow of Slavery: Peonage in the South, 1901–1969* (Urbana: University of Illinois Press, 1972), 24–25.
10 Daniel, *The Shadow of Slavery*, 34. Much of Daniel's interpretation came from Dan T. Carter's master's thesis at the University of Wisconsin, which made the case for local corruption and described the practice in places like Georgia of arresting a poor Black citizen on a minor charge, sentencing him to several months of hard labor, then arresting him immediately after his sentence as a vagrant and sentencing him again. Carter also described the organized practice of companies who watched courts and paid the fines of misdemeanor prisoners, then worked them for those companies. Dan T. Carter, "Prisons, Politics and Business: The Convict Lease System in the Post-Civil War South" (M.A. thesis: University of Wisconsin, 1964), 94–95.
11 Cohen, "Negro Involuntary Servitude in the South, 1865–1940: A Preliminary Analysis," 33–34. Quote from 33.
12 Roger L. Ransom and Richard Sutch, "Debt Peonage in the Cotton South after the Civil War," *Journal of Economic History* 32 (September 1972): 643. While there were critics of Ransom and Sutch's work, the most prominent were built on causal explanations of the economic forces that created the system, not on the existence of the system itself. See, for example, William W. Brown and Morgan O. Reynolds, "Debt Peonage Re-Examined," *Journal of Economic History* 33 (December 1973): 862–71.
13 Roger L. Ransom and Richard Sutch, *One Kind of Freedom: The Economic Consequences of Slavery*, originally published 1977 (New York: Cambridge University Press, 2001). For more on the influence of the book, see Peter A. Colcanis, "In Retrospect: Ransom and Sutch's *One Kind of Freedom*," *Reviews in American History* 28 (September 2000): 478–89.
14 Toombs quoted in "Peonage in Georgia," *Independent* 55 (December 24, 1903): 3079.
15 "Peonage in Georgia," 3079; "Does Slavery Exist in South Carolina," *Literary Digest* 22 (March 2, 1901): 244; and *New York Times*, February 17, 1901, 1.
16 "Does Slavery Exist in South Carolina," 244; and *New York Times*, March 8, 1901, 1, June 15, 1901, 3.
17 "An Act to abolish and forever prohibit the System of Peonage in the Territory of New Mexico and other Parts of the United States," March 2, 1867, Chapter 187, *Unit-*

ed States Statutes at Large, 39th Congress, 2nd sess, 546. For a more detailed account of how peonage worked in the territory, see William S. Kiser, *Borderlands of Slavery: The Struggle over Captivity and Peonage in the American Southwest* (Philadelphia: University of Pennsylvania Press, 2017).

18 *Slaughterhouse Cases*, 83 U.S. 36 (1873). For more on the *Slaughterhouse Cases*, see Michael A. Ross, "Justice Miller's Reconstruction: The Slaughter-House Cases, Health Codes, and Civil Rights in New Orleans, 1861–1873," *Journal of Southern History* 64 (November 1998): 649–76; Ronald M. Labbé and Jonathan Lurie, *The Slaughterhouse Cases: Regulation, Reconstruction, and the Fourteenth Amendment* (Lawrence: University Press of Kansas, 2003); and Kevin Christopher Newsom, "Setting Incorporationism Straight: A Reinterpretation of the *Slaughter-House Cases*," *Yale Law Journal* 109 (2000): 643–744.

19 *Civil Rights Cases*, 109 U.S. 3 (1883). For more on *Civil Rights Cases* and the Civil Rights Act of 1875, see Mark V. Tushnet, "'To Enable the Black Race to Take the Rank of Mere Citizens': The Civil Rights Cases, 1883," in *I Dissent: Great Opposing Opinions in Landmark Supreme Court Cases* (Boston: Beacon Press, 2008), 45–68; Tsesis, *The Thirteenth Amendment and American Freedom;* Leon A. Higginbotham Jr., "The Supreme Court's Sanction of Racial Hatred: The 1883 Civil Rights Cases," in *Shades of Freedom: Racial Politics and Presumptions of the American Legal Process* (New York: Oxford University Press, 1998), 94–107; Alan Friedlander and Richard Allan Gerber, *Welcoming Ruin: The Civil Rights Act of 1875* (London: Brill, 2018); Valeria W. Weaver, "The Failure of Civil Rights 1875–1883 and Its Repercussions," *Journal of Negro History* 54 (October 1969): 368–82; Patrick O. Gudridge, "Privileges and Permissions: The Civil Rights Act of 1875," *Law and Philosophy* 8 (April 1989): 83–130; James W. McPherson, "Abolitionists and the Civil Rights Act of 1875," *Journal of American History* 52 (December 1965): 493–510; and Carolyn Iona White, *Georgia's Reaction to the Civil Rights Act of 1875 and the Civil Rights Cases of 1883* (M.A. thesis: Atlanta University, 1971).

20 *Afro-American*, April 22, 1905, 1.

21 *United States v. Eberhart et al.*, 127 F. 252 (1899). The ruling, however, clearly discounted charges that the system imposed on the farm of William Eberhart in Oglethorpe County was, in fact, a version of slavery. Eberhart, it was charged, was conducting "a reign of terror," where "negroes are actually held in bondage, whipped almost into insensibility and forced to sign long termed [sic] contracts, and the children bound to said Eberhart until 21 years of age." H. O. Johnson to Ed. Angier, January 14, 1898, Casefile 909-1898, Reel 1, Peonage Files of the Department of Justice, 1901–1945. The original grand jury indictment in the case included multiple examples of that "reign of terror," not only chronicling the plight of individuals on Eberhart's farm, but also the strategy of Eberhart himself, who used the justice system to his advantage. His brother-in-law was the county's justice of the peace, allowing the plantation owner to submit trumped up charges against Black residents with relative surety that they would be convicted without evidence and allowed to be enslaved on his farm. *United States v. William Eberhart*, Indictment in the United States Circuit Court, Northern District of Georgia, April 19, 1898, No. 5357, Case-

file 909-1898, Reel 1, Peonage Files of the Department of Justice, 1901–1945; and *Oglethorpe Echo,* April 29, 1898, n.p., Casefile 909-1898, Reel 1, Peonage Files of the Department of Justice, 1901–1945.
22. *In re Lewis,* 114 Fed. 963 (1902).
23. *Peonage Cases,* 123 Fed. 671 (1903); and "Servitude for Debt in Georgia," *Outlook* 74 (June 27, 1903): 486. See also "The Peonage Cases," *Harvard Law Review* 17 (1903): 121–22.
24. *Peonage Cases,* 123 Fed. 676, 677, 678 (1903).
25. *Peonage Cases,* 123 Fed. 686 (1903).
26. *Peonage Cases,* 123 Fed. 687 (1903). At the same time that Jones was ruling on the class implications of debt peonage, the district court for the Eastern District of Arkansas was ruling on a race-based denial of a farmer's ability to lease a tract of farmland. It was a conspiracy by white people to "injure, oppress, and intimidate certain citizens of the United States, of African descent, in the free exercise or enjoyment of certain rights secured to them by the Constitution and laws of the United States, on account of their being negroes." The ruling, based on the Thirteenth Amendment, denounced such a conspiracy as unconstitutional, a different but tangential reckoning of racial limitations based on the amendment designed to end slavery. *United States v. Morris et al.,* 125 F. 322 (1903).
27. *Peonage Cases,* 123 Fed. 691 (1903). Jones was no consistent crusader for human rights, which gave his commentary all the more force. The following year, a case came before his docket alleging that a group of mining operators conspired to keep a union from organizing and that they responded to the attempt by violently accosting the organizer. Jones ruled that regulation of such instances was relegated to the states and was not under the purview of the federal courts. *United States v. Moore, et al.,* 129 F. 630 (1904).
28. Their relationship would falter after the creation of the NAACP later in the decade, but the two had a mutual disdain for peonage and a profitable working relationship in 1903. Cohen, "Negro Involuntary Servitude in the South," 50–52; *Afro-American,* August 8, 1903, 4, September 19, 1903, 2; Daniel, "Up from Slavery and Down to Peonage," 660; Booker T. Washington to Oswald Garrison Villard, June 16, 1903, Box 95, Part I: Special Correspondence, 1853–1915, Booker T. Washington Papers, 1853–1946, MSS44669, Manuscript Division, Library of Congress, Washington, D.C.; and *New York Evening Post,* June 25, 1903, 4, July 24, 1903, 4.
29. *Afro-American,* August 8, 1903, 4. See also Curtin, *Black Prisoners and Their World, Alabama, 1865–1900.*
30. *Afro-American,* July 4, 1903, 4. See also July 18, 1903, 4.
31. *Afro-American,* August 8, 1903, 4.
32. *Afro-American,* March 19, 1904, 1, July 16, 1904, 4. Benjamin Tillman was a segregationist firebrand from South Carolina whose combative style and overt white supremacy rankled many. He earned his nickname, "Pitchfork," from his threat to Grover Cleveland after the repeal of the Sherman Silver Purchase Act of 1890. "When Judas betrayed Christ, his heart was not blacker than this scoundrel, Cleveland, in deceiving the Democracy," said Tillman. "He is an old bag of beef and I am

going to Washington with a pitchfork and prod him in his fat ribs." For more on Tillman, particularly in relation to race, see Stephen Kantrowitz, *Ben Tillman and the Reconstruction of White Supremacy* (North Carolina: University of North Carolina Press, 2000); Francis Butler Simkins, "Ben Tillman's View of the Negro," *Journal of Southern History* 3 (May 1937): 161–74; and George B. Tindall, "The Question of Race in the South Carolina Constitutional Convention of 1895," *Journal of Negro History* 37 (July 1952): 277–303.

Chapter 4. Misdemeanor Leasing at the Turn of the Century

1 "Prison Commission Created, No. 340," December 21, 1897, *Acts and Resolutions of the General Assembly of the State of Georgia, 1897* (Atlanta: Franklin Printing and Publishing, 1898), 71–78; and Prison Industries Reorganization Administration, *The Prison Labor Problem in Georgia* (Washington: USGPO, 1937), 5.
2 "Prison Commission, Disposition of Convicts, No. 430," October 17, 1903, *Acts and Resolutions of the General Assembly of the State of Georgia, 1903* (Atlanta: Franklin Printing and Publishing, 1903), 65–71. The legislature would continue to tweak the law and the constitution of the Prison Commission in subsequent years but never change its basic original mission. "Hire of Felony Convicts, Disposition of, No. 150," August 23, 1905, *Acts and Resolutions of the General Assembly of the State of Georgia, 1905* (Atlanta: Franklin Printing and Publishing, 1905), 125–26; "Hire of Felony Convicts, Participation in By New Counties, No. 488," August 18, 1906, *Acts and Resolutions of the General Assembly of the State of Georgia, 1906* (Atlanta: Franklin Printing and Publishing, 1906), 113–14; and "Committee on Penitentiary, Inspections, Etc., No. 2," August 7, 1907, *Acts and Resolutions of the General Assembly of the State of Georgia, 1907* (Atlanta: Franklin-Turner Company, 1907), 1012–13.
3 The commission was also tasked with finding and purchasing land for a prison farm for minors, female prisoners, and "men who were infirm" to be kept segregated from those to be leased. The Prison Commission would also serve as the de facto board of pardons. The four commissioners serving during the first years of the twentieth century during Kinderlou's scrutiny were Joseph Sydney Turner, General Clement A. Evans, Jacob L. Beach, and Thomas Eason. Descriptive Inventory Number 1, Records of the Georgia Prison Commission, 1817–1936, A Part of the Records of the Georgia Board of Corrections, Record Group 21, 3–4, 19–20, Georgia Archives, Morrow, Georgia.
4 Francis M. Wilhoit, "An Interpretation of Populism's Impact on the Georgia Negro," *Journal of Negro History* 52 (April 1967): 116–27; and Alex Mathews Arnett, *The Populist Movement in Georgia: A View of the "Agrarian Crusade" in the Light of Solid-South Politics* (originally published 1922; Ithaca: Cornell University Library, 2009).
5 *First Annual Report of the Prison Commission of Georgia, 1898*, 3–4, Georgia Penitentiary Prison Commission's Reports, 21-1-40, Georgia Archives, Morrow, Georgia.
6 *First Annual Report of the Prison Commission of Georgia, 1898* (Atlanta: Franklin Printing Co., 1898), 35–36.

7 *First Annual Report of the Prison Commission of Georgia, 1898,* 37.
8 *First Annual Report of the Prison Commission of Georgia, 1898,* 37–38.
9 *First Annual Report of the Prison Commission of Georgia, 1898,* 38.
10 *First Annual Report of the Prison Commission of Georgia, 1898,* 38–39.
11 *First Annual Report of the Prison Commission of Georgia, 1898,* 40–41.
12 *First Annual Report of the Prison Commission of Georgia, 1898,* 36.
13 *Second Annual Report of the Prison Commission of Georgia, 1899* (Atlanta: Foote & Davies Co., 1899), 17.
14 *Second Annual Report of the Prison Commission of Georgia, 1899,* 18.
15 *Third Annual Report of the Prison Commission of Georgia, 1900,* 3–5, Georgia Penitentiary Prison Commission's Reports, 21-1-40, Georgia Archives, Morrow, Georgia.
16 *Third Annual Report of the Prison Commission of Georgia, 1900,* 7.
17 *Third Annual Report of the Prison Commission of Georgia, 1900,* 8–9.
18 *Third Annual Report of the Prison Commission of Georgia, 1900* (Atlanta: Foote & Davies Co., 1900), 16.
19 Italics in the original. *Third Annual Report of the Prison Commission of Georgia, 1900,* 18–19.
20 *Third Annual Report of the Prison Commission of Georgia, 1900,* 19.
21 *Third Annual Report of the Prison Commission of Georgia, 1900,* 20.
22 *Third Annual Report of the Prison Commission of Georgia, 1900,* 21.
23 *Third Annual Report of the Prison Commission of Georgia, 1900,* 21.
24 *Third Annual Report of the Prison Commission of Georgia, 1900,* 22.
25 *Third Annual Report of the Prison Commission of Georgia, 1900,* 11–12.
26 *Third Annual Report of the Prison Commission of Georgia, 1901,* 13.
27 *Fourth Annual Report of the Prison Commission of Georgia, 1901* (Atlanta: Franklin Printing Co., 1901), 9, 10–13.

Chapter 5. The Scandal of 1900–1901

1 *Macon Telegraph,* September 27, 1900, 3; and *Quitman Free Press,* September 28, 1900, 1. Several months later, for example, John Eagan, U.S. attorney for the Northern District of Florida, reported a variety of abuses in north Florida turpentine camps, where "colored men" were "treated outrageously by their employers." And yet there was no "report of any case prosecuted" for the various offenses. Eagan sought to change that, but the impunity with which such behavior occurred was a demonstration of not only its prevalence but law enforcement's complicity in the practice. John Eagan to Attorney General, July 13, 1901, Casefile 909-1898, Reel 1, Peonage Files of the Department of Justice, 1901–1945. Eagan was prompted by reports to his office that "many poor unfortunate negroes out in this section" were "being held by these turpentine men in abject bondage. It is impossible for one [of] them, the negroes, to get justice in the Justice of the Peace Courts, for the turpentine men have all the J.P.'s in their power, and as a result many negroes are being held by these turpentine men in a worse state than when they were slaves." The practice of advancing goods to Black employees, then using the debt to keep them in bondage,

beating them consistently throughout, was a regular occurrence. "So common has this most outrageous abuse become until it has become dangerous for one who is opposed to such treatment to open his mouth in defense of the poor negroe [sic]." W. O. Butler and John Cook to John Eagen, June 29, 1901, Casefile 909-1898, Reel 1, Peonage Files of the Department of Justice, 1901–1945. For more on the relationship between debt peonage and the turpentine industry, see Tegeder, "Prisoners of the Pines."

2 *Macon Telegraph,* September 27, 1900, 3; and *Atlanta Constitution,* September 27, 1900, 7.
3 *Quitman Free Press,* September 28, 1900, 1; and *Macon Telegraph,* September 27, 1900, 3.
4 *Atlanta Constitution,* September 27, 1900, 7. That legitimate scandal also permeated nationally. See *Indianapolis Journal,* September 27, 1900, 1; *Omaha Daily Bee,* September 27, 1900, 1; *Salt Lake Herald,* September 27, 1900, 1; and *Washington Post,* September 27, 1900, 1.
5 *Macon Telegraph,* September 27, 1900, 3; and *Atlanta Constitution,* September 27, 1900, 7.
6 *Macon Telegraph,* September 28, 1900, 3; *Atlanta Constitution,* September 28, 1900, 2; and *Thomasville Times-Enterprise,* February 26, 1901, 1.
7 *Atlanta Constitution,* October 2, 1900, 2.
8 Georgia's entire system was controlled by the Prison Commission, with no other state supervision for prisoners. In that way, it was similar to Arkansas, Alabama, Nevada, and Texas, which had similar commission systems. Frederick H. Guild, "Administration and Supervision of State Charities and Corrections," *American Political Science Review* 10 (May 1916): 327, 334.
9 *Quitman Free Press,* October 5, 1900, 1; and *Macon Telegraph,* October 3, 1900, 4.
10 *Macon Telegraph,* October 4, 1900, 4.
11 *Atlanta Constitution,* October 2, 1900, 7.
12 Though the commission's hearing featured thirty-three witnesses and was a high-profile and well-reported endeavor, any transcript of the event has disappeared from the historical record. It no longer resides at the Lowndes County or Brooks County courthouses, the state historical archives, Georgia's Southern Judicial Circuit, the Federal Court system in Georgia—either the Southern District of Georgia, which the region was part of at the time, or the Middle District of Georgia, which the region is part of in the twenty-first century—or the Georgia Department of Corrections, into which the Prison Commission was ultimately folded. Correspondence with all the aforementioned groups in possession of the author.
13 *Quitman Free Press,* October 19, 1900, 1; and *Macon Telegraph,* October 17, 1900, 4.
14 *Quitman Free Press,* October 19, 1900, 1.
15 For work on Black overseers, see William L. Van Deburg, *The Slave Drivers: Black Agricultural Labor Supervisors in the Antebellum South* (originally published 1979; New York: Oxford University Press, 1988); Randall Miller, "The Man in the Middle: The Black Slave Driver," *American Heritage* 30 (1979): 40–49; and Martin Reuf and Ben Fletcher, "Legacies of American Slavery: Status Attainment among Southern

Blacks after Emancipation," *Social Forces* 82 (December 2003): 445–90. For work on Jewish kapos (concentration camp guards), see Tuvia Friling, *A Jewish Kapo in Auschwitz: History, Memory, and the Politics of Survival* (Waltham: Brandeis University Press, 2014); Ross W. Halpin, *Jewish Doctors and the Holocaust: The Anatomy of Survival in Auschwitz* (Berlin: De Gruyter, 2018); and Dan Porat, *Bitter Reckoning: Israel Tries Holocaust Survivors as Nazi Collaborators* (Cambridge, Mass.: Harvard University Press, 2019).

16 *Quitman Free Press*, October 19, 1900, 1; and *Macon Telegraph*, October 17, 1900, 4.
17 *Quitman Free Press*, October 19, 1900, 1; and *Macon Telegraph*, October 19, 1900, 4.
18 *Macon Telegraph*, October 19, 1900, 4.
19 *Waycross Herald*, October 20, 1900, 4.
20 *Quitman Free Press*, October 19, 1900, 1.
21 *Fourth Annual Report of the Prison Commission of Georgia, 1901,* 10–12, Georgia Penitentiary Prison Commission's Reports, 21-1-40, Georgia Archives, Morrow, Georgia.
22 *Thomasville Times-Enterprise*, January 13, 1901, 1; and *Quitman Free Press*, March 1, 1901, 1.
23 John Dittmer, *Black Georgia in the Progressive Era, 1900–1920* (Urbana: University of Illinois Press, 1977), 74.
24 *Atlanta Constitution*, February 16, 1901, 7.
25 *Thomasville Times-Enterprise*, February 26, 1901, 1; and *Atlanta Constitution*, February 24, 1901, 7.
26 *Atlanta Constitution*, February 24, 1901, 7.
27 *Atlanta Constitution*, February 24, 1901, 7.
28 *Thomasville Times-Enterprise*, February 26, 1901, 1; and *Atlanta Constitution*, February 24, 1901, 7.
29 *Macon Telegraph*, October 6, 1900, 2. See *Third Annual Report of the Prison Commission of Georgia, 1900,* Georgia Penitentiary Prison Commission's Reports, 21-1-40, Georgia Archives, Morrow, Georgia.
30 *Macon Telegraph*, October 11, 1900, 4.
31 *Atlanta Constitution*, December 22, 1897, 5.
32 "1901—List of Insolvent Tax 1901, made out from filings returned," Records of the Georgia Board of Corrections, Record Group 21, 12-54-49-DOC2-894, Georgia Archives, Morrow, Georgia.
33 "Does Slavery Exist in South Carolina," *Literary Digest* 22 (March 2, 1901): 244.
34 *Savannah Morning News*, September 13, 1901, 3. The family bolstered its local ties by hiring people from the area. In April 1902, for example, Thomasville's David Libby was hired to be the McRees' stenographer and assistant bookkeeper. Ware Superior Court, April Term 1903, 395, Court Minutes Book F (unmarked volume), Ware County Clerk of Court, Waycross, Georgia; and *Thomasville Times-Enterprise*, April 23, 1902, 1.
35 *Macon Telegraph*, August 24, 1901, 3; and *Savannah Morning News*, August 24, 1901, 2.

36 Anthony M. Platt, *The Child Savers: The Invention of Delinquency*, 2nd ed. (Chicago: University of Chicago Press, 1977), 4–17; David S. Tanenhaus, *Juvenile Justice in the Making* (New York: Oxford University Press, 2004), 23–25; and Geoff K. Ward, *The Black Child-Savers: Racial Democracy and Juvenile Justice* (Chicago: University of Chicago Press, 2012), 5–8, 10–16, 77–78.

37 Blackmon, *Slavery by Another Name*, 7–8, 251–52; Douglas A. Blackmon, "Transcript of Keynote Speaker from Work in the South: Dixie Cotton, American Steel, and a Hurricane Named Katrina—a Reinvention Of Bondage," *Loyola Journal of Public Interest Law* 16 (Spring 2015): 449–51; and Robin Walker Sterling, "Fundamental Unfairness: *In re Gault* and the Road Not Taken," *Maryland Law Review* 72 (2013): 610–11. Blackmon also mentioned the same story in Douglas A. Blackmon, "America's Twentieth-Century Slavery," *Washington Monthly* (January/February 2013): https://washingtonmonthly.com/magazine/janfeb-2013/americas-twentieth-century-slavery/, accessed September 21, 2020. "Mr. President, I have a brother about 14-years old. A colored man came here and hired him from me and said that he would take good care of him and pay me five dollars a month for him and I heard of him no more. He went and sold him to McRee and they has been working him in prison for 12 months and I has tried to get them to send him to me and they wont let him go. He has no mother and no father. They are both dead and I am his only friend and they won't let me have him. He has not done nothing for them to have him in chains. So I write to you for you to help me get my poor brother. His name is James Robinson and the man that carried him off his name Dan Cal. He sold him to McRee at Valdosta Ga. Please let me hear from you at once." Letter dated July 21 and received July 31, 1903. No. 12007, file no. 3098., General Records of the Department of Justice, National Archives, Washington, D.C. The letter was popularized by Blackmon's *Slavery by Another Name* and was subsequently made part of the online collection of the National Archives, available at http://recordsofrights.org/records/279/sister-tries-to-save-her-kidnapped-brother/0, accessed September 27, 2020.

38 Senate Reports, 46 Cong., 2 Sess., No. 693: *Report and Testimony of the Select Committee of the United States Senate to Investigate the Causes of the Removal of Negroes from the Southern States to the Northern States*. Serial 1899, Washington, D.C., 1880, 117.

39 "Memorial of Republican Members of Legislature of Alabama to the Congress of the United States," in: Report: The subcommittee of the Committee on Privileges and Elections to inquire and report whether in any of the elections in the State of Alabama in the elections of 1874, 1875, and 1876 the right of male inhabitants of said State, being twenty-one years of age and citizens of the United States, to vote had been denied or abridged, Senate Report No. 704, 44th Congress, 2nd sess., 3 March 1877, in: *Report of the Committees of the Senate of the United States for the Second Session of the Forty-Fourth Congress, 1876–77*, vol. 1, United States Congressional Serial Set 1732 (Washington: USGPO, 1877), 662–69.

40 Green Berry Raum, *The Existing Conflict Between Republican Government and Southern Oligarchy* (New York: Charles M. Green Printing, 1884), 449.

41 *Fifth Annual Report of the Prison Commission of Georgia, 1902* (Atlanta: Lester Book and Stationery, 1902), 9.

42 "Authorizing Hiring Out of Misdemeanor Convicts, Etc., No. 679," October 16, 1891, *Acts and Resolutions of the General Assembly of the State of Georgia, 1890-'91, Vol. 1* (Atlanta: Franklin Publishing House, 1891), 212-13.

43 *Fifth Annual Report of the Prison Commission of Georgia, 1902*, 11-12.

44 *Fifth Annual Report of the Prison Commission of Georgia, 1902*, 15-16.

45 *Fifth Annual Report of the Prison Commission of Georgia, 1902*, 16.

46 *Fifth Annual Report of the Prison Commission of Georgia, 1902*, 17-20.

Chapter 6. The State Scandal of 1903

1 "In Ware Superior Court, April term, 1903. To the Honorable Superior Court of Ware County, Georgia.

> "We, the grand jurors, serving at said term of said court, beg leave to submit these, our general presentments...
>
> "8th. Testimony has been produced to us that McRee Brothers of Lowndes county Georgia, are coming into this county, paying the fines of misdemeanor convicts and carrying such convicts to their camps, and there keeping them illegally restrained of their liberty for long terms of servitude, subjecting them to harsh and cruel treatment at the hands of whipping bosses, and information coming to our body that there are now several citizens of this county so illegally restrained of their liberty by said McRee Brothers. We, therefore, recommend that the commissioners of roads and revenues of this county investigate this matter, and if they find such citizens to be restrained of their liberty, that they employ counsel to take proper legal steps to release such persons from custody, and if there has been a violation of the penal laws of the state, that prosecutions be instituted and carried on." *Quitman Free Press*, May 8, 1903, 1; and *Waycross Journal*, May 1, 1903, 1.

2 *Quitman Free Press*, May 15, 1903, 1, 4.

3 *Atlanta Constitution*, July 3, 1903, 5.

4 *Quitman Free Press*, July 17, 1903, 1; *Thomasville Times-Enterprise*, March 25, 1904, 11, May 6, 1904, 7; and *Journal of the House of Representatives of the State of Georgia, 1902* (Atlanta: Franklin Printing and Publishing Co., 1902), 7.

5 *Journal of the House of Representatives of the State of Georgia, 1902*, 140, 238; and *Thomasville Times-Enterprise*, November 22, 1902, 4. For more on the system in Alabama, see Blackmon, *Slavery By Another Name*; and Curtin, *Black Prisoners and Their World, Alabama, 1865-1900*.

6 Alton DuMar Jones, "The Administration of Governor Joseph M. Terrell Viewed in the Light of the Progressive Movement," *Georgia Historical Quarterly* 48 (September 1964): 271-90.

7 Joseph Merriwell Terrell, "Misdemeanor Convicts," *Journal of the House of Representatives of the State of Georgia, 1902* (Atlanta: Franklin Printing and Publishing Co., 1902), 48-52.

8 *Atlanta Constitution*, October 29, 1902, 7; and *Fifth Annual Report of the Prison Commission of Georgia, 1902* (Atlanta: Lester Book and Stationery, 1902), 30–31.
9 *Quitman Free Press*, July 24, 1903, 1.
10 *Atlanta Constitution*, August 2, 1903, B4.
11 *Quitman Free Press*, August 7, 1903, 1; and *Atlanta Constitution*, August 6, 1903, 7.
12 *Atlanta Constitution*, October 16, 1903, 1.
13 *Quitman Free Press*, August 21, 1903, 1.
14 *Quitman Free Press*, September 25, 1903, 1. The Brooks County decisions took place at a meeting of the county commissioners on September 23, 1903, but the minutes of those early-twentieth-century meetings no longer exist. Correspondence with Brooks County Clerk of Court.
15 *Atlanta Journal* article reprinted in *Quitman Free Press*, September 25 1903, 1. See also *Atlanta Journal*, September 18, 1903, 2.
16 *Quitman Free Press*, October 9, 1903, 1. Similar pleas from Quitman citizens appeared on October 16, 1903, 1, and October 23, 1903, 1.
17 "An Act to make it illegal for any person to procure money, or other thing of value, on a contract to perform services with intent to defraud, and to fix the punishment therefor, and for other purposes," No. 345, August 15, 1903, Casefile 909-1898, Reel 1, Peonage Files of the Department of Justice, 1901–1945; and *Townsend v. State*, 52 SE 293 (1905). Demonstrating the regional variation in southern thinking on the issue of peonage, at the same time that the Georgia Supreme Court was validating the state's fraud mandates that held debt peonage in place, the federal district court for the Eastern District of Arkansas was striking down peonage as constitutionally invalid. "If a man enters into such a contract with another, the laws of the United States say that it is void, and he may at any time he desires leave his employment, although the debt is still unpaid; and any attempt on the part of the employer to prevent him from leaving, either by force, threats, or intimidation, or by guarding him and locking him up to prevent his escape, is, within the meaning of the laws of the United States, an offense." *Peonage Cases*, 136 F. 707 (1905).
18 As were federal prosecutors. "I doubt the constitutionality of the act," said Alexander Ackerman, "and it seems to me to be in violation of the Thirteenth Amendment, as it provides for an involuntary servitude not as a punishment for crime. In the second place, it provides one rule of law for the laboring man who procures advances on a promise to work out a debt, while on the other hand there is no law which would punish me, for instance, criminally, for refusing to pay my bill to my tailor. Therefore the act seems to deny to the laboring class the equal protection of the laws given other classes of debtors." Alexander Ackerman to Attorney General, January 7, 1905, Casefile 909-1898, Reel 1, Peonage Files of the Department of Justice, 1901–1945.
19 *In re Peonage Charge*, 138 F. 686 (1905). It was clear, however, that not all federal courts were crafted from the same mold. Months after the ruling in the Northern District of Florida, a district court ruling in the Eastern District of North Carolina refused to rule against peonage, arguing that "the federal Constitution does not guaranty to citizens the right to a jury trial, except in courts of the United States,"

and a defendant not receiving a jury trial did not entitle them to a habeas corpus writ. Peonage, in that formulation, was unproblematic. In fact, "the due process of law provided for in the fourteenth amendment does not apply to state courts under any ironclad rule." *Ex parte Brown et al.,* 140 F. 461 (1905). For more on bound carceral labor in Florida, see Noel Gordon Carper, "The Convict-Lease System in Florida, 1866–1923" (Ph.D. diss, Florida State University, 1964).

20 Alexander Ackerman to Attorney General, July 20, 1903; Attorney General to Alexander Ackerman, July 27, 1903, Casefile 909-1898, Reel 1, Peonage Files of the Department of Justice, 1901–1945.

21 Alexander Ackerman to Attorney General, August 10, 1903, Casefile 909-1898, Reel 1, Peonage Files of the Department of Justice, 1901–1945.

22 Alexander Ackerman to Attorney General, August 10, 1903, Casefile 909-1898, Reel 1, Peonage Files of the Department of Justice, 1901–1945.

23 *Quitman Free Press,* November 27, 1903, 1; and *Augusta Chronicle,* November 27, 1903, 7.

24 Official Bond of Emory Speer, Solicitor General, Western Circuit, January 29, 1873, DOC 2174, C72142, Public Reference Service—File II, Georgia Archives, Morrow, Georgia.

25 Timothy S. Huebner, "Emory Speer and Federal Enforcement of the Rights of African Americans, 1880–1910," *American Journal of Legal History* 55 (January 2015): 38–42; Brent J. Aucoin, *A Rift in the Clouds: Race and the Southern Federal Judiciary, 1900–1910* (Fayetteville: University of Arkansas Press, 2007), 37–51; Schmidt Jr., "Principle and Prejudice," 657; and Mary Ann Hawkins, "He Drew the Lightning: Emory Speer, Federal Judge in Georgia, 1885–1918" (M.A. Thesis: Georgia State University, 1984), 23–24.

26 Huebner, "Emory Speer and Federal Enforcement of the Rights of African Americans," 42–46, quotes from 44 and 45; Pamela Brandwein, "A Lost Jurisprudence of the Reconstruction Amendments," *Journal of Supreme Court History* 41 (November 2016): 332; Emory Speer, *Argument of Emory Speer, United States Attorney, in the case of the United States versus Jasper Yarbrough, et al., in the United States Circuit Court for the Northern District of Georgia* (Atlanta: W. H. Scott, 1883), 57–59 (quotes); and *Ex parte Yarbrough,* 110 U.S. 651 (1884).

27 Every Democratic leader in Georgia opposed Speer's nomination. Huebner, "Emory Speer and Federal Enforcement of the Rights of African Americans," 46–47.

28 Schmidt Jr., "Principle and Prejudice," 659–60; and Huebner, "Emory Speer and Federal Enforcement of the Rights of African Americans," 38.

29 Blackmon, *Slavery by Another Name,* 249.

30 "I am informed that this is a part of the public records of the State and is open for the inspection of any citizen, but that there is no way of securing copies thereof," he explained of his trip to Atlanta. That insistence on maintaining only the one copy, bound in Moroccan leather, made it much easier for the report to disappear from Prison Commission records. Alexander Ackerman to Attorney General, July 6, 1903, Casefile 909-1898, Reel 1, Peonage Files of the Department of Justice, 1901–1945.

31 Dittmer, *Black Georgia in the Progressive Era, 1900–1920,* 72.
32 Miller was a longstanding sheriff in Ware County, serving off and on from 1882 to 1906. Ware County Sheriff's Office, correspondence with the author.
33 *Waycross Journal,* June 5, 1903, 1; and Alexander Ackerman to Attorney General, December 2, 1903, Casefile 909-1898, Reel 1, Peonage Files of the Department of Justice, 1901–1945.
34 *Waycross Journal,* June 5, 1903, 2; and Alexander Ackerman to Attorney General, March 27, 1905, Casefile 909-1898, Reel 1, Peonage Files of the Department of Justice, 1901–1945.
35 *Waycross Journal,* June 5, 1903, 2.
36 W. E. B. Du Bois, "The Spawn Of Slavery: The Convict-lease System In The South," in *W.E.B. Du Bois On Crime And Justice: Laying The Foundations Of Sociological Criminology,* ed. Shaun L. Gabbidon (Aldershot: Ashgate, 2007), 119; and Angela Davis, *Are Prisons Obsolete?* (New York: Seven Stories Press, 2003), 72.
37 Haley, "Like I Was a Man," 53, 55. Historian Fletcher Green even claimed that "in both Georgia and Florida there were lease camps containing at one time twenty-five or more illegitimate children born of convict mothers." Green, "Some Aspects of the Convict Lease System in the Southern States," 121.
38 LeFlouria, *Chained in Silence,* 9, 13. LeFlouria's text spends the majority of its time in Georgia. For a study of incarcerated women in Alabama, see Mary Ellen Curtin, "The 'Human World' of Black Women in Alabama Prisons, 1870–1900," in *Hidden Histories of Women in the New South,* ed. Virginia Bernhard, Betty Brandon, Elizabeth Fox-Genovese, Theda Purdue, and Elizabeth Hayes Turner (Columbia: University of Missouri Press, 1994), 11–30.
39 "Servitude for Debt in Georgia," *Outlook* 74 (June 27, 1903): 486. The *Outlook* account was one of many national stories on the charges, again thrusting the McRees and Kinderlou into the national spotlight. See *Washington Post,* July 1, 1903, 1; *Kinsley Graphic,* June 26, 1903, 2; *Baxter Springs (KS) News,* June 27, 1902, 4; and *Wichita Daily Eagle,* July 1, 1903, 14.
40 "Peonage in Georgia," 3080; *New York Times,* May 31, 1903, 2; and Dittmer, *Black Georgia in the Progressive Era,* 72–73.
41 "Peonage in Georgia," 3080.
42 Alexander Ackerman to Attorney General, March 27, 1905; Emory Speer to Attorney General, June 25, 1903, Casefile 909-1898, Reel 1, Peonage Files of the Department of Justice, 1901–1945. Ackerman's respect for Speer's sentencing was reciprocated. In a letter to the attorney general, Speer noted that "Ackerman I think deserves *great* credit for his conduct of these cases." Emory Speer to Attorney General, November 25, 1903, Casefile 909-1898, Reel 1, Peonage Files of the Department of Justice, 1901–1945.
43 *Augusta Chronicle,* November 27, 1903, 7.
44 "Peonage in Georgia," 3080.
45 *Augusta Chronicle,* November 27, 1903, 7.

Chapter 7. The National Scandal of 1903

1 *New York Times,* May 31, 1903, 2.
2 *New York Times,* May 31, 1903, 2.
3 *U.S. v. McClellan,* 127 F. 1 (1904). For a full description of the case from the view of the prosecutor, see Alexander Ackerman to Attorney General, December 2, 1903, Casefile 909-1898, Reel 1, Peonage Files of the Department of Justice, 1901–1945.
4 *Thomasville Times-Enterprise,* March 24, 1905, 4; and *Atlanta Constitution,* November 24, 1903, 5.
5 *Thomasville Times-Enterprise,* November 28, 1903, 4; Dittmer, *Black Georgia in the Progressive Era,* 74; and Donald Lee Grant, *The Way It Was in the South; The Black Experience in Georgia* (Athens: University of Georgia Press, 2001), 151. Though it was never charged, as Ackerman believed it to be an overreaction, the sheriff of Ware County, S. F. Miller, claimed that Crawley and McClellan "assaulted him and threatened his life because he testified before the grand jury." The charges against the two would solely be about their peonage actions, however, because Ackerman "decided that Miller was unnecessarily alarmed and that there had been no actual assault upon him, and in fact nothing to justify any action by the United States authorities at the present time." Alexander Ackerman to Attorney General, May 4, 1904, Casefile 909-1898, Reel 1, Peonage Files of the Department of Justice, 1901–1945.
6 *United States v. Thomas J. McClellan and William F. Crawley,* Indictments, Vio. 5526 R.S., Casefile 909-1898, Reel 1, Peonage Files of the Department of Justice, 1901–1945.
7 The debate about the validity of such indictments in relation to Georgia law was exhaustive and rehearsed all the arguments that played out in previous cases, in the press, and in the state legislature. *In Re: Peonage Cases,* Brief of Alexander Ackerman; *United States v. William P. Crawley and Thomas J. McClellan,* Indictment for Peonage Returned at November Term 1903, Brief of W. M. Toomer, John C. McDonald and Leon A. Wilson, Casefile 909-1898, Reel 1, Peonage Files of the Department of Justice, 1901–1945.
8 *United States v. McClellan,* 127 F. 971 (1904); William A. Cohen, *At Freedom's Edge: Black Mobility and the Southern White Quest for Racial Control, 1861–1915* (Baton Rouge: Louisiana State University Press, 1991), 278–79; Huebner, "Emory Speer and Federal Enforcement of the Rights of African Americans," 49–52; *Afro-American,* March 25, 1905, 2; Schmidt Jr., "Principle and Prejudice," 658, 669–71; "Negro Peonage and the Thirteenth Amendment," *Yale Law Journal* 13 (June 1904): 452–53; *Savannah Press,* March 20, 1905, 1; *Savannah Morning News,* March 23, 1905, 4; and Emory Speer to W. H. Moody, March 20, 1905, Casefile 909-1898, Reel 1, Peonage Files of the Department of Justice, 1901–1945.
9 *New York Times,* November 24, 1903, 2, November 25, 1903, 3; *Washington Post,* November 24, 1903, 1; and *Atlanta Constitution,* November 25, 1903, 5. For more on the shotgun policy, see Warren A. Ellem, "The Overthrow of Reconstruction in Mississippi," *Journal of Mississippi History* 54, no. 2 (1992): 175–201; and Vernon L.

Wharton, "The Race Issue in the Overthrow of Reconstruction in Mississippi: A Paper Read before the American Historical Association, 1940," *Phylon* 2 (4th Qtr., 1941): 362–70. Those alleged to have been held in involuntary servitude were John Wesley Boney, George Davis, Imla Durham, Dave Smith, Dave Brimmage, Ed Hardy, Henry Brimmage, Joe Holmes, John McMullen, John Spanger, Nealy Hardy, and Andrew Moore. *Atlanta Constitution,* November 24, 1903, 5.

10 "More Cases of Peonage," *Northwestern Christian Advocate,* December 2, 1903, 2.

11 *Thomasville Times-Enterprise,* November 28, 1903, 4; Dittmer, *Black Georgia in the Progressive Era,* 74; and Grant, *The Way It Was in the South,* 151.

12 "Remarks of Mr. Brantley," March 28, 1904, *Congressional Record,* 58th Congress, vol. 38 (Washington: USGPO, 1904), 3901. His defense was noticed by the court. Prosecuting attorney Ackerman noted that he "assisted in the preparation of the defendants' case although not retained" in the prosecution of Tifton's Samuel Clyatt. "These circumstances in connection with other information I have received convinces me that the crime is widely prevalent and demands the utmost attention of the officers of the Department of Justice." Alexander Ackerman to Attorney General, March 16, 1904, Casefile 909-1898, Reel 1, Peonage Files of the Department of Justice, 1901-1945.

13 "Remarks of Mr. Brantley," 3901–02.

14 "Remarks of Mr. Brantley," 3905; *Georgia Constitution,* Article 1, section 1, paragraph 23; *Pitts v. Allen,* 72 Ga. 69 (1883); *Willingham v. Hooven, Owens, Rentschler & Co.,* 74 Ga. 233 (1884); *Walton County v. Franklin,* 95 Ga. 538 (1894); and *Ryan v. State,* 45 Ga. 128 (1872).

15 "Remarks of Mr. Brantley," 3898–3906.

16 "Remarks of Mr. Littlefield," April 12, 1904, *Congressional Record,* 58th Congress, vol. 38 (Washington: USGPO, 1904), 4700–4702.

17 *Clyatt v. United States,* 197 U.S. 207 (1905); William Wirt Howe, "The Peonage Cases," *Columbia Law Review* 4 (April 1904): 282–84; N. Gordon Carper, "Slavery Revisited: Peonage in the South," *Phylon* 37 (1st Qtr. 1976): 87–89; *Afro-American,* December 24, 1904, 1; Herbert D. Ward, "Peonage in America," *Cosmopolitan* 39 (August 1905): 429–30; Schmidt Jr., "Principle and Prejudice," 660–63; *Florida Times-Union and Citizen,* March 27, 1902, 1; and John Egan to Attorney General, April 3, 1902, Casefile 909-1898, Reel 1, Peonage Files of the Department of Justice, 1901-1945.

18 Carper, "Slavery Revisited," 89; *Crescent City News,* September 5, 1901, 4; *Clyatt v. United States,* Memoranda for Defendant in Error, Supplemental, United States Circuit Court of Appeals, Fifth Circuit, No. 1151; and *Clyatt v. United States,* Transcript of Record, United States Circuit Court of Appeals, Fifth Circuit, No. 1151, Casefile 909-1898, Reel 1, Peonage Files of the Department of Justice, 1901-1945. Chimmie Fadden was the protagonist of an eponymous Cecil B. DeMille silent film from 1915, in which a man, Fadden, is saved from false arrest by a crusading socialite. Cecil B. DeMille, *Chimmie Fadden,* Paramount Pictures, 1915.

19 *Chicago Record-Herald* editorial reprinted in *Afro-American,* December 19, 1903, 4.
20 *Clyatt v. United States,* 197 U.S. 207 (1905). See also W. W. Howe to Attorney General, March 29, 1904; *Clyatt v. United States,* No. 659, Petition for an Order to Send up Entire Record; *Clyatt v. United States,* No. 659, Motion to Advance; and Attorney General to Alexander Ackerman, March 14, 1905, Casefile 909-1898, Reel 1, Peonage Files of the Department of Justice, 1901–1945.
21 William B. Sheppard to Attorney General, May 7, 1906; Attorney General to William B. Sheppard, June 4, 1906; William B. Sheppard to Attorney General, January 30, 1907; Fred C. Cubberly to Attorney General, May 18, 1909; and Attorney General to Fred C. Cubberly, June 2, 1909, Casefile 909-1898, Reel 1, Peonage Files of the Department of Justice, 1901–1945.
22 "To the Commissioners of Roads and Revenues of Oglethorpe County," June 25, 1903, Governor, Executive Department Minutes, 25 October 1902–1 September 1906, Vol. 3, 4758, Governor Joseph Meriwether Terrell, Georgia Archives, Morrow, Georgia; *New York Times,* June 27, 1903, 1; and *Atlanta Constitution,* June 26, 1903, 7, July 17, 1903, 12.
23 *New York Times,* July 15, 1903, 1; and *Journal of the House of Representatives of the State of Georgia, June 24, 1903* (Atlanta: Franklin Printing and Publishing Co., 1903), 284.
24 *Afro-American,* July 16, 1904, 4.
25 *Afro-American,* July 25, 1903, 4.
26 White newspapers at the time incorrectly listed him as J. M. Cobb. *R.L. Polk & Co.'s Valdosta City Directory, 1904* (Valdosta: R.L. Polk & Co., 1904), 191; *Twelfth Census of the United States, 1900,* Population Schedule, Valdosta District No. 663, Sheet 27B; *Thirteenth Census of the United States, 1910,* Population Schedule, Valdosta City, Sheet 6B; and Georgia, Lowndes County, Record of Marriages, Book D, 1897–1903, 399, County Marriage Records, 1828–1978, Georgia Archives, Morrow, Georgia. Cobb died of apoplexy brought on by hypertension on August 28, 1938, aged sixty. Certificate of Death, No. 19557, Georgia Department of Public Health, Bureau of Vital Statistics, Atlanta, Georgia.
27 *Banks County Journal,* December 2, 1903, 3; *Atlanta Constitution,* November 25, 1903, 5; Dittmer, *Black Georgia in the Progressive Era,* 73; and Alexander Ackerman to Attorney General, December 2, 1903, Casefile 909-1898, Reel 1, Peonage Files of the Department of Justice, 1901–1945.
28 Cohen, "Negro Involuntary Servitude in the South," 41–42.
29 "Peonage in Georgia," 3080. The case against Cobb and Hart was delayed, as Lula Durham, like so many witnesses before her, seemed to disappear when federal marshals attempted to locate her for testimony. She lived in White Springs, Florida, just south of Valdosta, Georgia, but was unavailable as of March 1904. It was a problem exacerbated by the fact that Durham had married in the interim and her name was now Lula Durham King. Cobb had traveled to White Springs, spoken with her new husband, and convinced him to take her away. In response, the attorney general authorized a marshal to go into Florida and search for her. Alexander Ackerman

to Attorney General, March 19, 1904, Western Union Telegraph; Alexander Ackerman to Attorney General, March 22, 1904; and Attorney General to John M. Barnes, March 24, 1904, Casefile 909-1898, Reel 1, Peonage Files of the Department of Justice, 1901–1945. The case was ultimately held over to 1905, when again marshals had to be employed to search for her in Florida. Alexander Ackerman to Attorney General, March 2, 1905, Western Union Telegraph; Attorney General to George F. White, March 21, 1905, Casefile 909-1898, Reel 1, Peonage Files of the Department of Justice, 1901–1945.

30 Cobb and Hart were indicted at the same time as the McRees for "causing a citizen to be held in Peonage." *United States v. J. M. Cobb and George P. Hart*, Lowndes County, Indictment No. 416, November 23, 1903, *Minutes*, U.S. District Court, Eastern Division, South District, Georgia, 460, 21.12.6, Records of the U.S. District Court for the Southern District, Records of the Eastern Division (Savannah), including minute books, 1789–1947, National Archives and Records Administration, Morrow, Georgia.

31 Daniel, *The Shadow of Slavery*, 36; and "Lowndes County Negroes Entered Pleas of Guilty," unidentified newspaper clipping enclosed in Alexander Ackerman to Attorney General, March 27, 1905, Casefile 909-1898, Reel 1, Peonage Files of the Department of Justice, 1901–1945. Like he had with the McRees, Speer fined the defendants $1,000 each, requiring only that they pay $300. Alexander Ackerman to Attorney General, March 27, 1905, Casefile 909-1898, Reel 1, Peonage Files of the Department of Justice, 1901–1945.

32 The original punishment was a $1,000 fine with Cobb and Hart to be imprisoned until payment was made, but Speer reduced the fine upon reconsideration and allowed both a suspended sentence pending payment and assuming the "good behavior" of both. *United States v. J. M. Cobb and George P. Hart*, Indictment, Peonage, March 22, 1905, *Minutes*, U.S. District Court, Eastern Division, South District, Georgia, 576, 21.12.6, Records of the U.S. District Court for the Southern District, Records of the Eastern Division (Savannah), including minute books, 1789–1947, National Archives and Records Administration, Morrow, Georgia.

33 *Jamison v. Wimbush*, 130 F. 351 (1904); Emory Speer, *Argument of Emory Speer, United States Attorney, in the case of the United States versus Jasper Yarbrough, et al., in the United States Circuit Court for the Northern District of Georgia* (Atlanta: WH Scott, 1883), 59; *Afro-American*, July 2, 1904, 1; Huebner, "Emory Speer and Federal Enforcement of the Rights of African Americans," 53–57; and Schmidt Jr., "Principle and Prejudice," 652. See also Emory Speer to Attorney General, 6 April 1905, Casefile 909-1898, Reel 1, Peonage Files of the Department of Justice, 1901–1945.

34 *Afro-American*, July 2, 1904, 4.

35 *Sixth Annual Report of the Prison Commission of Georgia, 1903*, 1–2, Georgia Penitentiary Prison Commission's Reports, Georgia Archives, Morrow, Georgia.

36 *Seventh Annual Report of the Prison Commission of Georgia, 1904*, 23, Georgia Penitentiary Prison Commission's Reports, Georgia Archives, Morrow, Georgia.

37 *Seventh Annual Report of the Prison Commission of Georgia, 1904* (Atlanta: Lester Book & Stationary, 1904), 11.

38 *Seventh Annual Report of the Prison Commission of Georgia, 1904,* 4, 15.
39 *Seventh Annual Report of the Prison Commission of Georgia, 1904,* 16.
40 *Eleventh Annual Report of the Prison Commission of Georgia, 1908* (Atlanta: Lester Book & Stationary, 1908), 7.
41 "Supplies Furnished for Convicts by Contractor, J.F. Fender at Camp Valdosta, April-December 1904," Prisons-State Prison Commission-Rations and Clothing Daily Records-1904–1909, 021-01-016, Georgia Archives, Morrow, Georgia. In 1904, labor shortages in nearby Newton, Georgia, led local law enforcement to make "wholesale arrests of idle Negroes," reported the *Atlanta Constitution,* "to scare them back to the farms from which they emanated." *Atlanta Constitution,* February 1, 1904, 2.
42 "Supplies Furnished for Convicts by Contractor, S.M. Stanley at Camp Valdosta, April 1908-March 1909," Prisons-State Prison Commission-Rations and Clothing Daily Records-1904–1909, 021-01-016, Georgia Archives, Morrow, Georgia.
43 Ward, "Peonage in America," 430.

Chapter 8. The Federal Crusade against Peonage

1 *Afro-American,* August 4, 1906, 4.
2 *Afro-American,* August 18, 1906, 1, September 23, 1906, 1.
3 *Eighth Annual Report of the Prison Commission of Georgia, 1905* (Atlanta: Lester Book & Stationary, 1905), 7–8.
4 Richard Barry, "Slavery in the South To-Day," *Cosmopolitan* 42 (March 1907): 482–483; and *Afro-American,* December 22, 1906, 2.
5 Barry, "Slavery in the South To-Day," 486, 490.
6 *Afro-American,* December 29, 1906, 1.
7 *Afro-American,* December 29, 1906, 4.
8 *Afro-American,* January 12, 1907, 1, January 19, 1907, 1.
9 Charles W. Russell, *Report on Peonage* (Washington: USGPO, 1908), 28, 31; and *Afro-American,* December 7, 1907, 5.
10 Russell, *Report on Peonage,* 16–17.
11 *Chicago Defender,* April 22, 1911, 3; and *Afro-American,* November 21, 1908, 2, September 18, 1909, 3, March 5, 1910, 4, February 25, 1911, 2.
12 *Pittsburgh Courier,* April 13, 1912, 1; and *Afro-American,* October 26, 1912, 2.
13 U.S. House of Representatives, 59 HR 383, December 4, 1905.
14 U.S. House of Representatives, "Hearing on the Bill (HR 383) to Prohibit Shanghaiing and Peonage in the United States," February 2, 1906, 20.
15 U.S. House of Representatives, 60 H. Res. 60, December 16, 1907; U.S. House of Representatives, 60 H. Res. 115, January 6, 1908; and U.S. House of Representatives, 60th Congress, 1st sess., Report No. 1287, "Call for Information Concerning Investigation of Alleged Peonage Cases in Florida by Department of Justice, Etc.," March 21, 1908.

Chapter 9. The Death of Leasing in Georgia

1 Byrd, *Report of Special Inspector of Misdemeanor Convict Camps of Georgia,* 7–8.
2 The committee was chaired by F. B. Sirmans of Clinch County and included McRee,

Bush, T. G. Simmons of Ellijay, Jake Moore, the state warden, A. K. Ramsey of Ramsey, J. S. Alesbrook of Woods Station, W. E. Prescott of Statenville, G. B. Holder of Rome, D. P. Rose of Owens Ferry, Nat D. Arnold of Arnoldsville, and J. C. Powell of Morgantown. *Valdosta Times,* March 10, 1906. The rivalries generated by the turpentine industry in the region could be substantive motivators for punitive actions and statements. See for example *Smith v. Willis,* 33 S.E. 667 (1899).

3   Green, "Some Aspects of the Convict Lease System in the Southern States," 121, 123.

4   Leon F. Litwack, *Trouble in Mind: Black Southerners in the Age of Jim Crow* (New York: Vintage Books, 1999), 100, 213, 221, 282–283; and Josephine Bone Floyd, "Rebecca Latimer Felton, Champion of Women's Rights," *Georgia Historical Quarterly* 30 (June 1946): 83–84. For more on the lynching of Sam Hose, see Edwin Arnold, *What Virtue There Is in Fire: Cultural Memory and the Lynching of Sam Hose* (Athens: University of Georgia Press, 2012); and Darren E. Grem, "Sam Jones, Sam Hose, and the Theology of Racial Violence," *Georgia Historical Quarterly* 90 (Spring 2006): 35–61.

5   *Atlanta Independent,* August 10, 1907, 4; and Eugene Pierce Walker, "Attitudes Towards Negroes as Reflected in the *Atlanta Constitution,* 1908–1918" (M.A. thesis: Emory University, 1969), 24.

6   *Atlanta Georgian,* July 7, 1908, 1; and Zimmerman, "Penal Systems and Penal Reforms in The South Since the Civil War," 282.

7   "Joint Committee to Investigate Convict System, No. 34, A Resolution," July 26, 1908, *Acts and Resolutions of the General Assembly of the State of Georgia, 1908* (Atlanta: Franklin Printing and Publishing, 1908), 1029–1032.

8   Interview with R. E. Davidson, *Georgia, House of Representatives Special Committees, Vol. 1,* July 20–July 26, 1908, 13-59-36, 252-14, GRG 1-705, 135–137, Georgia Archives, Morrow, Georgia.

9   Interview with W. R. Cheves (White), *Georgia, House of Representatives Special Committees, Vol. 2,* July 27–July 29, 1908, 13-59-36, 252-14, GRG 1-705, 455–466, quote from 460, Georgia Archives, Morrow, Georgia; and *Atlanta Constitution,* February 23, 1908, B1, July 28, 1908, 1, July 31, 1908, August 11, 1908, 1.

10 Interview with C. H. Lowe (white), *Georgia, House of Representatives Special Committees, Vol. 3,* July 30–August 3, 1908, 13-59-36, 252-14, GRG 1-705, p.748–755, Georgia Archives, Morrow, Georgia.

11 Gut-wrenching stories of prisoners abused and killed in the custody of convict camps are rampant throughout the volumes of printed testimony. For accounts of particularly brutal murders, see *Georgia, House of Representatives Special Committees, Vol. 4,* August 4–August 17, 1908, 13-59-36, 252-14, GRG 1-705, p. 1252–1272, Georgia Archives, Morrow, Georgia.

12 Thomas S. Felder, chairman, Convict Lease Investigating Committee, "Report of the Investigating Committee," August 20, 1908, *Acts and Resolutions of the General Assembly of the State of Georgia, 1908* (Atlanta: Franklin Printing and Publishing, 1908), 1063–1067; and *Atlanta Constitution,* August 3, 1908, 3, August 4, 1908, 1, August 5, 1908, 1.

13 Felder, "Report of the Investigating Committee," 1068–1070.

14 Felder, "Report of the Investigating Committee," 1070–1073.
15 Felder, "Report of the Investigating Committee," 1074–1089. The Georgia State Reformatory was established by state law in August 1905 for those convicted under the age of sixteen. "Georgia State Reformatory Established, No. 6," August 22, 1905, "Prison Commission Created, No. 340," December 21, 1897, *Acts and Resolutions of the General Assembly of the State of Georgia, 1905* (Atlanta: Franklin Printing and Publishing, 1905), 71–78.
16 "Examination of Books and Records Prison Commission, State Farm and Reformatory 1899 to May 31, and July 19, 1908," Report of the Convict Lease Investigating Committee," August 20, 1908, *Acts and Resolutions of the General Assembly of the State of Georgia, 1916* (Atlanta: Chas. P. Byrd, State Printer, 1916), 1092–1104.
17 *Eleventh Annual Report of the Prison Commission of Georgia, 1908* (Atlanta: Lester Book & Stationary, 1908), 8.
18 *Eleventh Annual Report of the Prison Commission of Georgia, 1908*, 8–9.
19 *Valdosta Times,* July 21, 1908, 6.
20 "Employment of Convicts; System of Penology, No. 4," September 19, 1908, *Acts and Resolutions of the General Assembly of the State of Georgia, 1916* (Atlanta: Chas. P. Byrd, State Printer, 1916), 1119–30; and Zimmerman, "Penal Systems and Penal Reforms in The South Since the Civil War," 286–87.
21 It would, however, at the very least, put all misdemeanants under the watchful purview of the Prison Commission, and for whatever blind spots the commission had evinced over the previous decade, it had been arguing for that purview since its inception. *First Annual Report of the Highway Department of Georgia to the Governor and General Assembly of the State of Georgia* (Atlanta, June 15, 1919), 43–45. This was not a rare phenomenon. Not only had prisoners maintained colonial streets in urban areas in the eighteenth century, but infrastructure systems throughout the South began post-Reconstruction roads programs that included convict labor. The poor quality of southern roads left legislatures hoping to cut costs however they could in pursuit of a better system. Carter, "Prisons, Politics and Business," (97–99. See also Myers and Massey, "Race, Labor, and Punishment in Postbellum Georgia," 269–70.
22 *First Annual Report of the Highway Department of Georgia to the Governor and General Assembly of the State of Georgia* (Atlanta, June 15, 1919), 43–45; Adamson, "Punishment after Slavery," 560; and Haley, "Like I Was a Man," 55. See also Hortense J. Spillers, "Interstices: A Small Drama of Words," in *Pleasure and Danger: Exploring Female Sexuality,* ed. Carole S. Vance (Boston: Routledge, 1984), 78; Evelyn Nakano Glenn, *Forced to Care: Coercion and Caregiving in America* (Cambridge, Mass.: Harvard University Press, 2010), 36; and Kathleen M. Brown, *Good Wives, Nasty Wenches, and Anxious Patriarchs: Gender, Race, and Power in Colonial Virginia* (Chapel Hill: University of North Carolina Press, 1996), 108. Another valuable resource that carries the broader discussion of women's imprisonment in the nineteenth century into the twenty-first is Nancy Kurshan, *Women and Imprisonment in the US: History and Current Reality* (Philadelphia: Prison Activist Resource Center and Monkeywrench Press, 1995).

23 McCallie, "Use of Convicts on the Public Roads of Georgia," 157; *Progress of Road Construction in the United States* (Washington: USGPO, 1897), 16; and U.S. Department of Agriculture, *Road Conventions in the Southern States and Object-Lesson Roads* (Washington: USGPO, 1902), 42–45, 49, 52–54. Though he dates the onset of convict road work to 1904, later than it actually started, Alex Lichtenstein noted in 1996 that the use of prisoners for road work "eroded" convict leasing even before its official demise in 1908. Lichtenstein, *Twice the Work of Free Labor*, 175.
24 McCallie, "Use of Convicts on the Public Roads of Georgia," 157–58.
25 "Procuring Money on Contract for Service," No. 345, *Acts and Resolutions of the General Assembly of the State of Georgia, 1903* (Atlanta: Franklin Printing and Publishing Co., 1903), 90–91; Carter, "Prisons, Politics and Business," 102; and Blake McKelvey, "A Half-Century of Southern Penal Exploitations," *Social Forces* 13 (October 1934): 113.
26 *Atlanta Georgian*, August 2, 1908, 1; Mancini, "Race, Economics, and the Abandonment of Convict Leasing," 342; and Taylor, "The Abolition of the Convict Lease System in Georgia," 278–81. As deadly and vicious as the system was, and as worthy of protest, there does not seem to be any correlation between the violence of convict leasing and the violence of lynchings and executions, as execution-level crimes were never subject to the possibility of lease labor and lynchings were a popular movement over and against the economic dictates of the state's best interest. There is no specific study of this correlation, but a study of the relationship between lynchings, executions, and disfranchisement statutes in Georgia provides the data that makes it easy to draw such conclusions. There were, for example, no dramatic spikes or dips corresponding with dates of legal changes to the system through the late nineteenth and early twentieth centuries. E. M. Beck, James L. Massey, and Stewart E. Tolnay, "The Gallows, the Mob, and the Vote: Lethal Sanctioning of Blacks in North Carolina and Georgia, 1882 to 1930," *Law & Society Review* 23, no. 2 (1989): 324–29. See in particular chart on page 326.
27 Mancini, "Race, Economics, and the Abandonment of Convict Leasing," 343, 348–49.
28 McCallie, "Use of Convicts on the Public Roads of Georgia," 157–58.
29 Myers and Massey, "Race, Labor, and Punishment in Postbellum Georgia," 270.
30 McKelvey, "A Half-Century of Southern Penal Exploitations," 114, 118, quote from 114.
31 Mancini, "Race, Economics, and the Abandonment of Convict Leasing," 339.
32 Oswald Garrison Villard to Booker T. Washington, September 10, 1908, Box 95, Part I: Special Correspondence, 1853–1915, Booker T. Washington Papers, 1853–1946, MSS44669, Manuscript Division, Library of Congress, Washington, D.C.
33 The NAACP would ultimately use its resources to investigate peonage and to advocate against it. Papers of the NAACP, Part 10: Peonage, Labor, and the New Deal, 1913–1939. See also Patricia Sullivan, *Lift Every Voice and Sing: The NAACP and the Making of the Civil Rights Movement* (New York: New Press, 2009); Kevern Verney and Lee Sartain, eds., *Long Is the Way and Hard: One Hundred Years of the NAACP* (Fayetteville: University of Arkansas, 2009); Gilbert Jonas, *Freedom's Sword: The*

NAACP and the Struggle Against Racism in America, 1909–1969 (New York: Routledge, 2005); and Robert L. Zangrando, *The NAACP Crusade Against Lynching, 1909–1950* (Philadelphia: Temple University Press, 1980).

34 *Valdosta Times,* October 9, 1909, 7.
35 *Valdosta Times,* April 9, 1909, 3.
36 *Bailey v. Alabama,* 211 U.S. 457 (1909); *Afro-American,* April 13, 1912, 2; and Daniel, "Up from Slavery and Down to Peonage," 662.
37 *Bailey v. Alabama,* 219 U.S. 231 (1911); and Daniel, "Up from Slavery and Down to Peonage," 664–67.
38 Lafayette M. Hershaw, *Peonage,* Occasional Papers, No. 15 (Washington: American Negro Academy, 1915), 14.
39 *United States v. Reynolds, United States v. Broughton,* 235 U.S. 133 (1914). Holmes concurred but made sure to note, "There seems to me nothing in the Thirteenth Amendment or the Revised Statutes that prevents a State from making a breach of contract, as well a reasonable contract for labor as for other matters, a crime and punishing it as such. But impulsive people with little intelligence or foresight may be expected to lay hold of anything that affords a relief from present pain even though it will cause greater trouble by and by. The successive contracts, each for a longer term than the last, are the inevitable, and must be taken to have been the contemplated outcome of the Alabama laws." *United States v. Reynolds, United States v. Broughton,* 235 U.S. 133 (1914), at 150.
40 *Taylor v. Georgia,* 315 U.S. 25 (1942). A similar case did much the same in Florida two years later in 1944. In *Pollock v. Williams* (1944), the Supreme Court ruled as it had in *Taylor,* citing that decision, *Reynolds, Bailey,* and *Clyatt* in its opinion. *Pollock v. Williams,* 322 U.S. 4 (1944).

Chapter 10. The Last Twilight of the Kinderlou Dynasty

1 Alexander Ackerman to Attorney General, January 7, 1905, Casefile 909-1898, Reel 1, Peonage Files of the Department of Justice, 1901–1945.
2 Alexander Ackerman to Attorney General, January 7, 1905, Casefile 909-1898, Reel 1, Peonage Files of the Department of Justice, 1901–1945.
3 Catherine McRee Carter, "History of Kinderlou, Georgia, 1860–1940," December 7, 1940, 25, Box 122, folder 1, Kinderlou Papers, Archive Row 1, Lowndes County Historical Society, Valdosta, Georgia. In April 1906, during his last full year in the legislature, Ed McRee was listed as owing $5,384.68 for his leased prisoners for the first quarter of 1906. *Atlanta Constitution,* April 6, 1906, 7.
4 Last Will and Testament of Edward J. McRee, State of Georgia, County of Lowndes, Box 192, folder 8, archive row 1, E. J. McRee Papers, Lowndes County Historical Society, Valdosta, Georgia; and *Atlanta Constitution,* March 28, 1908, 4.
5 *Atlanta Constitution,* January 29, 1907, 4.
6 *Atlanta Constitution,* March 28, 1908, 4.
7 *Atlanta Constitution,* February 18, 1909, 4, February 19, 1909, 7.
8 *Atlanta Constitution,* December 14, 19907, 4.
9 Daniel, "Up from Slavery and Down to Peonage," 655. For more on immigrant pe-

onage, see Alexander Irvine, "The Life Story of a Hungarian Peon," *Independent* 63 (September 5, 1907): 557–64; "White Peonage in North Carolina," *Outlook* 87 (October 19, 1907): 319–20; and "Southern Peonage and Immigration," *Nation* 85 (December 19, 1907): 557.

10 Immigration Commission, "Peonage," *Reports of the Immigration Commission* (Washington: USGPO, 1910), 446–47. Russell's 1908 Report on Peonage found much the same thing, telling a story of a group of Germans held in peonage in Newnan, Georgia, that was similar to that of the Austrians at Kinderlou. Russell, *Report on Peonage*, 21.

11 *Atlanta Constitution*, April 9, 1909, 7.

12 *Atlanta Constitution*, August 17, 1909, 1.

13 *Twelfth Annual Report of the Prison Commission of Georgia, 1909* (Atlanta: Atlanta: Lester Book & Stationery, 1909), 19–20, 21.

14 *Thirteenth Annual Report of the Prison Commission of Georgia, 1910* (Atlanta: Lester Book & Stationery, 1910), 14.

15 *Tifton Gazette*, October 16, 1908, 2; and *Valdosta Times*, June 21, 1910, 1. Quote from *Valdosta Times*.

16 *Valdosta Times*, July 11, 1911, 10.

17 *Athens Banner*, March 6, 1909, 7; and "The Valdosta Area . . . Central to the geographic reaches of 'The Fire Forest' Longleaf Pine-Wiregrass Ecosystem," poster display, Lowndes County Historical Society, Valdosta, Georgia.

18 *Valdosta Times*, January 10, 1911, 8; and Carter, "History of Kinderlou, Georgia, 1860–1940," 17.

19 *Valdosta Times*, May 23, 1911, 2.

20 *Valdosta Times*, March 2, 1912, 5.

21 *Thomasville Times-Enterprise*, April 4, 1913, 1.

22 *Thomasville Times-Enterprise*, November 24, 1914, 4. Fire had been a constant through the years for Kinderlou. In October 1904, a spark from a train arriving at the Kinderlou railroad stop created a forest fire that burned around two hundred acres of McRee timberland before a team of volunteers from Valdosta and surrounding areas arrived to help put it out. In March 1906, the plantation's crate and basket factory burned, causing an estimated $50,000 worth of damage. *Savannah Morning News*, October 17, 1904, 7; and *Montgomery Monitor*, March 22, 1906, 1. The bad luck that befell the operation even included, in July 1906, mountain lions stalking the plantation, escapees from an area just outside Norman Park in Colquitt County the previous year. *Tifton Gazette*, July 13, 1906, 6.

23 *Valdosta Times*, August 17, 1914, 8; and *Atlanta Constitution*, August 18, 1914, 11.

24 *McRee v. Frederick*, 18 Ga.App. 321 (1916). McRee's problems with local businesses in this era, as he was the last brother alive seeking to maintain the family business, were many. Two years prior, in 1913, a dispute with the Atlantic Coast Line Railroad Company over a lumber shipping dispute also ended in litigation. *Atlantic Coast Line R. Co. v. McRee*, 76 S.E. 1057 (1913). He brought another case against Quitman Oil Company over a failed partnership in 1915, *McRee v. Quitman Oil Co. et al.*, 84 S.E. 487 (1915); and *Quitman Oil Co. et al. v. McRee*, 88 S.E. 921 (1916).

25 Carter, "History of Kinderlou, Georgia, 1860–1940," 25.
26 The McRee legacy could also be seen in the perseverance of truck farming as a vital part of the regional economy, a push originally made by George McRee. *Valdosta Times*, February 6, 1910, 2; and *Valdosta Daily Times*, September 16, 1946, 5.
27 *Valdosta Daily Times*, October 25, 1946, 5.
28 *Afro-American*, May 5, 1917, 1; and *Atlanta Independent*, October 14, 1916, 4.
29 "Negroes Leave the South," *Messenger* 2 (March 1920): 2. Not everyone agreed with Randolph's publication. In 1897, Frederick Douglass insisted that the South was the place for Black Americans to be. "Not only is the South the best locality for the Negro on the ground of his political powers and possibilities, but it is best for him as a field of labor. He is there, as he is nowhere else, an absolute necessity." Douglass did not elaborate, however, on how that necessity could breed situations like convict leasing or debt peonage. Frederick Douglass, "The Negro Exodus from the Gulf States," *Journal of Social Science* 11 (May 1880): 18.
30 Nell Irvin Painter, *Exodusters: Black Migrants to Kansas After Reconstruction* (Lawrence: University Press of Kansas, 1986), 3–18; and Dernoral Davis, "Toward a Socio-Historical and Demographic Portrait of Twentieth-Century African-Americans," in *Black Exodus: The Great Migration from the American South*, ed. Alferdteen Harrison (Jackson: University Press of Mississippi, 1991), 1–19. See also Rick Halpern, *Down on the Killing Floor: Black and White Workers in Chicago's Packinghouses, 1904–1954* (Urbana: University of Illinois Press, 1997); James R. Grossman, *Land of Hope: Chicago, Black Southerners, and the Great Migration* (New York: St. Martin's Press, 1991); Isabel Wilkerson, *The Warmth of Other Sons: The Epic Story of America's Great Migration* (New York: Random House, 2010); and Douglas J. Massey and Nancy A. Denton, *American Apartheid: Segregation and the Making of the Underclass* (Cambridge, Mass.: Harvard University Press, 1998).
31 Daniel, *The Shadow of Slavery*, 110–31, quote on 116; Cohen, "Negro Involuntary Servitude in the South," 50–52; and *New York Times*, April 26, 1921, 9.
32 N. Gordon Carper, "Slavery Revisited: Peonage in the South," *Phylon* 37 (1st Qtr. 1976): 94–97.
33 For more on Rosewood, see Edward Gonzalez-Tennant, *The Rosewood Massacre: An Archaeology and History of Intersectional Violence* (Gainesville: University Press of Florida, 2018); and Maxine D. Jones, Larry E. Rivers, David R. Colburn, R. Tom Dye, and William W. Rogers, "Documented History of the Incident Which Occurred at Rosewood, Florida in January 1923," Florida Board of Regents, 22 December 1993, available online at https://web.archive.org/web/20090126110750/http://displaysforschools.com/rosewoodrp.html, accessed October 24, 2020.
34 Myers and Massey, "Race, Labor, and Punishment in Postbellum Georgia," 270–71, 281.
35 *First Annual Report of the Highway Department of Georgia to the Governor and General Assembly of the State of Georgia* (Atlanta, June 15, 1919), 7.
36 *First Annual Report of the Highway Department of Georgia to the Governor and General Assembly of the State of Georgia* (Atlanta, June 15, 1919), 57. There had been no substantial change in the department's analysis the following year. *Second Annual*

Report of the Highway Department of Georgia to the Governor and General Assembly of the State of Georgia (Atlanta, May 1, 1920), 26, 45.

37 Myers and Massey, "Race, Labor, and Punishment in Postbellum Georgia," 218; and *Fifteenth Report of the State Highway Board of Georgia to the Governor and General Assembly of the State of Georgia* (Atlanta: Stein Printing Co., 1934), 148, 277.
38 Prison Commission of Georgia, *Third [Fourth] Biennial Report*, 23–26, Records of the Georgia Prison Commission, 1817–1936, Record group 21, Georgia Archives, Morrow, Georgia; and U.S. Bureau of Labor Statistics, *Prison Labor in the United States, 1932* (Washington: USGPO, 1933), 205.
39 McKelvey, "A Half-Century of Southern Penal Exploitations," 115. For comparison, see Jane Zimmerman, "The Convict Lease System in Arkansas and the Fight for Abolition," *Arkansas Historical Quarterly* 8 (Autumn 1949): 171–88, describing the system in the western portion of the American South.
40 Green, "Some Aspects of the Convict Lease System in the Southern States," 119; and Schmidt Jr., "Principle and Prejudice," 651.
41 Ray Stannard Baker, *Following the Color Line: An Account of Negro Citizenship in the American Democracy* (New York: Doubleday, Page, 1908), 50; Russell, *Report on Peonage*, 17; C. Vann Woodward, *Origins of the New South, 1877–1913* (Baton Rouge: Louisiana State University Press, 1951), 215; and Schmidt Jr., "Principle and Prejudice," 651.
42 Massey and Myers, "Patterns of Repressive Social Control in Post-Reconstruction Georgia, 1882–1935," 459.
43 As Massey and Myers explain, there is "virtually no empirical support for the presence of a relationship among trends in the lynching, execution, and incarceration of black males in Georgia during the so-called 'Lynch Era.'" Such is not to deny a coordinated effect but instead to argue against a coordination of intent. Massey and Myers, "Patterns of Repressive Social Control in Post-Reconstruction Georgia, 1882–1935," 482.
44 Robinson, Ulman, Peck, Davis, and Collins, *The Prison Labor Problem in Georgia*, ii–iii.
45 Robinson et al., *The Prison Labor Problem in Georgia*, 6–7, quote from 8.
46 Robinson et al., *The Prison Labor Problem in Georgia*, 17.
47 Robinson et al., *The Prison Labor Problem in Georgia*, 25, 26, 32–33.

BIBLIOGRAPHY

Newspapers

Afro-American
Athens Banner
Atlanta Constitution
Atlanta Georgian
Atlanta Independent
Atlanta Journal
Augusta Chronicle
Bainbridge Democrat
Baltimore Sun
Banks County Journal
Baxter Springs (KS) News
Chicago Defender
Columbus Daily Enquirer
Crescent City News
Daily Inter Ocean
Florida Times-Union and Citizen
Illinois State Journal
Illinois State Register
Indianapolis Journal
Kinsley Graphic
Los Angeles Herald
Macon Telegraph
Montgomery Monitor
New York Evening Post
New York Herald
New York Times
Oglethorpe Echo
Omaha Daily Bee
Pittsburgh Courier
Quitman Free Press

Salt Lake Herald
Savannah Morning News
Savannah Press
Savannah Tribune
Thomasville Times-Enterprise
Tifton Gazette
Valdosta Daily Times
Valdosta Times
Washington Post
Waycross Herald
Waycross Journal
Wichita Daily Eagle

Court Cases

Allgeyer v. Louisiana, 165 U.S. 578 (1897).
Atlantic Coast Line R. Co. v. McRee, 76 S.E. 1057 (1913).
Bailey v. Alabama, 211 U.S. 457 (1909).
Bailey v. Alabama, 219 U.S. 219 (1911).
Civil Rights Cases, 109 U.S. 3 (1883).
Clyatt v. United States, 197 U.S. 207 (1905).
Ex parte Brown et al., 140 F. 461 (1905).
Ex parte Yarbrough, 110 U.S. 651 (1884).
Goode v. Nelson, 73 Fla. 29 (1917).
In re Lewis, 114 Fed. 963 (1902).
In re Peonage Charge, 138 F. 686 (1905).
Jamison v. Wimbush, 130 F. 351 (1904).
McRee v. Frederick, 18 Ga. App. 321 (1916).
McRee v. Quitman Oil Co. et al., 84 S.E. 487 (1915).
Peonage Cases, 123 Fed. 671 (1903).
Peonage Cases, 136 F. 707 (1905).
Pitts v. Allen, 72 Ga. 69 (1883).
Pollock v. Williams, 322 U.S. 4 (1944).
Quitman Oil Co. et al. v. McRee, 88 S.E. 921 (1916).
Ryan v. State, 45 Ga. 128 (1872).
Slaughterhouse Cases, 83 U.S. 36 (1873).
Smith v. Willis, 33 S.E. 667 (1899).
Taylor v. Georgia, 315 U.S. 25 (1942).
Townsend v. State, 52 S.E. 293 (1905).
United States v. Eberhart et al., 127 F. 252 (1899).
United States v. McClellan, 127 F. 971 (1904).
United States v. Moore, et al., 129 F. 630 (1904).
United States v. Morris et al., 125 F. 322 (1903).

United States v. Reynolds, United States v. Broughton, 235 U.S. 133 (1914).
Walton County v. Franklin, 95 Ga. 538 (1894).
Williams v. Fears, 179 U.S. 270 (1900).
Willingham v. Hooven, Owens, Rentschler & Co., 74 Ga. 233 (1884).
Wilson v. State, 138 Ga. 489 (1912).

Archival Material

Booker T. Washington Papers, 1853–1946, MSS44669, Manuscript Division, Library of Congress, Washington, D.C.
Carter, Catherine McRee. "History of Kinderlou, Georgia, 1860–1940." 7 December 1940. Box 122, folder 1, Kinderlou Papers, Archive Row 1, Lowndes County Historical Society, Valdosta, Georgia.
Civil War Records, 1861–1865, 022-01-017, Georgia Archives, Morrow, Georgia.
County Marriage Records, 1828–1978, Georgia Archives, Morrow, Georgia.
E.J. McRee Papers, Archive Row 1, Box 192, Lowndes County Historical Society, Valdosta, Georgia.
General Records of the Department of Justice, National Archives, Washington, D.C.
Georgia Department of Public Health, Bureau of Vital Statistics, Atlanta, Georgia.
Georgia Headright and Bounty Documents, 3-4-5, McRee, William, Georgia Archives, Morrow, Georgia.
Georgia Tax Digests, Georgia Archives, Morrow, Georgia.
Governor, Executive Department Minutes, October 25, 1902–September 1, 1906, vol. 3, 4758, Governor Joseph Meriwether Terrell, Georgia Archives, Morrow, Georgia.
Governor Joseph E. Brown Papers, 1-1-5, Georgia Archives, Morrow, Georgia.
Papers of the NAACP, Part 10: Peonage, Labor, and the New Deal, 1913–1939.
Peonage Files of the Department of Justice, 1901–1945.
Prisons-State Prison Commission-Corporal Punishment Monthly Reports-1884–1886; 1889– (aka Whipping Reports) Consignment # 2000-1022A, Georgia Archives, Morrow, Georgia.
Prisons-State Prison Commission-Rations and Clothing Daily Records-1904–1909, 021-01-016, Georgia Archives, Morrow, Georgia.
Public Reference Service—File II, Georgia Archives, Morrow, Georgia.
Records of the Georgia Board of Corrections, Record Group 21, 3-4, 19-20, Georgia Archives, Morrow, Georgia.
Records of the Georgia Prison Commission, 1817–1936, A Part of the Records of the Georgia Board of Corrections, Record Group 21, 3-4, 19-20, Georgia Archives, Morrow, GA.
W.S. McRee Papers, Archive Row 1, Box 192, Lowndes County Historical Society, Valdosta, Georgia.

Government Documents

1854 §4705, Part IV, Title I, Division 13. In *Annotated Penal Laws of Georgia*, ed. John L. Hopkins, 453. Macon, Ga.: JW Burke & Co., 1875.

§449 "Vagrants." Tenth Division, Article 15. *The Code of the State of Georgia, 1910*, vol. 2, 91–92. Atlanta: Foote & Davies Company, 1911.

§860 ($715) "Rules for Government of Convicts, etc." Seventh Title, Chapter 1, Article 2. *The Code of the State of Georgia, 1910*, Vol. 1, 222. Atlanta: Foote and Davies, 1911.

§861 ($716) "Superintendent, etc., Not Personally Liable for Damage to Convict." Seventh Title, Chapter 1, Article 2. *The Code of the State of Georgia, 1910*, vol. 1, 222. Atlanta: Foote and Davies, 1911.

"An Act in relation to Contracts of Persons of Color." Chapter 1470, no. 7, January 12, 1866. *Acts and Resolutions Adopted by the General Assembly of Florida, 1865*, 32–33. Tallahassee: Office of the Floridian, 1866.

"An Act in Relation to Obtaining Money or any other Personal Property under False Promises, or for Violation of Contracts, and Providing Penalties therefor." Chapter 4032, No. 23. *Acts and Resolutions Adopted by the Legislature of Florida, 1891*, 57–58. Jacksonville: Times Union Book and Job Office, 1891.

"An Act to abolish and forever prohibit the System of Peonage in the Territory of New Mexico and other Parts of the United States." March 2, 1867, Chapter 187, 546, *United States Statutes at Large*, 39th Congress, 2nd sess.

"An Act to alter and amend the 4435th Section of the Penal Code of Georgia." March 12, 1866. *Acts of the General Assembly of the State of Georgia, 1865 and 1866*, 234–35. Milledgeville, Ga.: Bougton, Nisbet, Barnes & Moore, 1866.

"An Act to alter and amend Sections 4596 and 4597 of the Code of Georgia." February 15, 1866, *Acts of the General Assembly of the State of Georgia, 1865 and 1866*, 235. Milledgeville, Ga.: Bougton, Nisbet, Barnes & Moore, 1866.

"An Act to amend section 2652 and 2653 Revised Code of 1871, in relation to Grand and Petit Larceny." Chapter LVII. *Laws of the State of Mississippi, Passed At a Regular Session of the Mississippi Legislature, Held in the City of Jackson, Commencing January 4th, 1876, and Ending April 15th, 1876*, 51–52. Jackson, Ga.: Power & Barksdale, 1876.

"An Act to authorize the hiring of a certain class of Convicts to private citizens, to prescribe the conditions thereof, and to regulate the relations between the parties, No. 25." March 2, 1874. *Acts of the General Assembly of the State of Georgia, 1874*, 29. Savannah, Ga.: J. H. Estill, 1874.

"AN ACT To Carry into Effect the Seventh Section of the Fourth Article of the Constitution." No. 22, section 6, 5 December 1801. *A Compilation of the Laws of the State of Georgia*, ed. Augustin Smith Clayton, 21–23. Augusta: Adams & Duyckinck, 1812.

"An Act to extend the provisions of an act entitled an act in relation to Contracts of Persons of Color to all persons without distinction of color." Chapter 1551, No. 18, 13 December 1866. *Acts and Resolutions Adopted by the General Assembly of the State of Florida, 1866*, 21–22. Tallahassee: Office of the Floridian, 1867.

"An Act to Provide a Penalty to Be Imposed Upon Any Person in This State Who Shall, With the Intent to Injure and Defraud, Obtain or Procure Money or Other Thing of Value on a Contract to Perform Labor or Service, and to Repeal Chapter 5678, Acts 1907." Chapter 6528, No. 108. *General Acts and Resolutions Adopted by the Legislature of Florida, 1913,* 417. Tallahassee: T. J. Appleyard, 1913.

"An Act to Provide a Penalty to be Imposed Upon Any Person in This State Who Shall, With Intent to Injure and Defraud, Obtain or Procure Money or Other Thing of Value on a Contract or Promise to Perform Labor or Service and Prescribing a Rule of Evidence Governing Same." Chapter 7917, No. 135. *General Acts and Resolutions Adopted by the Legislature of Florida, 1919,* 286. Tallahassee: T. J. Appleyard, 1919.

"An Act to provide for the punishment of persons for tampering with, persuading or enticing away, harboring, feeding or secreting laborers, servants or apprentices." No. 16, 21 December 1865. *Acts Passed by the General Assembly of the State of Louisiana at the Extra Session, 1865,* 24–26. New Orleans: J. O. Nixon, 1866.

"An Act to punish Vagrants and Vagabonds." Ch. 1467, No. 4, *Acts and Resolutions Adopted by the General Assembly of Florida, 1865,* 28–29. Tallahassee: Office of the Floridian, 1866.

Annual Report of the Principal Keeper of the Georgia Penitentiary, 1893–1894. Atlanta: Franklin Publishing House, 1894.

Annual Report of the Principal Keeper of the Georgia Penitentiary, 1895–1896. Atlanta: Franklin Printing and Publishing Co., 1896.

"Authorizing Hiring Out of Misdemeanor Convicts, Etc., No. 679." October 16, 1891. *Acts and Resolutions of the General Assembly of the State of Georgia, 1890-'91, Vol. 1,* 212–13. Atlanta: Franklin Publishing House, 1891.

Biennial Report of the Principal Keeper of the Georgia Penitentiary, 1890–1892. Atlanta: Franklin Publishing House, 1892.

"Committee on Penitentiary, Inspections, Etc., No. 2." August 7, 1907. *Acts and Resolutions of the General Assembly of the State of Georgia, 1907,* 1012–13. Atlanta: Franklin-Turner Company, 1907.

"Contracts That Must Be in Writing." Chapter 29. *A Digest of the Laws of the State of Florida from 1822 to 1881,* comp. James F. McClellan, 208–10. Tallahassee: Floridian Book and Job Office, 1881.

Eighth Annual Report of the Prison Commission of Georgia, 1905. Atlanta: Lester Book & Stationery, 1905. Georgia Penitentiary Prison Commission's Reports, Georgia Archives, Morrow, Georgia.

Eleventh Annual Report of the Prison Commission of Georgia, 1908. Atlanta: Lester Book & Stationery, 1908. Georgia Penitentiary Prison Commission's Reports, Georgia Archives, Morrow, Georgia.

"Employment of Convicts; System of Penology, No. 4." September 19, 1908. *Acts and Resolutions of the General Assembly of the State of Georgia, 1916,* 1119–30. Atlanta: Chas. P. Byrd, State Printer, 1916.

"Examination of Books and Records Prison Commission, State Farm and Reformatory 1899 to May 31, and July 19, 1908." Report of the Convict Lease Investigating

Committee, August 20, 1908. *Acts and Resolutions of the General Assembly of the State of Georgia, 1916,* 1092–1104. Atlanta: Chas. P. Byrd, State Printer, 1916.

Felder, Thomas S., Chairman, Convict Lease Investigating Committee, "Report of the Investigating Committee." August 20, 1908. *Acts and Resolutions of the General Assembly of the State of Georgia, 1908,* 1059–92. Atlanta: Franklin Printing and Publishing, 1908.

Fifteenth Report of the State Highway Board of Georgia to the Governor and General Assembly of the State of Georgia. Atlanta: Stein Printing Co., 1934.

Fifth Annual Report of the Prison Commission of Georgia, 1902. Atlanta: Lester Book and Stationery, 1902. Georgia Penitentiary Prison Commission's Reports, Georgia Archives, Morrow, Georgia.

First Annual Report of the Highway Department of Georgia to the Governor and General Assembly of the State of Georgia. Atlanta, June 15, 1919.

First Annual Report of the Prison Commission of Georgia, 1898. Atlanta: Franking Printing Co., 1898. Georgia Penitentiary Prison Commission's Reports, Georgia Archives, Morrow, Georgia.

Fourth Annual Report of the Prison Commission of Georgia, 1901. Atlanta: Franking Printing Co., 1901. Georgia Penitentiary Prison Commission's Reports, Georgia Archives, Morrow, Georgia.

Georgia Constitution

Georgia, House of Representatives Special Committees, Vol. 4, August 4–August 17, 1908, 13-59-36, 252-14, GRG 1-705, 1252–72, Georgia Archives, Morrow, Georgia.

"Georgia State Reformatory Established, No. 6," August 22, 1905. *Acts and Resolutions of the General Assembly of the State of Georgia, 1905,* 71–78. Atlanta: Franklin Printing and Publishing, 1905.

"Good Behavior of Misdemeanor Convicts." Part I, Title VIII, No. 319, October 9, 1885. In *Acts and Resolutions of the General Assembly of the State of Georgia, 1884–1885,* 89. Atlanta: James P. Harrison & Co., 1885.

"Hearing on the Bill (HR 383) to Prohibit Shanghaiing and Peonage in the United States," February 2, 1906. United States Congress. House. Committee on Merchant Marine and Fisheries. Washington, D.C.: USGPO, 1906.

"Hire of Felony Convicts, Disposition of, No. 150." 23 August 1905. *Acts and Resolutions of the General Assembly of the State of Georgia, 1905,* 125–26. Atlanta: Franklin Printing and Publishing, 1905.

"Hire of Felony Convicts, Participation in By New Counties, No. 488." August 18, 1906. *Acts and Resolutions of the General Assembly of the State of Georgia, 1906,* 113–14. Atlanta: Franklin Printing and Publishing, 1906.

Immigration Commission. "Peonage." *Reports of the Immigration Commission,* 439–49. Washington, D.C.: USGPO, 1910.

Interview with C. H. Lowe (white), *Georgia, House of Representatives Special Committees, Vol. 3,* July 30–August 3, 1908, 13-59-36, 252-14, GRG 1-705, 748–55, Georgia Archives, Morrow, Georgia.

Interview with R. E. Davidson, *Georgia, House of Representatives Special Committees, Vol. 1*, July 20–July 26, 1908, 13-59-36, 252-14, GRG 1-705, 135–37, Georgia Archives, Morrow, Georgia.

Interview with W. R. Cheves (White), *Georgia, House of Representatives Special Committees, Vol. 2*, July 27–July 29, 1908, 13-59-36, 252-14, GRG 1-705, 455–66, Georgia Archives, Morrow, Georgia.

"Joint Committee to Investigate Convict System, No. 34, A Resolution," July 26, 1908, *Acts and Resolutions of the General Assembly of the State of Georgia, 1908*, 1029–32. Atlanta: Franklin Printing and Publishing, 1908.

Journal of the House of Representatives of the State of Georgia, 1892. Atlanta: Franklin Publishing House, 1892.

Journal of the House of Representatives of the State of Georgia, 1895. Atlanta: Franking Printing and Publishing Co., 1896.

Journal of the House of Representatives of the State of Georgia, 1902. Atlanta: Franklin Printing and Publishing Co., 1902.

Journal of the House of Representatives of the State of Georgia, 1903. Atlanta: Franklin Printing and Publishing Co., 1903.

Journal of the Senate of the State of Georgia, 1892. Atlanta: Franklin Publishing House, 1892.

Journal of the Senate of the State of Georgia, 1895. Atlanta: Franklin Printing and Publishing Co., 1895.

Memorial of Republican Members of Legislature of Alabama to the Congress of the United States. In: Report: The subcommittee of the Committee on Privileges and Elections to inquire and report whether in any of the elections in the State of Alabama in the elections of 1874, 1875, and 1876 the right of male inhabitants of said State, being twenty-one years of age and citizens of the United States, to vote had been denied or abridged, Senate Report No. 704, 44th Congress, 2nd sess., 3 March 1877. In: *Report of the Committees of the Senate of the United States for the Second Session of the Forty-Fourth Congress, 1876–77*, vol. 1, 662–69. United States Congressional Serial Set 1732. Washington, D.C.: USGPO, 1877.

Ninth Annual Report of the Prison Commission of Georgia, 1906. Atlanta: Lester Book & Stationery, 1906. Georgia Penitentiary Prison Commission's Reports, Georgia Archives, Morrow, Georgia.

"Of Offenses against Chastity, Morality, and Decency." Chapter 8, sec. 24, *Acts and Resolutions Adopted by the Legislature of Florida, 1868*, 96–100. Tallahassee: Office of the Tallahassee Sentinel, 1868.

"Penitentiary Convicts, Amending Law As to Release of, No. 124." December 14, 1895. *Acts and Resolutions of the General Assembly of the State of Georgia, 1890-'91, Vol. 1*, 80. Atlanta: Franklin Printing and Publishing, 1896.

"Prescribing Penalties for Felonies, with Certain Exceptions, and for All Misdemeanors." No. 17, Part I, Title 7, November 27, 1895. In *Acts and Resolutions of the General Assembly of the State of Georgia, 1895*, 63–64. Atlanta: Franklin Printing and Publishing Co., 1896.

"Prison Commission Created, No. 340." December 21, 1897. *Acts and Resolutions of the General Assembly of the State of Georgia, 1897,* 71–78. Atlanta: Franklin Printing and Publishing, 1898.

"Prison Commission, Disposition of Convicts, No. 430." October 17, 1903. *Acts and Resolutions of the General Assembly of the State of Georgia, 1903,* 65–71. Atlanta: Franklin Printing and Publishing, 1903.

Prison Commission of Georgia. *Third [Fourth] Biennial Report,* Records of the Georgia Prison Commission, 1817–1936, Record group 21, Georgia Archives, Morrow, Georgia.

"Procuring Money on Contract for Service, No. 345." 15 August 1903. *Acts of the General Assembly of the State of Georgia, 1903,* 90–91. Atlanta: Franklin Printing and Publishing Co., 1903.

Progress of Road Construction in the United States. Washington, D.C.: USGPO, 1897.

"Providing for Establishment of Reformatory Prisons by Counties or Municipalities." No. 321, Part I, Title 10, December 19, 1893. In *Acts and Resolutions of the General Assembly of the State of Georgia, 1892,* 120–23. Atlanta: Franklin Publishing House, 1893.

Reagan, E. J. "Report of the Committee on Penitentiary." 11 December 1895, *Journal of the House of Representatives of the State of Georgia, 1895,* 828–30. Atlanta: Franklin Printing and Publishing Co., 1895.

"Remarks of Mr. Brantley." March 28, 1904. *Congressional Record,* 58th Congress, vol. 38, 3898–3906. Washington, D.C.: USGPO, 1904.

"Remarks of Mr. Littlefield." April 12, 1904. *Congressional Record,* 58th Congress, vol. 38, 4700–4702. Washington, D.C.: USGPO, 1904.

Russell, Charles W. *Report on Peonage.* Washington, D.C.: USGPO, 1908.

S. B. No. 214. *Journal of the Senate of the State of Mississippi at a Regular Session Thereof, Convened in the City of Jackson, January 4, 1876,* 495. Jackson: Power & Barksdale, 1876.

Second Annual Report of the Highway Department of Georgia to the Governor and General Assembly of the State of Georgia. Atlanta, May 1, 1920.

Second Annual Report of the Prison Commission of Georgia, 1899. Atlanta: Foote & Davies Co., 1899. Georgia Penitentiary Prison Commission's Reports, Georgia Archives, Morrow, Georgia.

Senate Reports, 46 Cong., 2 Sess., No. 693: *Report and Testimony of the Select Committee of the United States Senate to Investigate the Causes of the Removal of Negroes from the Southern States to the Northern States.* Serial 1899, Washington, D.C., 1880, 117.

Seventh Annual Report of the Prison Commission of Georgia, 1904. Atlanta: Lester Book & Stationery, 1904. Georgia Penitentiary Prison Commission's Reports, Georgia Archives, Morrow, Georgia.

Sixth Annual Report of the Prison Commission of Georgia, 1903. Georgia Penitentiary Prison Commission's Reports, Georgia Archives, Morrow, Georgia.

"Statement of Joseph E. Brown." February 12, 1883. *Congressional Record,* 47th Cong., 2nd sess., vol. 14, 1883, 14, 2493.

Tenth Annual Report of the Prison Commission of Georgia, 1907. Atlanta: Lester Book & Stationery, 1907. Georgia Penitentiary Prison Commission's Reports, Georgia Archives, Morrow, Georgia.

Terrell, Joseph Merriwell. "Misdemeanor Convicts." *Journal of the House of Representatives of the State of Georgia, 1902,* 48–52. Atlanta: Franklin Printing and Publishing Co., 1902.

Third Annual Report of the Prison Commission of Georgia, 1900. Atlanta: Foote & Davies Co., 1900. Georgia Penitentiary Prison Commission's Reports, Georgia Archives, Morrow, Georgia.

Thirteenth Annual Report of the Prison Commission of Georgia, 1910. Atlanta: Lester Book & Stationery, 1910. Georgia Penitentiary Prison Commission's Reports, Georgia Archives, Morrow, Georgia.

Twelfth Annual Report of the Prison Commission of Georgia, 1909. Atlanta: Atlanta: Lester Book & Stationery, 1909. Georgia Penitentiary Prison Commission's Reports, Georgia Archives, Morrow, Georgia.

United States v. J. M. Cobb and George P. Hart, Lowndes County, Indictment No. 416, November 23, 1903, *Minutes,* U.S. District Court, Eastern Division, South District, Georgia, 460, 21.12.6, Records of the U.S. District Court for the Southern District, Records of the Eastern Division (Savannah), including minute books, 1789–1947, National Archives and Records Administration, Morrow, Georgia.

United States v. J. M. Cobb and George P. Hart, Indictment, Peonage, March 22, 1905, *Minutes,* U.S. District Court, Eastern Division, South District, Georgia, 576, 21.12.6, Records of the U.S. District Court for the Southern District, Records of the Eastern Division (Savannah), including minute books, 1789–1947, National Archives and Records Administration, Morrow, Georgia.

U.S. Bureau of Labor. *Second Annual Report of the Commissioner of Labor, 1886: Convict Labor.* Washington, D.C.: USGPO, 1887.

U.S. Bureau of Labor Statistics. *Prison Labor in the United States, 1932.* Washington, D.C.: USGPO, 1933.

U.S. Department of Agriculture. *Progress of Road Construction in the United States.* Washington, D.C.: USGPO, 1897.

U.S. Department of Agriculture. *Road Conventions in the Southern States and Object-Lesson Roads.* Washington, D.C.: USGPO, 1902.

U.S. Department of Commerce, *Fifteenth Census of the United States, 1930.*

U.S. Department of Commerce, *Fourteenth Census of the United States, 1920.*

U.S. Department of Commerce. *Seventh Census of the United States, 1850,* Schedule 2, Slave Inhabitants in the County of Lowndes. Washington, D.C.: National Archives and Records Administration, 1850.

U.S. Department of Commerce. *Tenth Census of the United States, 1880.*

U.S. Department of Commerce. *Thirteenth Census of the United States, 1910.*

U.S. Department of Commerce. *Twelfth Census of the United States, 1900.*

U.S. House of Representatives, 59 HR 383, December 4, 1905.

U.S. House of Representatives, 60 H. Res. 60, December 16, 1907.

U.S. House of Representatives, 60 H. Res. 115, January 6, 1908.

U.S. House of Representatives, 60th Congress, 1st sess., Report No. 1287, "Call for Information Concerning Investigation of Alleged Peonage Cases in Florida by Department of Justice, Etc.," March 21, 1908.

"Vagrants Defined." §4560. *The Code of the State of Georgia*, 4th edition, 1190. Atlanta: Jason P. Harrison & Co., 1882.

Ware Superior Court, April Term 1903, 395, Court Minutes Book F (unmarked volume), Ware County Clerk of Court, Waycross, Georgia.

"Whipping Bosses for County and Municipal Chain Gangs, No. 398." 11 September 1891. *Acts and Resolutions of the General Assembly of the State of Georgia, 1890-'91, Vol. 1*, 211–12. Atlanta: Franklin Publishing House, 1891.

Wines, Frederick H. *Report on Crime, Pauperism, and Benevolence in the United States at the Eleventh Census: 1890*. Washington, D.C.: USGPO, 1895.

Other Primary Sources

Baker, Ray Stannard. *Following the Color Line: An Account of Negro Citizenship in the American Democracy*. New York: Doubleday, Page, 1908.

Barry, Richard. "Slavery in the South To-Day." *Cosmopolitan* 42 (March 1907): 481–91.

Byrd, Phill G. *Report of Special Inspector of Misdemeanor Convict Camps of Georgia*. Atlanta: Franklin Printing and Publishing, 1897. Georgia Archives, Morrow, Georgia.

Childs, Arney R., ed. *The Private Journal of Henry William Ravenel, 1859–1887*. Columbia: University of South Carolina Press, 1947.

DeMille, Cecil B. *Chimmie Fadden,* Paramount Pictures, 1915.

"Does Slavery Exist in South Carolina." *Literary Digest* 22 (March 2, 1901): 244.

Douglass, Frederick. "The Negro Exodus from the Gulf States." *Journal of Social Science* 11 (May 1880): 18.

Du Bois, W. E. B. "The Spawn Of Slavery: The Convict-lease System In The South." In *W. E. B. Du Bois On Crime And Justice: Laying The Foundations Of Sociological Criminology*, ed. Shaun L. Gabbidon, 117–24. Aldershot, U.K.: Ashgate, 2007.

Fourth Decennial Catalogue of the Chi Psi Fraternity. New York: Baker & Godwin, 1883.

Guild, Frederick H. "Administration and Supervision of State Charities and Corrections." *American Political Science Review* 10 (May 1916): 327–35.

Hershaw, Lafayette M. *Peonage*, Occasional Papers, No. 15. Washington, D.C.: American Negro Academy, 1915.

Howe, William Wirt. "The Peonage Cases," *Columbia Law Review* 4 (April 1904): 279–86.

Irvine, Alexander. "The Life Story of a Hungarian Peon." *Independent* 63 (September 5, 1907): 557–64.

Koestler, Arthur. *The Ghost in the Machine*. Originally published 1967; New York: Penguin, 1990.

McCallie, SW. "Use of Convicts on the Public Roads of Georgia." *Engineering Record* 64 (August 1911): 157–58.

McKelvey, Blake. "A Half-Century of Southern Penal Exploitations." *Social Forces* 13 (October 1934): 112–23.
"More Cases of Peonage." *Northwestern Christian Advocate,* December 2, 1903, 2.
"Negro Peonage and the Thirteenth Amendment." *Yale Law Journal* 13 (June 1904): 452–53.
"Negroes Leave the South." *The Messenger* 2 (March 1920): 2.
"The Peonage Cases." *Harvard Law Review* 17 (1903): 121–22.
"Peonage in Georgia." *Independent* 55 (24 December 1903): 3079–80.
R.L. Polk & Co.'s Valdosta City Directory, 1904. Valdosta: R.L. Polk & Co., 1904.
Raum, Green Berry. *The Existing Conflict Between Republican Government and Southern Oligarchy.* New York: Charles M. Green Printing, 1884.
Robinson, Louis N., Joseph N. Ulman, Gustav Peck, James P. Davis, and Linton M. Collins. *The Prison Labor Problem In Georgia.* Washington, D.C.: U.S. Prison Industries Reorganization Administration, 1937.
"Servitude for Debt in Georgia." *Outlook* 74 (June 27, 1903): 486.
"Southern Peonage and Immigration." *Nation* 85 (December 19, 1907): 557.
Speer, Emory. *Argument of Emory Speer, United States Attorney, in the case of the United States versus Jasper Yarbrough, et al., in the United States Circuit Court for the Northern District of Georgia.* Atlanta: W. H. Scott, 1883.
"The Valdosta Area . . . Central to the geographic reaches of 'The Fire Forest' Longleaf Pine-Wiregrass Ecosystem." Poster display, Lowndes County Historical Society, Valdosta, Georgia.
Ward, Herbert D. "Peonage in America." *Cosmopolitan* 39 (August 1905): 423–30.
"White Peonage in North Carolina." *Outlook* 87 (October 19, 1907): 319–20.
Wright, R.F. *Special Report of R.F. Wright on Misdemeanor Convicts of the State of Georgia, 1895.* Atlanta: Franklin Printing and Publishing, 1895. Georgia Archives, Morrow, Georgia.

Secondary Sources

Adamson, Christopher R. "Punishment after Slavery: Southern State Penal Systems, 1865–1890." *Social Problems* 30 (June 1983): 555–69.
Armstrong, Julie Buckner. *Mary Turner and the Memory of Lynching.* Athens: University of Georgia Press, 2011.
Arnett, Alex Mathews. *The Populist Movement in Georgia: A View of the "Agrarian Crusade" in the Light of Solid-South Politics.* Originally published 1922; Ithaca: Cornell University Library, 2009.
Arnold, Edwin. *What Virtue There Is in Fire: Cultural Memory and the Lynching of Sam Hose.* Athens: University of Georgia Press, 2012.
Aucoin, Brent J. *A Rift in the Clouds: Race and the Southern Federal Judiciary, 1900–1910.* Fayetteville: University of Arkansas Press, 2007.
Bancroft, Frederic. *Slave Trading in the Old South.* Originally published 1931; Columbia: University of South Carolina Press, 1996.

Banks, Taunya Lovell. "Dangerous Woman: Elizabeth Key's Freedom Suit—Subjecthood and Racialized Identity in Seventeenth Century Colonial Virginia." *Akron Law Review* 41, no. 3 (2008): 799–837.

Beck, E. M., James L. Massey, and Stewart E. Tolnay. "The Gallows, the Mob, and the Vote: Lethal Sanctioning of Blacks in North Carolina and Georgia, 1882 to 1930." *Law & Society Review* 23, no. 2 (1989): 317–31.

Berlin, Ira. *Many Thousands Gone: The First Two Centuries of Slavery in North America*. Cambridge: Belknap Press of Harvard University Press, 1998.

Bernstein, David E. *Only One Place of Redress: African Americans, Labor Regulations, and the Courts from Reconstruction to the New Deal*. Durham, N.C.: Duke University Press, 2001.

Berry, David. "Free Labor He Found Unsatisfactory: James W. English and Convict Lease Labor at the Chattahoochee Brick Company." *Proceedings and Papers of the Georgia Association of Historians* (1990): 117–25.

Blackmon, Douglas A. *Slavery by Another Name: The Re-Enslavement of Black Americans from the Civil War to World War II*. New York: Anchor Books, 2008.

———. "America's Twentieth-Century Slavery." *Washington Monthly* (January/February 2013): https://washingtonmonthly.com/magazine/janfeb-2013/americas-twentieth-century-slavery/. Accessed September 21, 2020.

———. "Transcript Of Keynote Speaker From Work In The South: Dixie Cotton, American Steel, And A Hurricane Named Katrina—a Reinvention Of Bondage." *Loyola Journal of Public Interest Law* 16 (Spring 2015): 423–60.

Boyd, Bill. *Blind Obedience: A True Story of Family Loyalty and Murder in South Georgia*. Macon, Ga.: Mercer University Press, 2000.

Brandwein, Pamela. "A Lost Jurisprudence of the Reconstruction Amendments." *Journal of Supreme Court History* 41 (November 2016): 329–46.

Brown, Kathleen M. *Good Wives, Nasty Wenches, and Anxious Patriarchs: Gender, Race, and Power in Colonial Virginia*. Chapel Hill: University of North Carolina Press, 1996.

Brown, William W., and Morgan O. Reynolds. "Debt Peonage Re-Examined." *Journal of Economic History* 33 (December 1973): 862–71.

Brundage, W. Fitzhugh. "The Roar on the Other Side of Silence: Black Resistance and White Violence in the American South, 1880–1940." In *Under Sentence of Death: Lynching in the South*, ed. W. Fitzhugh Brundage, 271–89. Chapel Hill: University of North Carolina Press, 1997.

Bryant, Jonathan M. "'We Have No Chance of Justice before the Courts': The Freedmen's Struggle for Power in Greene County, Georgia, 1865–1874." In *Georgia in Black and White: Explorations in the Race Relations of a Southern State, 1865–1950*, ed. John C. Inscoe, 13–37. Athens: University of Georgia Press, 1994.

Cable, George Washington. *The Silent South*. Montclair, Calif.: Patterson Smith, 1969.

Carper, Noel Gordon. "The Convict-Lease System in Florida, 1866–1923." Ph.D. diss: Florida State University, 1964.

———. "Slavery Revisited: Peonage in the South." *Phylon* 37 (1st Qtr. 1976): 85–99.

Carter, Dan T. "Prisons, Politics and Business: The Convict Lease System in the Post–Civil War South." Master's thesis, University of Wisconsin, 1964.

Chaplin, Joyce E. "Berlin's Two Concepts of Slavery." *Reviews in American History* 27 (June 1999): 188–93.

Cohen, William A. *At Freedom's Edge: Black Mobility and the Southern White Quest for Racial Control, 1861–1915.* Baton Rouge: Louisiana State University Press, 1991.

———. "Negro Involuntary Servitude in the South, 1865–1940." *Journal of Southern History* 42 (February 1976): 31–60.

Colcanis, Peter A. "In Retrospect: Ransom and Sutch's *One Kind of Freedom*." *Reviews in American History* 28 (September 2000): 478–89.

Curtin, Mary Ellen. *Black Prisoners and Their World, Alabama, 1865–1900.* Charlottesville: University Press of Virginia, 2000.

———. "The 'Human World' of Black Women in Alabama Prisons, 1870–1900." In *Hidden Histories of Women in the New South*, ed. Virginia Bernhard, Betty Brandon, Elizabeth Fox-Genovese, Theda Purdue, and Elizabeth Hayes Turner, 11–30. Columbia: University of Missouri Press, 1994.

Daniel, Pete. *The Shadow of Slavery: Peonage in the South, 1901–1969.* Urbana: University of Illinois Press, 1972.

———. "Up from Slavery and Down to Peonage: The Alonzo Bailey Case." *Journal of American History* 57 (December 1970): 654–70.

Dasher, Wayne, and Judy Dasher. *Personal Mentions from Our Research Papers, Vol. 2.* s.p.

Davis, Angela. *Are Prisons Obsolete?* New York: Seven Stories Press, 2003.

Davis, David Brion. *Inhuman Bondage: The Rise and Fall of Slavery in the New World.* New York: Oxford University Press, 2006.

Davis, Dernoral. "Toward a Socio-Historical and Demographic Portrait of Twentieth-Century African-Americans." In *Black Exodus: The Great Migration from the American South*, ed. Alferdteen Harrison, 1–19. Jackson: University Press of Mississippi, 1991.

Dittmer, John. *Black Georgia in the Progressive Era, 1900–1920.* Urbana: University of Illinois Press, 1977.

Dolovich, Sharon. "State Punishment and Private Prisons." *Duke Law Journal* 55 (December 2005): 437–546.

Drobney, Jeffrey A. "Where Palm and Pine Are Blowing: Convict Labor in the North Florida Turpentine Industry, 1877–1923." *Florida Historical Quarterly* 72 (April 1994): 411–34.

Eckert, Ralph Lowell. *John Brown Gordon: Soldier, Southerner, American.* Baton Rouge: Louisiana State University Press, 1993.

Ellem, Warren A. "The Overthrow of Reconstruction in Mississippi." *Journal of Mississippi History* 54, no. 2 (1992): 175–201.

Floyd, Josephine Bone. "Rebecca Latimer Felton, Champion of Women's Rights." *Georgia Historical Quarterly* 30 (June 1946): 81–104.

Flynn, Jr., Charles L. *White Land, Black Labor: Caste and Class in Late Nineteenth-Century Georgia.* Baton Rouge: Louisiana State University Press, 1983.

Fogel, Robert William. *Without Consent or Contract: The Rise and Fall of American Slavery.* New York: W. W. Norton, 1994.

Foner, Eric. *Nothing But Freedom: Emancipation and Its Legacy.* Baton Rouge: Louisiana State University Press, 1983.

Forte, David F. "Spiritual Equality, the Black Codes, and the Americanization of the Freedmen." *Loyola Law Review* 43 (1998): 569–611.

Friedlander, Alan, and Richard Allan Gerber. *Welcoming Ruin: The Civil Rights Act of 1875.* London: Brill, 2018.

Friling, Tuvia. *A Jewish Kapo in Auschwitz: History, Memory, and the Politics of Survival.* Waltham: Brandeis University Press, 2014.

Glenn, Evelyn Nakano. *Forced to Care: Coercion and Caregiving in America.* Cambridge, Mass.: Harvard University Press, 2010.

Goluboff, Risa L. "The Thirteenth Amendment and the Lost Origins of Civil Rights." *Duke Law Journal* 50 (2001): 1609–85.

Gonzalez-Tennant, Edward. *The Rosewood Massacre: An Archaeology and History of Intersectional Violence.* Gainesville: University Press of Florida, 2018.

Grant, Donald Lee. *The Way It Was in the South; The Black Experience in Georgia.* Athens: University of Georgia Press, 2001.

Green, Fletcher Melvin. "Some Aspects of the Convict Lease System in the Southern States." In *Essays in Southern History,* ed. Fletcher M. Green, 112–23. Chapel Hill: University of North Carolina Press, 1949.

Greene, Harlan, Harry S. Hutchins, Jr., and Brian E. Hutchins. *Slave Badges and the Slave-Hire System in Charleston, South Carolina, 1783–1865.* Jefferson, N.C.: McFarland, 2004.

Grem, Darren E. "Sam Jones, Sam Hose, and the Theology of Racial Violence." *Georgia Historical Quarterly* 90 (Spring 2006): 35–61.

Grossman, James R. *Land of Hope: Chicago, Black Southerners, and the Great Migration.* New York: St. Martin's Press, 1991.

Gudridge, Patrick O. "Privileges and Permissions: The Civil Rights Act of 1875." *Law and Philosophy* 8 (April 1989): 83–130.

Hahn, Steven. "Hunting, Fishing, and Foraging: Common Rights and Class Relations in the Postbellum South." *Radical History Review* 26 (October 1982): 37–64.

Haley, Sarah. "'Like I Was a Man': Chain Gangs, Gender, and the Domestic Carceral Sphere in Jim Crow Georgia." *Signs: Journal of Women in Culture and Society* 39, no. 1 (2013): 53–76.

Halpern, Rick. *Down on the Killing Floor: Black and White Workers in Chicago's Packinghouses, 1904–1954.* Urbana: University of Illinois Press, 1997.

Halpin, Ross W. *Jewish Doctors and the Holocaust: The Anatomy of Survival in Auschwitz.* Berlin: De Gruyter, 2018.

Hamilton, Howard Devon. "The Legislative and Judicial History of the Thirteenth Amendment." Ph.D. diss: University of Illinois, 1950.

Hart, Albert Bushnell. *The Southern South.* New York: D. Appleton & Co., 1910.

Hawkins, Darnell F. "State versus County: Prison Policy and Conflicts of Interest in North Carolina." *Criminal Justice History* 5 (1984): 91–128.

———. "Trends in Black-White Imprisonment: Changing Conceptions of Race or Changing Patterns of Social Control?" *Crime and Social Justice*, no. 24 (1985): 187–209.

Hawkins, Mary Ann. "He Drew the Lightning: Emory Speer, Federal Judge in Georgia, 1885–1918." Master's thesis, Georgia State University, 1984.

The Heritage of Lowndes County, Georgia. Valdosta: Lowndes County Historical Society, 2000.

Higginbotham Jr., Leon A. "The Supreme Court's Sanction of Racial Hatred: The 1883 Civil Rights Cases." In *Shades of Freedom: Racial Politics and Presumptions of the American Legal Process*, 94–107. New York: Oxford University Press, 1998.

Hodges, Fred H. *History of Lowndes County, Georgia, 1825–1941*. Valdosta: General James Jackson Chapter NSDAR, 1995.

Holloway, Pippa. "'A Chicken-Stealer Shall Lose His Vote': Disfranchisement for Larceny in the South, 1874–1890." *Journal of Southern History* 75 (November 2009): 931–62.

Huebner, Timothy S. "Emory Speer and Federal Enforcement of the Rights of African Americans, 1880–1910." *American Journal of Legal History* 55 (January 2015): 34–63.

Johnson, Walter. *Soul by Soul: Life Inside the Antebellum Slave Market*. Cambridge, Mass.: Harvard University Press, 1999.

Jonas, Gilbert. *Freedom's Sword: The NAACP and the Struggle Against Racism in America, 1909–1969*. New York: Routledge, 2005.

Jones, Alton DuMar. "The Administration of Governor Joseph M. Terrell Viewed in the Light of the Progressive Movement." *Georgia Historical Quarterly* 48 (September 1964): 271–90.

Jones, Maxine D., Larry E. Rivers, David R. Colburn, R. Tom Dye, and William W. Rogers. "Documented History of the Incident Which Occurred at Rosewood, Florida in January 1923." Florida Board of Regents, December 22, 1993. Available online at https://web.archive.org/web/20090126110750/http://displaysforschools.com/rosewoodrp.html. Accessed October 24, 2020.

Jordan, Winthrop D. *White Over Black: American Attitudes toward the Negro, 1550–1812*. Chapel Hill: University of North Carolina Press, 1968.

Kantrowitz, Stephen. *Ben Tillman and the Reconstruction of White Supremacy*. North Carolina: University of North Carolina Press, 2000.

Kiser, William S. *Borderlands of Slavery: The Struggle over Captivity and Peonage in the American Southwest*. Philadelphia: University of Pennsylvania Press, 2017.

Klein, Herbert S. *Slavery in the Americas: A Comparative Study of Virginia and Cuba*. Chicago: University of Chicago Press, 1976.

Kurshan, Nancy. *Women and Imprisonment in the US: History and Current Reality*. Philadelphia: Prison Activist Resource Center and Monkeywrench Press, 1995.

Labbé, Ronald M., and Jonathan Lurie. *The Slaughterhouse Cases: Regulation, Reconstruction, and the Fourteenth Amendment*. Lawrence: University Press of Kansas, 2003.

LeFlouria, Talitha L. *Chained in Silence: Black Women and Convict Labor in the New South*. Chapel Hill: University of North Carolina Press, 2015.

Lichtenstein, Alex. *Twice the Work of Free Labor: The Political Economy of Convict Labor in the New South*. New York: Verson, 1996.

Litwack, Leon F. *Trouble in Mind: Black Southerners in the Age of Jim Crow*. New York: Vintage Books, 1999.

Lomax, Louis E. "Georgia Boy Goes Home." *Harper's* 230 (April 1965): 152–53.

Mancini, Matthew J. *One Dies, Get Another: Convict Leasing in the American South, 1866–1928*. Columbia: University of South Carolina Press, 1996.

———. "Race, Economics, and the Abandonment of Convict Leasing." *Journal of Negro History* 63 (October 1978): 339–52.

Massey, Douglas J., and Nancy A. Denton. *American Apartheid: Segregation and the Making of the Underclass*. Cambridge, Mass.: Harvard University Press, 1998.

Massey, James L., and Martha A. Myers. "Patterns of Repressive Social Control in Post-Reconstruction Georgia, 1882–1935." *Social Forces* 68 (December 1989): 458–88.

McPherson, James W. "Abolitionists and the Civil Rights Act of 1875." *Journal of American History* 52 (December 1965): 493–510.

Miller, Randall. "The Man in the Middle: The Black Slave Driver." *American Heritage* 30 (1979): 40–49.

Morgan, Edmund S. *American Slavery, American Freedom: The Ordeal of Colonial Virginia*. New York: W. W. Norton, 1975.

Muller, Christopher. "Freedom and Convict Leasing in the Postbellum South." *American Journal of Sociology* 2 (September 2018): 367–405.

Myers, Christopher. "Killing Them by the Wholesale: A Lynching Rampage in South Georgia." *Georgia Historical Quarterly* 90 (Summer 2006): 214–35.

Myers, Martha A. *Race, Labor, and Punishment in the New South*. Columbus: Ohio State University Press, 1998.

Myers, Martha A., and James L. Massey. "Race, Labor, and Punishment in Postbellum Georgia." *Social Problems* 38 (May 1991): 267–86.

Newsom, Kevin Christopher. "Setting Incorporationism Straight: A Reinterpretation of the *Slaughter-House Cases*." *Yale Law Journal* 109 (2000): 643–744.

Novak, Daniel A. *The Wheel of Servitude: Black Forced Labor after Slavery*. Lexington: University Press of Kentucky, 1978.

Oshinsky, David M. *Worse than Slavery: Parchman Farm and the Ordeal of Jim Crow Justice*. New York: Free Press, 1996.

Painter, Nell Irvin. *Exodusters: Black Migrants to Kansas after Reconstruction*. Lawrence: University Press of Kansas, 1986.

Parks, Joseph Howard. *Joseph E. Brown of Georgia*. Baton Rouge: Louisiana State University Press, 1977.

Pendleton, Jr., Albert S. *Way Back When*, Vol. 1. Valdosta: self-published, undated, available in general collection of the Lowndes County Historical Society.

Perman, Michael. *The Road to Redemption: Southern Politics, 1869–1879*. Chapel Hill: University of North Carolina Press, 1984.

Platt, Anthony M. *The Child Savers: The Invention of Delinquency*, 2nd ed. Chicago: University of Chicago Press, 1977.

Porat, Dan. *Bitter Reckoning: Israel Tries Holocaust Survivors as Nazi Collaborators*. Cambridge, Mass.: Harvard University Press, 2019.

Ransom, Roger L., and Richard Sutch. "Debt Peonage in the Cotton South after the Civil War." *Journal of Economic History* 32 (September 1972): 641–69.

———. *One Kind of Freedom: The Economic Consequences of Slavery*. Originally published 1977. New York: Cambridge University Press, 2001.

Raza, A. E. "Legacies Of The Racialization Of Incarceration: From Convict-lease To The Prison Industrial Complex." *Journal of the Institute of Justice and International Studies* 11 (2011): 159–69.

Reuf, Martin, and Ben Fletcher. "Legacies of American Slavery: Status Attainment among Southern Blacks after Emancipation." *Social Forces* 82 (December 2003): 445–90.

Richardson, Joe M. "Florida Black Codes." *Florida Historical Quarterly* 47 (April 1969): 365–79.

Roark, James L. *Masters Without Slaves: Southern Planters in the Civil War and Reconstruction*. New York: W. W. Norton, 1977.

Roberts, Derrell C. *Joseph E. Brown and the Politics of Reconstruction*. Tuscaloosa: University of Alabama Press, 1973.

Ross, Michael A. "Justice Miller's Reconstruction: The Slaughter-House Cases, Health Codes, and Civil Rights in New Orleans, 1861–1873." *Journal of Southern History* 64 (November 1998): 649–76.

Russell, John Henderson. *The Free Negro in Virginia, 1619–1865*. Baltimore, Md.: Johns Hopkins University Press, 1913.

Schmidt Jr., Benno C. "Principle and Prejudice: The Supreme Court and Race in the Progressive Era. Part 2: The Peonage Cases." *Columbia Law Review* 82 (May 1982): 646–718.

Schmier, Louis. *Valdosta and Lowndes County: A Ray in the Sunbelt*. Northridge, Calif.: Windsor Publications, 1988.

Shelton, Jane Twitty. *Pines and Pioneers: A History of Lowndes County, Georgia, 1825–1900*. Atlanta: Cherokee Publishing Co., 1976.

Simkins, Francis Butler. "Ben Tillman's View of the Negro." *The Journal of Southern History* 3 (May 1937): 161–74.

Spillers, Hortense J. "Interstices: A Small Drama of Words." In *Pleasure and Danger: Exploring Female Sexuality*, ed. Carole S. Vance, 73–100. Boston: Routledge, 1984.

Sterling, Robin Walker. "Fundamental Unfairness: *In re Gault* and the Road Not Taken." *Maryland Law Review* 72 (2013): 607–81.

Sullivan, Patricia. *Lift Every Voice and Sing: The NAACP and the Making of the Civil Rights Movement*. New York: New Press, 2009.

Tanenhaus, David S. *Juvenile Justice in the Making*. New York: Oxford University Press, 2004.

Taylor, A. Elizabeth. "The Abolition of the Convict Lease System in Georgia." *Georgia Historical Quarterly* 26 (September–December 1942): 273–87.

———. "The Origin and Development of the Convict Lease System in Georgia." *Georgia Historical Quarterly* 26 (June 1942): 113–28.

Taylor, William B. *Brokered Justice: Race, Politics, and Mississippi Prisons, 1798–1992.* Columbus: Ohio State University Press, 1993.

Tegeder, Michael David. "Prisoners of the Pines: Debt Peonage in the Southern Turpentine Industry, 1900–1930." Ph.D. diss., University of Florida, 1996.

Tindall, George B. "The Question of Race in the South Carolina Constitutional Convention of 1895." *Journal of Negro History* 37 (July 1952): 277–303.

Tsesis, Alexander. *The Thirteenth Amendment and American Freedom: A Legal History.* New York: New York University Press, 2004.

Tushnet, Mark V. "'To Enable the Black Race to Take the Rank of Mere Citizens': The Civil Rights Cases, 1883." In *I Dissent: Great Opposing Opinions in Landmark Supreme Court Cases,* 45–68. Boston: Beacon Press, 2008.

Van Deburg, William L. *The Slave Drivers: Black Agricultural Labor Supervisors in the Antebellum South.* Originally published 1979; New York: Oxford University Press, 1988.

Verney, Kevern, and Lee Sartain, eds. *Long Is the Way and Hard: One Hundred Years of the NAACP.* Fayetteville: University of Arkansas Press, 2009.

Waldrep, Christopher. "Substituting Law for the Lash: Emancipation and Legal Formalism in a Mississippi County Court." *Journal of American History* 82 (March 1996): 1425–51.

Walker, Eugene Pierce. "Attitudes Towards Negroes as Reflected in the *Atlanta Constitution,* 1908–1918." Master's thesis, Emory University, 1969.

Ward, Geoff K. *The Black Child-Savers: Racial Democracy and Juvenile Justice.* Chicago: University of Chicago Press, 2012.

Weaver, Valeria W. "The Failure of Civil Rights 1875–1883 and its Repercussions." *Journal of Negro History* 54 (October 1969): 368–82.

Wharton, Vernon L. *The Negro in Mississippi, 1865–1890.* Originally published 1947; New York: Harper Torchbooks, 1965.

———. "The Race Issue in the Overthrow of Reconstruction in Mississippi: A Paper Read before the American Historical Association, 1940." *Phylon* 2 (4th Qtr., 1941): 362–70.

White, Carolyn Iona. *Georgia's Reaction to the Civil Rights Act of 1875 and the Civil Rights Cases of 1883.* Master's thesis, Atlanta University, 1971.

Wilhoit, Francis M. "An Interpretation of Populism's Impact on the Georgia Negro." *Journal of Negro History* 52 (April 1967): 116–27.

Wilkerson, Isabel. *The Warmth of Other Sons: The Epic Story of America's Great Migration.* New York: Random House, 2010.

Williamson, Joel. *After Slavery: The Negro in South Carolina During Reconstruction, 1861–1877.* Chapel Hill: University of North Carolina Press, 1965.

Wilson, Theodore Brantner. *The Black Codes of the South.* Tuscaloosa: University of Alabama Press, 1965.

Woodward, C. Vann. *Origins of the New South, 1877–1913.* Baton Rouge: Louisiana State University Press, 1971.

Zangrando, Robert L. *The NAACP Crusade Against Lynching, 1909–1950.* Philadelphia: Temple University Press, 1980.

Zimmerman, Hilda Jane. "Penal Systems and Penal Reforms in The South Since the Civil War." Ph.D. diss., University of North Carolina, 1947.

———. "The Convict Lease System in Arkansas and the Fight for Abolition." *Arkansas Historical Quarterly* 8 (Autumn 1949): 171–88.

INDEX

Ackerman, Alexander
   Charging choices of, 236n5
   Clyatt case and, 237n12
   Investigation of McRees, 122–124, 133, 198
   Peonage and, 233n18
   Prosecution of McRees, 125, 131
   Relationship with Speer, 235n42
Adamson, Christopher, 33
Alabama Supreme Court, 194
Alesbrook, J. S., 241n2
Allgeyer v. Louisiana (1897), 11
Allison, J. R., 44, 47
Anti-Convict League, 178
Arlington Lumber Co., 155, 158, 159, 163
Arnold, Nat D., 241n2
Arthur, Chester A., 124, 125
Ashley-Price Lumber Co., 183
A. T. Beach and Co., 43, 87, 110, 163, 169, 188
Atkinson, William Yates, 28–30
Atlanta and Birmingham Construction Co., 153–154
Auburn University, 18, 203

Babcock Bros. Lumber Co., 155, 159, 165, 183
Bailey, Alonzo, 194
Bailey v. Alabama (1911), 12, 194–196
Baker, John, 101
Baker, Ray Stannard, 209
Barry, Richard, 13, 155
Battle, C. E., 35
Beckham, Mark, 101
Bell, Alan, 103
Belview College, 17, 218n10
Benet, William Christie, 59
Bibb Brick Co., 155, 159, 165, 183

Bibb County Good Roads Association, 191
Bird, John, 101
Black Codes, 9–10, 12
Blackmon, Douglas, 125
Boatwright, Lizzie, 47
Bonaparte, Charles Joseph, 164, 165
Boney, John Wesley, 136, 237n9
Boyd, Bill, 26
Bradley, Joseph P., 61
Branson, George, 104
Brantley, William Gordon, 138–140
Brewer, David Josiah, 141
Brice, Mitchell, 28, 92
Brimmage, David, 122, 133, 237n9
Brimmage, Henry, 131, 237n9
Brimmage, Jeff, 131
Brisbane, Burton, 101
Broach, J. R., 142
Broach, W. P., 142
Brooks, R. F., 105
Brown, Alston, 207
Brown, Henry, 127
Brown, Joseph E., 34, 217n4
Brown, Nathan A., 153
Burton, J. R., 96
Bush, J. A., 177, 240n2
Butchers' Benevolent Association, 60
Butler, Johnnie, 104
Byrd, Phill G., 40, 48–49
Byron, Aaron, 34

Cain, Mathis, 103
Callahan, John W., 145
Camp Heardmont, 129
Canda Lumber Co., 74, 80, 107, 145

Candler, Allen, 92, 93, 97–99, 115, 118
Cannon, Bob, 47, 223n46
Carter, Dan T., 191, 224n10
Carter, Lucius, 101
Chattahoochee Brick Company
　Convict monopoly, 36, 39
　Listed in annual reports, 71, 74, 80, 85, 107, 145, 155, 159, 165, 183, 188
Cheeks, Lorenzo, 101
Cherokee Brick Co., 155, 159, 165, 183
Chickamauga Coal & Coke, 74, 80, 85, 107
Child Savers, 105
Civil Rights Act of 1875, 61
Civil War, 57–58
　29th Georgia Regiment, 17
　Battle of Chickamauga, 16
　As marker of time, 2, 6, 9, 15, 17, 31, 61, 154
　Veterans of, 191
Clark, Frank, 172
Clay, Henry, 52
Clements, Judson C., 117
Clyatt, D. T., 140
Clyatt, Samuel M., 140, 237n12
Clyatt and Tift, 140
Clyatt v. United States (1905), 137, 140–143, 177, 195–196
Cobb, Maurice Hugh, 143–144, 238nn26,29, 239nn30,32
Cohen, William, 57
Colbert, Will, 101
Cole, Tom, 90
Convict Investigating Committee (Georgia), 192
Cotton States Exposition, 125
County chain gangs, 115, 138, 151, 165, 197, 201, 212
　Bibb County and, 117, 144
　Considered public good, 3, 81, 115–116, 148, 182, 192
　Cruelty of, 93, 112, 144–145, 146
　Durability after 1909, 13, 52, 154, 184, 192, 197, 201, 208, 214n6
　Gender and, 129, 190
　Included in annual state reports, 68
　Influencing private misdemeanor camps, 13, 61, 68, 77, 129
　Lack of in various counties, 116, 120, 138

　Legislation and, 2–3, 31, 36, 48, 112, 184, 189–190, 209
　Lowndes County and, 99, 112, 148
　Oglethorpe County and, 164–165
　Operated by county officials, 36
　Public works and, 35, 55, 190, 197
　Punishment for misdemeanors, 35, 55, 79
　Regulation of, 29–30, 35, 38, 67, 95, 96, 146, 193
　Ware County and, 131
Covington, W. A., 185, 188
Crawley, William F., 125–126, 128, 131, 135–136, 236n5
Cruger & Pace
　Listed in annual reports, 74, 80, 85, 87, 107, 110, 145, 155, 158, 159, 165, 183
Cubberly, Fred, 1, 137, 140
Culbreath, T. G., 155, 158, 159, 165, 183
Cunningham, George J., 164

Dade Coal Company, 36, 39, 71
Daniel, Pete, 1, 56–58, 200
Davis, Angela, 129
Davis, Benjamin, 178–179, 205
Davis, George, 237n9
Davis, Will, 101
Day, William R., 196
De Vancey, Jesse, 34
Debt peonage
　After convict lease, 189, 194
　Anderson, South Carolina, and, 59, 102
　Compared to wage slavery, 205–206
　Counties profiting from, 37
　Court decisions about, 12, 61, 62–65, 122, 124, 130–131, 134, 138–139, 140–143, 144, 154–155, 192, 194–197, 226n26, 233nn17–19, 236n7
　Criticism of, 7, 58, 61, 64–66, 124, 132, 137, 139–140, 152, 160, 170–171, 226n26, 243n33
　Defense of, 58, 121–122
　Driving Black migration, 204, 246n29
　Federal report on, 165–170
　Florida and, 62, 153, 169–170, 207
　Georgia and, 27, 55, 58, 61–62, 91, 121, 135, 143, 148, 169–170, 206
　Historiography of, 55–58

Immigrants and, 200, 245n10
Lack of government oversight of, 25
Legislation about, 36, 108, 111, 171–172, 223n48
McRees and, 1, 4, 5, 13, 17, 18, 23, 29, 56, 68, 89, 98, 100, 102, 108, 114, 126, 132, 135–136, 143–144, 199
New Mexico and, 59–60, 61, 63, 140
Race and, 2, 24–25, 64, 199–200
Rebellion of peons, 27
Representation in media, 1, 3, 58, 114, 132, 137, 138, 141, 152, 153, 155
Structure of, 1, 35
Thirteenth Amendment and, 60, 61, 63, 136, 195, 197
Turpentine belt and, 1, 121, 173
Working with convict leasing, 2–4, 6, 14, 27, 35–36, 50, 69, 129, 130–131, 137–138, 173, 206, 210, 211–212
Working with county chain gangs, 13
Deen, J. R., 140
DeMille, Cecil B., 237n18
Denmark, E.P.S., 94
Dickey, Henry C., 122, 123
Disfranchisement, 139, 192, 205
  Convictions used for, 106–108, 132
  Correlation with racial violence, 243n26
Dixon, Merritt W., 74, 80, 85, 107
Donalson Lumber Co., 74, 80, 107
Dorminy-Palmer Co., 155, 159
Dorminy-Price Lumber Co., 159, 165, 183
Douglass, Frederick, 246n29
Du Bois, W. E.B., 129, 170, 194
Dunbar, Paul Lawrence, 64
Dunn, Jeff, 103
Durham, Imla, 237n9
Durham, Lula, 144, 238n29
Durham Coal & Coke Co., 145, 155, 159, 165, 183, 191

Eason, Thomas, 94, 95, 227n3
Edmonson, J. W., 89–92, 94, 113
E. E. Foy Manufacturing Co., 110, 145, 150
Emigrant agents, 10–11, 144
English, James W., Jr., 74, 80, 85, 107, 145
Ensign, J. Lee, 145

Enterprise Lumber Co., 74, 80, 85, 107, 150, 155, 159
Erskine, John, 125
Evans, Clement A., 94, 191, 227n3
Eve, W. F., 190
Ewing, J. A., 202
Ex parte Yarbrough (1884), 124, 136

Fadden, Chimmie, 141, 237n18
Fai, Ed, 101
Federal Aid Road Act (1916), 193
Felder, Thomas S., 117, 184
Felony convict lease
  Beginning of, 31–32, 50, 118
  Bidding of, 13, 132
  Bureaucracy of, 39
  Contracts for, 23, 26
  Corporate contracts, 2, 36–37
  Corruption of, 180–181, 183
  Criticism of, 3, 6, 51, 52–53, 55, 61, 91, 124, 178–179, 212
  Death rates of, 5, 6, 67, 70, 78, 84, 117, 151, 182
  Defense of, 34–35, 42, 65, 77, 93, 112, 182
  Division of camps, 36, 68, 148
  End of in Georgia, 5, 173, 179–180, 183–184, 185, 188–189, 193, 197, 214n6
  End of in other states, 209
  Expense of, 12, 31
  Facilitated by state legislation, 33–34
  Geographic shift of, 173
  Historiography of, 51–52, 56
  Inspection of, 3
  Labor Commission report on, 51
  Less violent than misdemeanor lease, 42, 46, 49, 65, 67
  McRees and (early), 4, 17, 18, 29, 46, 50, 52, 96
  McRees and (late), 100, 119, 143, 148, 154, 160, 200–201, 211
  Number of prisoners involved: in 1894, 38; in 1890, 52; in 1899, 73; in 1904, 151; in 1905, 154; in 1907, 160; in 1908, 184
  Private nature of, 116
  Race and, 24–25, 26–27, 70, 77, 81, 210
  Reauthorization of, 117–118
  Replacement for slavery, 2, 31

272 · Index

State oversight of, 3, 29, 67, 81, 91, 93, 117, 118, 143
State revenue from, 13, 32, 67, 119, 135, 170, 192
Tables describing, 71, 74, 80, 85, 107, 145, 155, 159, 165, 183
Unlike misdemeanor lease, 3, 70
Working with debt peonage, 2–4, 6, 14, 27, 35–36, 50, 69, 129, 130–131, 137–138, 173, 206, 210, 211–212
Working with misdemeanor lease, 55–56
Felton, Rebecca Latimer, 178
Ferguson, Jessie, 103
Field, Stephen J., 60
Fields, Rheuben, 103
Flender, J. F., 152
Flowers Lumber Company, 110, 145, 155, 159, 165, 183
Flynn, Charles, 24
Ford, Phillip, 103
Fort, William A., 31
Fourteenth Amendment, 60, 61, 64, 234n19
Foy, John, 142, 143
Frazier, Jack, 103
Frazier, Lula, 125–130, 133, 142, 143
Frederick, Floyd, 204
Friling, Tuvia, 95
Fuller, Melville, 11

Garrison, William Lloyd, 64
Gaudidate, Tom, 101
Georgia and Alabama Railroad, 31
Georgia Department of Corrections, 229n12
Georgia Highway Commission, 193
Georgia House of Representatives, 114, 135
  Committee on the Penitentiary, 32
  Investigating leasing, 142, 179, 181
  Regulating leasing, 35, 38, 118, 179, 184
Georgia Immigration Association, 200
Georgia Iron & Coal Co., 155, 159, 165, 183
Georgia Prison Commission
  Annual reports: 1898, 67–68, 69; 1899, 73–74; 1900, 77–78, 84; 1901, 84; 1902, 108; 1903, 148; 1904, 148–151; 1905, 154; 1906, 160; 1907, 164; 1908, 180, 182–183
  Atlanta Constitution and, 90–91

  Charges against McRee filed with, 89, 123
  Corruption of, 181–182, 201
  End of convict leasing and, 208, 211
  Felony convict leasing and, 117–119, 137, 154, 229n8
  Folded into Department of Corrections, 229n12
  Founding of, 32, 67, 68, 180, 191, 227n2
  Hearing about Kinderlou, 92–95
  Investigations of (non-McRee), 143
  Lacking regulatory jurisdiction over debt peons, 148
  Lacking regulatory jurisdiction over misdemeanor camps, 30, 69, 131, 174, 176
  Lowcounting death numbers, 84
  Making felons available for county infrastructure work, 120, 189, 193, 197
  Records used in federal trial, 125
  Report on Kinderlou, 97–99, 108, 234n30
  Rules for misdemeanor chain gangs, 95
  Wanting jurisdiction over misdemeanor camps, 79, 100, 116, 118, 135, 139, 148, 242n21
Georgia Senate, 135
  Investigating leasing, 142, 177
  Regulating leasing, 35, 38, 184
Georgia State Agricultural Society, 178
Georgia State Penitentiary, 33, 36, 38, 40, 49
  Construction of, 6
  Reorganization of, 191
  Superintendent of, 39, 100
Georgia Supreme Court, 12, 121–122, 133, 233n17
Georgia Technical Institute, 18, 199
Gilbert, Robb, 101
Glenn, William C., 142
G. M. Sherouse and Co., 43
Good Roads Movement, 190–191
Gordon, John Brown, 51
Gordon, Will, 140, 141–142
Grant, Alexander, and Co., 32
Great Migration, 205–206
Green, Fletcher, 34, 235n37
Grier, Moses, 104
Griffin, J. H., 47
Griffin, Shep, 65

G. S. Baxter & Co., 74, 80, 85, 87, 107, 110, 159, 165, 183
G. V. Gress Co., 145, 155, 159

Hackett, A. T., 35
Haley, Sarah, 5, 129, 190
Hall, John I., 37
Hamby, W. B., 181, 201
Hamby & Toomer, 145, 155, 158
Hardy, Ed, 237n9
Hardy, Maggie, 127
Hardy, Nealy, 237n9
Harlan, John Marshall, 195
Harlem Renaissance, 205
Hart, George, 144, 238n29, 239nn30,32
Heard, Bedford J., 49
Henderson, Ed, 103
Hershaw, Lafayette, 7, 195
Hicks, John, 102
Hill, Mettie, 143
Hodges, John, 101
Holder, G. B., 241n2
Holder, John, 179, 184, 188
Holloway, Pippa, 34
Holmes, J.B.S., 112, 148
    Listed in annual reports, 110, 150, 155, 158, 159, 160, 163, 165, 183
Holmes, Joe, 237n9
Holmes, Oliver Wendell, Jr., 194–195, 244n39
Holmes, Sam, 122
Howard Association, 52, 55
Howell, W. S., 118
H. Stevens & Sons Co., 165, 183
Hudgins, J. C., 49
Huebner, Timothy, 125
Hughes, Charles Evans, 195
Humphreys, W. S., 94

Jackson, Fanny, 90
Jackson, Lucius, 101
Jackson, Thomas "Stonewall," 55
Jackson Lumber Company, 154
James, Charles, 101
James, Thomas J., 36, 38, 71
Jamison, Henry, 144–146, 148
January, Dan, 160

Jenkins, Arthur, 103
Jenkins, H. A., 38
J. N. Bray Company, 204
Johnson, Hexby, 104
Johnson, Jim, 101
Johnson, Sam, 28–29
Jones, Ben, 191
Jones, Berry, 15
Jones, Francis, 15, 16
Jones, Henry, 142
Jones, Mitchell, 17
Jones, R. R., 47
Jones, Thomas G., 62–63, 160, 226n27
Jones, Tom, 15

Kaigles, John, 101
Kidnapping
    Anderson, South Carolina, and, 58–59
    At Kinderlou, 4–5, 81, 84, 89–92, 94, 97–100, 114, 116, 178, 180, 211
    Criticism of, 5, 93, 136, 139, 172, 212
    Florida and, 62, 140–141, 160
    Georgia and, 61, 84, 106, 130, 142, 177
    Race and, 2, 96
Kinderlou
    Abuse of misdemeanor convict labor at, 4, 13, 26, 81, 84, 90, 93, 113, 122, 127, 177, 194
    Controversy surrounding, 89–100, 102, 105–106, 113–117, 122–128, 131–133, 134–140, 142–148
    Creation of, 15, 17–18
    Diversification of, 18–23, 25–26
    Early use of felony convict lease, 4, 17, 18, 29, 46, 50, 52, 96
    Late use of felony convict lease, 100, 119, 143, 148, 154, 160, 200–201, 211
    Naming of, 17
    Slave labor and, 16–17, 18–19, 23
    Truck crops and, 19–23, 246n26
    Use of debt peonage at, 1, 4, 5, 13, 17, 18, 23, 29, 56, 68, 89, 98, 100, 102, 108, 114, 126, 132, 135–136, 143–144, 199
    Use of misdemeanor convict lease, 50, 52, 96, 106, 143
King, Henry, 103
Kingsberry, S. T., 94

Kinnebrew, E. C., 164
Knight, Jonathan Perry, 118
Knox, Philander Chase, 61

LeFlouria, Talitha, 5, 130
Lessons, Caesar, 104
Lew, John, 104, 106
Lewis, James, 90
Lewis, Robert W., 62
Lewis, Will, 90
Lichtenstein, Alex, 1, 243n23
Lincoln, Abraham, 25
Littlefield, Charles, 139
Lomax, Louis, 27
Lookout Mt. Coal & Coke Co., 155, 159, 165, 183
Lowe, W. B., 36, 71
Lynching, 26, 141, 205, 210
    Bondage and, 55, 170, 210, 243n26, 247n43
    Sam Hose and, 178
    White women and, 178

Maddox, W. H., 36
Mancini, Matthew J., 33–34, 51–52, 192, 193
Martin, Joe, 104
Massey, James, 26, 247n43
Mathis, Jasper, 202
Mauldin, Tip, 28
McCalla, John W., 49, 74, 80, 85, 87, 107
McCallie, S. W., 191, 193
McClellan, Thomas, 125–126, 131, 134–136, 236n5
McCoy, John, 101
McCranie, Archibald, 105
McKelvy, Blake, 194
McKinnon, Joseph, 103
McLeod, Clayton B., 135
McLeod, John A., 135
McMullen, John, 237n9
McRay, Frank, 47, 223n46
McRee, Edward Jones, 17, 199, 218nn4,8
    Abuse of, 94, 100, 126–127
    Claims of corruption by, 92
    Death of, 198–199, 203
    Felony lease and, 119, 145, 244n3
    Indictment of, 124, 142
    Injury of, 105
    Insolvency of, 102
    Kidnapping of, 126
    Peonage and, 23, 131
    Political career of, 23, 115, 124, 131–132, 135, 142–143, 177–180
McRee, Edward Lawrence, 15–16
McRee, Francis Inman (Frank), 17–18, 199, 218n8, 219n26
    Abuse of, 100
    Convict camp of, 94, 100
    Death of, 202–203
    House of, 102, 199
    Indicted, 124
    Kidnapping of, 144
    Social life of, 23–24
McRee, George Randolph, 15, 17–19, 24, 218n4, 246n26
McRee, George Young, 17, 199, 201–202, 218n8
    Abuse of, 90, 100
    Death of, 203, 204
McRee, Jerry, 204
McRee, Lou G., 17, 199
McRee, William Spain, 17, 198, 199–201, 202, 218n8
    Abuse of, 90, 95, 127
    Death of, 204
    Farm tenancy and, 202
    Investigation of, 92, 97
    Kidnapping of, 94, 95
    Murder by, 203
    Property of, 92, 94, 100, 199
McRee family
    Abuse of misdemeanor convict labor of, 4, 13, 26, 81, 84, 90, 93, 113, 122, 127, 177, 194
    Combination misdemeanor and felony lease, 4, 50
    Controversy surrounding, 89–100, 102, 105–106, 113–117, 122–128, 131–133, 134–140, 142–148, 232n1
    Early use of felony convict lease, 4, 17, 18, 29, 46, 50, 52, 96
    Kidnapping related to misdemeanor convict lease, 4–5, 81, 84, 89–92, 94, 96–100, 113–114, 116, 141–142, 178, 180, 211
    Late use of felony convict lease, 100, 119, 143, 148, 154, 160, 200–201, 211
    Profits from misdemeanor convict lease, 13

Slave labor and, 16–17, 18–19, 23
Use of debt peonage, 1, 4, 5, 13, 17, 18, 23, 29, 56, 68, 89, 98, 100, 102, 108, 114, 126, 132, 135–136, 143–144, 199
Use of misdemeanor convict lease, 50, 52, 96, 106, 143
Methodist Freedman's Aid and Southern Educational Society, 6
Miller, Stephen F., 126, 235n32, 236n5
Milltown Lumber Co., 165, 180, 183
Misdemeanor convict lease
Abuse in (non-McRee), 29, 49, 81, 135, 142, 173, 174, 177, 180–182
Beginning of, 3, 13, 27, 31, 35, 57
Black guards in, 95
County profits from, 65, 67, 112
Criticism of, 49, 91, 111, 114–117, 121, 124, 182, 184
Death rate in, 67, 70, 77, 83–84, 88, 151, 154
Defense of, 69, 112, 177–178
End of, 148, 189, 191–193, 201
End of in Lowndes County, 160
Gender and, 5
Geography of, 173–176
Historiography of, 5
Lack of oversight, 3, 4, 5, 30, 37, 67, 78, 89–91, 139, 183
Legislation concerning, 12–13, 29, 35–37, 38–39, 81, 111–112, 115–120, 128
McRee abuse of, 4, 13, 26, 81, 84, 90, 93, 113, 122, 127, 177, 194
McRee combination with felony lease, 4, 50
McRee controversy over, 91–92, 96–100, 102, 115–116, 119, 135, 232n1
McRee kidnapping and, 4–5, 81, 84, 89–92, 94, 96–100, 113–114, 116, 141–1142, 178, 180, 211
McRee profits from, 13
McRee use of, 50, 52, 96, 106, 143
Number of camps: in 1898, 67; in 1899, 77; in 1901, 88; in 1902, 100; in 1904, 148; in 1905, 154; in 1907, 160; in 1908, 184
Number of prisoners: in 1898, 70; in 1901, 88; in 1902, 100; in 1904, 148, 151; in 1905, 154; in 1907, 160; in 1908, 184
Prison Commission lacking regulatory jurisdiction over, 30, 69, 131, 174, 176
Prison Commission wanting jurisdiction over, 79, 100, 116, 118, 135, 139, 148, 242n21
Prison Commission oversight, 68, 78, 91, 93, 95
Prison Commission report: of 1898, 68–69; of 1899, 73; of 1900, 78–79; of 1901, 87–88; of 1902, 100, 108; of 1904, 148–149
Profit from, 31, 36
Public invisibility of, 3, 7, 55, 61, 130, 137, 138, 172, 179
Race and, 16, 24–25, 28–29, 52, 70, 81, 96, 97, 112, 164, 184
Relationship with county chain gangs, 5, 35, 38, 197
Relationship with debt peonage, 4, 5, 14, 18, 129, 131, 137, 141, 192, 197, 210–212
Relationship with felony convict lease, 6, 14, 51, 55, 129, 197, 210–212
State reports on, 39–48, 66, 173
Tables describing, 72, 75, 81, 86, 101, 102–104, 109, 149, 157, 162, 167, 186
Turpentine work and, 68
Mitchell, Titus, 142
Monro, George P., 38
Moore, Alf, 26
Moore, Andrew, 237n9
Moore, Jacob C., 68, 95, 100, 240n2
Corruption of, 180–181, 201
Morgan, Joseph, 104
Morrell, Edward, 171
Morris, George, 103
Morris, Will, 47
Murphy, Holliston, 104
Muscogee Brick Co., 183
Mussane, Ed, 104
Myers, Martha, 26, 247n43

Newman, William T., 61–62
Niagara Movement, 170

Otey, Charles, L., 107–108
Owen, Chandler, 205

Palmer Brick Co., 155, 159, 165, 183
Parrott Lumber Co., 74, 80, 85, 87, 107, 110
Patrick, James, 160
Payne Whitney Plantation, 15

Peonage Cases (1903), 64, 122, 130, 134
Pig laws, 33–34
Pinson, T. J., 120, 150, 159, 164, 169
Platt, Anthony, 105
Pollard, Orange, 101
Populism, 68, 178
Porter, Will, 203–204
Postell, Will, 194
Powell, J. C., 241n2
Powell, Sallie, 127
Prescott, W. E., 241n2
Price, James, 43
Prison Industries Reorganization Administration, 210
Profit, P. P., 49

Ramsey, A. K., 240n2
Randolph, A. Philip, 205, 246n29
Ransom, Roger, 57–58, 224n12
Ravenel, Henry William, 9, 10
Rawlston, George, 103
Reagan, E. J., 38
Rease, Tom, 104
Recidivism, 6–7, 51
Reconstruction, 9, 12, 50
　Amendments, 10, 170
　Black life after, 24, 33, 58, 61, 106
　Bourbon Redeemers after, 10–11, 124, 137
　Prisons after, 4, 211, 212, 242n21
Ridley, Mose, 140, 141–142
Rivers, Ed, 195–196
Robinson, James, 105–106, 231n37
Robinson, Will, 104
Rodgers, Sallie, 103
Roosevelt, Franklin, 210
Roosevelt, Theodore, 64, 105, 153, 160, 170
Root, Elihu, 170
Rose, D. P., 241n2
Rosewood Massacre, 207
Royster Guano Co., 155, 159, 165, 183
Ruger, Thomas H., 31
Russell, Charles W., 165, 169–170, 200, 210
Russell, Ed, 104

Segregation, 40, 144, 192, 205
　Gendered, 45, 47, 50, 70, 95, 130, 190, 211
　In prison camps, 45–46, 70, 208, 211, 227n3

Seward, Jim, 104
S. F. Floyd and Co., 43
Shields, John H., 153
Shorter, Henry, 103
Simmons, T. G., 240n2
Sirmans, F. B., 240n2
Slaughterhouse Cases (1873), 60
Slavery, 7–9, 10, 16, 17, 18, 23, 25–26, 34, 33, 51, 52, 57, 178, 221, 226n26
　As predecessor of convict leasing, 193
　Convict leasing as, 2, 7, 13, 27–28, 50, 58, 66, 68, 128–129, 131, 137, 141, 152, 207, 225n21
　Peonage as a form of, 25, 59–65, 98, 121, 134, 144, 153, 160, 164, 170–171, 173, 195, 200, 204, 228n1
　Slave Codes, 8, 9
　Slave leasing, 8–9
　Wage slavery, 34, 205–206
Smith, Aaron, 103
Smith, Blanche, 101
Smith, Dave, 131, 237n9
Smith, David, 122
Smith, Hampton, 27
Smith, James M., 36
　In annual reports, 71, 74, 80, 83, 85, 87, 111, 150, 158, 164, 169, 188
Smith, James Milton (governor), 50
Smith, James W., 107
Smith, M. Hoke, 208
South Georgia Flying Service, 204
Southern Lumber Co., 183
Southern Mining Co., 74, 80
Spain, John William, 15
Spain, Rachel, 15
Spain, Rachel Inman, 15
Span, Rachel Lavinia, 17
Spain, Sallie, 15
Spanger, John, 237n9
Spanish-American War, 18
Speer, Emory, 124–125, 139, 148, 151
　Cobb trial and, 144, 239nn31,32
　Complimented by Roosevelt, 160
　McClellan trial and, 136–137, 146
　McRee trial and, 124, 130, 131, 135
　Relationship with Ackerman, 235n42
Spencer, Mackey, 122
Spivey, Oscar, 103

Stanley, John, 101
Stanley, S. M., 152, 154, 155, 159, 165, 183
Steed, Walter E., 118
Stetson Lumber Co., 159, 164, 165, 168, 183, 187
Strickland, J. M., 181
Sutch, Richard, 57–58, 224n12
Swartz, S. H., 153

Taft, William Howard, 170
Tanenhaus, David S., 105
Tatum, J. W., 49
Taylor v. Georgia (1942), 196
Taylor, Cy, 199
Taylor, Mamie, 199
Taylor-Colquitt Company, 204
Tenant farming, 21–23, 26, 57–58, 201–202
Terrell, Joseph Meriwether, 115–117, 134, 142
Thacel, Elura, 101
Thirkield, Wilbur Patterson, 6–7
Thirteenth Amendment, 2, 63, 139, 171, 233n18
  McClellan and Crawley trial and, 136
  McRees and, 135
  New Mexico and, 60
  Peonage Cases and, 63–64, 226n26
  Slaughterhouse Cases and, 60–62
  Supreme Court and, 195–197, 244n39
Thomas, Doak, 103
Tift, H. H., 140
Tillman, Benjamin, 226n32
Tillman, Dave, 103
Toombs, Robert, 58
Toomer, W. M., 155, 159, 165
Townsend, Jim, 121
Troy, Harry, 101
Tucker, Buster, 46
Turner, H. G., 94
Turner, Joseph, 92, 94, 227n3
Turner, Mary, 27
Tuskegee Institute, 64
Tutwiler, Julia, 178

Union College, 15–16
United States Department of Agriculture, 190
  Office of Road Inquiry, 190
United States Department of Justice, 106, 122, 174, 198

United States House of Representatives, 135, 138, 140, 171
  Judiciary Committee, 135, 172
United States Labor Commission, 51
University of Georgia, 17–18, 124, 135

Vagrancy, 6, 10–12, 41, 57, 64, 165, 170, 224n10
Valdosta Pecan Plantation Company, 203
Villard, Oswald Garrison, 64, 194
Virginia House of Burgesses, 8

Wade, Frank, 104
Walton County v. Franklin (1894), 12
Ward, Geoff, 105
Ward, Herbert, 152
Ware County Board of Commissioners, 126
Washington, Annie, 104
Washington, Booker T., 64, 194
Washington, George, 52
Watson, Tom, 68
Wharton, Vernon Lane, 33–34
Whitaker, G. A., 94
Wickersham, George Woodward, 170
Wildwood Plantation, 17, 18
Wilenski, Benjamin, 153
Willingham, Mary, 164
Williams, John S., 206
Williams, Mollie, 90
Williams, R. A., 11
Williams, Rich, 101
Williams v. Fears (1900), 11
Williamson, Lester, 135
Willis, Anna, 103
Wilson, Henry, 122
Wilson, Ida, 127
Winn, Abe, 191
Woods, Harry, 103
Woods, Tom, 103
Woodward, C. Vann, 210
Wright, R. F., 39–40

Yancey, Goodloe, 201
Young, Elizabeth, 15

Thomas Aiello is professor of history and Africana studies at Valdosta State University. He is the author of more than twenty books and more than sixty peer-reviewed journal articles. His work helped amend the Louisiana constitution to make nonunanimous juries illegal and was cited in the United States Supreme Court as part of its decision ruling them unconstitutional. His books have won multiple awards and have been nominated for others, including the Pulitzer Prize. He holds PhDs in history and anthrozoology. He lives in Valdosta, Georgia. Learn more at www.thomasaiellobooks.com.

www.ingramcontent.com/pod-product-compliance
Lightning Source LLC
Chambersburg PA
CBHW030610230426
43661CB00053B/1923